TRIAL PRACTICE PROBLEMS AND CASE FILES

TRIAL PRACTICE PROBLEMS AND CASE FILES

Supplement to The Trial Process: Law, Tactics, and Ethics, FOURTH EDITION

J. Alexander Tanford
Professor of Law
Indiana University Maurer School of Law — Bloomington

Carolina Academic Press
Durham, North Carolina

ISBN: 978-1-42247-553-9 (Print)
ISBN: 978-0-32717-811-8 (eBook)

Carolina Academic Press
700 Kent Street
Durham, North Carolina 27701
Telephone (919) 489-7486
Fax (919) 493-5668
www.caplaw.com

Printed in the United States of America
2021 reprint

PREFACE

This supplement contains seven case files that may be used either as full trials or as bases for individual exercises. The case files and problems derived from them are designed specifically to raise the legal, ethical and tactical issues discussed in **THE TRIAL PROCESS: LAW, TACTICS AND ETHICS FOURTH EDITION** (LexisNexis 2009), but also may be used effectively with any one of the trial advocacy textbooks that emphasizes skills and tactics.

Part one of this supplement contains a basic series of problems derived from *State v. Hunter* (case file A) and *Kesler v. Burnside* (case file B). In full-semester courses, I have tried both using one case file for the entire semester and using two case files, switching at mid-semester. Both approaches work well. I do not recommend changing case files more often; the fact patterns are too complex for students to master more than two files in a typical one-semester trial practice course. In an intensive course of four weeks or less, I recommend using a single case file throughout the course for problems

Part two of this supplement contains seven case files -- four criminal cases and three civil cases. Each case file is self-contained, including complete jury instructions. All cases are designed to be tried with either one or two student attorneys on each side. Case File F (*Kane v. Bond and the City of Bayshore*) can be tried as a three-party lawsuit with separate counsel to represent each of the two defendants in the event that a class has an odd number of students. I have strived to make the cases evenly balanced, so that both sides have realistic chances for favorable verdicts. I also have tried within cases to make all direct and cross-examinations of equivalent complexity and difficulty. The cases are set in the fictional city of Bayshore (pop. 150,000) in the imaginary state of Columbia. The location closely resembles my home town of Bloomington, Indiana, but all characters and events are fictitious. Any resemblance to any actual person or event is pure coincidence.

I am grateful to Indiana University Maurer School of Law in Bloomington for the support it has given me in the preparation of these case files. My medical consultant was the late Dr. John M. Guthrie of Green Bay, Wisconsin; my consultant on the battered woman syndrome was Lynne Henderson; Ken Dau-Schmidt led me through the economics of lost future earning capacity; Philippa M. Guthrie provided moral support. Thanks.

March 1, 2010

James Alexander Tanford
Bloomington, Indiana

TABLE OF CONTENTS

PART TWO: CASE FILES

PART ONE: PROBLEMS

A. TRIAL PREPARATION PROBLEMS

PROBLEM A-1.

Prepare a written theory of the case for the State in *State v. Hunter*. Your theory should include the crimes you think you can prove, what issues you think will be contested, what the most important pieces of evidence will be, and what theme(s) you will use. It should also anticipate your opponent's strengths and probable strategy, and how you are going to meet them.

PROBLEM A-2.

Prepare a written theory of the case for the Defendant in *State v. Hunter*. Your theory should include how you will disprove the crimes charged, what issues you think will be contested, what the most important pieces of evidence will be, and what theme(s) you will use. It should also anticipate your opponent's strengths and probable strategy, and how you are going to meet them.

PROBLEM A-3.

Prepare a written theory of the case for the Plaintiff in *Kesler v. Burnside*. Your theory should include which theory (or theories) of negligence you will pursue, what issues you think will be contested, what the most important pieces of evidence will be, and what theme(s) you will use. It should also anticipate your opponent's strengths and probable strategy, and how you are going to meet them.

PROBLEM A-4.

Prepare a written theory of the case for the Defendants in *Kesler v. Burnside*. Your theory should include which defense(s) you think you can prove, what issues you think will be contested, what the most important pieces of evidence will be, and what theme(s) you will use. It should also anticipate your opponent's strengths and probable strategy, and how you are going to meet them.

PROBLEM A-5.

Prepare a written theory of the case for the State in *State v. Hunter*. Your theory should include the crimes you think you can prove, what issues you think will be contested, what the most important pieces of evidence will be, and what theme(s) you will use. It should also anticipate your opponent's strengths and probable strategy, and how you are going to meet them. Assume the following additional facts.

(1) When Cheryl Pearlman was at the hospital, she noticed that her blouse was torn and several buttons were missing. She now recalls feeling the attacker's hand grab her breasts just before he choked her.

(2) Richard Hunter was arrested twice for forcible rape when he was a juvenile. In both cases the alleged victims were classmates (age 16) with whom Hunter was acquainted. Neither alleged victim would testify or cooperate with the police, and charges were dropped. Hunter

has claimed both victims consented to sexual intercourse, but both had visible bruises after the alleged assaults.

(3) After holding a full evidentiary hearing, the trial judge suppressed any testimony about the pretrial identification procedures and also suppressed any in-court identification by Cheryl Pearlman.

(4) Hunter has broken up with his girlfriend, Becky Collins. Collins now says that Hunter beat her on two or three occasions and was prone to fits of violent temper, during which he would scream that women in general, and his own mother in particular, were the source of evil in the world.

PROBLEM A-6.

Prepare a written theory of the case for the Defendant in *State v. Hunter*. Your theory should include how you will disprove the crimes charged, what issues you think will be contested, what the most important pieces of evidence will be, and what theme(s) you will use. It should also anticipate your opponent's strengths and probable strategy, and how you are going to meet them. Assume the following additional facts.

(1) When Cheryl Pearlman was at the hospital, she noticed that her blouse was torn and several buttons were missing. She now recalls feeling the attacker's hand grab her breasts just before he choked her.

(2) Richard Hunter was arrested twice for forcible rape when he was a juvenile. In both cases the alleged victims were classmates (age 16) with whom Hunter was acquainted. Neither alleged victim would testify or cooperate with the police, and charges were dropped. Hunter has claimed both victims consented to sexual intercourse, but both had visible bruises after the alleged assaults.

(3) After holding a full evidentiary hearing, the trial judge suppressed any testimony about the pretrial identification procedures and also suppressed any in-court identification by Cheryl Pearlman.

(4) Hunter has broken up with his girlfriend, Becky Collins. Collins now says that Hunter beat her on two or three occasions and was prone to fits of violent temper, during which he would scream that women in general, and his own mother in particular, were the source of evil in the world.

B. JURY SELECTION PROBLEMS

PROBLEM B-1.

Assume this jurisdiction is one in which Voir Dire is conducted exclusively by the judge. Prepare written requests for questions you would like the court to ask prospective jurors on behalf of the State in *State v. Hunter*. The judge has announced that she will entertain no more than 25 requests from each attorney.

PROBLEM B-2.

Assume this jurisdiction is one in which Voir Dire is conducted exclusively by the judge. Prepare written requests for questions you would like the court to ask prospective jurors on behalf of the Defendant in *State v. Hunter.* The judge has announced that she will entertain no more than 25 requests from each attorney.

PROBLEM B-3.

Assume this jurisdiction is one in which Voir Dire is conducted exclusively by the judge. Prepare written requests for questions you would like the court to ask prospective jurors on behalf of the Plaintiff in *Kesler v. Burnside.* The judge has announced that she will entertain no more than 25 requests from each attorney.

PROBLEM B-4.

Assume this jurisdiction is one in which Voir Dire is conducted exclusively by the judge. Prepare written requests for questions you would like the court to ask prospective jurors on behalf of the Defendants in *Kesler v. Burnside.* The judge has announced that she will entertain no more than 25 requests from each attorney.

PROBLEM B-5.

Assume this jurisdiction is one that uses six-person juries and in which the attorneys are entitled to ask questions. Based on juror questionnaires, you already have the information listed below about the first six jurors. Prepare additional questions for your side of the case in *State v. Hunter.* Anticipate that you will have only 30 minutes per attorney to question these six prospective jurors.

JUROR NUMBER ONE: Cynthia Stanton

1. Secretary -- county resident -- two years of college -- age 34.
2. Married -- husband Tom Stanton is a dentist -- two children who attend Lighthouse Christian School.
3. No prior jury service.
4. No criminal record.
5. No involvement in any way with this case.
6. Does not know any of the parties or attorneys.
7. Knows nothing of the facts and has formed no opinion on the merits of the case. Reads the local newspaper sometimes. Active in Mt. Pleasant Christian Church.
8. Is in good health with no defects in hearing or vision.
9. Has a cousin who is a police officer in Springfield, Illinois.
10. Will be fair and impartial.

JUROR NUMBER TWO: Daniel Holtz

1. Retired postal worker -- county resident -- high school education -- age 62.
2. Married -- wife Mary Holtz is housewife -- three grown children.

3. Served on criminal jury in 1999 as foreman, served on civil jury in 1993. Both juries reached verdicts.
4. No criminal record.
5. No involvement in any way with this case.
6. Does not know any of the parties or attorneys.
7. Knows nothing of facts and has formed no opinion on the merits of the case. Does not regularly read a newspaper.
8. Is in good health with no defects in hearing or vision.
9. No friends or relatives connected with law enforcement.
10. Will be fair and impartial.

JUROR NUMBER THREE: Gregory Dudley

1. Sales clerk at sporting goods store -- county resident -- B.A. in business from University of Columbia -- age 28.
2. Married -- wife Carol Urich -- used to work as sales clerk at department store, now home with infant daughter.
3. No prior jury service.
4. No criminal record.
5. No involvement in any way with this case.
6. Name Richard Hunter sounds familiar, might have seen him on campus, but does not know him -- does not know attorneys.
7. Remembers reading newspaper story about attempted rape on campus in January, but does not remember details, and has formed no opinion on the merits of the case.
8. Is in good health with no defects in hearing or vision.
9. No friends or relatives connected with law enforcement.
10. Will be fair and impartial.

JUROR NUMBER FOUR: Ivette Rodriguez

1. Case worker, county welfare department -- county resident -- M.S.W. degree from Temple University School of Social Work -- age 46.
2. Married -- husband Hector Rodriguez is unemployed, laid off from assembly line at RCA plant -- four children, one in Community College.
3. No prior jury service.
4. No prior criminal record.
5. No involvement in any way with this case.
6. Knows assistant district attorney and judge, is vaguely acquainted with defense attorney, all from job as welfare case worker.
7. Knows nothing about facts and has formed no opinion on merits of case. Regularly reads the local newspaper.
8. Is in good health with no defects in hearing or vision.
9. Knows a number of police officers because of job, none are close friends.
10. Will be fair and impartial.

JUROR NUMBER FIVE: Susan Rothstein

1. Copy editor for Bayshore Business Monthly Magazine -- county resident -- B.A. from University of Minnesota -- age 51.
2. Married -- husband Donald Bush is a professor of sociology at University of Columbia -- no children.

3. No prior jury service.
4. No criminal record.
5. No involvement in any way with this case.
6. Does not know any of the parties or attorneys.
7. Is familiar with facts of case because the Bayshore chapter of NOW (of which she is a member) publicized this incident as part of a petition drive to request better lighting around campus, but has formed no opinion on the merits of this case.
8. Is in good health with no defects in hearing or vision.
9. No friends or relatives connected with law enforcement.
10. Will be fair and impartial.

JUROR NUMBER SIX: George Ferry

1. Automobile mechanic -- county resident -- high school graduate -- age 37.
2. Divorced -- wife ran beauty parlor -- three children -- wife has custody.
3. Served once as juror before in a civil case -- case settled during trial.
4. Prior misdemeanor conviction for public intoxication and resisting arrest in 2001.
5. No involvement in any way with this case.
6. Knows the defendant, Richard Hunter, slightly. They live in same neighborhood. Does not know any of the attorneys.
7. Knows nothing about facts of case and has formed no opinion on the merits. Does not regularly read newspaper.
8. Is in good health but has no depth perception because of eye injury.
9. Former brother-in-law was deputy sheriff, did not like him very much.
10. Will be fair and impartial.

PROBLEM B-6.

Assume this jurisdiction uses six-person juries in civil cases, and is one in which the attorneys are permitted to ask questions. Based on their answers to questionnaires, you know the following information about the first six jurors. Prepare additional questions for your side in *Kesler v. Burnside.* Anticipate that you will have only 30 minutes per attorney to question these six prospective jurors.

JUROR NUMBER ONE: Cynthia Stanton

1. Secretary -- county resident -- two years of college -- age 34.
2. Married -- husband Tom Stanton is a dentist -- two children who attend Lighthouse Christian School.
3. No prior jury service.
4. No criminal record.
5. No involvement in any way with this case.
6. Does not know any of the parties or attorneys.
7. Knows nothing of the facts and has formed no opinion on the merits of the case. Seldom reads newspaper.
8. Is in good health with no defects in hearing or vision.
9. Owns and drives a YR-2 Dodge SUV insured by State Farm.
10. Has been involved in two minor accidents, both the other driver's fault -- no injuries -- both required car repair.
11. Had high school friend killed in automobile accident.

12. Has never been involved in a lawsuit.
13. Will be fair and impartial.

JUROR NUMBER TWO: Daniel Holtz

1. Retired postal worker -- county resident -- high school education -- age 62.
2. Married -- wife Mary Holtz is a housewife -- three grown children.
3. Served on criminal jury in 2000 as foreman, served on civil jury in 1994. Both juries reached verdicts.
4. No criminal record.
5. No involvement in any way with this case.
6. Does not know any of the parties or attorneys except familiar with Macklin Furniture Company and has purchased furniture there in the past.
7. Knows nothing of facts and has formed no opinion on the merits of the case. Does not read the local newspaper.
8. Is in good health with no defects in hearing or vision.
9. Owns and drives a YR-3 Ford pick-up truck insured by Allstate.
10. Was once involved in motorcycle accident (he ran off the road), but has never been in vehicle collision.
11. No friends or family killed or injured in automobile accidents.
12. Has been involved in several property lawsuits with neighbor over boundary dispute.
13. Will be fair and impartial.

JUROR NUMBER THREE: Gregory Dudley

1. Sales clerk at sporting goods store -- B.A. in business from Univ. of Columbia -- age 28.
2. Married -- wife Carol Dudley used to work as sales clerk at department store, now home with infant daughter.
3. No prior jury service.
4. No criminal record.
5. No involvement in any way with this case.
6. Has met Kesler once when she showed him and wife a house three years ago -- does not know any attorneys.
7. Knows nothing about facts and has formed no opinion on merits. Regularly reads local paper.
8. Is in good health with no defects in hearing or vision.
9. Owns and drives a YR-2 Honda insured by State Farm.
10. Wife was involved in accident, rammed from side by car running red light -- she suffered minor injuries.
11. Never personally been in automobile accident.
12. Has never been involved in any kind of civil lawsuit.
13. Will be fair and impartial.

JUROR NUMBER FOUR: Ivette Rodriguez

1. Case worker, county welfare department -- county resident -- M.S.W. degree from Temple University School of Social Work -- age 46.
2. Married -- husband Hector Rodriguez is unemployed, laid off from assembly line at RCA plant -- four children, one at Community College..
3. No prior jury service.
4. No prior criminal record.

5. No involvement in any way with this case.
6. Knows judge and defense attorney from job with welfare department, neither one is personal friend.
7. Knows nothing about facts and has formed no opinion on merits of case.
8. Is in good health with no defects in hearing or vision.
9. Owns YR-7 Ford SUV insured by Geico.
10. Has never been personally involved in accident.
11. Has known a number of welfare clients who were involved in accidents -- several seriously hurt and some suffered severe economic hardships because of injuries.
12. Has been involved tangentially in many lawsuits involving welfare clients -- frequent testimony in juvenile delinquency, child abuse, divorce, paternity, adoption, and civil commitment cases.
13. Will be fair and impartial.

JUROR NUMBER FIVE: Susan Rothstein

1. Copy editor for Bayshore Business Monthly Magazine -- county resident -- B.A. from University of Minnesota -- age 48.
2. Married -- husband Donald Bush is a professor of sociology at University of Columbia -- no children.
3. No prior jury service.
4. No criminal record.
5. No involvement in any way with this case.
6. Does not know any of the parties or attorneys.
7. Is acquainted with facts of case because magazine for which she works did a feature on the need for business interruption insurance, using Kesler's injuries as example -- has formed no opinion on merits of case.
8. Is in good health with no defects in hearing or vision.
9. Owns and drives YR-1 Toyota -- does not know the insurance company.
10. Has been involved in one accident through her own fault -- hit a mailbox while turning around -- not injured, but car required repairs.
11. Had sister seriously injured in accident when rammed by drunk driver, three weeks in hospital, complete recovery -- other driver had no insurance.
12. Once brought small claims action against dry cleaner for ruining a suede jacket -- lost case but is not sure why.
13. Will be fair and impartial.

JUROR NUMBER SIX: George Ferry

1. Automobile mechanic -- county resident -- high school graduate -- age 51.
2. Divorced -- wife ran beauty parlor -- three children, all grown.
3. Served once before as juror in a civil case -- case settled during trial.
4. Prior misdemeanor conviction for public intoxication and resisting arrest in 2002.
5. No involvement in any way with this case.
6. Knows the defendant, Jeffrey Burnside, slightly. They live in same neighborhood. Does not know any of the attorneys.
7. Knows nothing about facts of case and has formed no opinion on' the merits.
8. Is in good health but has no depth perception because of eye injury.
9. Owns and drives a YR-6 Dodge 4x4 truck, insured by American Family.
10. Has never been involved in an accident.

11. Has known a number of people involved in accidents -- knows of no one seriously injured -- has worked on several cars badly damaged in accidents.
12. Will be fair and impartial.

PROBLEM B-7.

Assume this is a jurisdiction that permits attorney-conducted Voir Dire in criminal cases. Prepare to question prospective jurors for the State in *State v. Hunter*. The judge has announced that jurors will be questioned in panels of six, with a 20-minute time limit for each attorney per panel.

PROBLEM B-8.

Assume this is a jurisdiction that permits attorney-conducted Voir Dire in criminal cases. Prepare to question prospective jurors for the Defendant in *State v. Hunter*. The judge has announced that jurors will be questioned in panels of six, with a 20-minute time limit for each attorney per panel.

PROBLEM B-9.

Assume this is a jurisdiction that permits attorney-conducted Voir Dire in civil cases. Prepare to question prospective jurors for the Plaintiff in *Kesler v. Burnside*. The judge has announced that jurors will be questioned in panels of six, with a 20-minute time limit for each attorney per panel.

PROBLEM B-10.

Assume this is a jurisdiction that permits attorney-conducted Voir Dire in civil cases. Prepare to question prospective jurors for the Defendants in *Kesler v. Burnside*. The judge has announced that jurors will be questioned in panels of six, with a 20-minute time limit for each attorney per panel.

C. OPENING STATEMENT PROBLEMS

PROBLEM C-1.

Prepare the opening statement for the State in *State v. Hunter*. Ignore the instructions for use as a full trial on page A-3. You are free to try the case any way you see fit, and will be able to call any available witnesses. Try to limit your statement to ten minutes.

PROBLEM C-2.

Prepare the opening statement for the Defense in *State v. Hunter*. Ignore the instructions for use as a full trial on page A-3. You are free to try the case any way you see fit, and will be able to call any available witnesses. Try to limit your statement to ten minutes.

PROBLEM C-3.

Prepare the opening statement for the Plaintiff in *Kesler v. Burnside*. Ignore the instructions for use as a full trial on page B-3. You are free to try the case any way you see fit, and may call any available witnesses. Assume that the parties have stipulated that total damages are $400,000 and that the case is being tried solely on the issues of negligence and comparative fault. Try to limit your statement to ten minutes.

PROBLEM C-4.

Prepare the opening statement for the Defendants in *Kesler v. Burnside*. Ignore the instructions for use as a full trial on page B-3. You are free to try the case any way you see fit, and may call any available witnesses. Assume that the parties have stipulated that total damages are $400,000 and that the case is being tried solely on the issues of negligence and comparative fault. Try to limit your statement to ten minutes.

PROBLEM C-5.

Prepare the opening statement for the Plaintiff in *Kesler v. Burnside*. Ignore the instructions for use as a full trial on page B-3. You are free to try the case any way you see fit, and may call any available witnesses. Try to limit your statement to no more than fifteen minutes.

PROBLEM C-6.

Prepare the opening statement for the Defendants in *Kesler v. Burnside*. Ignore the instructions for use as a full trial on page B-3. You are free to try the case any way you see fit, and may call any available witnesses. Try to limit your statement to no more than fifteen minutes.

PROBLEM C-7.

Prepare the opening statement for Plaintiff in *Kesler v. Burnside*. Ignore the instructions for use as a full trial on page B-3. You will be free to try the case any way you see fit and call any available witnesses. Assume the following additional facts:

(1) At the time of the accident, the National Automobile Dealers' Association "blue book" listed the retail value of Kesler's car as $14,200.
(2) Kesler's father is the mayor of Bayshore.
(3) At the time of the accident, Kesler admits she was trying to restart her car, which had stalled. She had been having trouble with the car for two weeks and it was overdue for service, but she had been too busy to take it in for servicing.

Try to limit your statement to fifteen minutes.

PROBLEM C-8.

Prepare the opening statement for Defendant in *Kesler v. Burnside*. Ignore the instructions for use as a full trial on page B-3. You will be free to try the case any way you see fit and call any available witnesses. Assume the following additional facts:

(1) At the time of the accident, the National Automobile Dealers' Association "blue-book" listed the retail value of Kelser's car as $14,200.
(2) Kesler's father is the mayor of Bayshore.
(3) At the time of the accident, Kesler admits she was trying to restart her car, which had stalled. She had been having trouble with the car for two weeks and it was overdue for service, but she had been too busy to take it in for servicing.

Try to limit your statement to fifteen minutes.

PROBLEM C-9.

Prepare the opening statement for the State in *State v. Hunter*. Ignore the instructions for use as a full trial on page A-3. You will be free to try the case any way you see fit and to call any available witnesses. Assume the following additional facts:

(1) When Cheryl Pearlman was at the hospital, she noticed that her blouse was torn and several buttons were missing. She now recalls feeling the attacker's hand grab her breasts just before he choked her.
(2) Richard Hunter was arrested twice for forcible rape when he was a juvenile. In both cases the alleged victims were classmates (age 16) with whom Hunter was acquainted. Neither alleged victim would testify or cooperate with the police, and charges were dropped. Hunter has claimed both victims consented to sexual inter-course, but both had visible bruises after the alleged assaults.
(3) After holding a full evidentiary hearing, the trial judge suppressed any testimony about the pretrial identification procedures and also suppressed any in-court identification by Cheryl Pearlman.
(4) Hunter and Becky Collins have broken up. Collins now says that Hunter beat her on two or three occasions, and was prone to fits of violent temper during which he would scream that women in general, and his own mother in particular, were the source of evil in the world.

Try to limit your statement to no more than fifteen minutes.

PROBLEM C-10.

Prepare the opening statement for the Defendant in *State v. Hunter*. Ignore the instructions for use as a full trial on page A-3. You will be free to try the case any way you see fit and to call any available witnesses. Assume the following additional facts:

(1) When Cheryl Pearlman was at the hospital, she noticed that her blouse was torn and several buttons were missing. She now recalls feeling the attacker's hand grab her breasts just before he choked her.
(2) Richard Hunter was arrested twice for forcible rape when he was a juvenile. In both cases the alleged victims were classmates (age 16) with whom Hunter was acquainted. Neither alleged victim would testify or cooperate with the police, and charges were dropped. Hunter

has claimed both victims consented to sexual inter-course, but both had visible bruises after the alleged assaults.

(3) After holding a full evidentiary hearing, the trial judge suppressed any testimony about the pretrial identification procedures and also suppressed any in-court identification by Cheryl Pearlman.

(4) Hunter and Becky Collins have broken up. Collins now says that Hunter beat her on two or three occasions and was prone to fits of violent temper during which he would scream that women in general, and his own mother in particular, were the source of evil in the world.

Try to limit your statement to no more than fifteen minutes.

D. MAKING AND MEETING OBJECTIONS PROBLEMS

PROBLEM D-1.

For the State in *State v. Hunter*, prepare a written outline of objections that you could make to the testimony of Richard Hunter.

PROBLEM D-2.

For the Defense in *State v. Hunter*, prepare a written outline of objections that you could make to the testimony of Donald Adair.

PROBLEM D-3.

For the State in *State v. Hunter*, prepare a written outline of objections that you could make to the testimony of Diane Howard.

PROBLEM D-4.

For the Defense in *State v. Hunter*, prepare a written outline of objections that you could make to the testimony of Cheryl Pearlman.

PROBLEM D-5.

For the State in *State v. Hunter*, prepare a written outline of objections that the defendant might make to your direct examination of Donald Adair. Prepare an outline indicating how you will respond to those objections.

PROBLEM D-6.

For the Defense in *State v. Hunter*, prepare a written outline of objections that the prosecutor might make to your direct examination of Richard Hunter. Prepare an outline indicating how you will respond to those objections.

PROBLEM D-7.

For the State in *State v. Hunter*, prepare a written outline of objections that the defendant might make to your direct examination of Cheryl Pearlman. Prepare an outline indicating how you will respond to those objections.

PROBLEM D-8.

For the Defendant in *State v. Hunter*, prepare a written outline of objections that the prosecutor might make to your direct examination of Diane Howard. Prepare an outline indicating how you will respond to those objections.

PROBLEM D-9.

For the Plaintiff in *Kesler v. Burnside*, prepare a written outline of objections that you could make to the testimony of Jeffrey Burnside.

PROBLEM D-10.

For the Defendant in *Kesler v. Burnside*, prepare a written outline of objections that you could make to the testimony of Susan Kesler.

PROBLEM D-11.

For the Plaintiff in *Kesler v. Burnside*, prepare a written outline of objections that you could make to the testimony of Judy Larson.

PROBLEM D-12.

For the Defendant in *Kesler v. Burnside*, prepare a written outline of objections that you could make to the testimony of Mary Ewing.

PROBLEM D-13.

For the Plaintiff in *Kesler v. Burnside*, prepare a written outline of objections that the defendants might make to your direct examination of Susan Kesler. Prepare an outline indicating how you will respond to those objections.

PROBLEM D-14.

For the Defendant in *Kesler v. Burnside*, prepare a written outline of objections that the defendants might make to your direct examination of Jeffrey Burnside. Prepare an outline indicating how you will respond to those objections.

PROBLEM D-15.

For the Plaintiff in *Kesler v. Burnside*, prepare a written outline of objections that the defendants might make to your direct examination of Mary Ewing. Prepare an outline indicating how you will respond to those objections.

PROBLEM D-16.

For the Defendant in *Kesler v. Burnside*, prepare a written outline of objections that the defendants might make to your direct examination of Judy Larson. Prepare an outline indicating how you will respond to those objections.

PROBLEM D-17.

Be prepared to make and respond to objections to the direct and cross-examination of Edwin Mills, Susan Kesler and Judy Larson, in *Kesler v. Burnside.*

PROBLEM D-18

Be prepared to make and respond to objections to the direct and cross-examination of Cheryl Pearlman, Donald Adair, and Diane Howard, in *State v. Hunter.*

E. EXHIBITS AND DEMONSTRATIVE EVIDENCE PROBLEMS

PROBLEM E-1.

For the State in *State v. Hunter*, introduce Cheryl Pearlman's purse and the money allegedly taken from it. You may call any witness(es) in order to lay an appropriate foundation.

PROBLEM E-2.

For the Defendant in *State v. Hunter*, introduce the raincoat he was wearing on the night of the crime to prove that it had no stain on its sleeve. You may call any witness(es) in order to lay an appropriate foundation.

PROBLEM E-3.

For the Plaintiff in *Kesler v. Burnside*, introduce the broken wristwatch found by Officer Mills on the pavement near the scene of the accident, to help prove that Kesler was giving an arm signal. You may call any witness(es) to lay the appropriate foundation.

PROBLEM E-4.

For the Defendants in *Kesler v. Burnside*, assume you will call as an expert witness an auto mechanic who examined Kesler's car after it had been towed from the scene of the accident. He will testify that he took the driver's side door apart and discovered that the window glass was missing and the window mechanism was in the "closed" position. That means that the window must have been rolled all the way up at the time of the accident. The mechanic says that anyone can tell this by looking at the disassembled door, because the frame that holds the window glass is at the top of its tracks. You have had Kesler's car towed to the courthouse parking lot. Introduce the car door into evidence. You may call any witness(es) in order to lay the foundation.

PROBLEM E-5.

For the State in *State v. Hunter*, introduce the diagram of the parking lot (page A-39) to aid Cheryl Pearlman in describing the attack. The original diagram was sketched by Donald Adair. You may call any witness(es) to lay the appropriate foundation.

PROBLEM E-6.

For the Defense in *State v. Hunter*, introduce the diagram of the area around Maxwell Street and South Henderson (page A-37) to aid Richard Hunter in describing his movements on the night of the crime. The original diagram was sketched by Paul Swain, a private investigator. You may call any witness(es) to lay the appropriate foundation.

PROBLEM E-7.

For the Plaintiff in *Kesler v. Burnside*, introduce the diagram of the scene of the accident (page B-14) to aid Mary Ewing in describing the events. The original was sketched by Police Officer Edwin Mills. You may call any witness(es) in order to lay the appropriate foundation.

PROBLEM E-8.

For the Defendants in *Kesler v. Burnside*, introduce the diagram of the scene of the accident (page B-14) to aid Jeffrey Burnside in describing the events. The original was sketched by Edwin Mills. You may call any witness(es) in order to lay the appropriate foundation.

PROBLEM E-9.

In order to prove that Cheryl Pearlman was injured, the State in *State v. Hunter* wants to introduce her hospital record (page A-43) into evidence. Lay the necessary foundation to introduce it, calling any appropriate witness(es).

PROBLEM E-10.

In order to corroborate Richard Hunter's alibi, the Defendant wants to prove that "South Park" was scheduled for 8:00 p.m. on January 12, YR-0, using the listing from the Bayshore Herald (page A-49). Lay the necessary foundation to introduce it, calling any appropriate wit-ness(es).

PROBLEM E-11.

In order to prove the amount of damages, Plaintiff in *Kesler v. Burnside* wants to introduce the two hospital bills sent to Susan Kesler by her doctor (page B-23) and Monroe County Hospital (page B-25). Lay the necessary foundation to introduce them, calling any appropriate witness(es).

PROBLEM E-12.

In order to establish contributory negligence, the Defendants in *Kesler v. Burnside* want to introduce the warning ticket issued to Kesler by Officer Dougherty (page B-27). Lay the necessary foundation to introduce it, calling any appropriate witness(es).

PROBLEM E-13.

In *State v. Hunter*, Donald Adair is called as a prosecution witness. When asked what time he first saw Richard Hunter and why he is certain about the time, he says he cannot remember. Try to refresh his recollection using the arrest report (page A-9) and/or the patrol log (page A-45). Be prepared to introduce either document as a record of past recollection if you are unsuccessful in refreshing recollection.

PROBLEM E-14.

In *State v. Hunter*, Diane Howard is called as a defense witness. When asked what time she arrived at Becky Collins' house and why she is certain about the time, she says she cannot remember. Try to refresh her recollection using the statement she made to Jennifer MacPherson (page A-31). Be prepared to introduce the statement as a record of past recollection if you are unsuccessful in refreshing recollection.

PROBLEM E-15.

In *Kesler v. Burnside*, Officer Edwin Mills is called as a witness for the plaintiff. When asked to describe Kesler's appearance when he first arrived at the scene, Officer Mills says he cannot remember. Try to refresh his recollection using either his field report (page B-13) or his narrative statement (page B-15). Be prepared to attempt to introduce either statement as a record of past recollection if you are unsuccessful in refreshing recollection.

PROBLEM E-16.

In *Kesler v. Burnside*, Judy Larson is called as a witness for the defendants. When she is asked how fast the delivery van was going, she says she cannot remember. Try to refresh her recollection using her statement (page B-39). Be prepared to attempt to introduce the statement as a record of past recollection if you are unsuccessful in refreshing recollection.

PROBLEM E-17.

In *State v. Hunter*, the owner of the Ozark Store had installed an automatic closed-circuit television camera to monitor the parking lot after suffering from a series of break-ins. The camera is aimed at the parking lot and records a continuous digital image on a computer. This system recorded the assault on Cheryl Pearlman and the attacker's flight. The image of the attacker is grainy but appears to be Richard Hunter. For the State, lay the necessary foundation to play a DVD copy of the recording for the jury, calling any appropriate witness(es).

PROBLEM E-18.

In *Kesler v. Burnside*, a group of film students from the University of Columbia had been engaged in a project near the accident scene. They had set up a video camera on a tripod overlooking the portion of Highway 451 on which the accident occurred. The camera was pointed at the railroad crossing, and was set to record one image every two seconds automatically. At the time of the accident, none of the students was watching the road. When they looked at the recording, they discovered that one image clearly showed Kesler's car stopped in the road near the Ewing driveway with her left arm extended out the window giving a left turn signal. The truck is not in the picture. For Plaintiff, call any appropriate witness(es) to lay a foundation for the introduction of a two by three-foot photo-enlargement made from that image.

F. DIRECT EXAMINATION PROBLEMS

PROBLEM F-1.

For the State in *State v. Hunter*, prepare and conduct the direct examination of Donald Adair. Assume that the court has granted a defense motion to suppress any use of Hunter's written statement in the state's case-in-chief.

PROBLEM F-2.

For the State in *State v. Hunter*, prepare and conduct the direct examination of Cheryl Pearlman.

PROBLEM F-3.

For the Defendant in *State v. Hunter*, prepare and conduct the direct examination of Richard Hunter. Assume that the court has granted a defense motion to suppress any use of Hunter's written statement in the state's case-in-chief, but has ruled that the statement may be used to impeach Hunter if he testifies at trial.

PROBLEM F-4.

For the Defendant in *State v. Hunter*, prepare and conduct the direct examination of Diane Howard.

PROBLEM F-5.

For the Plaintiff in *Kesler v. Burnside*, prepare and conduct the direct examination of Susan Kesler. Follow the instructions on page B-3 for use of the case file as a full trial without experts.

PROBLEM F-6.

For the Plaintiff in *Kesler v. Burnside*, prepare and conduct the direct examination of Mary Ewing. Follow the instructions on page B-3 for use of the case file as a full trial without experts.

PROBLEM F-7.

For the Defendants in *Kesler v. Burnside*, prepare and conduct the direct examination of Jeffrey Burnside. Follow the instructions on page B-3 for use of the case file as a full trial without experts.

PROBLEM E-8.

For the Defendants in *Kesler v. Burnside*, prepare and conduct the direct examination of Judy Larson. Follow the instructions on page B-3 for use of the case file as a full trial without experts.

G. CROSS-EXAMINATION PROBLEMS

PROBLEM G-1.

For the State in *State v. Hunter*, conduct the cross-examination of Richard Hunter. Base your cross-examination on the direct examination actually conducted by the defense in problem F-3.

PROBLEM G-2.

For the State in *State v. Hunter*, conduct the cross-examination of Diane Howard. Base your cross-examination on the direct examination actually conducted by the defense in problem F-4.

PROBLEM G-3.

In *State v. Hunter*, the defense calls Diane Howard as a witness. For the State, prepare and conduct the cross-examination of this witness. The following new information has come to your attention:

(1) Diane Howard has a prior criminal record. She pleaded guilty to misdemeanor check deception (CCC 240.2 -- passing a bad check knowing it was bad) in Monroe County Court on November 13, YR-1. She was fined $100. She also was adjudicated a juvenile delinquent in Monroe County Juvenile Court on April 30, YR-7, for possession of cocaine (it would have been a felony if she had been tried as an adult) and for committing perjury during the juvenile hearing (she denied possessing the cocaine).

(2) Larry Zollman says that he and Diane needed to talk about a personal matter, so they parked the car on Fess Street between First Street and University Avenue from approximately 8:25 to 8:35, so they could finish their conversation before arriving at Becky's house. He states they would have seen or heard anyone run by, but no one did.

Base your cross-examination on the following direct examination:

DIRECT EXAMINATION OF DIANE HOWARD:

Q: State your name and address, please.
A: Diane Reynolds Howard, 1703 North Maple Street, Bayshore.

Q: How old are you?
A: Twenty-two.

Q: Are you acquainted with the defendant, Richard Hunter?
A: Yes. He is Becky Collins' boyfriend. I have known Becky all my life. We went to school together. She's one of my best friends, so I've met Rich lots of times, like when we all go out together.

Q: Do you know him well enough to recognize him on the street?
A: Of course.

Q: At night?
A: Sure, if there was any light.

Q: Now, directing your attention to January 12 of this year, at about 8:00 p.m., where were you?
A: At Cutter's Supermarket, waiting to pick up my boyfriend, Larry Zollman, and drive to Becky's. We were going to go out with Becky and Rich.

Q: When did you leave?
A: At 8:10 or so. I'm not sure of the time exactly. I did not have my watch with me.

Q: Where did you go?
A: Down Route 45 into town, south on Dunn Street, then left on Atwater, and right on Fess Street. I drove down Fess to the corner of Maxwell Street. Well, we stopped for a minute on Fess, but then drove to Maxwell.

Q: Who was driving?
A: I was.

Q: What time did you get to the corner of Maxwell and Fess?
A: 8:28 or 8:29.

Q: How are you certain?
A: Because it normally takes fifteen or twenty minutes to get to town from Cutter's Market. Larry and I drive it all the time. Also, because I heard the clock chime 8:30 when we got to Becky's house only one or two minutes later.

Q: What happened at the corner of Fess and Maxwell Streets?
A: I saw Richard Hunter on the corner, standing on the south side of Maxwell Street, just as I made the turn.

Q: Are you certain?
A: Yes. There was a streetlight and I saw his face clearly for five or ten seconds. I remember thinking he and Becky must have had a fight and he must have left.

Defense Attorney: No further questions.

PROBLEM G-4.

In *State v. Hunter*, the defense calls Becky Collins as an alibi witness. For the State, assume that you did not call her in your own case-in-chief. Prepare and conduct the cross-examination of Collins based on the following direct examination:

DIRECT EXAMINATION OF BECKY L. COLLINS

Q: State your name and address.
A: Becky Collins. I live in Bayshore, mostly with my boyfriend, Richard Hunter.

Q: Were you living with Richard on January 12th of this year?
A: No, I was living at my parents' home. They were on vacation. They live here in Bayshore, at 906 South Henderson.

Q: On January 12, where were you?
A: I was at work from 11:00 to 7:30, and then I went home -- I mean, to my parents' house.

Q: Was Richard there?
A: Yes. He was watching TV.

Q: What happened next?
A: I got a phone call from my friend, Diane Howard, saying she would be over about 8:30 and we could all go out for drinks. I asked Rich if he wanted to go too, but he said no. He said he was going to play cards to try to win back some of the money he had lost earlier in the week.

Q: Did the two of you have an argument?
A: Sort of. I told him he was playing cards too much and he couldn't afford it because he didn't have a steady job. He said he was tired of me complaining But it blew over and we watched TV until 8:30. I think we watched "South Park."

Q: When did Richard leave?
A: At 8:30 pm. He said he wanted to leave before Diane got there because he didn't like her very much.

Q: Did your friend Diane Howard arrive a few minutes later?
A: Yes. Rich had left and I had turned off the TV. I was cleaning the kitchen when Diane and Larry rang the doorbell.

Q: What happened next?
A: When I answered the door, Diane said she had just seen Richard walking down the street, and asked whether he was going with us. She pointed back down Maxwell Street. I looked and saw Richard about a block away, walking east on Maxwell Street.

Q: What time was this?
A: I didn't look at my watch, but it must have been right around 8:35.

Q: So at 8:35 pm on January 12th, Richard Hunter was near the corner of Fess and Maxwell Streets?
A: Yes.

Attorney: No further questions.

PROBLEM G-5.

For the Defendant in *State v. Hunter*, prepare and conduct the cross-examination of Donald Adair. Assume that the court has granted a defense motion to suppress any use of Hunter's written statement in the state's case-in-chief, but will permit it to be used for impeachment or rebuttal purposes. Base your cross-examination on the direct examination actually conducted by the state in Problem F-1.

PROBLEM G-6.

For the Defendant in *State v. Hunter*, prepare and conduct the cross-examination of Cheryl Pearlman. Base your cross-examination on the direct examination actually conducted by the state in Problem F-2.

PROBLEM G-7.

For the Defendant in *State v. Hunter*, prepare and conduct the cross-examination of Cheryl Pearlman. Base your cross-examination on the following direct examination:

DIRECT EXAMINATION OF CHERYL PEARLMAN

Q: State your name and address.
A: Cheryl Pearlman. I live with my parents at 1000 Pleasant Valley Road.

Q: What is your occupation?
A: I am a graduate student in social psychology at the University of Columbia. I am currently studying problems of behavior modification and socialization among law students for my Ph.D. thesis.

Q: Do you ever go to the law school?
A: Yes, often.

Q: Did you go to the law school on January 12th of this year?
A: Yes. I got there about 8:35 pm.

Q: How can you be sure of the time?
A: I left home at 8:15 by the kitchen clock, and it always takes me about 20 minutes to get to the law school.

Q: Describe what happened when you got to the parking lot.
A: I got out of my car, put my purse over my right shoulder, gathered up my books, and started to walk to the law school. I took four or five steps when a man grabbed me from behind in a choke hold. With his other hand he grabbed me between the legs and said, "Lie down and shut up. I have to have it real bad." He pushed me face down on the pavement, pulled my coat up around my shoulders, and started tugging at my pants.

Q: What happened next?
A: I started to scream and a car drove into the parking lot. We were illuminated in the car's headlights and the man jumped up and ran off. As he ran, he stopped for a minute and looked back at me. I got a good look at his face.

Q: Do you see that man here in the courtroom?
A: Yes, it's the defendant, Richard Hunter.

Q: What happened to your purse?
A: The defendant ran off with it.

Q: Did it have any money in it?
A: Yes, forty-five dollars. Four tens and a five.

Q: Did you ever see the defendant again?
A: Yes. They brought him back to the parking lot only a few minutes after the attack, and I also saw him in a lineup next day at the police station.

Q: Were you injured in the attack?
A: Yes, I had to go to the hospital.

Prosecutor: No further questions.

PROBLEM G-8

In *Kesler v. Burnside*, the defendants call Jeffrey Burnside as a witness. For the Plaintiff, cross-examine this witness. Base your cross-examination on the direct examination actually conducted by defendants.

PROBLEM G-9.

In *Kesler v. Burnside*, the defendants call Judy Larson as a witness. For the Plaintiff, cross-examine this witness. Base your cross-examination on the direct examination actually conducted by defendants.

PROBLEM G-10.

In *Kesler v. Burnside*, the defendants call Judy Larson as a witness. For the Plaintiff, cross-examine this witness. Base your cross-examination on the following direct examination:

DIRECT EXAMINATION OF JUDY LARSON:

Q: What is your name?
A: Judy Larson.

Q: Where do you live?
A: In Johnson's Trailer Court, Route 2, Bayshore.

Q: Are you married?
A: Yes.

Q: Any children?
A: Yes, two boys age 6 and 8.

Q: What does your husband do?
A: My husband got laid off at the plant. He used to work for RCA but they shut down the plant. So I have to work, and he has to take care of the kids. We hope he'll find another job soon.

Q: What kind of work do you do?
A: Housekeeping. I work for two families, cleaning and helping out.

Q: Who are these families?
A: The Robertsons who live on University Avenue, and the Ewings out on 451.

Q: When do you work for the Ewings?
A: Tuesdays and Fridays.

Q: Directing your attention to Friday, August 14, YR-2, did you work that day?
A: Yes, I worked at the Ewing's as usual.

Q: Do you recall where you were at approximately 2:45 p.m.?
A: Yes, I was in the kitchen. I was washing and drying the dishes.

Q: Is there a window in the kitchen?
A: Yes, near the sink.

Q: Did you happen to look out that window at about that time?
A: Yes, I looked out.

Q: Please tell the jury what you could see out the window?
A: Well, the window looks down over the side lawn and a stretch of highway 451 about 75 feet away. From where I was, I could see the lawn sloping down to the road, and the driveway which was on my left. I could see along 451 from the place where it crosses the railroad

tracks, which is on my right, to about 100 feet past the driveway on my left. Mind you, it was raining kind of hard at the time, but the carport roof keeps the window clear.

Q: Excuse me, what carport?
A: Well, there's a carport connected to the kitchen. The window looks out into the carport.

Q: Does this carport have walls like a garage?
A: Oh, no. It's just a roof supported by some posts.

Q: All right. Tell the jury in your own words what you saw.
A: Well, I saw a little yellow or beige foreign car slow down and stop in the road across from the Ewing's driveway. I mean, it just stopped there in the middle of the road. It didn't pull into the driveway or pull off the road. It just stopped right there in the lane of traffic and sat there for a minute or so.

Q: Could you see any turn signals or other lights on the car?
A: No. The car did not have its headlights on. I didn't see any flashing turn signals, but I couldn't clearly see the back of the car. I am sure that the car did not have its signal on as it approached, because I could see the front of it.

Q: Was the driver giving a hand signal when the car stopped?
A: No. There was no arm sticking out of the window.

Q: Are you sure?
A: Yes. I could see her left hand. It was holding a cell phone up at the side of her face.

Q: Had you been drinking alcohol that day?
A: If you mean beer, yeah, I'd had a beer at lunch.

Q: Had it affected you?
A: Of course not. I wasn't drunk or anything like that.

Q: All right. What happened next?
A: I saw a furniture delivery van from Macklin Furniture Company come flying around the corner and cross the tracks, heading east in a big hurry. He never had a chance to slow down, but ran into the back of the yellow car and there was a big crash. It all happened very fast.

Q: How fast was the truck going?
A: About 45 miles per hour.

Q: Do you know the speed limit on Highway 451?
A: Sure, I drive it all the time. It's 45 miles per hour.

Q: How far is it from the railroad tracks to the point of impact?
A: About 100 feet or so.

Q: Now, could the driver of the truck have seen a hand signal from the railroad tracks when he was still 100 feet away?

Plaintiff's Attorney: Objection, your honor, that calls for speculation.

Q: I'll rephrase. Is there any object about the size of a human hand that's 100 feet from where you were?
A: Yes, there's a bird feeder in one of the neighbor's trees just across the road.

Q: Considering the hard rain, how clearly could you see this bird feeder?
A: Not very clearly at all. Because of the rain, I could barely make out what it was. If I hadn't already known it was a bird feeder, I probably could not have made it out.

Q: Thank you. What happened next?
A: Well, I called the police, I turned around and picked up the Ewing's kitchen phone and called 911. I told them that there had been an accident, to send an ambulance out highway 451. Then I hung up and ran down to the road. Ms. Kesler, she was sitting in her car. Her car -- the yellow one -- had been knocked onto the shoulder. The van was also off on the shoulder, and Mr. Burnside was still sitting in the driver's seat. Mr. Burnside looked kind of stunned.

Q: What happened next?
A: Mr. Burnside got out of the truck, and we tried to make Ms. Kesler comfortable. About five minutes later, the police and an ambulance arrived. The ambulance took Ms. Kesler to the hospital and I went back to work.

Defense Attorney: No further questions.

PROBLEM G-11

In *Kesler v. Burnside*, the plaintiff calls Susan Kesler as a witness. For the Defendants, cross-examine this witness. Base your cross-examination on the direct examination actually conducted by plaintiffs.

PROBLEM G-12.

In *Kesler v. Burnside*, the plaintiff calls Mary Ewing as a witness. For the Defendants, cross-examine this witness. Base your cross-examination on the direct examination actually conducted by plaintiffs.

PROBLEM G-13.

In *Kesler v. Burnside*, the plaintiff calls Mary Ewing as a witness. For the Defendants, cross-examine this witness. Base your cross-examination on the following direct examination:

DIRECT EXAMINATION OF MARY EWING

Q: What is your name and address?
A: Mary Ewing. My husband David and I live at 5351 East Highway 451 in Bayshore.

Q: Are you employed?

A: I am a writer, so I work mostly at home.

Q: Were you at home on August 14, about 2:30 pm?
A: Yes. I was waiting for Susan Kesler to arrive. She is a real estate agent whom I met at a business luncheon, who was going to give me some advice on selling our home. It had been listed with another agent, one of the big ones, and we were not getting the kind of service I wanted. We had no serious offers on our house after ten weeks on the market.

Q: Was it raining?
A: Yes, but I think it had let up around 2:30.

Q: Were you watching the road?
A: Yes. From the living room, you can see the highway clearly. It has a big picture window that runs almost the entire 12-foot length of the front wall.

Q: What did you see?
A: I saw Ms. Kesler's car slow down. It was hard to miss -- the car is bright yellow and it had its lights on, and Susan was giving a left-turn arm signal in the rain. You couldn't help but notice it.

Q: What happened next?
A: A big truck from Macklin Furniture came barreling around the corner from the west, and started skidding when it crossed the railroad tracks. It weaved from side to side and slammed into the back of Susan's car. It was driving way too fast, probably 60 or 65 miles per hour. There was a horrible accident, and I saw Susan Kesler thrown through the windshield of her car. I thought she was dead.

Plaintiff's attorney: No further questions.

PROBLEM G-14.

In *State v. Hunter*, Diane Howard testifies for the defense on direct examination that after seeing Hunter on the street, she told Larry Zollman that she saw him and Larry responded, "So did I. I wonder what he's doing out in the cold at 8:25." For the State, impeach this witness using her prior statement (page A-31).

PROBLEM G-15.

In *State v. Hunter*, Donald Adair testifies for the state on direct examination that when he showed Cheryl Pearlman a group of photos, she recognized Hunter's picture and identified it. For the Defendant, impeach this witness using his supplemental report (page A-11).

PROBLEM G-16.

In *Kesler v. Burnside*, Judy Larson testifies on direct examination for the defendants that the furniture van was going about 20 miles per hour when it crossed the railroad tracks. For the Plaintiff, impeach this witness using her prior statement (page B-39).

PROBLEM G-17.

In *Kesler v. Burnside*, Mary Ewing testifies for the plaintiff on direct examination that Kesler's car had its headlights on when it stopped to make the left turn. For the Defendants, impeach this witness using her prior statement (page B-41).

H. EXPERT WITNESS PROBLEMS

PROBLEM H-1.

In *Kesler v. Burnside*, one of the disputed issues is the appropriate measure of damages for Susan Kesler's lost income. To aid the jury in valuing the loss to Kesler's real estate business for the six-month period following the August 14 accident, both sides have retained consultants with expertise in real estate. Their reports can be found at pages B-55 through B-62. Plaintiff should prepare to conduct the direct examination of Shirley Master and the cross-examination of Sandra Hawkins. Defendants should prepare the direct examination of Sandra Hawkins and the cross-examination of Shirley master.

PROBLEM H-2.

March v. Brown Jug Tavern (Case File D) involves a truck-pedestrian accident. It raises the issue whether the victim was within or outside the cross-walk when she was struck by the truck. For the plaintiffs in that case, prepare and present the testimony of Officer Gerald Adams as an accident reconstruction expert. His report is on pages D-13 through D-20)

PROBLEM H-3.

One of the damages issues in *March v. Brown Jug Tavern* (Case File D) is the present value of lost future earnings of the victim. For the defendant in that case, prepare and conduct the testimony of Dr. Jane Moore as an economics expert. Her report is on pages D-71 to 72.

PROBLEM H-4.

In case file E (*State v. Townsley*), the Defendant is charged with attempted murder. She asserts a battered woman defense. For the state, prepare and conduct the testimony of Dr. Linda Cochran on the battered woman syndrome. For the defense, be prepared to oppose the evidence and to cross-examine the witness. Her report is on pages E-59 to 62.

J. CLOSING ARGUMENT PROBLEMS

PROBLEM J-1.

Prepare and present the closing argument for the State in *State v. Hunter*. Assume that the attempted rape charge was dismissed by the judge at the close of the evidence, and limit your argument to the robbery and theft charges. Try to limit your argument to fifteen minutes.

PROBLEM J-2.

Prepare and present the closing argument for the State in *State v. Hunter*. Assume that the attempted rape charge was dismissed by the judge at the close of the evidence, and limit your argument to the robbery and theft charges. Assume we are in a jurisdiction in which the State goes first and last. Be prepared to present both an opening and a final argument. You have a maximum of twenty minutes total time for both arguments.

PROBLEM J-3.

Prepare and present the closing argument for the State in *State v. Hunter*. Assume that the attempted rape charge is still in the case. Try to limit your argument to twenty minutes.

PROBLEM J-4.

Prepare and present the closing argument for the Defendant in *State v. Hunter*. Assume that the attempted rape charge was dismissed by the judge at the close of the evidence, and limit your argument to the robbery and theft charges. Assume we are in a jurisdiction in which the State goes first and last. Try to limit your argument to fifteen minutes.

PROBLEM J-5.

Prepare and present the closing argument for the Defendant in *State v. Hunter*. Assume that the attempted rape charge is still in the case. Assume we are in a jurisdiction in which the State goes first and last. Try to limit your argument to twenty minutes.

PROBLEM J-6.

Prepare and present the closing argument for the Plaintiff in *Kesler v. Burnside*. Assume that the parties have stipulated that the defendant was 80% negligent and the plaintiff was 20% negligent. Limit your argument to the issue of damages, and follow the instructions on page B-3 for trying the case with experts. Try to limit your argument to fifteen minutes. In this jurisdiction, plaintiffs have the right to argue first and last.

PROBLEM J-7.

Prepare and present the closing argument for the Plaintiff in *Kesler v. Burnside.* Assume that the parties have stipulated that the total amount of damages is $400,000. Limit your argument to the issues of negligence and comparative fault, and follow the instructions on page B-3 for trying the case without experts. Try to limit your argument to fifteen minutes. In this jurisdiction, plaintiffs have the right to argue first and last.

PROBLEM J-8.

Prepare and present closing argument for the Plaintiff in *Kesler v. Burnside.* Argue all issues, including liability, comparative negligence, and damages. Follow the instructions on page B-3 for use as a full trial with experts. Try to limit your argument to twenty-five minutes. In this jurisdiction, plaintiff has the right to go first and last. For purposes of this exercise, plaintiff's attorney must reserve at least ten minutes of his or her time for final argument.

PROBLEM J-9.

Prepare and present the closing argument for the Defendant in *Kesler v. Burnside.* Assume that the parties have stipulated that the defendant was 80% negligent and the plaintiff was 20% negligent. Limit your argument to the issue of damages, and follow the instructions on page B-3 for trying the case with experts. Try to limit your argument to fifteen minutes. Plaintiffs have the right to argue first and last.

PROBLEM J-10.

Prepare and present the closing argument for the Defendant in *Kesler v. Burnside.* Assume that the parties have stipulated that the total amount of damages is $400,000. Limit your argument to the issues of negligence and comparative fault, and follow the instructions on page B-3 for trying the case without experts. Try to limit your argument to fifteen minutes. In this jurisdiction, plaintiffs have the right to argue first and last.

PROBLEM J-11.

Prepare and present closing argument for the Defendant in *Kesler v. Burnside.* Argue all issues, including liability, comparative negligence, and damages. Follow the instructions on page B-3 for use as a full trial with experts. Try to limit your argument to twenty-five minutes. In this jurisdiction, plaintiff has the right to go first and last.

PART TWO: CASE FILES

CASE FILE A:

STATE OF COLUMBIA

v.

RICHARD HUNTER

ROBBERY
ATTEMPTED RAPE

STATE v. HUNTER
CONTENTS OF FILE

GENERAL INSTRUCTIONS

This is a criminal case. The defendant is charged with attempted rape, robbery, and theft. He says he is not guilty and is the victim of mistaken identity. All events took place in January in a fictional city called Bayshore, Columbia (population 150,000).

Potential Witnesses

Cheryl Pearlman -- victim.
James Corbin, University of Columbia Police Department -- first officer on the scene.
Donald Adair, Bayshore Police Department -- arresting officer and chief investigator.
Dr. Stanley Reed, Monroe County Hospital -- physician who examined Cheryl Pearlman.
Richard Hunter -- defendant.
Becky Collins -- defendant's girlfriend.
Diane Howard -- friend of Becky Collins.

Instructions Concerning Exhibits

1. The state may use any purse and wallet as Cheryl Pearlman's.

2. The defense may use any raincoat as Richard Hunter's.

Instructions for Use as a Full Trial

1. The state must call Cheryl Pearlman and Donald Adair as witnesses in its case-in-chief.

2. The defense must call Richard Hunter and Diane Howard as witnesses in its case-in-chief.

3. Either side may call James Corbin, Dr. Reed, and/or Becky Collins; or the parties may stipulate to any or all of their testimony.

Stipulations

1. The FBI Identification Record on Richard Hunter (page A-17) is an accurate copy of the official record on file with the FBI.

2. The Bayshore Transit bus timetable (page A-47) is a true and accurate copy of the official bus schedule for January, YR-0. Bayshore Transit is operated by the City of Bayshore.

3. Douglas Wyatt, the assistant district attorney who conducted the preliminary hearing, has moved to Washington, D.C., and taken a job with the Solicitor General's Office.

4. Jennifer MacPherson, Richard Hunter's original defense attorney, has been appointed a state appeals court judge and withdrawn from the case.

5. Richard Hunter has been out on bail since February 19, YR-0. His coat was returned to him when he left jail.

6. Any criminal offense listed as a misdemeanor is one for which the maximum statutory penalty is one year or less. Any offense listed as a felony is one for which the maximum penalty is more than one year.

Note on Dates

The designation YR-0 refers to the present year; YR-1 is last year; YR-2 is two years ago, etc.

STATE OF COLUMBIA
County of Monroe

FILE # 012350N

THE STATE OF COLUMBIA)
)
vs.) **INDICTMENT**
)
RICHARD HUNTER,)
Defendant)

THE GRAND JURORS FOR THE STATE UPON THEIR OATH PRESENT:

That on or about the 12th day of January, YR-0, at or about 8:30 p.m., in Monroe County, RICHARD HUNTER unlawfully and willfully did feloniously:

COUNT I: Attempt to rape Cheryl Pearlman, female, forcibly and against her will, by pushing her to the ground and attempting to remove her clothes, with the intent to compel her to submit to sexual intercourse by force; in violation of Columbia Criminal Code § 213.1.

COUNT II: Take and carry away from the person of Cheryl Pearlman her purse and the contents of it, without her consent and with the intent to deprive her thereof, by pulling the purse from her possession; in violation of Columbia Criminal Code § 223.2.

COUNT III: During the course of committing the theft set forth in Count II, inflict serious bodily injury upon Cheryl Pearlman, and threaten to inflict immediate serious bodily injury by choking her and attempting to rape her; in violation of Columbia Criminal Code § 222.1.

Douglas Wyatt
Assistant District Attorney

WITNESSES:
Cheryl Pearlman
Ofc. Donald Adair, BPD ✘
Ofc. James Corbin, UCPD

The witnesses marked with an X were sworn by the undersigned foreperson of the Grand Jury, and this bill was found to be ✔ a True Bill/___ not a True Bill.

This the 21st of January, YR-0

Bruce Beddow
Grand Jury Foreperson

EXCERPTS FROM COLUMBIA CRIMINAL CODE

§ 213.1. Rape. (a) A male who has sexual intercourse with a female is guilty of rape if:

(1) he compels her to submit by force or by threat of imminent death, serious bodily injury, or extreme pain; or

(2) he has substantially impaired her power to appraise or control her conduct by administering or employing without her knowledge drugs, intoxicants or other means for the purpose of preventing resistance; or

(3) the female is unconscious.

(b) Rape is a felony of the second degree unless in the course thereof the actor inflicts serious bodily injury upon her, in which case the offense is a felony of the first degree.

§ 5.01. Criminal Attempt. (a) A person is guilty of an attempt to commit a crime if, acting with the kind of culpability otherwise required for commission of the crime, such person purposely does or omits to do anything which, under the circumstances as such person believes them to be, is an act or omission constituting a substantial step in a course of conduct planned to culminate in such person's commission of the crime.

(b) An attempt to commit a felony constitutes an offense of the next lower degree, except that an attempt to commit a felony of the third degree shall constitute a misdemeanor.

§ 223.2. Theft. (a) A person is guilty of theft if such person unlawfully takes, or exercises unlawful control over, the movable property of another with purpose to deprive the other person thereof.

(b) Theft constitutes a felony of the third degree if the amount involved exceeds $500, or if the property stolen is a firearm, automobile, airplane, motorcycle, motorboat or other motor-propelled vehicle, or in the case of theft by receiving stolen property, if the receiver is in the business of buying or selling stolen property.

© Theft not within the preceding paragraph constitutes a misdemeanor, except that if the property was not taken from the person or by threat, or in breach of a fiduciary obligation, and the actor proves by a preponderance of the evidence that the amount involved was less than $100, the offense constitutes a petty misdemeanor.

§ 222.1 Robbery. (a) A person is guilty of robbery if, in the course of committing a theft, the actor:

(1) inflicts serious bodily injury upon another; or

(2) threatens another with or purposely puts another in fear of immediate serious bodily injury; or

(3) commits or threatens immediately to commit any felony of the first or second degree.

(b) An act shall be deemed "in the course of committing a theft" if it occurs in an attempt to commit theft or in flight after the attempt or commission. An injury shall be deemed "serious" if it creates a substantial risk of death, causes permanent disfigurement, or causes loss or impairment of the function of any bodily member or organ.

© Robbery is a felony of the second degree unless the actor is armed with a weapon, in which case it is a felony of the first degree.

BAYSHORE POLICE DEPARTMENT ARREST REPORT

1 DATE OF REPORT: **1/12/YR-0**
2 TIME: **11:10 pm**
3 ARRESTING OFFICER'S NAME: **Donald Adair**
4 RANK: **PO**
5 BADGE: **235**

6 DEFENDANT NAME: **Richard Hunter**
7 ADDRESS: **314 E 11th St, Bayshore**
8 CRIMES: **213.1 Att rape, 222.1 Robbery, 223.2 Theft**

9 VICTIM NAME: **Cheryl Pearlman**
10 SEX: **F**
11 AGE: **24**
12 ADDRESS: **1000 Pleasant Valley Rd, Bayshore**
13 CONTACT INFORMATION: **339-7138, cpearl733@aol.com**
14 EMPLOYER: **Univ of Columbia student**

15 DATE OF CRIME: **1/12/YR-0**
16 TIME: **8:30 pm**
17 LOCATION: **Between 3rd & 4th Streets west side of Henderson St**
18 TYPE OF PREMISES: **Parking lot**
19 WEATHER: **cold, wet**
20 HOW ATTACKED OR COMMITTED: **Victim grabbed from behind, choked, pushed to ground, suspect pulled clothing and stole purse**
21 WEAPON/TOOLS: **No**
22 PERSON REPORTING CRIME: **Jim Corbin, UCPD**
23 ADDRESS: **UCPD, Donner Hall, Univ of Columbia**
24 CONTACT INFORMATION: **335-2886**
25 TIME/DATE OF REPORT: **8:35 pm 1/12/YR-0**
26 TOTAL VALUE STOLEN: **$100**
27 TOTAL VALUE RECOVERED: **$0**
28 CURRENCY: **unknown**
29 JEWELRY:
30 AUTOS:
31 COMPUTERS/TV ETC:
32 FIREARMS:
33 OTHER: **Purse, wallet, credit cards, cell phone**

34 TOTAL PERSONS INVOLVED: **1**
35 TOTAL ARRESTED: **1**
36 ADULTS ARRESTED: **1**
37 JUVENILES ARRESTED: **0**
38 TOTAL AT LARGE: **0**

39 OTHER BPD OFFICERS INVOLVED:

40 NARRATIVE: **At about 8:40 pm I responded to radio run and LOF in area of southwest corner of UC campus. I was proceeding west on Maxwell Street when suspect matching description was seen crossing street from north to south. Suspect began to run upon seeing my patrol vehicle. Suspect ordered to halt but continued running. Suspect detained without incident, gave spontaneous admission of guilt without being prompted, stated he was unlucky to have been caught so quickly. I returned to scene with suspect, where he was identified by victim. Victim was taken to hospital by Ofc James Corbin, UCPD. Suspect was placed under arrest and given Miranda warnings and indicated he understood them. Suspect made no request for lawyer, stating he did not mean to hurt victim but admitting he took the money. Behavior consistent with guilt. Suspect made no further statement.**

41 OFFICER'S SIGNATURE: *Donald Adair 235*

BAYSHORE POLICE DEPARTMENT SUPPLEMENTAL REPORT

1 DATE OF REPORT: **1/13/YR-0**
2 OFFICER'S NAME: **Donald Adair 235**
3 DEFENDANT NAME: **Richard Hunter**

4 NARRATIVE: **On today's date I returned to vicinity of Fess and Maxwell Sts location of arrest. Upon arrival, caught two juveniles looking through victim's purse and wallet. Juveniles said they found purse in bushes, were looking for ID to return purse, not detained. Wallet contained ID for victim Pearlman, who identified purse as one taken in robbery. Victim states that $45 missing from wallet, but all credit cards still there. Stated cell phone had been in purse and was missing. Currency was four tens and a five. Checked suspect's inventory of possessions at jail, discovered suspect was in possession of currency when arrested. I interrogated suspect further. He said he won the money gambling. When confronted with the purse, suspect showed recognition by facial expression and stated "Look, I'll tell you the truth. I saw some guy running down the street who threw the purse into the bushes. All I did was pick it up and take the money. You arrested me right after that." Suspect appeared nervous. I believe he was lying. Later, victim arrived at station to make a statement. She was unable to identify Hunter from photo array, although she seemed to recognize Hunter's photo. She asked for live line-up to be sure and said she would not make an ID unless she was sure. Suspect showed to victim in 3-person lineup and she gave a positive identification. Standard protocol followed. I asked her to take her time and be sure and made no suggestive statements. Victim stated immediately that she recognized Hunter, saying "How could I ever forget him." I telephoned Monroe County Hospital and talked to Dr. Stanley Reed in the ER who stated that victim's injuries were potentially serious because located near larynx part of throat.**

With victim's consent, currency and purse retained as exhibits; wallet and its contents returned to victim.

5 OFFICER'S SIGNATURE: *Donald Adair 235*

CITY OF BAYSHORE

POLICE DEPARTMENT "TO SERVE AND PROTECT"

LEGAL RIGHTS ADVICE FORM

Before we ask you any questions, you must understand your rights.

1. You have the right to remain silent.

2. Anything you say can and will be used against you in court.

3. You have the right to consult with a lawyer before we ask you any questions, and to have the lawyer present with you during questioning.

4. If you cannot afford a lawyer, one will be appointed for you before any questioning if you wish.

5. If you decide to answer questions now without a lawyer present, you will still have the right to stop answering at any time.

WAIVER

I have read this statement of my rights and I understand what my rights are. I understand that I may ask for clarification and explanation of my rights if I do not understand them. I am willing to make a statement and answer questions. I do not want a lawyer at this time. I understand and know what I am doing. No promises or threats have been made to me, and no pressure or coercion of any kind has been used against me.

Date: Jan. 13, YR-0 Signature: Richard Hunter

Witness: Donald S Adair 235 Witness: Todd Bowers

Time: 2:40 pm Place: Bayshore PD Building

CITY OF BAYSHORE

POLICE DEPARTMENT "TO SERVE AND PROTECT"

STATEMENT OF RICHARD HUNTER
Made to Donald Adair, BPD
Transcribed from tape recorded interrogation
1/13/YR-0

My name is Richard Hunter, 314 East Eleventh Street, Bayshore, Columbia. I am twenty-two years old and have lived in Bayshore all my life. I am unmarried but have a girlfriend named Becky Collins who lives at 906 South Henderson, Bayshore. My parents also live in Bayshore, at 1616 West Allen Street. I am unemployed and a part-time student at the University of Columbia. I went to a small college in Indiana called Butler on a basketball scholarship, but was kicked out my freshman year because they said I cheated on an exam. A couple of us broke into the English department office and stole a copy of the mid-term exam. I paid a smart kid to prepare an answer for me. When they caught me, I lied and said I hadn't cheated but they kicked me out anyway. Then I came back to Bayshore and went to work for Bayshore Ford where my father works, but got laid off in YR-2. For the last two years I have been looking for work, doing odd jobs, borrowing money from my parents, and going to college part time. I am taking classes in the Physical Education and Recreation Department. I'd like to be a high school coach, because I thought the best thing I got out of school was the chance to play football and basketball.

I play in a medium-stakes poker game every Tuesday night with some guys I know from Bayshore Ford. This week there were two guys from Chicago who I didn't know. They must have been cheating, because I lost almost $500.00. That left me flat broke. So I spent most of Wednesday and Thursday at my girlfriend's house. On Thursday, January 12, I was at Becky's house all day, mostly watching television. Becky was at work at Rick's Café.

Becky came home about 7:00 p.m. She showered and changed, and spent about fifteen minutes on the telephone talking to her friend, Diane Howard. At 8:00, we started watching South Park. It was a re-run of one of my favorite episodes where Chef gets arrested for harassing a record company defended by Johnnie Cochran who comes up with the Chewbacca defense. He keeps telling the jury that if Chewbacca lives on Endor, you must acquit, but no one understands what he means. Becky said that Diane was coming over and they were going out and she asked if I wanted to come. I told her she should have asked me first, because what if I wanted to have a quiet romantic evening at home? She criticized me for always sitting around watching television and not having a job. We had our usual fight over my not making any money and always borrowing from her, and I told her I was looking for a job. Finally, I just couldn't stand it anymore, and I needed to get out of there. I told her I wasn't going to go out with her, put on my coat, and left. It was just a minute or two before 8:30, because South Park was over and the next show had not started yet. It was my favorite episode and I missed most of it because Becky was being bitchy. I left the house and walked east on Maxwell Street to calm down. I was pretty angry, I guess.

I had gone one block when I saw a guy in a tan coat or long jacket run around the northwest corner of Fess and Maxwell Streets. He had been coming south on Fess. He saw me and threw something into the bushes, then ran across Maxwell Street and disappeared. I walked across the street and found a woman's purse in the bushes. I took out the wallet and removed forty-five dollars. I had been walking on the south side of the street. I returned to the south side of Maxwell Street. I decided to go home, so I started to jog toward Henderson Street. I thought I could catch a bus there that would go northwest toward my apartment. I do not ride the bus very much. I was jogging because it was cold. As I was jogging toward Henderson Street, I was stopped by the police. I did not stop at first because I wanted to get home and was afraid I might miss the bus. Officer Adair ordered me to stop, and I did. I know I said something like "What a time for you to come along, you don't get something for nothing," but I only meant finding the purse. I did not take the purse from the woman who was attacked. I was never in the parking lot or anywhere near the campus that night. I was at Becky's home, and she can vouch for the fact that I was there.

I was taken to the Law School parking lot by Officer Adair. We parked about twenty feet from a campus police car. A young woman was there screaming and crying. I was confused. I heard the campus cop say she had been attacked at 8:25 that night but I didn't know if that had anything to do with why I was arrested. At one point Officer Adair asked me if I had heard what the woman said. I did not hear anything she said, so I just shrugged because I did not know what he was talking about. I was at Becky's at 8:25. I was given a card to read with my constitutional rights on them, but I did not actually read it. I watch television and I know my rights and I have nothing to hide. I told Officer Adair then that I never touched the woman, didn't have anything to do with whatever happened to her, and I didn't know why she was screaming. Then the cop made me get out of the car and he put handcuffs on me. He took me to the police station, and they took all my possessions and put me in jail. I've been in jail before. I was arrested a couple of times for possession of marijuana. You know, I'd be at a party where lots of people were using drugs, and we'd all get arrested. I never got convicted of anything, though, and I don't use or sell any drugs anymore. Just say no to drugs and all that crap.

On January 13, they came and got me in my cell and took me to see Adair. I complained because they only give you one blanket and it looks like it's never been washed. Also, there was no coffee for breakfast because the jailer said the coffee machine was broken. Officer Adair asked me about the money. At first I thought he meant the money I had lost, so I told him I had been playing poker. Then he held up a purse I recognized as the one I had found, and I realized he meant the forty-five dollars. I told him the truth, that I had seen a guy running along Maxwell Street who threw the purse in the bushes, and I took the money out of it. I told him that I was flat broke and needed money because Becky did not have any to lend me. I had nothing to do with attacking that woman in the parking lot.

I have read the foregoing and it is true and accurate. There is nothing I want to change or add.

Richard Hunter

Richard Hunter

UNITED STATES DEPARTMENT OF JUSTICE
FEDERAL BUREAU OF INVESTIGATION
IDENTIFICATION DIVISION
WASHINGTON, D.C. 20537

The following FBI record, NUMBER 4 207 733 P13 , is furnished for OFFICIAL USE ONLY. Information shown on this Identification Record represents data furnished FBI by fingerprint contributors. WHERE DISPOSITION DATA IS NOT SHOWN OR FURTHER EXPLANATION OF CHARGE OR DISPOSITION IS DESIRED, COMMUNICATE WITH AGENCY CONTRIBUTING THOSE FINGERPRINTS.

CONTRIBUTOR: IDENTIFIER (ORI) NAME CASE NUMBER (OCA)	SUBJECT: NAME STATE NUMBER	ARRESTED OR RECEIVED	C - CHARGE D - DISPOSITION
CO203010 PD BAYSHORE COL 3N2001	HUNTER, RICHARD CO3722480N	07/02/-5 07/10/-5	C - CCC 415.4 MISD POSS DRUGS D - DISMISSED
CO203010 PD BAYSHORE COL 3P2147	HUNTER, RICHARD CO3722480N	03/16/-1 04/10/-1	C - CCC 415.4 MISD POSS DRUGS D - GUILTY 415.9 PUBLIC NUISANCE FINE $50
CO203010 PD BAYSHORE COL 5R3133	HUNTER, RICHARD CO3722480N	01/12/-0	C - CCC 213.1 ATT RAPE CCC 222.1 ROBBERY

CITY OF BAYSHORE

POLICE DEPARTMENT "TO SERVE AND PROTECT"

STATEMENT OF CHERYL PEARLMAN
Made to Donald Adair, BPD
Transcribed from tape recorded interrogation
1/13/YR-0

My name is Cheryl Pearlman. I live with my parents at 1000 Pleasant Valley Road, Bayshore. I was born on May 6, YR-24, in Indianapolis. I am unmarried and a graduate student in social psychology at the University of Columbia. I went to Park-Tudor Preparatory School and received a B.A. from Smith College in YR-2. My father is a physician in general practice and my mother is a housewife. I am seeing a psychiatrist, Dr. Rachel Lieberman, for anxiety and depression, but I never had any problems with delusions. I am currently taking Prozac, an antidepressant. I was taking that medication on January 12th, but it does not affect me outwardly. All it does is prevent major depressions. I have never experienced any side effects other than insomnia. Since the attack, however, I have had nightmares.

On January 12th, I met with my major professor, Jeffrey Mitchell, in the morning, regarding my research on behavior modification and socialization among law students. I had almost no money with me, so I stopped at the campus union and got $50.00 from the ATM. I met a friend, Melodee Butler, for lunch at the union. My bill came to $6.80. I paid it, and that meant I had about forty-five dollars in bills in my wallet. I am certain I had four tens and one five, and I may have had one or two one-dollar bills also. I spent no more money that day.

money discrepancy

I ate dinner with my parents at our usual time of 7:00 p.m. I helped clean up and then decided to go to the law school to do some research for my master's thesis. I remember checking my watch and noticing that it was 8:15 p.m. It was cold, so I put on a coat and hat. I was wearing wool slacks. It took me about ten minutes to drive to the law school. It had rained earlier, but had stopped by late afternoon. I'm not sure exactly what time I got to the law school, but it was between 8:25 and 8:30.

When I got to the parking lot, it was dark and cloudy. There were lights on outside of the law school, and I think there is a street light on the corner of Henderson and Fourth Street. There were also lights coming from the Ozark Store. I could see fairly well. I parked in the center of the lot, at the median on the law school side. There were very few other cars in the lot, all unoccupied as far as I could tell. I have a new YR-0 Honda, and I did not want it to get scratched, so I parked away from the other cars. I got out, put my purse over my right shoulder, and gathered up my notebooks. I locked the car, and started to walk toward the law school front entrance. I took four or five steps when I was grabbed from behind in a choke hold. A man's right arm was around my throat, choking me. The man said, "Lie down and shut up. I have to have it real bad." I knew he would kill me if I resisted. I felt him pulling at my coat, trying to get it off me. He pushed me to the ground, still pulling at my coat. I noticed the sleeve of his coat. It was a raincoat-type material, and had a stain on the sleeve. I fell on all fours, with my head pointed in the direction of the law building front door. I felt him get on top of me and then something hit the back of my head. I was stunned for a second, and then I think I started to scream. The man stopped attacking me and ran off.

He ran toward the Ozark Store. I saw the headlights of a car pulling into the parking lot from Henderson Street. When he was about twenty feet away, he turned to look at me. I thought he was going to come back and rape me. He took a step toward me and I got a good look at his face. I remember he was a tall, young man, brown hair, medium build, wearing a dark colored raincoat. He was about six feet tall and had either a beard or moustache. He was not carrying a gun or knife as far as I remember. Then he changed his mind, turned, and ran around the music store and disappeared south on Henderson Street.

I was very upset because I had almost been raped, so I'm not too clear about what happened next. A campus police officer named Corbin tried to calm me down. I gave him a description of the man who attacked me. I was sitting in the front seat of his patrol car when a city police car drove up. I really have no idea of how long it had been since I was attacked. The city police car parked about ten feet away. As the city policeman was walking over, I saw the man who had attacked me sitting in the back of his police car. I am sure it was the same man. I remember crying, "Keep him away from me. Then I must have fainted because the next thing I remember is waking up in the hospital. Officer Corbin was with me. I realized my purse was missing and had this vague recollection that maybe it was pulled from me when the attacker ran off. I described it to Officer Corbin and told him it contained forty-five dollars and my cell phone. When I realized I wasn't hurt, I refused medication. They released me from the hospital and Officer Corbin took me home.

The next day, January 13th, I was called by Officer Adair of the Bayshore Police. He asked me to come down and make a statement. I went down around noon. I identified my purse which Officer Adair said he found on Maxwell Street. Luckily, my debit card and keys were still there, but the cell phone was gone. I looked at some photographs. One or two looked like the man who attacked me, but I couldn't be sure. I asked to see a lineup. A short time later, Officer Adair asked me to look in a room through one-way glass. All he said to me was to look at all three people carefully. They were sitting around a table, talking. They were all casually dressed. I immediately recognized one as the man who had attacked me. I told Officer Adair, "That's him. How could I ever forget his face?" He told me the guy's name was Richard Hunter. The name didn't mean anything to me, but I was sure I'd seen his face somewhere before -- maybe in the library. One of the other police officers told me that Mr. Hunter was a suspect in a series of assaults on women in the University Library. I then voluntarily gave this statement.

I have read the foregoing and it is true. I do not want to add or change anything. I do not wish to speak personally with Richard Hunter's attorneys, but I authorize them to have a copy of this statement.

Cheryl Pearlman

Cheryl Pearlman

State of Columbia File # 012350
County of Monroe

State of Columbia)
)
vs.) In the Circuit Court
)
Richard Hunter) January 19, YR-0

TRANSCRIPT OF PRELIMINARY HEARING

COURT: Case of State v. Hunter, docket number 012350. Are both sides ready?
MR. WYATT: The state is ready, your honor.
MS. MACPHERSON: The defense is ready.
COURT: You may proceed.
MR. WYATT: Call Officer Donald Adair.
[whereupon the witness was duly sworn]
Q: State your name and occupation.
A: Donald Adair, patrolman, Bayshore Police Department.
Q: How long have you been on the force?
A: Seven years. In that time I've been mostly a patrolman, although I've also been temporarily assigned to the detective bureau.
Q: So you handled the Hunter case?
A: Yes I did. We're short-handed right now, and since I'd worked as a detective before, Lieutenant Callahan put me in charge of the case instead of assigning a regular detective to it. That's a little unusual, but Callahan told me that since I had won the Police Officer of the Year Award last year, he thought I could handle it.
Q: Tell us about yourself.
A: I'm married and have two kids. I grew up in Bayshore, graduated from Bayshore High School in YR-10. I did three years as an Army M.P., with a tour in Iraq, and then joined the force here in Bayshore.
Q: Were you on duty January 12th and 13th of this year?
A: Yes.

Q: And did you arrest the defendant, Richard Hunter?

A: Yes.

Q: Why?

A: We suspect him of being the person who attacked and attempted to rape Cheryl Pearlman. Ms. Pearlman has made a voluntary statement to me that at 8:35 p.m. on January 12th, she was grabbed from behind, choked and pushed to the ground by the defendant who tried to subdue her and pull her clothing off and then ran off with her purse containing $45.00.

Q: Where did you arrest Hunter?

A: At about 8:40 p.m. January 12th I was on routine patrol. I was driving west on Maxwell, between Park and Stull Streets. I received an LOF -- that's a "look out for" -- for a young man, medium build, brown coat, last seen near the University of Columbia Law School. I pulled over between Stull and Fess Streets to note the call in my logbook. When I looked up, I saw a person fitting that description crossing Maxwell from north to south, about 50 feet away. I drove up and he must have seen me, because the suspect started to run away from me, west on Maxwell. I rolled down the window and yelled at him to stop. He kept running and called out that he had to catch a bus. I knew he was lying because the buses stop running at 8:30 p.m. on that line. I pulled in front of him, blocking his path, and jumped out. I ordered him to stop, at which point he threw up his hands in disgust and said, "Jesus, what a time for you to come along; nobody gets something for nothing." I asked him to accompany me, and he got in the car. I radioed that I had a suspect and dispatch said the victim was still at the scene, so I returned to the scene of the crime.

Q: What happened next?

A: I drove to the parking lot across from the law school and parked about 15 feet north of a campus patrol vehicle. I recognized Officer James Corbin, a campus police officer, who was standing next to a young woman sitting in the front seat of his car. I gave Hunter a card with his rights on them, exited my vehicle, and proceeded over to Corbin's vehicle. I asked if this was the victim, and Corbin said yes, she was Cheryl Pearlman. I told him I had a suspect I had just picked up on Maxwell Street. I asked him what time the attack had occurred, and he said about 8:35. I had first seen Hunter at 8:41.

Q: Could Hunter have gotten from the parking lot to Maxwell Street in six

minutes?
A: Sure. It's only one-half mile. He could do it at a slow jog.
Q: Go on.
A: About this time, Pearlman looked up -- she had been sobbing -- and saw Hunter in my vehicle. She screamed, "It's him. Keep him away from me," and then fainted. Corbin took her to the hospital and I formally arrested Hunter and put wrist restraints on him.
Q: Did he make a statement?
A: Yes. He told me he understood his rights, then he said, "I needed the money but I never touched the girl." He was nervous and shaky when he said it. I asked him if he had heard her accusation, and he shrugged and said, "I don't know nothing about it."
Q: What else happened?
A: Corbin called me later that evening and reported that Pearlman's purse was missing which contained forty-five dollars. I went down to the jail and looked in the envelope containing Hunter's possessions, and found four tens and a five. The jailer said it had been in Hunter's pocket, not in his wallet, when they inventoried his possessions during booking.
Q: Did you do any further investigation?
A: Yes. Next morning I drove back to the corner of Fess and Maxwell where I had first seen Hunter. I found Pearlman's purse and wallet in the bushes. The wallet had no money in it, but contained Pearlman's identification and credit cards. Also her cell phone was in the purse. I called Pearlman and asked her to come down to the station.
Q: Did she?
A: Yes. She identified her purse and verified that it had contained four tens and one five at the time she was attacked. This was a little after noon. I showed her five photographs, one was of Hunter. She seemed to hesitate over Hunter's photo, like she recognized him, but said she would have to see him in person to be sure. I set up a line-up, with Hunter and two detectives, all sitting around a table. She looked through one-way glass, and immediately said, "That's him; how could I ever forget?" She identified her assailant as the one on the left end, which was Hunter. I took her statement and she left.
Q: What did you do next?
A: I brought Hunter to my office and repeated his constitutional rights.

I asked him where he had gotten the forty-five dollars. He said he had won it in a poker game. Then I took the purse out of the desk. He looked at it and appeared startled, and changed his story. He said, "Look, I'll tell the truth. I took the money from the purse, but some other guy robbed that woman." I asked if he wanted to make a full statement. I have it here.

MR. WYATT: We offer this as state's exhibit 1, and also Ms. Pearlman's statement as state's exhibit 2.

COURT: Received. Anything else?

MR. WYATT: No, your honor.

MS. MACPHERSON: I have some brief cross-examination.

Q: How can you be sure of the times?

A: We set our watches by the clock at the police station before each shift.

Q: Have you had any training in fingerprint identification?

A: Not much.

Q: Did you send the purse to the lab for fingerprint tests, or do anything to test it for fingerprints?

A: No. I figured since it had sat out on a cold rainy night, there was no point.

Q: Are you aware that fingerprints can last for weeks even if the object is left outside?

A: I didn't know that.

Q: You didn't believe Mr. Hunter's statement about the other man, did you?

A: No I didn't.

Q: But if you'd tested the purse for fingerprints, you might have found this other man's prints, isn't that true?

A: Not likely, since Pearlman positively identified Hunter as her assailant.

Q: Her cell phone was missing, is that right? And it has not been recovered? You didn't find it on Hunter, right?

A: That's right.

Q: Let's talk about the identification. Did you preserve the photo array?

A: No.

Q: Was anyone other than Hunter in both the photo array and the line-up?

A: No.

Q: What exactly did you say to Ms. Pearlman about the line-up?

A: Just to take her time and look carefully at all three people.

Q: What did you tell her on the phone?

A: To come down to the station to make a statement and identify her purse.

Q: Did you tell her you wanted her to view a suspect?
A: No, only that we had a suspect in custody. I didn't volunteer that -- she asked.
Q: Was Hunter wearing his coat during the line-up?
A: No. We told him to remove it so all three persons would be dressed the same. He put it over the chair next to him.
Q: Do you remember if his coat had a stain on the sleeve?
A: I never looked.
Q: Isn't it true you told Ms. Pearlman not to talk to me?
A: No. I told her she didn't have to if she didn't want to, and that quite frankly it would be your job to try to twist her words so it would look like she was lying.
Q: Speaking of twisting words, isn't it true you were accused of witness tampering in your rookie year for coaching witnesses on what to say?
A: Yes, by a drug dealer. The charge was ridiculous.
Q: You went to a disciplinary hearing on November 11, YR-7, didn't you?
A: Yes.
Q: And you were suspended for thirty days, correct?
A: Yes, but I never did anything. I certainly never tampered with witnesses. It was a frame-up by drug dealers.
Q: In your police report, you said two juveniles were looking through Pearlman's wallet when you arrived on January 13. Tell us about that.
A: No, the wallet was still in the purse, I think. The two juveniles were simply in the vicinity. I determined they had no connection to the crime.
Q: Did you search them for any money or other property that might have come from the purse, such as the missing cell phone?
A: No.
Q: When you took Hunter to the parking lot, where was he sitting?
A: In the back seat, driver's side.
Q: Did you inform Hunter of his right to counsel before putting him in the line-up?
A: Yes. I told him to read the warning which was written in big print on the wall of the line-up room. He said he knew his rights.
Q: In the car, you only gave him a Miranda card -- you didn't actually read him his rights, correct?
A: Correct.

MS. MACPHERSON: Nothing further.
MR. WYATT: We call Officer James Corbin.
[Whereupon the witness was duly sworn]
Q: State your name and occupation.
A: James Corbin, Public Safety Officer for the University of Columbia Police Department. I've been working there two years after graduating from Jefferson Community College in police science.
Q: Do you recall the events of January twelfth?
A: Yes, I do. I was on routine patrol in the southwest quadrant of the campus when the Pearlman woman -- what's her first name?
Q: Cheryl.
A: Yes, when Cheryl Pearlman was assaulted in Lot "L" across from the Law School.
Q: Tell us in your own words what happened.
A: I had just turned the corner from Third Street onto Henderson. I was going northbound, when I heard screaming. I rolled down my window and determined that the screams were coming from the Law School parking lot.
Q: What time was this?
A: I did not check my watch, but I'm sure it was between 8:30 and 8:34, because I looked at my watch after locating Ms. Pearlman and obtaining a description. It was 8:36 at that point, and five minutes or less had elapsed.
Q: What was the weather like?
A: Cold and damp. It had been raining earlier in the day.
Q: What did you do next?
A: Drove into the Law School lot. I saw someone on the ground, and noticed it was a young woman. I drove around her and parked my vehicle. I got out and quieted her down. She was crying but managed to tell me she had been grabbed, pushed down, and almost raped and gave me a description. I radioed the description to headquarters who transmitted the information to the city police. We're on different radio frequencies, you see. I ascertained that the victim's name was Cheryl Pearlman, a graduate student. She was extremely upset but did not appear seriously injured.
Q: Did a city police cruiser arrive a few minutes later?
A: Yes. Five to ten minutes later, Officer Adair pulled up and parked next to my vehicle. He had a suspect in the car -- the defendant, Richard Hunter.

At this time, Pearlman saw the suspect and screamed, "Oh my God, keep him away from me." Then she fainted. I took her to the Monroe County Hospital emergency room. When she regained consciousness, she told me her purse was missing and that she thought it had been yanked from her during the assault. She indicated that it contained $45, keys, some credit cards and her cell phone. I radioed this information to my dispatcher and asked that it be passed along to Officer Adair. She also said the assailant had hit her several times with some kind of weapon.
Q: What is the lighting like in the parking lot across from the law school?
A: Fair. Not as good as we'd like, but there's plenty of light to see by. There are two bright lights, one on each side of the entrance to the law school, and there's a streetlight on the southwest corner of Henderson and Fourth Street. In addition, there's a music store – called Ozark something -- at the southeast corner of the parking lot. It has a light on the back, and when it's open, light shines out from inside through a large window -- maybe 8 feet high and 12 feet wide -- on the north side of the building facing the parking lot.
MR. WYATT: No further questions.
MS. MACPHERSON: Officer, did you see anyone running from the scene?
A: No, I don't think so. Not that I remember, anyway.
Q: No one ran past you?
A: No.
Q: How exactly did Ms. Pearlman describe the incident?
A: To the best of my recollection, she said, "A man grabbed me from behind and pushed me to the ground. He got on top of me, grabbed at my clothes, and said he had to have it. He hit me and tried to rape me but he ran off."
Q: And how did she describe her assailant? Please be precise.
A: She said he was a young man, medium build, wearing a tan or brown coat. I asked her if he was tall or short, and she said tall. Then she started crying again, so I made no attempt to obtain any more details.
Q: When Adair came over to your vehicle, did he say he had a suspect?
A: Yes, to me. I don't think Pearlman heard him.
Q: Did you ever search the parking lot for evidence?
A: No.
MS. MACPHERSON: That's all.
MR. WYATT: The state rests.

MS. MACPHERSON: Your honor, we move to suppress Hunter's statements for violation of Miranda, and to suppress all identification testimony because Hunter was not adequately informed of his right to counsel and because the process was impermissibly suggestive.
MR. WYATT: We oppose the motions. The officer was clearly acting in good faith. We ask that the defendant be bound over for the grand jury and that his $20,000 bail be continued.
COURT: The motions to suppress are denied. The defendant is bound over for the grand jury under the same bail. We stand in recess.

Certified as an accurate transcription of court proceedings.

January 31, YR-O.

Dodie Bowman
Dodie Bowman
Court Reporter

OFFICE OF THE PUBLIC DEFENDER
309 West Washington Street, Suite 1200
Bayshore, Columbia Phone 232-2475

STATEMENT BY: BECKY L. COLLINS
MADE TO: JENNIFER MACPHERSON
PLACE: 309 W. WASHINGTON ST., RM. 241
DATE: JANUARY 28, YR-0

My name is Becky Lynn Collins. I was born August 19, YR-22. I am a close friend of Richard Hunter's. We have been romantically involved off and on for about three years. I lived with him for about six months up until December, YR-1. I dropped out of the University of Columbia after my Freshman year and now work as a waitress at Rick's Café. During December and January I have been living in my parents' home at 906 South Henderson Street while they are vacationing in Florida. They are retired.

Rich is unemployed and is constantly short of cash. He's always borrowing from me or from his parents. He used to sell marijuana to the fraternity houses along Third Street, but he doesn't even do that anymore. He either goes over to the gym to play basketball or sits around watching television. I love him, but couldn't get serious unless he gets himself together and gets a job.

On January 12, YR-0, I was working from 11:30 to 7:30. I got off work at 7:30 and went home. I got home about 7:45. Richard was there watching television. He has a key to the house. We talked for a while. I told Rich I was going out at 8:30 with some friends and asked if he wanted to come along. Diane Howard had called earlier and we had decided to go out drinking and dancing. Rich said he had no money and would need to borrow some. I told him I only had twenty dollars to get me through till payday on the fifteenth. Rich said he did not want to go out without money because it would be too embarrassing. We watched "South Park" on television. It's Rich's and my favorite show because we watched it on our first date. This was a classic episode where Chef was on trial and the other side hired the famous lawyer, Johnnie Cochran. It's very funny because there are lots of Star Wars references mixed in. Rich was pretty silent throughout the show. He gets that way when he's embarrassed. Suddenly, he got up, slammed his hand against the wall, and said he couldn't stand all this bull about money, and he sure didn't want to have to talk to Diane about his money problems. He put on his coat and left the house, slamming the door behind him. The time was about 8:30. I am sure of the time because there were commercials on about upcoming television shows like the kind they run between programs. I cannot remember specifically what the commercials were, and I did not look at my watch, but it must have been about 8:28 or 8:29 when he left. My friends, Diane Howard and her boyfriend Larry Zollman, arrived about five minutes after Rich left.

We got in Diane's car and drove downtown. I did not see Rich again until the next Tuesday, which was visiting day at the jail. He tells me he did not attack the woman and I believe him. He's never struck me even when he gets angry. I don't think he could hit a woman.

I have talked to Rich once at the jail since his arrest. He assures me he did not have anything to do with the attack on the student. I believe him. I've known him long enough to know when he's lying.

This statement is true and accurate to the best of my recollection.

Becky L. Collins

Becky L. Collins

OFFICE OF THE PUBLIC DEFENDER

309 West Washington Street, Suite 1200
Bayshore, Columbia Phone 232-2475

STATEMENT BY: DIANE R. HOWARD
MADE TO: JENNIFER MACPHERSON
PLACE: 309 W. WASHINGTON ST. RM. 241
DATE: JANUARY 28, YR-0

My name is Diane Reynolds Howard. I live at 1703 North Maple Street on the northwest edge of town. I am twenty-two years old. I have known Becky Collins most of my life. We went to middle school and high school together here in Bayshore. Becky has been seeing Richard Hunter for about three years. I do not know much about him, but I know who he is. We have been out together many times. He's nice enough but has no ambition.

I was convicted two years ago for forgery. I had my wisdom teeth out and they gave me a prescription for pain-killers. When it ran out, I changed the "0" to a "1" where the label says "number of refills," and tried to get it refilled because I was still in a lot of pain. They said it was forgery. I got probation.

credibility

On January 12, YR-0, I called Becky about 7:45 to see if she and Rich wanted to go out drinking with me and my boyfriend, Larry Zollman. I called Becky's parents' house, because I knew that was where Becky was staying. Before that, she had lived with Rich at his apartment on Eleventh Street. Becky said she wanted to go out, but was not sure about Rich. I said we'd be by about 8:30.

A little before 8:00, I drove to Cutter's Supermarket where Larry worked. He gets off at 8:00. He was late, so I had to wait about ten minutes. About 8:10 we started to drive to Becky's. I called on my cell phone to say we were on our way but she didn't answer. I am certain of the time because I kept checking my watch while I was waiting. I was driving the car and Larry was in the front passenger seat. We often drive into town from the store where Larry works, and it usually takes about twenty minutes. Since Becky's parents live about a mile south of the center of town, my best estimate is that we got to Becky's right after 8:30. I remember distinctly hearing a clock chime once when we got into Becky's house.

I drove into Bayshore on route 45. I drove south on Dunn past Third Street, where Dunn becomes Atwater Avenue. I could not turn onto Henderson, because that's one way north, so I drove another block and turned south onto Fess Street. I drove down to Maxwell Street and turned right to drive the one block over to Becky's house. As I made the right turn, I saw Richard Hunter standing on the south side of Maxwell Street about 20 feet away. He was just standing there, sort of looking around. I waved, but he did not respond. I guess he could not see me because the windows of the car were rolled up because it was cold and rainy. I could see him clearly because there is a streetlight at the corner of Fess and Maxwell. I think he was wearing an overcoat of some kind but I am not certain. I had a good view of him for about five seconds. I said to Larry that I'd just seen Rich, and Larry said he had not been looking. This was right about 8:30.

I got to Becky's a minute or so later. She said she had a fight with Rich, and that he was not coming. That's not uncommon. They quarreled often. Rich didn't have a job and was always borrowing money and living hand-to-mouth. I told her I had just seen him on the corner. We got into my car and drove up Henderson Street going north. Becky said they had argued over money. Becky said she thought Richard would be walking up Henderson Street. I said I'd stop and pick him up if we saw him. I was driving, so I asked Becky and Larry to watch for him, but they told me when we got to Third Street that they had not seen him. We drove past the University, but I don't remember seeing any police cars.

I am familiar with Rich's reputation in town. We know a lot of the same people. His reputation is not very good. People think of him as a gambler and small-time drug dealer with an angry streak. But I think his reputation is exaggerated. He's never been involved in any serious crime like rape or robbery and sells marijuana only to make a little money because he's unemployed. I cannot imagine that he would be capable of any assault and robbery like they charged him with.

This has been a true and accurate statement to the best of my recollection.

Diane R. Howard

Diane R. Howard

Monroe County Circuit Court
Criminal Division
State of Columbia

CERTIFICATE OF DISPOSITION

Court Number: 3216-CR-2

Judge: Carlton

Case: State v. Diane Reynolds Howard

Original Offense(s): CCC 224-1 Felony Forgery

Disposition: CCC 224-2 Misd Forgery

Guilty Plea: Feb 9, YR-2

Trial:

Appeal:

Final Judgment Entered: Probation 1 year and costs

Date: April 11, YR-2

I hereby certify that this is a true excerpt from the records of the Monroe County Circuit Court, Criminal Division, State of Columbia.

Camille Johnson, Clerk of the Circuit Court

By: Robert Hamilton, Deputy Clerk

Date: January 29, YR-0

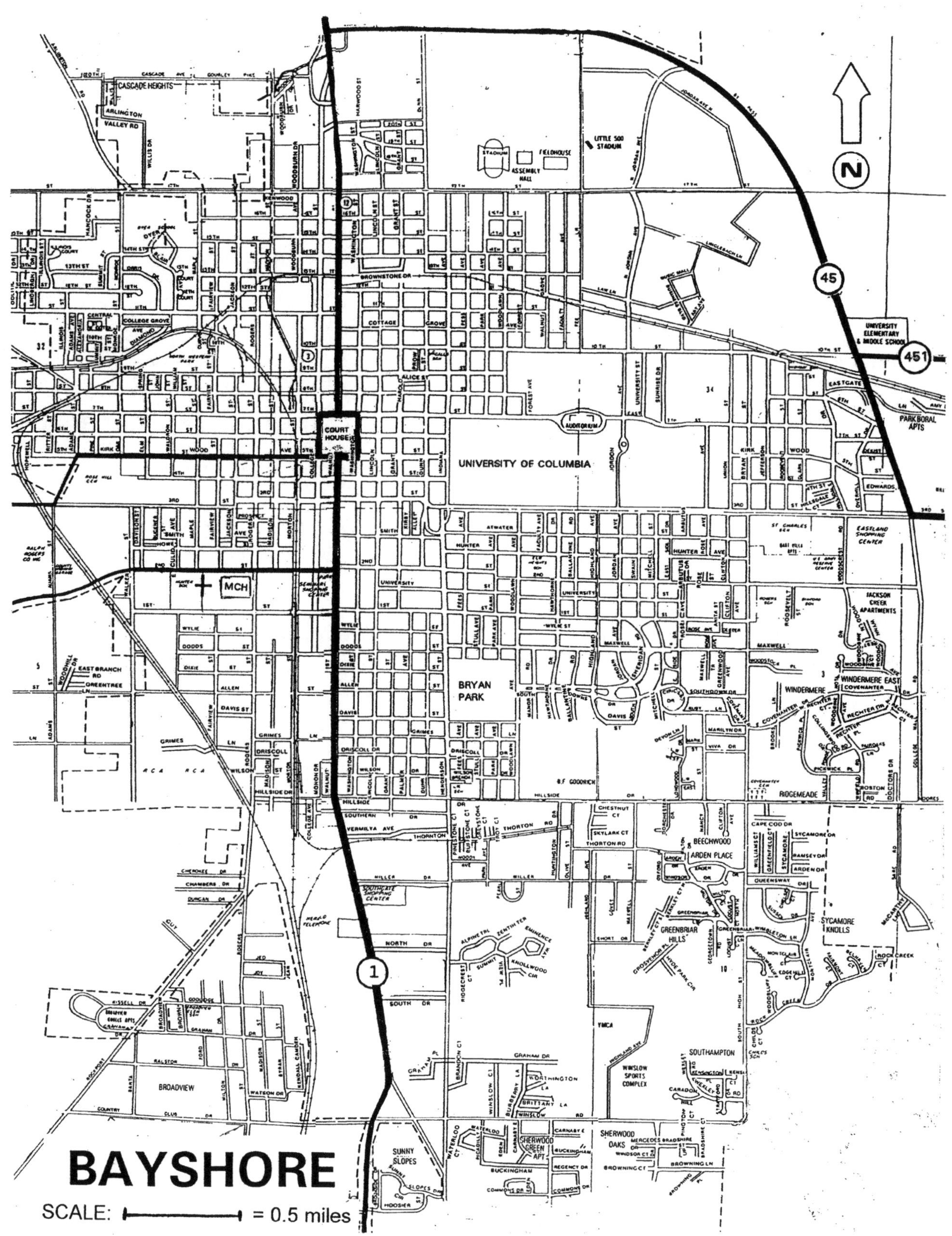
BAYSHORE
SCALE: = 0.5 miles
N
45
451
1
UNIVERSITY OF COLUMBIA
BRYAN PARK
COURT HOUSE
MCH
CASCADE HEIGHTS
UNIVERSITY ELEMENTARY & MIDDLE SCHOOL
PARKBORAL APTS
WINDERMERE
WINDERMERE EAST
RIDGEMEADE
BEECHWOOD
ARDEN PLACE
GREENBRIAR HILLS
SYCAMORE KNOLLS
SOUTHAMPTON
WINSLOW SPORTS COMPLEX
YMCA
BROADVIEW
SUNNY SLOPES
SHERWOOD OAKS
SHERWOOD GREEN APT
LITTLE 500 STADIUM
FIELDHOUSE
ASSEMBLY HALL
AUDITORIUM

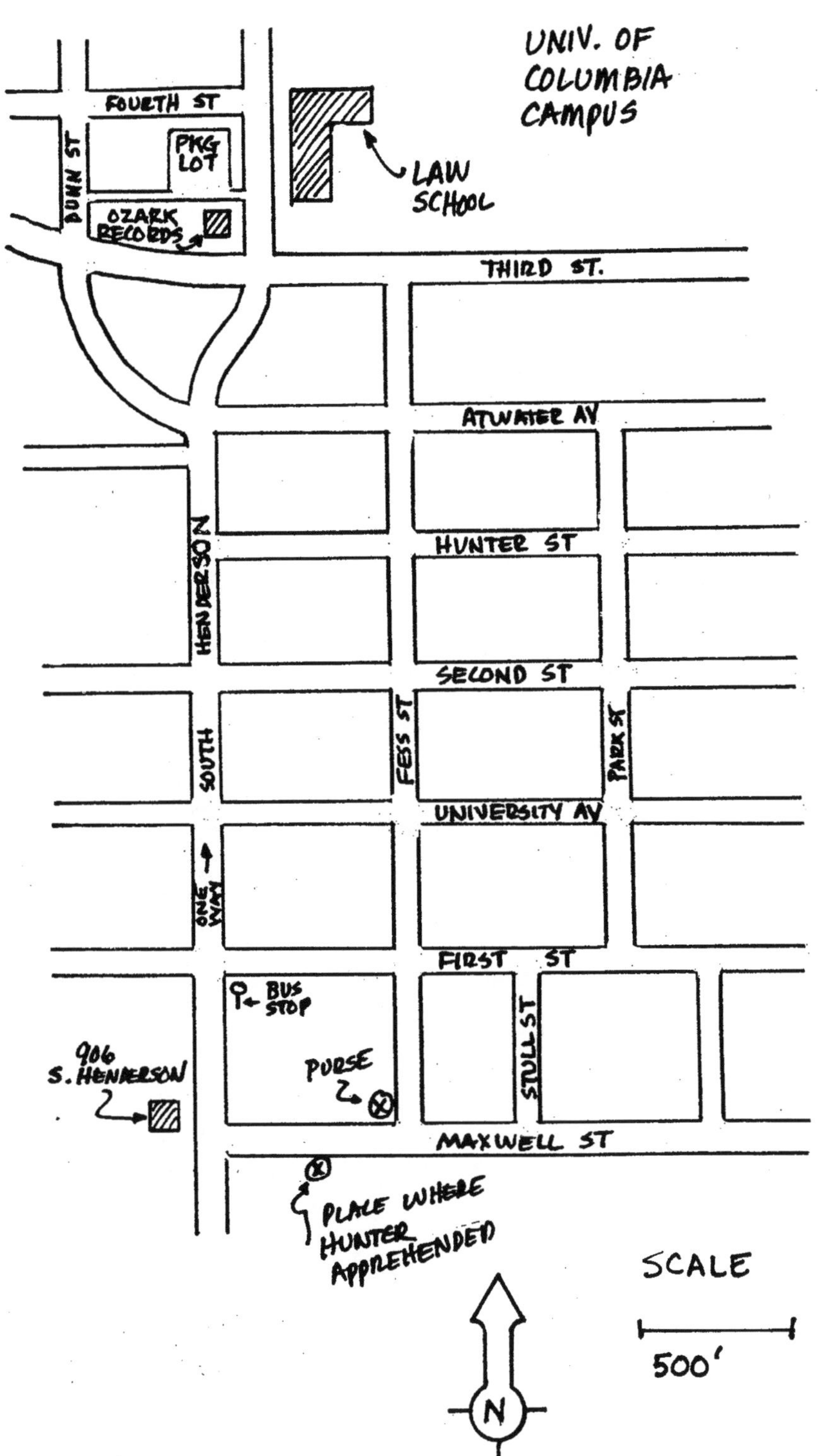
UNIV. OF
COLUMBIA
CAMPUS
FOURTH ST
PKG
LOT
LAW
SCHOOL
BOHN ST
OZARK
RECORDS
THIRD ST.
ATWATER AV
HUNTER ST
HENDERSON
SECOND ST
SOUTH
FESS ST
PARK ST
UNIVERSITY AV
ONE
WAY
FIRST ST
BUS
STOP
STULL ST
906
S. HENDERSON
PURSE
MAXWELL ST
PLACE WHERE
HUNTER
APPREHENDED
SCALE
500'
N

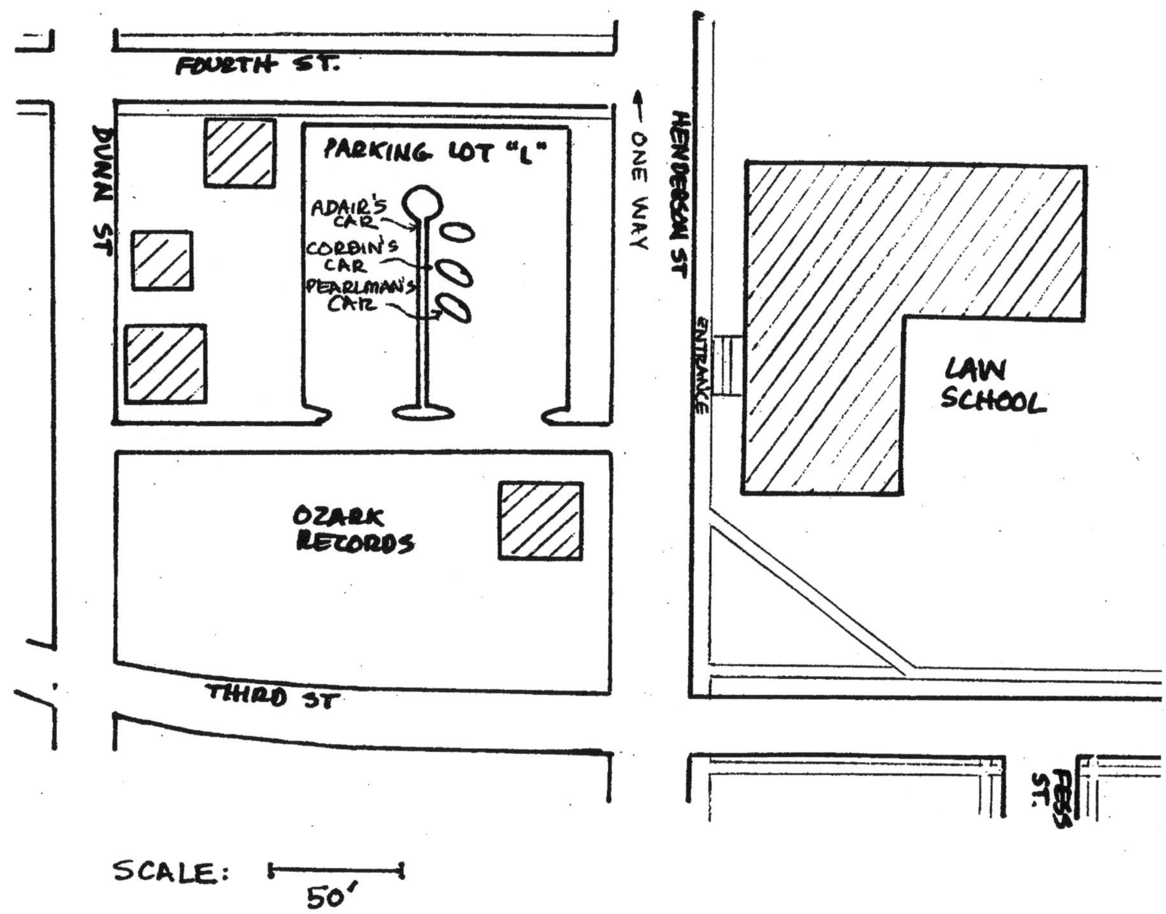
NORTH
FOURTH ST.
DUNN ST
PARKING LOT "L"
ONE WAY
HENDERSON ST
ADAIR'S CAR
CORBIN'S CAR
PEARLMAN'S CAR
ENTRANCE
LAW SCHOOL
OZARK RECORDS
THIRD ST
FESS ST.
SCALE:
50'

✣ Monroe County Hospital

Emergency Care Department
684-3597

TO: Attorneys

Attached please find a photocopy of the emergency room report I prepared on Ms. Cheryl Pearlman. This is the only record we have on her admittance for January 12. We fill out this standard report on every emergency room patient, but do not complete a full admissions form unless the patient must be admitted overnight to the hospital. In this case, the patient's abrasions were not serious. They involved some loss of skin, and their origin was impossible to determine.

Sincerely,

Stanley Reed

Stanley Reed, M.D.

✣ Monroe County Hospital

EMERGENCY ROOM REPORT

PATIENT'S NAME AND ADDRESS
PEARLMAN, CHERYL
1000 PLEASANT VALLEY RD
BAYSHORE COL

ACCOUNT NUMBER
02 47 86A

INSURANCE INFORMATION
BC/BS 222-33-2323
JOHN L. PEARLMAN

DATE ADMITTED
01/12/YR-0

DATE DISCHARGED
01/12/YR-0

POSTING DATE	PHYSICIAN	DESCRIPTION	TOTAL CHARGES
01/12/YR-0	REED	PATIENT UNCONSCIOUS, ADMITTED BY OFC CORDIN, UC POLICE. CORDIN STATED PATIENT HAD BEEN ASSAULTED. EXAMINATION REVEALED ABRASIONS ON THROAT, OTHERWISE UNREMARKABLE. PATIENT HIGHLY ANXIOUS UPON REGAINING CONSCIOUSNESS. DECLINED TRANQUILIZER. DISCHARGED.	ER 220.00

BAYSHORE POLICE DEPARTMENT
PATROL OFFICER LOG

DATE: JANUARY 12, YR-0
OFFICER: ADAIR 235
SHIFT: C
CAR: 12
DAY OF WEEK: THURSDAY
TIME LOGGED ON: 1607
TIME LOGGED OFF: 2354

4:07
11:54

TIME	EVENT
1607	ON DUTY. COMPUTER CHECK. RADIO CHECK.
1610	TA HILLSIDE & HENDERSON. NO INJURY. D1 LARRY FLYNN 25634-28787 06 CHEV SILVERADO D2 HYUNG LIU CHENG NO DL 08 HONDA CIVIC CITED NO DL
1835	OFF DUTY SUPPER LONGS CAFÉ
1937	ON DUTY 7:37
2040	LOF Y-M MED TAN COAT NR UNIV CAMPUS ASSAULT 8.40
2127	OFF PATROL RICHARD HUNTER ARRESTED ATT RAPE ASSAULT 9:27 BOOKED INTO JAIL
2245	RESUME PATROL
2354	OFF DUTY. PRINT LOG.

dispatch log

1

BAYSHORE TRANSIT

South Walnut / Arbor Glen

Call 336-RIDE

ROUTE MAP

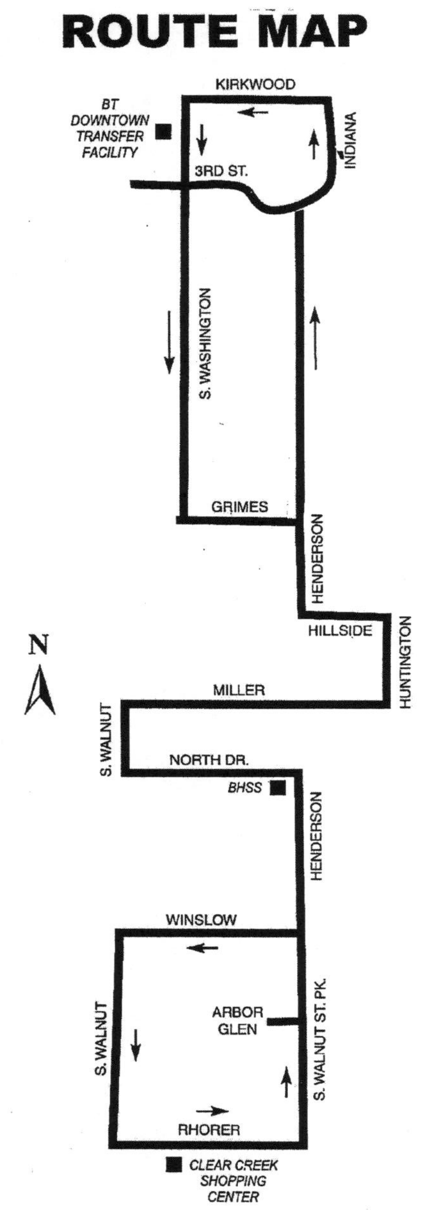

1 South Walnut / Arbor Glen

DOWNTOWN TO BHS SOUTH / CLEAR CREEK SHOPPING CENTER / ARBOR GLEN

LEAVE 4TH/WASH	GRIMES & WASHI	BHS SOUTH	CLEAR CREEK SHOPPING CENTER	ARBOR GLEN APTS	BHS SOUTH	GRIMES & HENDERSON	INDIANA & 4TH	ARRIVE 4TH/WASH
			6:25 AM	6:30 AM	6:34 AM	6:41 AM	6:47 AM	7:00 AM
			6:55 AM	7:00 AM	7:04 AM	7:11 AM	7:17 AM	7:30 AM
7:10 AM	7:14 AM	7:19 AM	7:25 AM	7:30 AM	7:34 AM	7:41 AM	7:47 AM	8:00 AM
7:40 AM	7:44 AM	7:49 AM	7:55 AM	8:00 AM	8:04 AM	8:11 AM	8:17 AM	8:30 AM
8:10 AM	8:14 AM	8:19 AM	8:25 AM	8:30 AM	8:34 AM	8:41 AM	8:47 AM	9:00 AM
8:40 AM	8:44 AM	8:49 AM	8:55 AM	9:00 AM	9:04 AM	9:11 AM	9:17 AM	9:30 AM
9:10 AM	9:14 AM	9:19 AM	9:25 AM	9:30 AM	9:34 AM	9:41 AM	9:47 AM	10:00 AM
10:10 AM	10:14 AM	10:19 AM	10:25 AM	10:30 AM	10:34 AM	10:41 AM	10:47 AM	11:00 AM
11:10 AM	11:14 AM	11:19 AM	11:25 AM	11:30 AM	11:34 AM	11:41 AM	11:47 AM	12:00 PM
12:10 PM	12:14 PM	12:19 PM	12:25 PM	12:30 PM	12:34 PM	12:41 PM	12:47 PM	1:00 PM
1:10 PM	1:14 PM	1:19 PM	1:25 PM	1:30 PM	1:34 PM	1:41 PM	1:47 PM	2:00 PM
1:40 PM	1:44 PM	1:49 PM	1:55 PM	2:00 PM	2:04 PM	2:11 PM	2:17 PM	2:30 PM
2:10 PM	2:14 PM	2:19 PM	2:25 PM	2:30 PM	2:34 PM	2:41 PM	2:47 PM	3:00 PM
2:40 PM	2:44 PM	2:49 PM	2:55 PM	3:00 PM	3:04 PM	3:11 PM	3:17 PM	3:30 PM
3:10 PM	3:14 PM	3:19 PM	3:25 PM	3:30 PM	3:34 PM	3:41 PM	3:47 PM	4:00 PM
3:40 PM	3:44 PM	3:49 PM	3:55 PM	4:00 PM	4:04 PM	4:11 PM	4:17 PM	4:30 PM
4:10 PM	4:14 PM	4:19 PM	4:25 PM	4:30 PM	4:34 PM	4:41 PM	4:47 PM	5:00 PM
4:40 PM	4:44 PM	4:49 PM	4:55 PM	5:00 PM	5:04 PM	5:11 PM	5:17 PM	5:30 PM
5:10 PM	5:14 PM	5:19 PM	5:25 PM	5:30 PM	5:34 PM	5:41 PM	5:47 PM	6:00 PM
5:40 PM	5:44 PM	5:49 PM	5:55 PM	6:00 PM (OUT OF SERVICE)				
6:10 PM	6:14 PM	6:19 PM	6:25 PM	6:30 PM	6:34 PM	6:41 PM	6:47 PM	7:00 PM
7:10 PM	7:14 PM	7:19 PM	7:25 PM	7:30 PM	7:34 PM	7:41 PM	7:47 PM	8:00 PM
8:10 PM	8:14 PM	8:19 PM	8:25 PM	8:30 PM (OUT OF SERVICE)				

Excerpt from page 18, *Bayhore Herald* for Thursday, January 12, YR-0

THURSDAY EVENING

LOCAL	6:00	6:30	7:00	7:30	8:00	8:30	9:00	9:30	10:00	10:30
4 WTTV 29 WTTK	**My Name Is Earl** (CC)	**My Name Is Earl** Stripper Catalina.	**Two and a Half Men** (CC)	**Two and a Half Men** (CC)	**One Tree Hill** Brooke gets life-changing news; Dan returns to Tree Hill. (CC)		**Gossip Girl** "Dan De Fleurette" (CC)		**Seinfeld** "The Bottle Deposit"	**Seinfeld** "The Soup Nazi" (CC)
6 WRTV ABC	**6 News at Six** (N) (CC)	**ABC World News**	**6 News at Seven** (N)	**The Insider** (N) (CC)	**Happy New Year, Charlie Brown** (CC)	**The Middle** "The Cheerleader"	**Modern Family** (CC)	**Cougar Town** (CC)	**(10:01) Eastwick** Joanna tries to help Penny find closure. (N) (CC)	
8 WISH CBS	**WISH-TV News 8 at 6** (N) (CC)	**CBS Evening News With Katie Couric**	**Inside Edition** (N) (CC)	**Entertainment Tonight** (N) (CC)	**The New Adventures of Old Christine**	**Gary Unmarried** (CC)	**Criminal Minds** "Amplification" Deadly virus is released. (CC)		**CSI: NY** "Help" (CC)	
13 WTHR NBC	**News** (N) (CC)	**NBC Nightly News** (N) (CC)	**Wheel of Fortune** (N) (CC)	**Jeopardy!** (N) (CC)	**The Office** Michael feels left out.	**The Office** "The Lover" (CC)	**The Office** "Double Date" (CC)	**The Office** Oscar has a secret crush.	**The Jay Leno Show** (N) (CC)	
20 WFYI PBS	**PBS NewsHour** (N) (CC)		**Nightly Business Report** (N) (CC)	**Indianapolis Public School**	**A Girl's Life** Four teenage girls. (N) (CC)		**P.O.V.** "Patti Smith: Dream of Life" Singer Patti Smith's career. (N) (CC)			
59 WXIN FOX	**The Simpsons** (CC)	**The Simpsons** (CC)	**Family Guy** "Boys Do Cry" (CC)	**The Office** "Diversity Day" (CC)	**Glee** "Vitamin D" Terri tries to keep an eye on Will. (CC)		**Glee** "Throwdown" (CC)		**Fox 59 News** (N) (CC)	

CABLE	6:00	6:30	7:00	7:30	8:00	8:30	9:00	9:30	10:00	10:30
A&E	**Dog**	**Dog**	**Dog the Bounty Hunter**		**Dog**	**Dog the Bounty Hunter**		**Dog**	**Seagal**	**Seagal**
AMC	**Rambo: First Blood Part II** ★★ (R) ('85) Action. (CC)				**Aliens** ★★★★ (R) ('86) A task force goes to eradicate a horrific space predator.					
ANIMAL	**Untamed and Uncut** (CC)		**Untamed and Uncut** (CC)		**I Shouldn't Be Alive** (CC)		**I Shouldn't Be Alive** (CC)		**I'm Alive** "Journeys" (CC)	
BET	**Beauty Shop** ★★ (PG-13) ('05) (Queen Latifah) (CC)				**Juwanna Mann** ★ (PG-13) ('02) (Miguel A. Núñez, Jr.)				**The Mo'Nique Show** (CC)	
BIG TEN	**Best**	**Tip Off**	**College Basketball** Texas-Arlington at Michigan State.				**College Basketball** Northwestern at Illinois. (Live)			
BRAVO	**Launch My Line**		**Launch My Line**		**Launch My Line**		**Men in Black II** ★★ (PG-13) ('02) (Tommy Lee Jones)			
CART'N	**Agent Cody Banks** ★★ (PG) ('03) (Frankie Muniz)				**Destroy**	**Dude**	**Star Wars**	**Teen Titans**	**King of Hill**	**King of Hill**
CMT	**Extreme Makeover: Home Edition** "Correa/Medeiros"				**Smarter**	**Smarter**	**Police Academy** ★★ (R) ('84) (Steve Guttenberg)			
CNBC	**Mad Money** (N)		**Kudlow Report** (Live)		**Ultimate Fighting: Fistful**		**Biography on CNBC**		**Inside the Mind of Google**	
COMEDY	**Scrubs** (CC)	**Scrubs** (CC)	**RENO 911!**	**Jeff Dunham**	**South Park**	**South Park**	**Futurama**	**Futurama**	**South Park**	**South Park**
DISC	**Everest: Beyond the Limit**		**Everest: Beyond the Limit**		**Everest: Beyond the Limit**		**Everest: Beyond the Limit**		**Everest: Beyond the Limit**	
E!	**Kardashian**	**Kardashian**	**E! News** (N)	**The Daily 10**	**Bank of Hollywood**		**Evan Almighty** ★★ (PG) ('07) (Steve Carell) Comedy.			
ESPN	**College Basketball** Connecticut at Cincinnati. (Live)				**College Basketball** Baylor at Arkansas. (Live)				**SportsCenter**	**NFL Live** (N)
FAM	**Gilmore Girls** (CC)		**Fresh Prince**	**Fresh Prince**	**'70s Show**	**Practical Magic** ★★ (PG-13) ('98) (Sandra Bullock) (CC)				
FOOD	**Contessa**	**Down Home**	**Cooking**	**Minute**	**Challenge** "Shrek Cakes"		**Snacks Unwrapped**		**Bobby Flay**	**Bobby Flay**
FOX NEWS	**Glenn Beck** (N)		**Special Report**		**FOX Report**		**The O'Reilly Factor** (N)		**Hannity** (N)	
FOX SPORTS	**The Final Score Review**		**Game 365**	**Pacers Live**	**NBA Basketball** Memphis Grizzlies at Indiana Pacers. (Live)					**Pacers Live**
FX	**'70s Show**	**'70s Show**	**Alien vs. Predator** ★★ (PG-13) ('04) (Sanaa Lathan)				**Rocky Balboa** ★★★ (PG) ('06) (Sylvester Stallone)			
GAME	**Deal or No Deal** (CC)		**Newlywed**	**Catch 21**	**Deal or No Deal** (CC)		**Family Feud**	**Family Feud**	**Newlywed**	**Catch 21**

SELECTED COLUMBIA PATTERN JURY INSTRUCTIONS

Preliminary Instructions Before Trial

Members of the Jury: Before we begin the trial, I would like to describe how the trial will be conducted and explain what we will be doing -- you, the lawyers for both sides, and I. At the end of the trial I will give you more detailed guidance on how you are to go about reaching your decision.

This criminal case has been brought by the state of Columbia. The defendant has been charged with three violations of the law: attempted rape, robbery, and theft. The defendant pleaded not guilty to the charges and denies committing these offenses. He is presumed innocent and may not be found guilty by you unless all of you unanimously find that the State has proved his guilt beyond a reasonable doubt.

The first step in the trial will be the opening statements. The attorneys in their opening statements will tell you about the evidence which they intend to put before you, so that you will have an idea of what the case is going to be.

Next the state will offer evidence that it says will support the charges against the defendant. The evidence will consist of the testimony of witnesses as well as documents and exhibits.

After the state's evidence, the defendant's lawyer may present evidence in the defendant's behalf, but he is not required to do so. I remind you that the defendant is presumed innocent and the government must prove the guilt of the defendant beyond a reasonable doubt. The defendant does not have to prove his innocence.

After you have heard all the evidence, the attorneys will each be given time for their final arguments. In their closing arguments the lawyers will be attempting to summarize their cases and help you understand the evidence that was presented.

The final part of the trial occurs when I instruct you about the rules of law which you are to use in reaching your verdict. You must base your decision only on the evidence in the case and my instructions about the law.

During the course of the trial, you should not talk with any witness, or with the defendant, or with any of the lawyers in the case. Also, you should not discuss this case among yourselves until I have instructed you on the law and you have gone to the jury room to make your decision at the end of the trial. It is important that you wait until all the evidence is received and you have heard my instructions on rules of law before you deliberate among yourselves. Please keep your cell phones turned off and you may not use them for any reason during trial. There is a telephone in the jury room if you need to call home.

All people in this trial are fictional, and the events take place in an imaginary city called Bayshore, in the state of Columbia.

Concluding Instruction: The Charge

Members of the Jury: You will soon leave the courtroom and begin discussing this case in the jury room.

During the course of the trial you received all the evidence you may properly consider to decide the case. Your decision in this case must be made solely on the evidence presented at the trial. You may not do your own investigation nor look things up on the Internet nor may you text your friends and ask their opinions.

It is my job to decide what rules of law apply to the case. This is my job; it is not the job of the lawyers. So, while the lawyers may have commented during the trial on some of these rules, you are to be guided only by what I say about them. You must follow all of the rules as I explain them to you. You may not follow some and ignore others. Even if you disagree or don't understand the reasons for some of the rules, you are bound to follow them.

In criminal cases, the State must prove that the defendant is guilty beyond a reasonable doubt. Proof beyond a reasonable doubt is proof that leaves you firmly convinced of the defendant's guilt. There are very few things in this world that we know with absolute certainty, and in criminal cases the law does not require proof that overcomes every possible doubt. If, based on your consideration of the evidence, you are firmly convinced that the defendant is guilty of the crime charged, you must find him guilty. If on the other hand, you think there is a real possibility that he is not guilty, you must give him the benefit of the doubt and find him not guilty.

An important part of your job will be making judgments about the testimony of the witnesses who testified in this case. You should decide whether you believe what each person had to say, and how important that testimony was. In making that decision I suggest that you ask yourself a few questions: Did the person impress you as honest? Did he or she have any particular reason not to tell the truth? Did he or she have a personal interest in the outcome of the case? Did the witness seem to have a good memory? Did the witness have the opportunity and ability to observe accurately the things he or she testified about? Did he or she appear to understand the questions clearly and answer them directly? Did the witness's testimony differ from the testimony of other witnesses? These are a few of the considerations that will help you determine the accuracy of what each witness said.

The state must prove, beyond a reasonable doubt, that the crimes charged in this case were actually committed. But more than that, the state must also prove beyond a reasonable doubt that the defendant, Richard Hunter, committed them. Therefore, the identification by Cheryl Pearlman is an important part of the state's case. As with any other witness, you must first decide whether she is telling the truth as she understands it. But you must do more than that. You must also decide how accurate the identification was, whether the witness saw what she thought she saw. You should consider:

(1) Whether the witness knew the defendant before the crime took place,
(2) Whether the witness had a good opportunity to see the person,
(3) Whether the witness was paying careful attention to what was going on,
(4) Whether the description given by the witness was close to the way the defendant actually looked,

(5) How much time had passed between the crime and the first identification by the witness,
(6) Whether, at the time of the first identification by the witness, the conditions were such that the witness was likely to make a mistake,
(7) Whether at an earlier time, the witness failed to identify the defendant, and
(8) Whether the witness seemed certain at the time of the first identification and again when she testified here in court.

If you are not convinced beyond a reasonable doubt that it was the defendant who committed the crime, you must find him not guilty.

The state has charged the defendant with attempted rape. To convict the defendant of this crime, the state must prove the following elements beyond a reasonable doubt:
(1) That the defendant intended to compel Cheryl Pearlman to submit to sexual intercourse against her will;
(2) That the defendant intended to use force or the threat of death or serious injury; and
(3) That the defendant committed an act constituting a substantial step in a course of conduct intended to culminate in rape.

The state has also charged the defendant with the crimes of robbery and theft. Of these, robbery is the more serious. To find the defendant guilty of robbery, the state must prove the following elements beyond a reasonable doubt:
(1) That the defendant took property belonging to Cheryl Pearlman; and
(2) That the taking was accomplished by the use of force resulting in serious injury or the threat of immediate serious injury.

An injury is serious if it creates a substantial risk of death or causes permanent disfigurement, loss or impairment of the function of any body part.

If you find beyond a reasonable doubt that the defendant took and carried away property from Cheryl Pearlman's person, but you do not find that the taking was accomplished by force resulting in serious injury or the threat of immediate serious injury, then you should find the defendant not guilty of robbery but guilty of theft. You may not convict the defendant of both robbery and theft.

If the defendant proves the following elements by a preponderance of evidence, the offense is reduced to petty theft:
(1) That the property was not taken from Cheryl Pearlman's person; and
(2) That the total value of the property taken was less than $100.00.

Your verdict must be unanimous. Please notify the bailiff upon reaching a verdict.

CIRCUIT COURT OF MONROE COUNTY
CRIMINAL DIVISION

CASE NO. 025-CR-9

STATE OF COLUMBIA
COUNTY OF MONROE

THE STATE OF COLUMBIA	)	
	)	
vs.	)	VERDICT
	)	
RICHARD HUNTER,	)	
	)	
Defendant	)	

We, the jurors of Monroe County in the above titled action, find the defendant:

1. __________ Guilty of attempted rape.

   __________ Not Guilty of attempted rape.

2. __________ Guilty of robbery.

   __________ Guilty of theft.

   __________ Guilty of petty theft.

   __________ Not Guilty of robbery or theft.

Signed: ______________________
Jury Foreperson

CASE FILE B:

SUSAN D. KESLER

v.

JEFFREY C. BURNSIDE and MACKLIN FURNITURE COMPANY

PERSONAL INJURY
TRAFFIC ACCIDENT

KESLER V. BURNSIDE
CONTENTS OF FILE

GENERAL INSTRUCTIONS

This is a civil case arising out of a truck-car collision. The plaintiff alleges that negligent driving by the defendant's employee caused the accident. She seeks recovery for her personal injuries, property damage, pain and suffering, and lost income. The defendants deny negligence and plead contributory negligence, unavoidable accident, and that a third party was at fault. The accident took place two years ago in August on a rural road just outside the fictional city of Bayshore, Columbia (population 150,000). Columbia is a comparative negligence jurisdiction.

Potential Witnesses

Susan Kesler -- plaintiff.
Edwin Mills -- Bayshore police officer.
Dr. Bradley Craig -- plaintiff's doctor.
Jeffrey Burnside -- defendant truck driver.
Judy Larson -- eyewitness.
Mary Ewing -- eyewitness.
Paul Swain -- private investigator.
Shirley Master -- real estate broker.
Sandra Hawkins -- professor in business school

Instructions for use as a full trial (without experts)

1. The plaintiff must call Susan Kesler and Mary Ewing as witnesses in her case-in-chief.

2. The defendants must call Jeffrey Burnside and Judy Larson as witnesses in their case-in-chief.

3. Either side may call Dr. Bradley Craig or use stipulation number two below.

4. Other witnesses may be called only with the approval of the court.

5. The original attorneys have withdrawn from this case, citing conflicts of interest.

Instructions for use as a full trial with experts

1. The plaintiff must call Susan Kesler, Mary Ewing, and Shirley Master as witnesses in her case-in-chief.

2. The defendants must call Jeffrey Burnside, Judy Larson, and Sandra Hawkins as witnesses in their case-in-chief.

3. Either side may call Dr. Bradley Craig or use stipulation number two below.

4. Other witnesses may be called only with the approval of the court.

5. The original attorneys have both withdrawn from the case.

Stipulations

1. The Bayshore Police Department Officer Field Report and Narrative Report are required to be filed by the investigating officer within 24 hours after every traffic accident and are regularly maintained by the Police Department.

2. In lieu of calling Dr. Bradley Craig, the parties may introduce his statement (pages B-43 to B-44) into evidence. The statement is stipulated to be fully admissible.

3. Any criminal offense listed as a misdemeanor is one for which the maximum statutory penalty is one year or less. Any offense listed as a felony is one for which the maximum penalty is more than one year.

Note on dates

The designation YR-0 means the present year, YR-1 is one year ago, YR-2 (the year in which the events took place) is two years ago, etc.

In the Monroe County Circuit Court
State of Columbia

SUSAN D. KESLER Plaintiff vs. JEFFREY C. BURNSIDE and MACKLIN FURNITURE CO., INC. Defendants	)))))))))))	Civil No. 09 CV 1127

COMPLAINT FOR COMPENSATORY DAMAGES FOR NEGLIGENT OPERATION OF A MOTOR VEHICLE

Plaintiff, Susan D. Kesler, by her counsel, alleges as her complaint against the defendants the following:

1. The jurisdiction of this Court is based on the Columbia Constitution, Article 5, §1, and Columbia Code §§14-13-80 and 14-15-6.

2. Plaintiff is and at all times herein mentioned was a resident of the City of Bayshore, County of Monroe, State of Columbia.

3. Defendant Macklin Furniture Co., Inc. is and at all times hereinafter mentioned was a corporation organized and existing under the laws of the State of Columbia, having its principle place of business in Bayshore, Columbia.

4. Defendant Jeffrey C. Burnside is and at all times herein mentioned was a resident of the City of Bayshore, County of Monroe, State of Columbia.

5. Defendant Jeffrey C. Burnside is employed by defendant corporation as a truck driver, and at all times hereinafter mentioned was engaged in the scope and course of his employment for defendant corporation.

6. On or about August 14, YR-2, plaintiff, in the exercise of due care, was proceeding eastward and stopped in her automobile, a YR-2 Toyota, on Highway 451 in the County of Monroe, State of Columbia.

7. Defendant, Jeffrey C. Burnside, was proceeding eastward on said highway, and at a point approximately 100 feet before Ratcliff Road intersects Highway 451, defendant Burnside so carelessly and negligently operated a YR-6

Ford 24-foot truck, owned by the defendant Macklin Furniture Co., Inc., and driven by the defendant Jeffrey C. Burnside, that the same was violently propelled against plaintiff's automobile causing severe damage to plaintiff's automobile and personal injury to the plaintiff.

8. The defendants, and each of them, hereinbefore alleged, were then and there guilty of one or more of the following negligent acts or omissions:

a. Negligently failed to keep the proper lookout for stopped vehicles;

b. Negligently operated a vehicle at a speed that was greater than reasonable and proper speed considering the conditions and use of the road;

c. Negligently and carelessly failed to have the vehicle under sufficient control as to avoid collision with plaintiff's vehicle.

9. As a proximate result of the negligent conduct of defendants, hereinbefore alleged, plaintiff sustained multiple broken bones and lacerations, and was compelled to expend $43,620 in medical expenses for treating said injury.

10. As a proximate result of the collision and of said negligence of the defendants, and each of them, caused as aforesaid, plaintiff was compelled to expend the sum of $15,400 in having her automobile repaired, which repair took thirty days, during which plaintiff rented a replacement vehicle, which was reasonably worth the sum of $50.00 per day.

11. That as a proximate result of said accident and the injuries received, plaintiff was unable to engage in her occupation as a real estate broker for a period of 180 days, to her further loss in the sum of $50,000.

12. That as a proximate result of said accident and the injuries received, plaintiff was in great pain and suffered for a period of six months, which was reasonably worth the sum of $2,000,000.00.

WHEREFORE, plaintiff asks this Court to enter judgment in her favor against defendants, jointly and severally, for $2,110,520.00 in compensatory damages, plus interest and costs.

Signed: Deb~h Huxtable

Deborah Huxtable
Attorney for Plaintiff
Law Offices of Stanley Lerner
3131 East Third Street
Bayshore, Columbia

In the Monroe County Circuit Court
State of Columbia

Susan D. Kesler *Plaintiff*	)	
v.	)	
Jeffrey C. Burnside	)	Civil No. 09 CV 1127
and	)	
Macklin Furniture Company, Inc. *Defendants*	)	

ANSWER TO COMPLAINT AND
STATEMENT OF AFFIRMATIVE DEFENSES

COME NOW the defendants Jeffrey C. Burnside and Macklin Furniture Company, Inc., by counsel, and answer plaintiff's complaint as follows:

1. The defendants admit the allegations asserted in paragraph one of the plaintiff's complaint.

2. The defendants are without sufficient knowledge upon which to form a belief as to the truth or falsity of the allegations contained in paragraph two of the plaintiff's complaint.

3. Defendants admit the allegations contained in paragraph three of plaintiff's complaint.

4. Defendants admit the allegations contained in paragraph four of plaintiff's complaint.

5. Defendants admit the allegations contained in paragraph five of plaintiff's complaint.

6. The defendants are without sufficient knowledge upon which to form a belief as to the truth or falsity of the allegations contained in paragraph six of the plaintiff's complaint.

7. The defendants deny the allegations asserted in paragraph seven of the plaintiff's complaint.

8. The defendants deny the allegations contained in paragraph eight of plaintiff's complaint and each subparagraph contained therein.

9. As to paragraph nine of the complaint, the defendants admit that plaintiff was billed for $43,620 in medical expenses, but deny each and every other allegation contained therein.

10. The defendants are without sufficient knowledge upon which to form a belief as to the truth or falsity of the allegations contained in paragraph ten of the plaintiff's complaint.

11. The defendants deny the allegations contained in paragraph eleven of the plaintiff's complaint.

12. The defendants are without sufficient knowledge upon which to form a belief as to the truth or falsity of the allegations contained in paragraph twelve of the plaintiff's complaint.

FIRST AFFIRMATIVE DEFENSE: CONTRIBUTORY NEGLIGENCE

13. If plaintiff was injured as alleged in the complaint, her injuries were the result of plaintiff's own negligence in whole or in part, in one of the following ways:

a. By talking on her cell phone and failing to maintain a proper lookout for other vehicles on the road;

b. By failing to properly maintain her vehicle's safety devices, to wit: the left electric turn signal.

c. By failing to use the vehicle's safety devices, including turn signals, head and tail lights and seat belts.

d. By failing to give proper indication, by signal or other means, of her intention to stop or turn.

e. By stopping her vehicle at a place and in such a manner as to unreasonably impede the flow of traffic.

SECOND AFFIRMATIVE DEFENSE: UNAVOIDABLE ACCIDENT

14. If plaintiff was injured as alleged in the complaint, her injuries were solely the result of an unavoidable accident in which neither party was negligent.

THIRD AFFIRMATIVE DEFENSE: THIRD-PARTY LIABILITY

15. If plaintiff was injured as alleged in the complaint, her injuries were caused in whole or in part, by the actions of an unknown third party, who drove their vehicle across the center line causing defendant Jeffrey Burnside to swerve and lose control of his vehicle immediately before it impacted with plaintiff's vehicle.

WHEREFORE, the defendants pray this Court for judgment dismissing the complaint and awarding defendants costs and expenses incurred herein.

Barry J. Greenberg

Barry J. Greenberg
Attorney for Defendants
Houston Minnick & Dos Santos
100 North Walnut Street
Bayshore, Columbia

CERTIFICATE OF SERVICE

I hereby certify that a true copy of the foregoing Answer was mailed, postage prepaid, to Deborah Huxtable, 3131 East Third Street, Bayshore, Columbia, attorney for plaintiff; this 3rd day of May, YR-1.

Barry J. Greenberg

Barry J. Greenberg

EXCERPT FROM COLUMBIA STATUTES

§ 9-4-180. Stopping Distances -- Judicial Notice. All courts of general jurisdiction in this state may take judicial notice of the following table:

Table of Average Speed and Stopping Distances (in feet)

For vehicles with brakes and tires in good condition on dry level pavement free from loose material. For wet pavement add 10% for all-season tires and ABS, 20% for all-season tires and no ABS, 30% for high-performance tires, and 40% for tires with visibly worn tread.

SPEED IN:		AVERAGE STOPPING DISTANCES				TOTAL STOPPING DISTANCES		
Miles per hour	Feet per second	Cars	Vans, SUVs & pickups	Trucks to 36 feet	Driver reaction time	Cars	Vans etc	Trucks
10	14.7	5	5	6	22	27	27	28
15	22.0	11	12	14	33	44	45	47
20	29.3	19	21	25	44	63	65	69
25	36.6	30	33	40	55	85	88	95
30	44.0	43	48	57	66	109	114	123
35	51.3	58	65	78	77	135	142	155
40	58.7	76	85	102	88	164	173	190
45	66.0	96	107	129	99	195	243	228
50	73.3	119	133	159	110	229	207	242
55	80.7	144	161	192	121	265	282	288
60	88.0	171	191	229	132	303	323	336
65	95.3	201	224	268	143	344	367	387
70	102.6	233	259	311	154	387	413	444
75	109.9	268	298	357	165	433	463	504
80	117.2	305	339	406	176	481	481	568
85	124.7	344	384	459	187	531	565	646
90	132.0	386	430	514	198	584	628	706

George HOOVER, Appellant
(Defendant below)

v.

Cathleen MINTER, Appellee
(Plaintiff below)

No. 977S725

Supreme Court of Columbia

June 20, YR-3

DAUBER, Associate Justice

This action was brought to recover damages allegedly caused in an automobile accident. The defendant tried unsuccessfully to raise the issue of plaintiff's failure to wear a seat belt. This appeal asks us to clarify Columbia law with respect to the so-called seat belt defense.

The defendant Hoover was driving to school on January 18, Yr-7. At about 8:15 a.m., defendant lost control of his car in a curve and struck head-on a pickup truck being driven by the plaintiff Minter. Minter was not wearing a seat belt at the time, and was seriously injured. The evidence indicated that the defendant was driving in excess of ninety miles an hour at the time of the accident. Trial resulted in a verdict against the defendant for $1,500,000.00 actual damages.

In Count 14 of his answer to the complaint, the defendant alleged that the plaintiff had been guilty of contributory negligence for failure to wear a seat belt. In Count 15 of the answer, defendant pleaded that plaintiff's failure to wear a seat belt contributed to the severity of plaintiff's injuries, and should be considered by the jury in mitigation of damages. The trial court dismissed both defenses on motion by the plaintiff, and defendant appeals from these rulings.

I.

We first turn to the issue of whether failure to wear a seat belt constitutes negligence. Although state law requires the wearing of a seat belt, no statute addresses whether such nonuse constitutes negligence. In the absence of such a statute, we have previously held that the plaintiff must prove negligence in fact and may not rely on the old doctrine of negligence per se. Anchors v. Lathrop, 334 Col.2d 299 (1995).

In order for failure to wear a seat belt to constitute negligence, there must be a common law duty to wear one, and the breach of that duty must increase the risk that an accident will happen. The majority of courts answer both questions in the negative [citations omitted]. We agree.

"Duty" is the obligation to use care to avoid endangering others. Nonuse of a seat belt does not endanger anyone other than the nonwearer him- or herself. Although there may be a strong public policy favoring seat belt use, that is not the same thing as a duty. If the legislature wished to make failure to wear a seat belt an act of negligence, it could have done so by statute. Nor is failure to wear a seat belt usually the "cause" of an accident in the ordinary sense. In Wheatland v. Farkas, 311 Col.2d 122 (1992), we held that a motorcyclist's failure to wear a helmet did not constitute contributory negligence. Otherwise, "a perfectly innocent motorcyclist injured by a drunk driver could conceivably recover nothing, just because he was not wearing a helmet." *Id* at 127.

For these reasons, we hold that failure to wear a seat belt does not constitute negligence in and of itself.

II.

Courts are divided on the issue whether failure to wear a seat belt can be shown in mitigation of damages [citations omitted]. Under common law, the mitigation doctrine applied only to post-accident conduct. However, a number of courts have held that this doctrine has been modified by the Uniform Comparative Fault Act, which defines "fault" to include "unreasonable failure to avoid an injury or mitigate damages." [Citations omitted]. The commentary to the UCFA says that failure to use a seat belt should be considered as reducing damages for those injuries directly attributable to lack of seat belt restraint. Thus, we hold that as far as the calculation of damages is concerned, the comparative negligence statute extends the doctrine of avoidable consequences to pre-accident conduct. The trial court should not have dismissed this defense.

We reverse the judgment of the trial court, and remand for proceedings consistent with this opinion.

B. P. D. AND M. C. S. D. OFFICER FIELD REPORT

DATE OF ACCIDENT AUG 14 -2 (Month Day Year) DAY OF WEEK Friday TIME ____ A.M. 234 P.M.

1/2 mile OUTSIDE CITY LIMITS COUNTY Monroe CITY OR TOWN ____

____ INSIDE CITY LIMITS TOWNSHIP ____

SPECIFIC LOCATION Hwy 451, 120' E of RR tracks, 100' NW of Ratliff Rd

VEHICLE NO. 1

YEAR -2 MAKE Toyota TYPE 2-door

LICENSE NO. ABX 210 ST. Col. YR. -2

DRIVER Susan D. Kesler

ADDRESS 2225 Montclair Av
Bayshore PHONE unk

DRIVER'S LIC. NO. C219-02-1104

D.O.B. 6/4/Yr-29 AGE 27 SEX F

OWNER ——

ADDRESS ——

VEHICLE DAMAGE Total loss

INS. CO. OR AGENT unk.

ADDRESS ____

VEHICLE NO. 2

YEAR -6 MAKE Ford TYPE Truck

LICENSE NO. T 10992 ST. Col. YR. -2

DRIVER Jefrey C. Burnside

ADDRESS 813 N. Washington
Bayshore PHONE 227-1031

DRIVER'S LIC. NO. C 308-33-1022

D.O.B. 2/18/Yr-47 AGE 45 SEX M

OWNER Macklin Furniture

ADDRESS 104 S. Walnut, Bayshore

VEHICLE DAMAGE front end

INS. CO. OR AGENT Aetna 014-H227-
ADDRESS 33-1792

PERSONAL INJURIES

NAME	DESCRIPTION OF INJURY
Susan Kesler	seriously injured, bleeding, partially conscious, removed to hospital by EMT.

DESCRIPTION OF ACCIDENT Vehicle #2 hit #1 from rear as #1 stopped for left turn. Vehicle #2 driving too fast for conditions, given ticket for following too close.

INVESTIGATING OFFICER Edwin M. Mills DEPT. BPD

WITNESSES: Judy Larson Rte 2 Bayshore 221-9219
Mary Ewing, 5351 E. Hwy 451 Bayshore 829-0371

PREPARE DIAGRAM OF ACCIDENT ON BACK OF THIS FORM

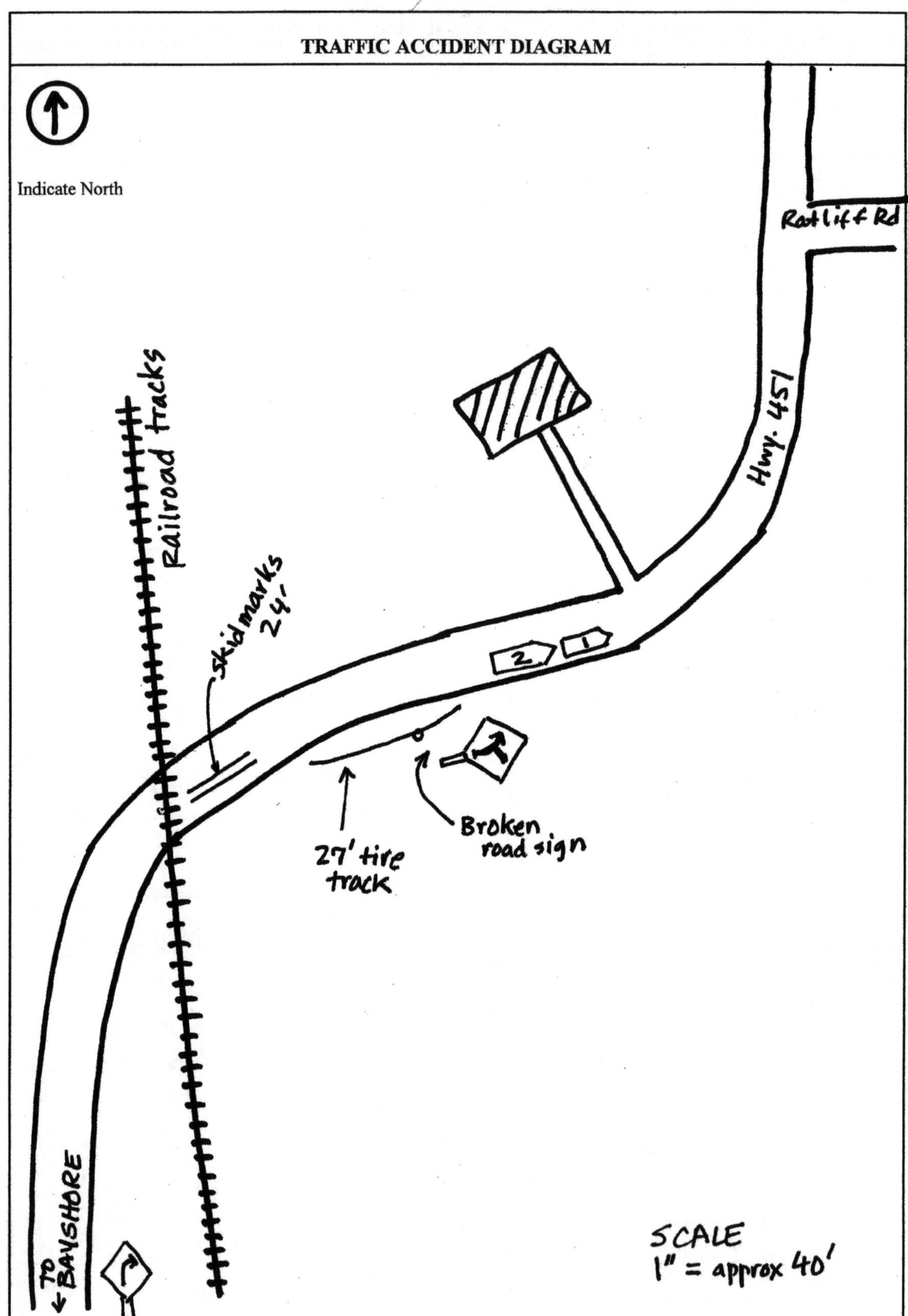

TRAFFIC ACCIDENT DIAGRAM
Indicate North
Ratliff Rd
Hwy. 451
Railroad tracks
skidmarks 24'
2
1
27' tire track
Broken road sign
TO BAYSHORE
SCALE
1" = approx 40'

B. P. D. AND M. C. S. D. OFFICER NARRATIVE REPORT

DATE OF ACCIDENT Aug. 14, Yr-2 DATE OF REPORT Aug. 14, YR-2

SPECIFIC LOCATION Hwy 451, 120 ft East of RR crossing, 100 ft SW of Ratliff Rd

NAME(S) OF PARTIES #1 -- Susan Kesler #2 - Jeffrey Burnside

NAME OF OFFICER Edwin Mills DEPARTMENT BPD

NARRATIVE DESCRIPTION OF ACCIDENT:

On August 14, YR-2, I investigated a car-truck traffic accident at 5351 E. Highway 451 in Monroe County approximately 1/2 mile outside the city limits. It was raining heavily. When I arrived at the scene, I observed Susan Kesler on the pavement 3 feet NE of wrecked Toyota, bleeding heavily from the face. She was semi-conscious. She stated she had been stopped in the road and was hit from behind. She stated she was not wearing her seat belt. The Toyota's windshield was broken and there was some blood on the dashboard area. There was extensive broken glass on the road. The victim's wristwatch was found approximately 20' NE of the Toyota.

I identified the driver of the truck as Jeffrey Burnside, who works for Macklin Furniture. The truck was located half off the shoulder of the road behind the Toyota. The driver stated he had been driving 40 m.p.h., did not see the Toyota, lost control of his truck when he tried to stop quickly, and hit the car. There were 24 feet of skidmarks beginning 118 feet before the point of impact and one set of tire tracks for 27 feet in the mud approximately 90 feet before the point of impact that look like truck tires, indicating that the driver hit brakes, skidded off the road, the right wheels of the truck swerved off the road and back on. The truck hit a road sign when it swerved off the road which I observed lying in the ditch 20 feet away.

Two witnesses verified that the car had been stopped and was hit by the truck from the rear. The witnesses did not believe the truck driver had been speeding, but I could not verify this because the skid marks was interrupted. Issued driver (Burnside) a ticket for following too closely. There was no evidence of impairment.

120 feet SW of point of impact is a level grade railroad crossing in good repair. I do not believe it contributed to the accident. The speed limit was 45 m.p.h.

Susan D. Kesler Plaintiff v. Jeffrey C. Burnside and Macklin Furniture Co., Inc. Defendants	)))))))))))	**DEPOSITION OF SUSAN D. KESLER**

This deposition taken this 3rd day, August YR-1, pursuant to notice at the offices of Houston, Minnick and Dos Santos, 100 North Walnut Street, Bayshore, Columbia, before Diana Watts, A.S.W. certified shorthand reporter.

Appearances: DEBORAH HUXTABLE, Esquire
on behalf of Plaintiff
and
BARRY J. GREENBERG, Esquire
on behalf of Defendants

STIPULATIONS

It is hereby stipulated by and between all parties present at this Deposition that the reading and signing of the Deposition by the deponent is hereby waived, and it may be treated for all purposes as if it had been so read and signed.

The witness being first duly sworn the follow proceedings were had:

Q: (By Mr. Greenberg) State your name, address and age.
A: Susan D. Kesler, 2225 Montclair Avenue. I was born in YR-29.
Q: Your present occupation?
A: I'm a self employed real estate broker and agent.
Q: How long have you been doing that?
A: Since YR-6.
Q: Are you married?
A: Yes, I have a husband named Michael and two children.

Q: What does your husband do?
A: He is the manager of the Book Nook in Bayshore.
Q: Where do the children go to school?
A: University School.
Q: I thought you had to work for the University of Columbia before your children could attend that school?
A: My husband's father is a vice president of the university so they are allowed to attend.
Q: Any criminal record?
A: No.
Q: Do you remember where you were on the 14th of August of last year?
A: Yes sir.
Q: And where was that?
A: I was on my way to go try and get a listing on the Ewing house east of town on highway 451 and when I stopped to make a turn into the driveway a big furniture van hit me from behind.
Q: Was the property listed with another agency at the time?
A: Yes, Century 21 I think, but Mary Ewing was not happy with it. She asked me out to talk about re-listing with me.
Q: Why did you stop to make the turn?
A: It was raining and difficult to see the names and numbers on the mailboxes and I had never been to this house before, so I was having a hard time making sure -- you see, the house I wanted was not on my side of the street -- I had to turn left into the drive and it was raining pretty hard and I wanted to make sure it was the right house. Mrs. Ewing had told me on the telephone the house was hard to find, but that I should look for "Ewing" on the mailbox.
Q: Describe the road for me, please.
A: It was very wet, it had been . . .
Q: No, I mean, what was its shape, number of lanes. . .
A: Oh, I see. It's one lane of traffic in each direction and it's pretty narrow. It has dirt shoulders. At the point where the guy hit me I had just come around a corner and across some railroad tracks.
Q: When you stopped to turn was there any other traffic?
A: Oh, no. There were very few cars on the road, probably because of the rain.
Q: What kind of car were you driving?

A: A Toyota.
Q: Which model?
A: Camry. It was new.
Q: What kind of transmission does it have?
A: Automatic.
Q: At the time of the accident where were you coming from?
A: Bayshore. My place of business, Kesler Agency, on South Lincoln.
Q: What time did you leave your business?
A: It was just after lunch -- about one-thirty.
Q: What time was the accident?
A: Well, let's see. It takes me about twenty minutes to get out there, but with the stops I made it must have been closer to an hour -- so maybe around 2:30.
Q: What were the purposes of the stops that you made?
A: One was because I was pulled over by Bayshore policeman. He informed me that my left signal was not working and told me that I should be sure to use hand signals until I got it fixed.
Q: Did he issue you a citation?
A: No, he told me that if I promised to get the signal fixed that day that he would only give me a warning ticket, so he only gave me a warning.
Q: When did you get the turn signal fixed?
A: I didn't have a chance because I got rear-ended by your client's truck.
Q: How do you know it was my client's truck?
A: I saw the words "Macklin Furniture" in my rear-view mirror just before I got creamed.
Q: And the other stop?
A: I dropped some clothes off at the dry cleaner.
Q: Let's go back to the actual collision for a moment. Were you stopped to make a turn?
A: Yes.
Q: Was your window up or down?
A: I think it was down because I was looking for the name on the mailbox.
Q: Was your foot on the brake?
A: I don't remember.
Q: Was it a left turn or a right turn?
A: A left turn.
Q: And your signal lights weren't working?

A: No, I was signaling with my arm.
Q: What signal were you making?
A: My arm was extended straight out, the hand signal for a left turn.
Q: What was the weather like at that point?
A: I think it was raining real hard.
Q: Were your headlights or tail lights on?
A: No. It was daytime.
Q: What happened next?
A: I heard a noise like a big truck, and glanced at my rear-view mirror.
Q: Inside or outside mirror?
A: Inside.
Q: Go on.
A: I saw a yellow truck that said Macklin Furniture on it bearing down on me, only 50 feet away. It was clearly going too fast and I knew I didn't have time to get out of the way. The truck never even slowed down. It hit me and everything went black. I think I was thrown through the windshield.
Q: Could you see the face of the truck driver?
A: Not really, only the outline.
Q: Is your car equipped with seat belts?
A: Yes.
Q: What type of belts?
A: It has regular shoulder belts.
Q: Was your seat belt fastened at the time of the collision?
A: No, I don't think so.
Q: Do you normally use seat belts?
A: Sometimes I do and sometimes I don't. I always wear them on long trips.
Q: Have you had any previous accidents in the same automobile that you were operating on August 14th?
A: I've never had an accident.
Q: Have you ever been convicted of a moving violation?
A: I had one speeding ticket when I was in college.
Q: For the last full taxable year before the collision of August 14th,YR-2, what was your personal gross income?
A: Approximately $50,000 for YR-3 after office expenses.
Q: And what did you earn in YR-4?
A: I'm not sure. About the same or a little less.
Q: How long were you out of work following the accident?

A: 6 months, from August YR-2 until early February, YR-1.
Q: Was your husband working during this time? How much did he make?
A: Yes. He is on a salary of $65,000 a year at the Book Nook.
Q: You have asked for $50,000 in lost earnings in your complaint for six month's work, which is the same as you earned all the year before. Why?
A: Business had been growing steadily and it was going to be a good year. I had several big clients who were giving me multiple listing. The business was about to really take off after all my hard work. Then this happened and I had to give up my listings to other agents and lost all my income.
Q: In YR-2 and YR-1, wasn't there a national housing crisis?
A: Yes. Lots of people defaulted on mortgages and the market slowed down.
Q: Why wouldn't the mortgage crisis have brought your income down?
A: Bayshore never really experienced much housing price inflation in the 1990s, so the local market wasn't hit too hard because buyers hadn't gotten in over their heads trying to finance million dollar homes, so there weren't many defaulted mortgages. Nothing much changed here.
Q: Why did you have to be out of work for six months?
A: My doctor recommended it. When he released me from the hospital, he said that based on the nature and extent of my injuries, it was his opinion that I might need up to five more months to fully recover.
Q: All right. You claim $15,400 for property damage to your car, a YR-2 Toyota. How did you arrive at that figure?
A: That's what the dealer charged me to fix the car. It took a month to finish, and I had to rent a car for my family to get around in.
Q: How much did that cost?
A: It was $50.00 a day for thirty days.
Q: Your husband already owned a car, didn't he?
A: Yes, but it went into the shop to get re-painted.
Q: You've alleged medical damages in the amount of $43,620, the amount of the hospital bill. Are there any other medical expenses?
A: No.
Q: Who was your doctor?
A: Dr. Bradley Craig.
Q: Were you treated by anyone else?
A: No.
Q: Can you describe the injuries that you sustained during this collision?
A: My face got cut up real bad when I went through the windshield. I also

broke my left arm.
Q: Can you be more specific about your facial injuries?
A: I had deep and wide cuts around my eyes. For a while I couldn't see from the swelling. The cut on my forehead was through to the skull. I also had cuts on my nose and my nose was broken.
Q: Had you ever broken your nose before?
A: Yes, once when I was in high school in a skiing accident.
Q: As best you can, please describe your pain and suffering.
A: Well, the first week in the hospital was real bad. Everything was hazy and they gave me a lot of drugs for pain, but they didn't really work very well. I couldn't sleep because of headaches and body aches. The pain got better and the next three weeks I was just sore and stiff. I still couldn't see because my eyes were bandaged and swollen. It was agony not knowing if my eyes had been damaged. I was thirsty all the time but couldn't drink. After a month in the hospital, the swelling went down so I could see all right, and they sent me home. I had a prescription for a painkillers which helped, but I still got frequent bad headaches -- maybe once or twice a week. The headaches got gradually better and I was able to go back to work in February. The scars and facial surgery took four months to fade away to the point where I could face the public again. Those five months recuperating at home were emotionally trying because we had lost my income and I was bored and tense.
Q: Do you remember telling the doctor in the emergency room that you wanted to go home because you felt alright?
A: I don't remember. Things were real hazy. I do remember telling Dr. Craig a few days later to give me whatever it took to make me well again.
Q: Do you have copies of your medical bills?
A: Yes, my attorney does.
Q: One more thing. Were you using your cell phone at any time?
A: I had called Mrs. Ewing to verify her address maybe a minute before I was hit, but I was definitely not using it when I was hit.
Q: Do you receive itemized cell phone bills that record each call?
A: Yes.
Mr. Greenberg: That's all. Will you send us the medical bills and phone record?
Ms. Huxtable: Of course.

END OF DEPOSITION

REMIT TO: RECONSTRUCTIVE SURGERY GROUP, INC.
P.O. BOX 1330
BAYSHORE COLUMBIA
811-775-3626

NOV 15, YR-2

ACCOUNT: 702503 13
SUSAN D. KESLER
2225 MONTCLAIR AV
BAYSHORE, COLUMBIA

AMOUNT DUE: $3598.00

AMOUNT
ENCLOSED __________

PLEASE DETACH AND RETURN THIS STUB WITH YOUR REMITTANCE

- -

DATE OF SERVICE	REFERENCE	DESCRIPTION	CHARGES	CREDITS
AUG 24	024786	EMERGENCY SURGE	3990.00	
AUG 24	024786	FACIAL RECONSTRUCT SURGERY	5910.00	
SEP 2	024786	FACIAL RECONSTRUCT SURGERY	5090.00	
SEP 28	702503	OFFICE VISIT	200.00	
OCT 19	702503	OFFICE VISIT	200.00	
NOV 5	113-H7	INS PAYMENT		11,992.00
NOV 11	702503	OFFICE VISIT	200.00	

TOTAL

PAY THIS AMOUNT ➡ 3598.00

✣ Monroe County Hospital

STATEMENT

PATIENT'S NAME AND ADDRESS
SUSAN D. KESLER
2225 MONTCLAIR AV
BAYSHORE, COLUMBIA

ACCOUNT NUMBER
20 716 66Q

INSURANCE INFORMATION
BC/BS 238284998

DATE ADMITTED
AUG 14 YR-2

DATE DISCHARGED
SEP 11 YR-2

POSTING DATE	PHYSICIAN	DESCRIPTION	TOTAL CHARGES
AUG 14		EMERGENCY ROOM GROUP	680.00
AUG 14		RADIOLOGY	540.00
AUG 14	DUVALL	ANAESTHESIA	670.00
AUG 14		OPERATING ROOM CHARGE	550.00
AUG 14	BOWLEN	ASSIST AT SURGERY	1200.00
AUG 14		AMBULANCE	220.00
AUG 21		1 WK PRIVATE ROOM	3575.00
AUG 21		PHARMACY	355.00
AUG 22		LAB	360.00
AUG 23	GORDON	CONSULTATION	580.00
AUG 24		RADIOLOGY	610.00
AUG 24	DUVALL	ANAESTHESIA	910.00
AUG 24		OPERATING ROOM CHARGE	1090.00
AUG 24	ZEITLIN	ASSIST AT SURGERY	1640.00
AUG 28		PHARMACY	255.00
AUG 28		1 WK PRIVATE ROOM	3575.00
AUG 30		LAB	360.00
AUG 31		RADIOLOGY	640.00
SEP 02	DUVALL	ANAESTHESIA	690.00
SEP 02	ZEITLIN	ASSIST AT SURGERY	1260.00
SEP 02		OPERATING ROOM CHARGE	610.00
SEP 04		1 WK PRIVATE ROOM	3575.00
SEP 04		PHARMACY	255.00
SEP 11		PHARMACY	255.00
SEP 11		1 WK PRIVATE ROOM	3575.00
SEP 30		ANTHEM PAYMENT	[22,424.00]
		BALANCE DUE	5606.00

508006

THIS IS NOT A CITATION. IT IS ONLY A WARNING

STATE OF COLUMBIA
DEPARTMENT OF PUBLIC SAFETY
STATE OFFICE BUILDING
LINCOLN, COLUMBIA

Date: Aug 14 Time: 2:03 pm

Location: 2900 block of Hillside Drive
Bayshore, Columbia

Driver's Name: Susan D. Kesler

Address: 2225 Montclair Ave
Bayshore, Columbia

Operator number: C2190211 Type: Operator

Restrictions: none Expires: June 4, Yr+1

Vehicle Make: Toyota Year: -2 Type: 4 door

Registration: ABX-210 State: Columbia

Nature of Violation: Inoperative left turn signal

THIS IS NOT A CITATION
YOU DO NOT HAVE TO APPEAR IN COURT

This is not a citation. It is a warning ticket. You have five (5) days within which to remedy the above defect. When you have done so, you must have the garage, dealer or service station performing the work send confirmation to the above address. If you perform the repairs yourself, you must present yourself to your local police or sheriff's department with proof that the defect has been corrected. Failure to make these repairs within five days will result in a citation being issued.

DRIVE SAFELY. THE LIFE YOU SAVE MAY BE YOUR OWN.

Issuing Officer: William Dougherty

Department: Bayshore PD

AUTOROYAL
TOYOTA-SUBARU
3333 S WALNUT STREET
BAYSHORE, COLUMBIA

INVOICE

MICHAEL KELSER
2225 MONTCLAIR
BAYSHORE, COL

COLOR: BEIGE
YEAR: YR-2
MAKE: TOYOTA CAMRY
VIN: 3TOCA214CX274363565

MILEAGE: 9935
DROP OFF: AUG 14, YR-2 (L & C TOWING)
COMPLETED: SEP 13, YR-2
SERVICE ADVISOR: BEATTY

A CUST AUTHORIZES REPAIR AND CLEANUP OF CAR FROM ACCIDENT. USE GENUINE TOYOTA PARTS

34 BODY SHOP SUBCHARGE PARTS	9956.00
35 BODY SHOP SUBCHARGE LABOR	5125.00
B OIL CHANGE/LUBE SERVICE	38.00
C CK ENGINE & COOLING SYS	
13P BELT DRIVE	23.40
63 HOSES	42.10
99 ANTIFREEZE	11.00
02 OIL PAN	66.90
02 OIL PAN SEAL	10.20
01 LABOR CHARGE	165.50

☞ PLEASE PAY THIS AMOUNT 15,400.10

AUTOROYAL
TOYOTA-SUBARU
3333 S WALNUT STREET
BAYSHORE, COLUMBIA

INVOICE

TO: MICHAEL KESLER
2225 MONTCLAIR AV
BAYSHORE COL

ACCOUNT NUMBER: 6352878-93

SALES ASSOCIATE: E. GREENEBAUM

DATE OF SALE: SEP. 14, YR-2

SHORT TERM LEASE, YR-1 TOYOTA CAMRY LXE @ 49.99 PER DAY

START OF LEASE: AUG 15, YR-2

END OF LEASE: SEP 14, YR-2

SUBTOTAL: 1499.70
TAX: 0

PLEASE PAY THIS AMOUNT: 1499.70

Susan D. Kesler)
Plaintiff)
)
v.) **DEPOSITION OF**
) **JEFFREY C. BURNSIDE**
Jeffrey C. Burnside)
)
and)
)
Macklin Furniture Co..)
Defendants)

This deposition is taken this 3rd day of August YR-1, pursuant to notice at the offices of Houston, Minnick & DosSantos, 100 North Walnut, Bayshore, Columbia, before Diana Watts, A.S.W. certified shorthand reporter.

Appearances: DEBORAH HUXTABLE, Esquire
on behalf of Plaintiff
and
BARRY J. GREENBERG, Esquire
on behalf of Defendants

STIPULATIONS

It is hereby stipulated by and between all parties represented at this Deposition that the reading and signing of the Deposition by the deponent is hereby waived, and it may be treated for all purposes as if it had been so read and signed.

The witness being first duly sworn the following proceedings were had:

Q: (By Ms. Huxtable) State your name.
A: Jeffrey C. Burnside.
Q: What is your home address?
A: 813 North Washington Street, Bayshore, Columbia.
Q: When were you born?
A: In YR-47.
Q: Are you employed?
A: Yes, I work for Macklin Furniture Co.

Q: In what capacity?
A: I work in the warehouse loading and unloading furniture.
Q: Were you employed on August 14, YR-2?
A: I was employed by Macklin Furniture Co. but as a truck driver.
Q: Why do you no longer drive a truck?
A: Because Mr. Macklin decided I would be better in the warehouse.
Q: When did you change jobs?
A: A week after the accident.
Q: Are you married?
A: I'm divorced.
Q: Any children?
A: Three: Jennifer, Joshua, and Kimberly.
Q: Any military service?
A: Navy. I was in the Navy for four years.
Q: How long have you been working for Macklin Furniture?
A: 22 years.
Q: How long have you had a drivers license in this state?
A: Since I was 16.
Q: Have you ever lost your driving privilege?
A: No.
Q: Have you ever had a traffic ticket before?
A: Yes. Three speeding tickets I think. None in the last few years.
Q: Had you ever been involved in a traffic collision prior to August 14, YR-2?
A: Yes, twice in YR-2, once in March and again in May. Both were my fault. My boss, Jerry Macklin, told me he'd fire me if I caused another accident. Luckily, this one wasn't my fault, and Mr. Macklin told me he was satisfied this one wasn't my fault so my job was secure.
Q: Directing your attention to August 14, YR-2, you stated earlier that you were employed by Macklin Furniture Co. Were you working on that day?
A: Yes, I was delivering furniture.
Q: Were you operating a truck?
A: Yes, I was driving a Ford furniture van.
Q: Do you recall the weather on that day?
A: Yes, it rained all day, at times very heavy.
Q: Where were you at approximately 2:00 p.m. on August 14th?
A: Making deliveries. I was unloading chairs at a place called the Old Timey

General Store and Café on Route 45.
Q: How long did you stay at the store?
A: I was there for about an hour.
Q: When did you leave?
A: About 2:30 p.m. I didn't look at my watch. I was running a little late.
Q: What happened when you left the store?
A: I drove south to Route 451 and then drove east on Route 451 towards my next delivery but I never got there.
Q: Where were you headed?
A: To a home in Unionville, about 10 miles east of Bayshore.
Q: Had you been there before?
A: No.
Q: How did you know where it was?
A: There's a GPS thing in the truck so I just entered the address.
Q: What happened to keep you from your delivery?
A: I got in an accident with Ms. Kesler.
Q: Could you describe that accident?
A: I was driving east on 451, approaching the railroad tracks. It was raining real hard. As I got to the tracks, a car coming the other way very fast crossed the center line, forcing me off the road. I fought to get the truck under control. I didn't even see Ms. Kesler's car until I was about 50 feet away. I slammed on the brakes but with all the rain I skidded into the rear of her car. She didn't have any lights on or anything. No taillights, no turn signal, nothing.
Q: Was she giving a hand signal?
A: Not that I could see.
Q: How fast were you driving directly before the collision?
A: I guess about 40 mph. The speed limit there is 45 mph.
Q: Can you describe this car that supposedly ran you off the road?
A: No. It flashed by.
Q: Are you familiar with route 451?
A: Yes, I've driven probably 20 times on the road each year for the past 20 years.
Q: Can you describe route 451 where the collision took place?
A: It's one lane each way with a soft shoulder.
Q: What did you do after you hit Ms. Kesler's car.
A: Well, I jumped out of the truck and ran over to the car to see if I could do anything to help. She had been thrown through the windshield because she

had not been wearing her seat belt. I didn't hit her car all that hard so she would have been okay if she had been wearing her seat belt like the law says. She was bleeding around her face and I gave her my shirt to press against the wounds. I ran back to my truck, got my cell phone, and called the police and told them to get an ambulance.

Q: Did anything else happen?

A: Well, oh yes, after I got back from calling the cops I was talking to the injured woman to try to keep her conscious. I saw that on TV, that you're not supposed to let a person with a head injury fall into a coma. She said to me, "I'm sure sorry I wasn't wearing that damn seat belt."

Q: Did she say anything else?

A: Nothing other than to ask me to call her family and tell them she was ok.

Q: Did you do that?

A: No, I didn't know her name or phone number.

Q: Did anything else happen with respect to this accident?

A: The police gave me a ticket for following too close.

Q: Do you recall the officer's name?

A: No.

Q: Did you make any statements to the police officer?

A: I told him I was driving safely, well under the speed limit, and that the car didn't have its lights on.

Q: Did anyone else make any statements?

A: There were three or four people standing around. I heard one woman say that the driver of the car was not giving a signal, but I don't know her name.

Q: What happened to the traffic ticket?

A: I pleaded guilty on the advice of the lawyer from the insurance company, even though I had not been at fault. I mean, the woman's car was stopped without any lights on.

By Ms. Huxtable: Nothing further.

By Mr. Greenberg: Just before the accident, were you watching the road?

A: Of course.

Q: Were you keeping a lookout for stopped vehicles?

A: Of course.

Q: Did you see any other vehicles on the road before the accident?

A: Yes, a car passed me going towards town just as I crossed the tracks. It was the one that forced me off the road.

Q: Was there any way for you to avoid the accident?
A: No. When I first saw the car I was almost on top of it.
Q: How fast were you going?
A: 40 mph pretty much all the way along 451.
Q: Did any other cars pass you headed into town?
A: Several cars passed me going 50 or 55 mph.
Q: Describe exactly what happened just before the accident.
A: As I crossed the tracks, another car coming toward me crossed the center line and forced me to the right. The road curves at the same time as it crosses the tracks and there's no shoulder. I've always thought that was a bad corner. When I tried to move to the right, the right wheels of the truck slipped off the pavement, causing the truck to fishtail a little. I got the truck back on the road, and then I saw a foreign car stopped in the road. I hit the brakes but it was too late.
Q: Had you been watching the road during all this time?
A: Yes, of course. The little car just appeared suddenly out of the darkness. If she had had her lights on, I'd have seen the car and this whole thing would never have happened.
Q: Were you distracted by anything? Cell phone, computer, anything like that?
A: No.
Q: Had you had anything to drink?
A: You mean like alcohol? No, of course not.
Mr. Greenberg: That's all.
Ms. Huxtable: One more thing. Did you have a cell phone with you?
A: Yes.
Q: Did you make any calls that day while driving?
A: Not while driving, but I called in a couple of times to let them know when I was finished with a delivery.
Q: Is there a computer in the truck?
A: No.
Q: There's a GPS device, you said earlier?
A: Yes, so we can find addresses for deliveries.
Q: Was it on at the time of the accident?
A: Yes. It's always on.
Ms. Huxtable: That's all.

END OF DEPOSITION

STATEMENT OF JUDY LARSON

MADE TO: Robert C. Weber
Investigator for Aetna Insurance Company

DATE: October 11, YR-2

This statement is a summary prepared by Robert C. Weber from notes taken at an interview with Judy Larson at her home in Bayshore, Columbia, on October 9, YR-2. It is being given to Ms. Larson to read and approve on today's date.

My name is Judy Larson. I live in Johnson's Trailer Court, Route 2, Bayshore, Columbia. I am 37 years old, married, with three children. My husband currently is unemployed, and I support the family by doing housework. I work for Mrs. David Ewing on route 451 on Tuesdays and Fridays.

I was at work on Friday, August 14, YR-2. Mrs. Ewing was also home, but in a different part of the house. At about 2:45 p.m. I was in the kitchen doing the dishes. You can see the road clearly from the kitchen window. It was raining kind of hard. I looked out the window and saw a yellow foreign car stop in the road near the Ewing's driveway. That's about 75 feet away. I saw a furniture van come around the corner from the west and run into the small car. I think the truck was going 30 to 40 miles an hour, but I'm not absolutely sure. The driver was obviously driving carefully, but never had a chance. There was a terrible accident and I called the police on the kitchen phone. I told the police I thought a man was dead. I meant Mrs. Kesler, but could not tell until I went down to the road that the driver was a woman.

Because I was looking at the side of the car, I couldn't be absolutely certain whether it had headlights, tail lights or turn signals on. I don't think so, because it was dark enough that I think I would have seen them. But I could clearly see the drivers' side of the car. The window was rolled up and the driver definitely was not giving a hand signal. She could not have given a hand signal anyway because I could see her left hand up at the side of her head and she was talking on her cell phone. She must have been looking for the Ewing driveway which is kind of hard to find because of some bushes, because she was stopped in the road for several seconds. My best estimate is that the car sat there stopped for about five seconds. No cars passed in either direction during that time and nothing blocks my view.

After I called the police, I ran down to the road and saw Mrs. Kesler lying there, bleeding real bad. She had been thrown through the windshield. It was hard to see her face clearly because of all the blood. I was the first person at the scene. Mrs. Kesler saw me, and asked why the truck never stopped. She said, "I'm not going to make it. Tell the cops that I was driving safely and that maniac ran into me." I looked around for the truck driver and he was sitting in the truck talking on his cell phone. Then he came up to where I was, and we tried to keep the poor woman comfortable in all the rain. She was unconscious. I know this sounds bizarre, but Mr. Burnside was not wearing a shirt. A few minutes later an ambulance arrived and a police officer. I told the officer what I had seen and went back to work.

I visited Mrs. Kesler in the hospital two weeks later. I don't know why -- curiosity, I guess. She thanked me for helping her at the scene of the accident. She was bandaged up and her eyes were covered and she looked pretty bad.

I also went to court at the end of September, YR-2, when Mr. Burnside, the truck driver, was charged with speeding. I had been a witness and they said they might need my testimony. They didn't, because Mr. Burnside pleaded guilty. Mrs. Kesler was also there and I went up to talk to her to see how she was doing. She said she was feeling better but her face still looked a little beat up and was black and blue. Mr. Burnside must have seen me talking to Mrs. Kesler, because he came up to me a little later and told me to tell her that he didn't mean to run into her. I think his exact words were, "Tell her I'm sorry, I didn't mean to run into her. I hit the brakes but couldn't stop in time because the truck skidded."

I knew Mr. Burnside from before the accident. He used to live near us. He was a neighbor until he moved away about five years ago. He used to ride to work with my husband.

On August 14, YR-2, I had had two beers that day around lunch time, along with my sandwich, but I wasn't drunk or anything. I weigh about 155 pounds.

I have read the foregoing, and it is true and accurate.

Judy Larson
Judy Larson

Witnessed: *Robert C. Weber*
Robert C. Weber

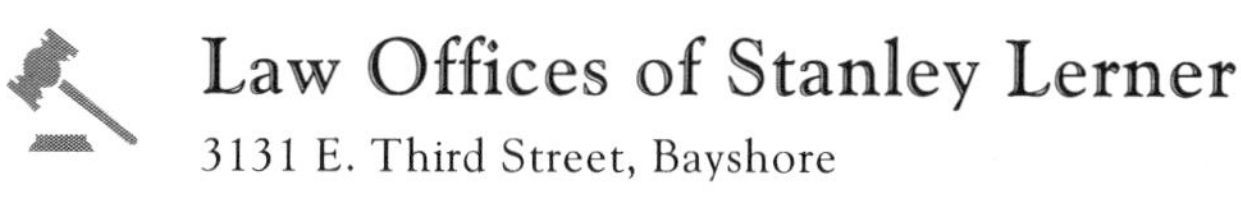
Law Offices of Stanley Lerner
3131 E. Third Street, Bayshore

Phone 811-JUSTICE
Your Attorneys in the College Mall

STATEMENT OF MARY LOUISE EWING

Made to: Deborah Huxtable, Esq.
Place: 3131 E. Third Street
Bayshore, Columbia
DATE: November 16, YR-2

STATEMENT OF MARY EWING

My name is Mary Louise Ewing. I was born September 30, YR-36. I live at 5351 East Highway 451. The house is a one-story ranch house on a small hill overlooking Route 451. It is located about one-half mile from the Bayshore city limits.

My husband's name is David Ewing. He is the deputy administrator of the Monroe County School Corporation. We have been married for 12 years. We met in college and got married in Washington, D.C. when we were both doing internships with the government after graduation. We have two children, Derek and Kathleen. Derek is nine and Kathleen is seven. Both children were in school the day of the accident.

I am a homemaker and writer. When the kids were small, I devoted most of my time to raising them. Now that they are in school, I have returned to my writing. Like all writers, I am working on my novel. I want it to raise the dilemma of the post-modern woman, by focusing on two sisters, one a homemaker and one a single career woman. During the novel, each re-examines her choice, and they end up with their roles reversed. However, to actually bring in a paycheck, I write articles profiling successful women that I sell to magazines.

Because of the additional income from my writing, we decided to move to a larger house. In July, we listed our house with Gaston Real Estate. We had few inquiries and no formal offers. In early August, Susan Kesler called me. She's a real estate agent I had met at a Leadership Bayshore luncheon several months before. Susan said she heard that we weren't getting much response on our home, and that she wanted to come talk to me about listing the house with her because she could give me more personal attention. I agreed to talk to her. I told her to come out the afternoon of August 14th about 2:30.

At about 2:45, I was sitting in the living room waiting for Susan to arrive. The living room looks out over the road. It has a large plate glass window, maybe 6 feet high and 8 feet wide, with a clear view down to the highway. There is one small evergreen tree in the yard, about ten feet high, but it is fairly spindly and does not significantly block my view. I think it is a cedar tree of some kind. I was watching the road for Ms. Kesler because she was late. I remember that it was raining. At times the rain was so hard that you couldn't see the road clearly, but it had let up slightly at 2:45. It was still unusually dark, but I could see the road without too much difficulty.

I remember seeing a car, maybe a Toyota or Honda, slow down and stop across from the driveway. The car was a bright color, maybe yellow. I watched it because I wondered if it was Ms. Kesler. As the car came to a stop, I noticed that the driver's side window was rolled down and she was giving a left turn signal with her arm. I thought this was silly because it was raining, and I wondered why she did not use her automatic signals. I do not remember for sure whether the headlights or parking lights were on, but I don't think so. There were no other cars on the road. Then the phone rang, and I looked away for a moment -- maybe one or two seconds. It only rang once and then stopped. When I looked back at the road, Ms. Kesler's car was just starting to turn into our driveway. I don't know why she had waited. I assume she was looking at the mailbox to make sure she had the right house. Her window was still rolled down but her arm was now inside the car in order to turn the steering wheel. As she was starting to turn left into our driveway, a truck came barreling around the corner, started skidding when it hit the railroad tracks, and slammed into the back of Ms. Kesler's car. It looked to me like the truck driver was going too fast, not watching the road, and lost control going around the curve. In fact, one of my neighbors named Nancy Dempsey told me later she heard the truck driver tell the police that he lost control of the truck because he was trying to adjust the GPS navigation system and wasn't watching the road. I estimate the truck's speed as about 50 mph.

After the accident, several people came running over to the scene. I don't know where they came from, but there are several houses nearby. I did not go down. It looked like there were enough gawkers without me. I did not call the police at first, because I didn't want to become involved and have to spend a lot of time in court. I later realized that it was my duty, and I called to say I had been a witness. They took my name but no one ever came to talk to me.

At the time of the accident, our maid Judy Larson was in the house, probably in the kitchen, so she probably saw the accident too. The kitchen window also overlooks the highway. I never discussed the accident with her. We had to fire her shortly after the accident because she had a drinking problem. She would drink several beers and one or two glasses of Bourbon every day that she worked.

I have never met Mr. Burnside. I am familiar with Macklin Furniture Company. They are one of the two big furniture stores in town. I once bought something from them -- a double chest of drawers. It arrived damaged. When I complained, they claimed my children had caused the damage and refused to replace it. I sent a nasty letter to the Better Business Bureau, and have not done business with them since. I have no idea if Mr. Burnside was the driver who delivered the chest.

This statement was prepared by Dorothy Schott, a stenographer, based on my conversation with Deborah Huxtable, an attorney at the law offices of Stanley Lerner, 3131 E. Third Street, in Bayshore. I have read it over. It is complete and accurate.

Mary L. Ewing

Mary Louise Ewing

✣ Monroe County Hospital

Surgical Department
684-3771

STATEMENT OF DR. BRADLEY CRAIG

This statement is being dictated by Bradley Craig in response to written questions submitted by attorneys involved in a case concerning injuries to Susan D. Kesler.

I am a plastic surgeon on the staff of the Monroe County Hospital and a member of the Reconstructive Surgery Group here in Bayshore. I was Ms. Kesler's attending physician in August and September, YR-2, during her hospitalization. I am a graduate of the University of Florida Medical School. I interned at Methodist Hospital in Indianapolis, and completed a plastic surgery residency at Boston Children's Hospital. I am board-certified in plastic surgery, a member in good standing of the state and local medical association, and have taught courses in facial reconstruction surgery at the University of Columbia Medical School. I am 52 years old, and have been practicing plastic surgery for twenty years.

Ms. Kesler was in the hospital for 28 days. She underwent three operations to reconstruct extensive damage to her face and nose. There was evidence of a pre-existing injury to her nose that complicated the surgery slightly. However, the surgery was successful, and her prognosis is excellent for a full recovery, with only minimal scarring around one eye from skin grafts lasting longer than six months. Consultation with Dr. Sharon Gordon revealed no permanent damage to her eyes. I was assisted in my surgery by Dr. Zeitlin.

Ms. Kesler demonstrated unusually high anxiety over the prospect of losing her eyesight during the first three weeks in the hospital. During that time her eyes were shut due to excessive swelling. She seemed more helpless and less self-reliant than most patients.

These injuries and surgery were probably very painful during her entire stay in the hospital. The first surgical operation to reattach facial tissue and reconstruct her nose had to be conducted without anesthetic because it was a massive head injury. We can give adrenalin shots, but they only partially alleviate pain. After the first surgery, based on my experience with many patients, I would expect that the demerol she was taking would only partially alleviate her pain. According to her chart, Ms. Kesler asked for (but did not receive) additional pain medication on 12 of the 28 nights she was in the hospital. The nurses reported that she had difficulty sleeping, and complained constantly about the pain. After her discharge from the hospital, she was prescribed Vicodin which should have been sufficient to alleviate further pain, but there would be stiffness and discomfort similar to clogged sinuses for a month or so after discharge. The pain should have disappeared completely by mid-December.

Ms. Kesler's face would have been disfigured from scarring, swelling, and discoloration through late December with slight residual discoloration visible for several weeks thereafter.

I saw Ms. Kesler briefly three times after her discharge from the hospital. She was making satisfactory progress. I saw her for the last time on November 11, YR-2.

I have read this statement after it was transcribed, and it is accurate.

Bradley Craig

Bradley Craig, M.D.

Date: 02/06/YR-1

Paul Swain Investigations
809 W 6th Street, Bayshore, Columbia
(811) 332-8544 sherlockswain@zipper.net

RE: KESLER V. MACKLIN FURNITURE

FROM: PAUL SWAIN

DATE: December 10, YR-1

SUBJECT: Results of Investigation

1. A check of police department records shows that Ms. Judy Larson was arrested and convicted for larceny five years ago. She was convicted in District Court of Larceny as a misdemeanor on April 20, YR-5, and given a suspended sentence. A check of courthouse records shows that she pleaded guilty. A copy of the record is attached. Also, she is currently under indictment charged with extortion. She and her husband are charged with trying to extort money from Kroger supermarket for falsely claiming she had been poisoned by food bought there. No trial date has been set.

2. The reports indicated that Nancy Dempsey was a possible witness who lives near the accident site. She was interviewed and denies being a witness or knowing anything about the accident.

3. I visited the Ewing home. Mrs. Ewing let me into the house. You can see the accident site clearly from the kitchen window but not from the kitchen sink. You can see most of the accident site from the living room, except for a tree that blocks part of the view. A full diagram is attached.

4. According to other real estate agents, it is considered unethical and dishonest to try to get someone to list their home with you when it is already listed with another agent. This is called "stealing a listing" and that is what Susan Kesler was apparently trying to do when she went to visit Mary Ewing.

5. A copy of Mary Ewing's letter to the Better Business Bureau is attached.

Monroe County Circuit Court
Criminal Division
State of Columbia

CERTIFICATE OF DISPOSITION

Court Number: 1326-CR-5

Judge: Marks

Case: State v. Judy Larson

Original Offense(s): CCC 220-3 Misd Larceny Under $500

Disposition: CCC 220-3 Misd Larceny Under $500

Guilty Plea: Apr 20, YR-5

Trial:

Appeal:

Final Judgment Entered: 30 days suspended on condition that defendant pay restitution and court costs

Date: Apr 20, YR-5

I hereby certify that this is a true excerpt from the records of the Monroe County Circuit Court, Criminal Division, State of Columbia.

Camille Johnson, Clerk of the Circuit Court

By: Robert Hamilton, Deputy Clerk

Date: January 29, YR-0

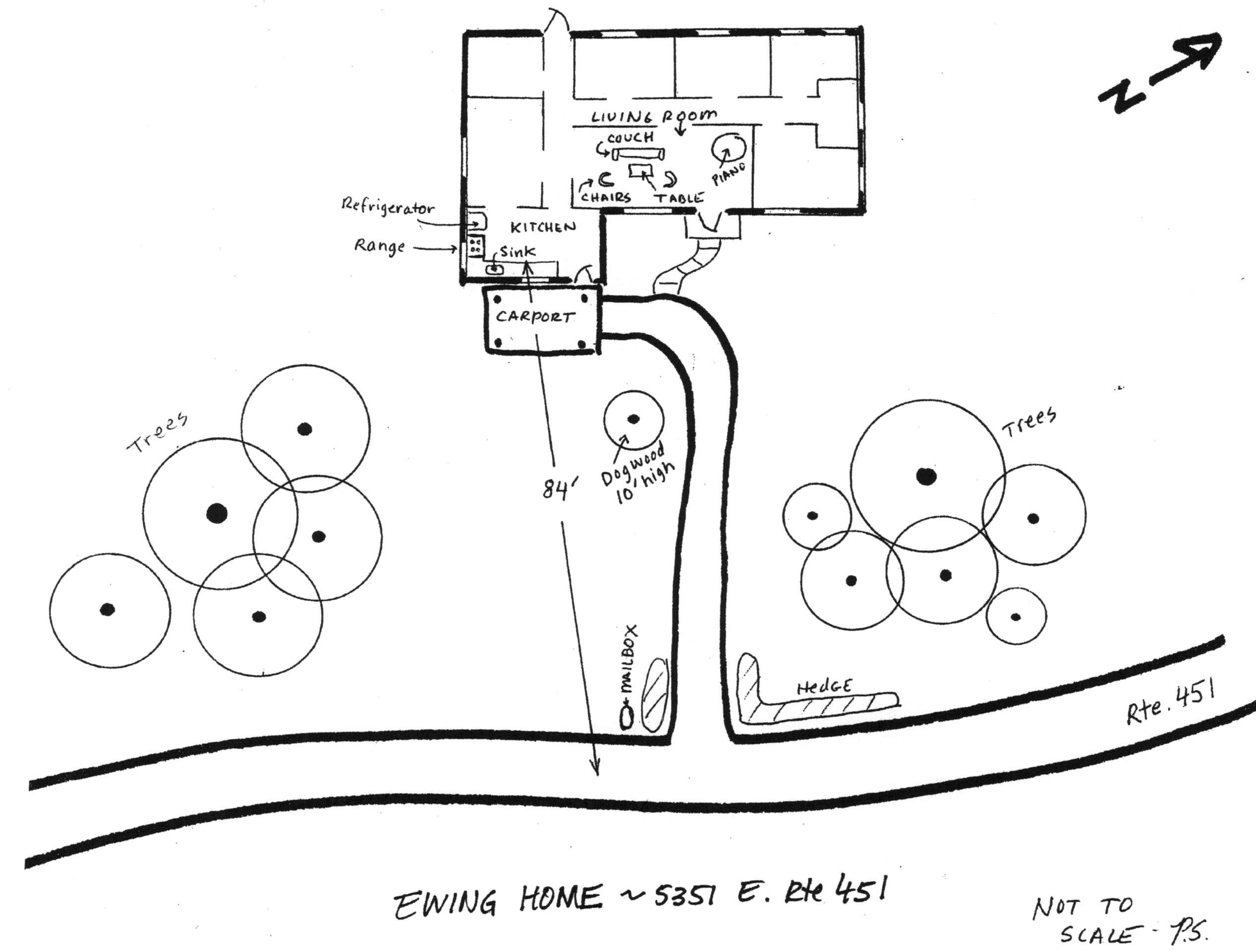
N
LIVING ROOM
COUCH
CHAIRS
TABLE
PIANO
Refrigerator
Range
KITCHEN
Sink
CARPORT
Trees
84'
Dogwood 10' high
Trees
MAILBOX
Hedge
Rte. 451
EWING HOME ~ 5351 E. Rte 451
NOT TO SCALE - P.S.

5351 E. Highway 451
Bayshore, Columbia
October 23, YR-4

Better Business Bureau
123 W. Kirkwood
Bayshore, Columbia

To whom it may concern:

I purchased a chest of drawers from Macklin Furniture Company of Bayshore at the Labor Day Sale. It was a floor model, so I was able to examine it closely. It was in perfect shape when I bought it. The price was $795.00, delivery included.

When they delivered the chest, it had been damaged. One of the legs was split and a corner of the chest was cracked. Obviously, their delivery person had dropped the chest when loading or unloading it. Unfortunately, I did not notice the damage for several days. When I called the store, and spoke to a manager named Mr. Sims, he said he would call me back. When he did, he said that they had delivered the chest in perfect condition, and that my children must have damaged it. He said he would not replace it and hung up on me!

I am angry at them, and will not shop there any more. I want this complaint on file so other innocent customers will be warned about the way they do business.

Sincerely,

Mary L. Ewing

Mary L. Ewing

MONROE COUNTY

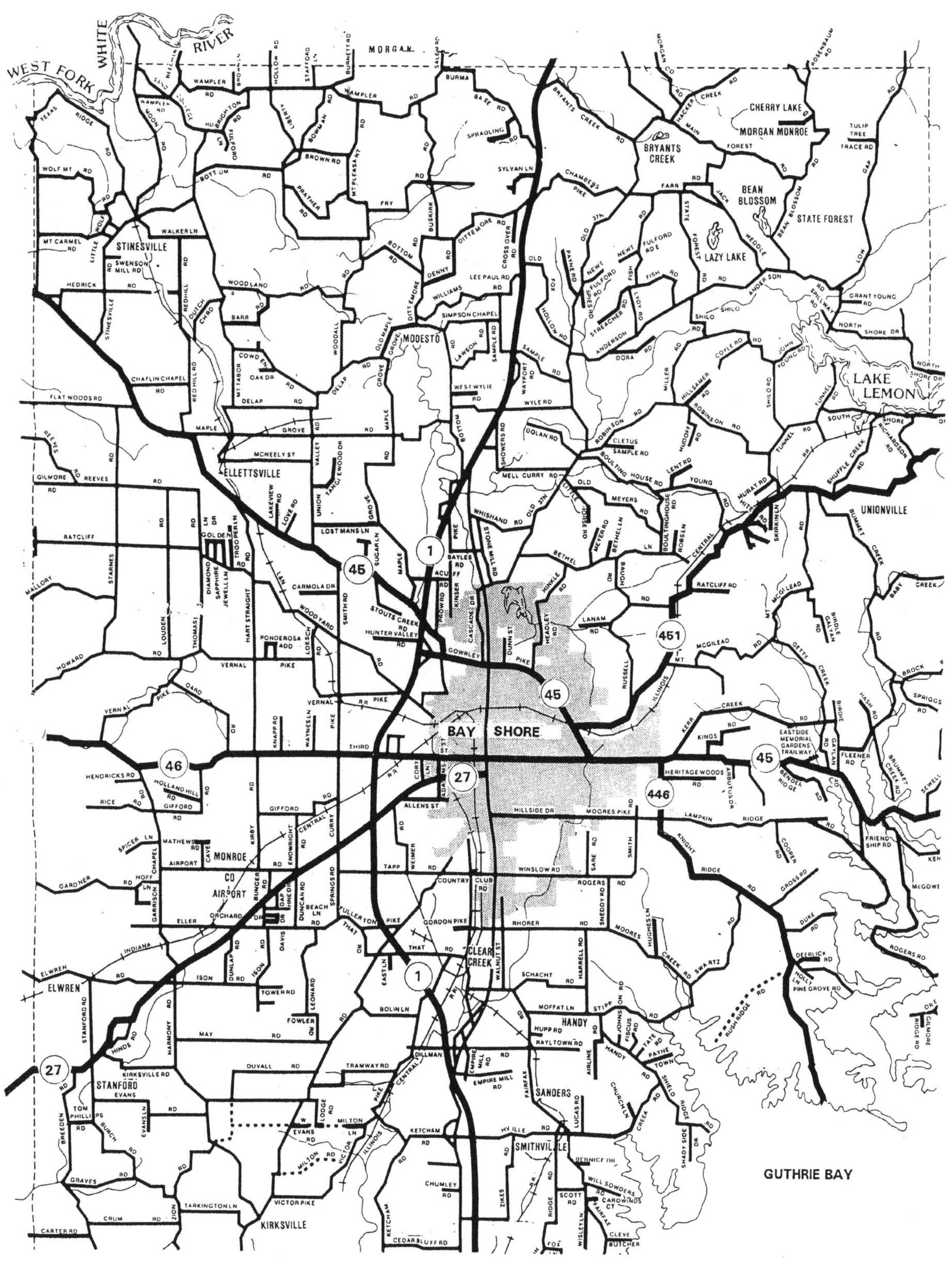

MASTER REAL ESTATE

704 N. Walnut Street, Bayshore, Columbia 336-7713

TO: PLAINTIFF'S ATTORNEY
FROM: SHIRLEY MASTER
DATE: APRIL 28, YR-1
RE: SUSAN KESLER

This memorandum is in response to your request that I evaluate the probable loss of business to Susan Kesler for being out of work for six months from August 14, Yr-2, until February 15, Yr-1. I am in a good position to do this because I know Ms. Kesler personally. She often came to me for advice when she first started her agency, and we have kept in touch throughout. In addition, I am familiar with the Kesler Agency by word of mouth. I have been in real estate in Bayshore for over twenty-five years, running my own agency with fifteen brokers working for me. Bayshore is a small town in many ways, and I know almost every real estate agent in town. I have been president of the Bayshore Real Estate Board three times in the last ten years, and I keep in touch with what is going on in the market. I have been selected Realtor of the Year three times (YR-12, YR-8, and YR-3), and have served on the city Zoning and Planning Board since YR-4.

Susan Kesler ran a small, one-person agency. She started it about five or six years ago. I admire her courage. Most brokers work for one of the large agencies rather than trying to make a go of it by themselves. Kesler ran a one-woman shop. That means there is no one to cover for her when she is in the hospital. As far as I know, she did not even have a secretary, but did her own paperwork and record-keeping.

The real estate business of any solo broker tends to grow steadily during her first five or six years, as the broker becomes familiar with the local market and attracts more clients. Maximum profit comes from obtaining exclusive listings, because then you make a commission regardless of who sells the listed property. When you first start out, you attract mostly people who want to buy, not sell. That means you have to split your commissions with the listing agent. However, most people who sell their homes list it with the agent who helped them buy it. It takes five or six years before any substantial number of your former clients decide to sell their homes. So business is usually very weak the first five years, and you make ends meet by handling the management of rental units. If you survive five years, your business begins to take off in the sixth and seventh years.

Most of Susan's business is residential listings in the university fringe neighborhoods (properties within a mile of the University of Columbia campus). These are good homes to list, because they have a high turnover and are always in demand. I estimate that Susan's business would have steadily increased by 30% to 50% a year over her first five years as a broker. All other things being equal, her business in YR-2 would have been 30% to 50% higher than the year before.

There were two problems, however. First, and obvious to everyone, was the general downturn in the housing market caused by the nationwide mortgage crisis. Across the country, people had bought houses they could not afford on the assumption that they could continually refinance as housing prices inflated. When the bubble collapsed and home values went down, millions of people could neither pay their mortgages nor refinance, and lost their homes to foreclosures. That meant that banks had houses rather than cash and had little money to lend for new mortgages. With mortgages harder to get, people put off buying homes, or bought cheaper ones, so the overall market declined. Monroe County was not hit too hard because prices here had never inflated like they had in California, but it still had a negative impact on the income of real estate brokers. Also, in the summer of YR-2, the RCA plant closed down after being in Bayshore for thirty years. This was a major industry in Bayshore, employing about four hundred people. All were either put out of work or moved to other cities where RCA still had a plant. This caused an additional economic slump in the area and also caused many homes of RCA employees to flood the market, driving down prices. These two factors meant for most brokers that the second half of YR-2 and all of YR-1 were worse than previous years. In Susan's case, it is hard to say. She had a small business concentrating on the high-turnover university community, which was largely unaffected by the plant closing, so she would probably have fared better than most brokers. It is impossible to predict the income of any individual broker, however, because income can go up or down by as much as $50,000 a year based on the sale or non-sale of two expensive homes.

In general, there are two busy seasons in Bayshore: April through June, and late August through mid-October. The two periods are about equally busy for most brokers. It's hard for me to be more precise about Susan's business, because I do not handle much university housing. I concentrate on the new developments going up all over the outskirts of town.

Commissions in Bayshore generally run 7% of selling price, split equally between the selling agent and the listing agent. The expenses of running the business, including the enormous cost of maintaining your automobile, eat up approximately 50% of gross receipts, so a broker has to sell houses worth a total of approximately $500,000 to make $10,000 taxable income.

Under state law, only a real estate broker can list property and handle sales and closings. You have to have a broker's license, which requires that you pass a test about property law and financing and all the federal housing law and disclosure requirements. You have to take continuing education classes. Both Susan and I are brokers. There also are lots of real estate "agents" in town. Anyone can be an agent and sell real estate, but you have to work for a licensed broker.

If you need me to be a witness, I will be happy to testify. Susan is a good friend, and I know that she suffered financially by being unable to work for six months.

Shirley Master

UNIVERSITY OF COLUMBIA
SCHOOL OF BUSINESS
Wentworth Building
Bayshore, Columbia
811-855-8100

To: Defense Attorney	From: Prof. Sandra Hawkins SAH
Re: Kesler v. Macklin Furniture	Date: September 19, YR-1

In reference to the dispute concerning the value of lost business to Kesler Real Estate Agency, I have reviewed the file as you requested.

According to the file, Kesler ran a small real estate agency in Bayshore from March, YR-7, until August 14, YR-2. On that date, Kesler was in an automobile accident and was unable to work for six months. She returned to work on February 15, YR-1. She estimates that she lost $50,000 in income (I assume she means net taxable income) during this period.

In my opinion, Kesler's estimate of her lost revenue is far too optimistic. As you know from our telephone call, I am engaged in a long-term study of the Bayshore residential real estate market. Commercial real estate sales have not been included. I have been collecting data from a random sample of real estate brokers who concentrate on the sale of private residences since YR-8. Kesler is not one of the brokers in the study. The data show that YR-2 and YR-1 were bad years in the real estate market. Only 10% of brokers made more money than they had in YR-3. Of those whose incomes increased, the increases averaged only 13% (although one broker doubled his income); 33% made within 5% of the same amount they had made in YR-3; and 57% made over 5% less than they had the previous year. I attribute this to the fact that we were in a recession during those years triggered by the collapse of the financial industry. There was a further aggravating factor that there was a glut of houses on the Bayshore market. There were too many houses on the market at both the high and low ends simultaneously, which is unusual. There were expensive homes on the market due to mortgage foreclosures and the inability or unwillingness of buyers to spend top dollar. At the same time, there were too many low-end homes on the market because one of Bayshore's major blue-collar employers, RCA, closed its local plant. With fewer homes selling and prices going down, real estate agents' incomes went down.

I have reviewed the report by Ms. Shirley Master. She claims that relatively new brokers generally show steady increases in the first five or six years. That may be true in a boom market, but was not true in YR-2 and YR-1. While I had seen the young brokers in my sample increase their business by 20-25% a year for the first five years up until YR-2, the new agents were hardest hit by the recession. Of the nine brokers in my sample that had six or fewer years' experience in YR-2, one showed an increase in income (46%), two maintained a constant income, four experienced decreases averaging 25%, and two went out of business altogether.

From YR-5 to the present, brokers in their first five years have averaged $25,000 to $60,000 taxable income (after deducting office and automobile expenses); in their next five years, they average about $35,000 to $80,000 depending on all sorts of factors. Throughout Bayshore over the last five years, the busiest season for real estate sales is May and June; the slowest is December through February. The rest of the year is variable.

I am willing to testify as an expert if needed. My resume is attached. I am a tenured full professor of real estate in the University of Columbia School of Business. I have written three books and a dozen articles on the microeconomics of real estate marketing. I graduated from Harvard Business School in YR-12, and have been here at the University of Columbia for 11 years. For three of those years, I was the associate chairperson of the Real Estate Department in the Business School. My fee is $200 an hour against a guarantee of at least $2000.

I am attaching three charts derived from my ongoing study that may be useful.

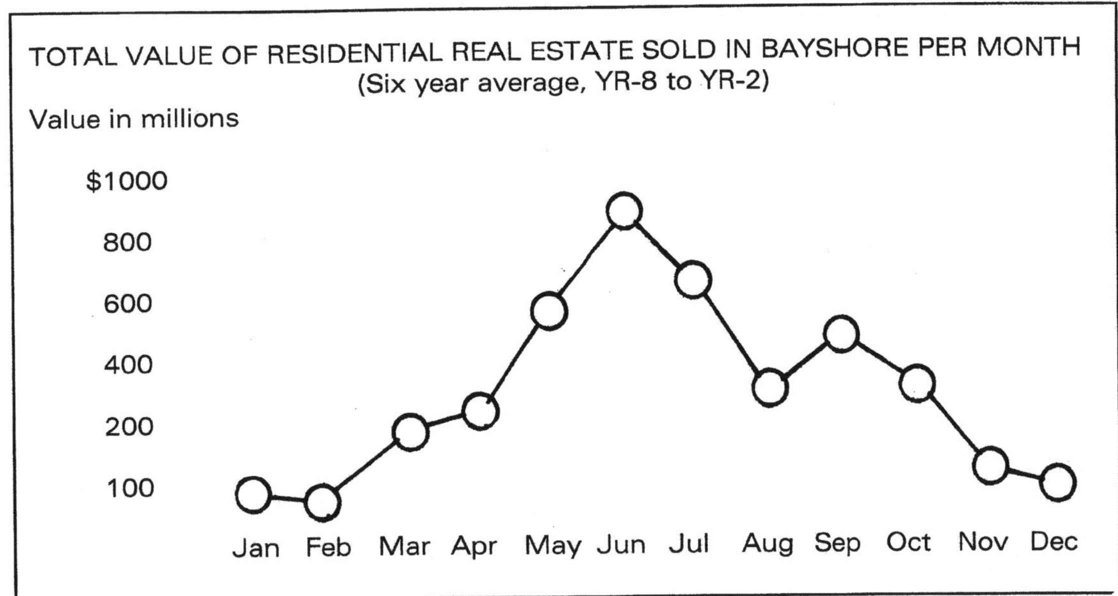
TOTAL VALUE OF RESIDENTIAL REAL ESTATE SOLD IN BAYSHORE PER MONTH
(Six year average, YR-8 to YR-2)
Value in millions
$1000
800
600
400
200
100
Jan
Feb
Mar
Apr
May
Jun
Jul
Aug
Sep
Oct
Nov
Dec

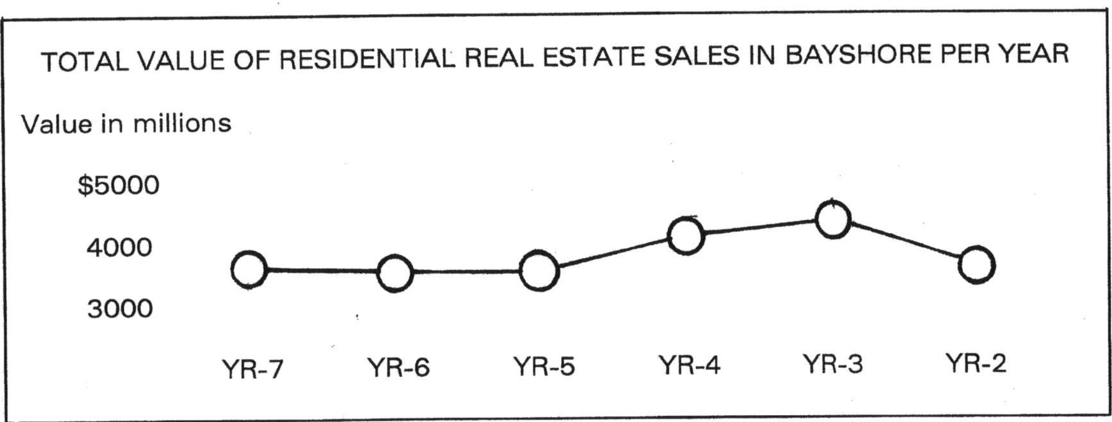
TOTAL VALUE OF RESIDENTIAL REAL ESTATE SALES IN BAYSHORE PER YEAR
Value in millions
$5000
4000
3000
YR-7
YR-6
YR-5
YR-4
YR-3
YR-2

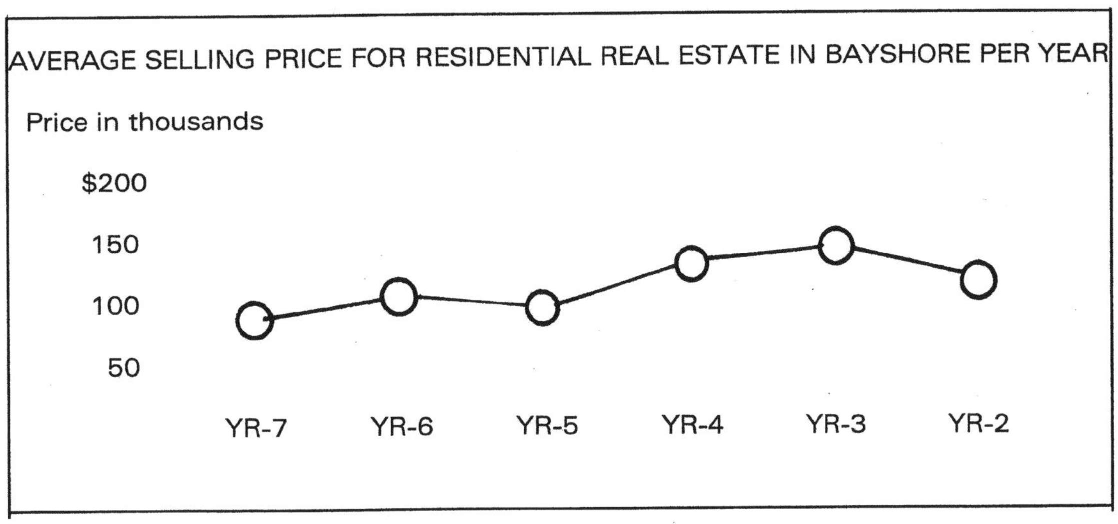
AVERAGE SELLING PRICE FOR RESIDENTIAL REAL ESTATE IN BAYSHORE PER YEAR
Price in thousands
$200
150
100
50
YR-7
YR-6
YR-5
YR-4
YR-3
YR-2

SANDRA A. HAWKINS

University of Columbia School of Business
Bayshore, Columbia
tel: (811) 555-4846
fax: (811) 555-0555
shawkins@ucolum.edu

CURRENT POSITION

Professor of Business, University of Columbia

TEACHING AREAS

Real Estate, Business Economics, Small Business (seminar)

ACADEMIC POSITIONS

University of Columbia, YR-11 to present
 Ira C. Zimmerman Research Award, YR-3
 Associate Chair, Real Estate Department, YR-4 to YR-1
University of Iowa College of Business
 Visiting Scholar, fall YR-4

BACKGROUND

MBA, YR-12. Harvard University
BA in Business (with High Honors), YR-14. Duke University Fuqua School.
Affiliations: AAUP, Business Law Society

HONORS AND DISTINCTIONS

Teaching Excellence Recognition Award, YR-2
Ira C. Zimmerman Research Award, YR-3
Appointed Senior Research Fellow, Private Enterprise Institute, YR-6
Business Student of the Year, YR-14

MAJOR PUBLICATIONS

BOOKS

The Real Estate Financing Process (YR-1)

The Economics of Gentrification (YR-4)

Changing Economics of Real Estate Markets in the Midwest (YR-8)

ARTICLES

The Enterprise Zone Controversy, **Northwestern Univ. Business Journal** 33:637 (YR-1).

Patterns of Real Estate Ownership in Transition Neighborhoods, **Journal of Urban Real Estate** 17:423 (YR-3).

Keeping Property Taxes Under Control in Small Markets, 18 **American Business Journal** 52: 245 (YR-4)

Century 21 Meets Joe's Real Estate: The Plight of the Small Broker, **Real Estate Review** 6:45 (YR-6)

SELECTED COLUMBIA PATTERN JURY INSTRUCTIONS

Preliminary Instructions:

This is a civil case concerning a traffic accident brought by Susan Kesler against Jeffrey Burnside and the Macklin Furniture Company.

You are the triers of fact. You are to decide, after considering all the evidence presented, what happened and what the facts are. You are to apply the facts as you determine them to be to the instructions of law I will give you at the end of the trial. You should use your common sense in considering the evidence, and you may draw reasonable inferences from the evidence.

To begin the case the lawyers may make opening statements. In these opening statements, the lawyers may tell you what they expect the evidence to be. This should help you to understand the evidence as it is presented through the witnesses later and make you aware of conflicts and differences that may arise in the testimony. What the lawyers say is not evidence; you must not consider it as evidence.

After opening statements, you will hear and see the evidence. The witnesses are first examined by the lawyer who calls them and may then be cross-examined by the lawyer for the other side. There may be objections, and you must not consider any evidence that is stricken or that you are told to disregard.

After all the evidence has been presented, the lawyers make their closing arguments. In their closing arguments the lawyers will refer to and summarize the testimony you have heard. Again, what they say is not evidence. Their statements are only their recollection of the testimony.

There will be occasional recesses during the trial. During these recesses you must not discuss the case with anyone, not even your friends. Nor may you look things up on the Internet. Please keep your cell phones turned off.

Please keep an open mind as the evidence is presented. Remember that your job is to reach your verdict only after you have heard and considered all the evidence, the instructions of law, and the final arguments of the lawyers.

All people in this trial are fictional, and the events take place in an imaginary city called Bayshore, in the state of Columbia.

Concluding Instructions

You have now heard the evidence and the arguments of counsel. It is my task to instruct you on the law, which you are obliged to follow.

You are the judges of the facts, the credibility of the witnesses, and the weight of the evidence. In deciding the credibility of witnesses, you may consider the appearance and manner of the witnesses on the stand, their intelligence, their opportunity for knowing the truth and for having observed the things about which they testified, their interest in the outcome of the case, their bias, and, if any have been shown, their prior inconsistent statements, or whether they have knowingly testified untruthfully as to any material fact in the case.

The only evidence you may consider is the evidence that was properly admitted at trial. You may not consider any matter that was rejected or stricken by the Court. You may not consider anything you read in the paper or hear from your friends about this case, nor may you do your own investigation or look anything up on the Internet.

The amount sued for is not evidence in this case; you should not consider it in arriving at the amount of your verdict, if any.

You must not base your verdict in any way upon sympathy, bias, guesswork or speculation. Your verdict must be based solely upon the evidence and instructions of the court.

There are six issues in this case. The plaintiff, Susan Kesler, has the burden of proof on three issues:

(1) Was the defendant Jeffrey Burnside negligent?

(2) Was his negligence a proximate cause of the accident?; and

(3) What is the amount of the damages suffered by the plaintiff, Susan Kesler, as a result of the accident?

The defendants, Jeffrey Burnside and Macklin Furniture Company, have the burden of proof on three issues:

(1) Was the plaintiff Susan Kesler also negligent?

(2) Was her negligence a proximate cause of the accident? and

(3) What portion of the damages suffered by the plaintiff are attributable to her own negligence?

When a party has the burden of proof on an issue, then he or she must prove that issue by the greater weight of all the evidence.

Negligence is the failure to use ordinary care. Ordinary care is the care a reasonable person would have used under the circumstances of this case.

The drivers of vehicles have a duty to use ordinary care:

(1) to keep a proper lookout;

(2) to keep their vehicles under proper control;

(3) to operate their vehicles at reasonable speeds under existing conditions.

(4) to give visible signals before turning or stopping; and

(5) to avoid obstructing a street or highway with their vehicles in ways that may be dangerous to others.

An unavoidable accident is one which ordinary care and diligence could not have prevented, or one which occurred in the absence of negligence by any party to this action.

A proximate cause of an accident, injury, or damage is a cause which in natural and continuous sequence produces the accident, injury, or damage. It is a cause without which the accident, injury, or damage would not have occurred. There may be only one proximate cause of an accident, or there may be more than one.

If you reach a verdict for the plaintiff, then you must determine damages. In determining the damages to which she is entitled, you may consider any of the following which you believe by the greater weight of the evidence resulted from the accident:

(1) any bodily injuries she sustained;

(2) any physical pain and mental anguish she suffered;

(3) any disfigurement or deformity and any associated humiliation or embarrassment;

(4) any medical expenses incurred;

(5) any earnings she lost because she was unable to work at her calling;

(6) any property damages she sustained.

It is now your time to retire and deliberate to a verdict. Upon retiring to the jury room you should select one of your members to act as Foreperson. The Foreperson will preside over your deliberations. Your verdict must be unanimous.

In the Monroe County Circuit Court
State of Columbia

Susan D. Kesler Plaintiff	)))	
v.	))	Civil No. 09 cv 1127
Jeffrey C. Burnside	))	**VERDICT**
and	))	
Macklin Furniture Co., Inc. Defendants	))	

We, the jurors of Monroe County in the above titled action, find:

(1) Was the defendants' negligence a proximate cause of the accident?

YES _______ NO ______

(2) What is the total amount of damages suffered by plaintiff as a result of the accident?

$ _________________

(3) Did the plaintiff's own negligence contribute to causing the accident?

YES ______ NO ______

(4) By what percentage should the damage award be reduced to reflect plaintiff's own fault? __________________%

(5) What is the actual damage award to be given by defendant to plaintiff?

$ _________________

Signed:_____________________________
Jury Foreperson

CASE FILE C:

STATE OF COLUMBIA

v.

WAYNE B. WALKER

ARMED ROBBERY
ATTEMPTED MURDER

STATE v. WALKER
CONTENTS OF FILE

GENERAL INSTRUCTIONS

This is a criminal case. The defendant is charged with armed robbery and attempted murder in connection with a hold-up at the Nite Owl Convenience Store. The defendant has pleaded not guilty and asserted an alibi defense. All events take place in August of last year in a fictional city called Bayshore, Columbia (population 150,000).

Potential Witnesses

Gerald Culler -- night manager, Nite Owl Convenience Store
Peter Scott -- detective, Bayshore Police Department
Wayne Walker -- defendant
Albert Moore -- alibi witness
Elizabeth Knoll -- Director of Medical Records, Monroe County Hospital

Instructions concerning exhibits

If either side wishes to use a gun or bandana as an exhibit, they may do so. No objections may be made on grounds that an exhibit does not precisely match its description in the file. For example, if a toy gun is used, no objections may be made that it is the wrong size, wrong manufacturer, wrong caliber, lacks the correct serial number, etc.

Instructions for use as a full trial

1. The state must call Gerald Culler and Peter Scott as witnesses in its case-in-chief, and may call other witnesses only with the approval of the court.

2. The defense must call Wayne Walker and Albert Moore as witnesses in its case-in-chief, and may call other witnesses only with the approval of the court.

3. The original attorneys have withdrawn from this case, citing conflicts of interest.

Stipulations

1. The fingerprints appearing on the fingerprint card (page C-21) are those of the defendant, Wayne Walker.

2. Detective Peter Scott is a qualified fingerprint expert.

3. Carl Dawson and Michael Kearny are unavailable because no one has been able to locate them. Michael Butler is unavailable because he is beyond the reach of process for the reasons described in his statement.

4. Wayne Walker has been out on bail since September 20, YR-1.

5. Any criminal offense listed as a misdemeanor is one for which the maximum statutory penalty is one year or less. Any offense listed as a felony is one for which the maximum penalty is more than one year.

Note on dates

The designation YR-0 means the present year, YR-1 (the year in which the events took place) is one year ago, YR-2 is two years ago, etc.

STATE OF COLUMBIA
County of Monroe

THE STATE OF COLUMBIA	)	Y 20476 CR
	)	
vs.	)	**INDICTMENT**
	)	
WAYNE WALKER	)	
Defendant	)	

THE GRAND JURORS FOR THE STATE UPON THEIR OATH PRESENT:

That on or about the 12th day of August, YR-1, at or about 11:00 p.m., in Monroe County, WAYNE WALKER unlawfully, willfully and feloniously:

COUNT I: Committed the crime of robbery, in that while armed with a gun, he took two hundred and sixty dollars belonging to the Nite Owl Convenience Store, 609 West First Street, Bayshore, Columbia, in the course of which he threatened to kill Gerald Culler and put Gerald Culler in fear of immediate serious bodily injury by firing a gun; in violation of section 222.1 of the Columbia Criminal Code.

COUNT II: Committed the crime of attempted murder of Gerald Culler by purposely and knowingly firing a gun at Gerald Culler with the intent to kill him; in violation of section 210.2 of the Columbia Criminal Code.

Marian Jacobi
Assistant District Attorney

WITNESSES:
Gerald Culler
✘ Det. Peter Scott, BPD

The witnesses marked with an X were sworn by the undersigned foreperson of the Grand Jury, and this bill was found to be _✘_ a True Bill/___ not a True Bill.

This the _16_ of _September_, YR-0 _Jon Bricker_
Grand Jury Foreperson

EXCERPTS FROM COLUMBIA CRIMINAL CODE

Section 222.1 -- Robbery. (a) A person is guilty of robbery if the actor unlawfully takes and carries away property of another with purpose to permanently deprive the owner thereof, in the course of which the actor:

(1) inflicts serious bodily injury upon another;

(2) threatens another with a deadly weapon; or

(3) purposely puts another in fear of immediate serious bodily injury.

(b) Robbery is a felony of the second degree, except that it is a felony of the first degree if in the course of committing the robbery, the actor is armed with a deadly weapon.

Section 210.2 -- Murder; attempted murder. (a) A person is guilty of murder if the actor purposely or knowingly causes the death of another human being. Murder is a felony of the first degree.

(b) A person is guilty of attempted murder if the actor purposely or knowingly does anything which constitutes a substantial step in a course of conduct planned to culminate in murder. Attempted murder is a felony of the second degree.

District Court of Monroe County
State of Columbia

State of Columbia	)	
	)	NO. Y20476CR
vs.	)	
	)	**NOTICE OF ALIBI**
Wayne Walker,	)	
Defendant	)	

Comes now the defendant, Wayne Walker, by counsel, and serves notice that he may raise the defense of alibi to the charges against him, by offering proof that he was at J.B. Smith's Mobil Station, 740 E. 17th St., Bayshore, or in Denny's Restaurant on N. Walnut St., Bayshore, at the time of the offense, and may call the following witness in support of that defense:

Albert E. Moore
808 Jackson Street
Apartment 3-B
Bayshore, Columbia

A copy of this notice has been sent this day to the office of the District Attorney for Monroe County.

Robert Hartwell
Robert Hartwell
Public Defender

September 30, YR-1

BAYSHORE POLICE DEPARTMENT ARREST REPORT

1 DATE OF REPORT: **8/17/YR-1**
2 TIME: **11:55 pm**
3 ARRESTING OFFICER'S NAME: **Peter Scott**
4 RANK: **Det**
5 BADGE: **77**

6 DEFENDANT NAME: **Wayne Brooks Walker**
7 ADDRESS: **214 Fairview, Bayshore**
8 CRIMES: **222.1 Robbery (armed); 210.2 Att. murder**

9 VICTIM NAME: **Gerald Culler**
10 SEX: **M**
11 AGE: **25**
12 ADDRESS: **415 W Hill, Bayshore**
13 CONTACT INFORMATION: **286-2112, gcull77@aol.com**
14 EMPLOYER: **Nite Owl Convenience Store, 609 W 1st St**

15 DATE OF CRIME: **8/12/YR-1**
16 TIME: **10:55 pm**
17 LOCATION: **609 W 1st St, Bayshore**
18 TYPE OF PREMISES: **Nite Owl Convenience Store**
19 WEATHER: **warm, dry**
20 HOW ATTACKED OR COMMITTED: **Suspect robbed store with gun, fired at victim, stole $260**
21 WEAPON/TOOLS: **.32 H & R Revolver #AP-45225**
22 PERSON REPORTING CRIME: **unknown**
23 ADDRESS:
24 CONTACT INFORMATION:
25 TIME/DATE OF REPORT: **11:01 pm 8/12/YR-1**
26 TOTAL VALUE STOLEN: **$260**
27 TOTAL VALUE RECOVERED: **$0**
28 CURRENCY: **$260**
29 JEWELRY:
30 AUTOS:
31 COMPUTERS/TV ETC:
32 FIREARMS:
33 OTHER:

34 TOTAL PERSONS INVOLVED: **1 (possible accomplice not verified)**
35 TOTAL ARRESTED: **1**
36 ADULTS ARRESTED: **1**
37 JUVENILES ARRESTED: **0**
38 TOTAL AT LARGE: **0**

39 OTHER BPD OFFICERS INVOLVED:

40 NARRATIVE: **On August 12, YR-1, I investigated the armed robbery of Nite Owl Convenience Store, 609 W. First St., Bayshore. I was notified by dispatcher at 11:01 p.m. that an armed robbery had just occurred at that address. I proceeded to the scene, arriving at 11:10 p.m. The night manager, Gerald Culler, informed me that two males had approached the store on foot, one entered wearing a red bandana, carrying a small black revolver believed to be a .32 in right hand. Suspect pointed gun at Culler and said, "Don't do nothing funny or you'll get hurt. Give me all the money in the register." Culler emptied both registers into brown lunch bag (no identifying marks), and gave it to the suspect. Estimated to be over $200. Suspect did not obtain money from safe in office. Culler reports that bandana slipped off suspect's face and he would be able to identify him again. Culler reported a college student was also present during robbery, last name believed to be Hall. Suspect forced Culler and Hall into back room office, threatened to kill them, then fired one shot and fled. No reported injuries. Bullet believed to have broken window in office. Culler appeared nervous throughout investigation. Culler described perpetrator as tall thin male, 18-25 years old, dark brown hair, white T-shirt. Customer described as young male, medium height, blond hair, 21, believed to be named Hall. Culler unable to describe accomplice who waited outside. I phoned in descriptions and called the University of Columbia police with same information. I dusted the doors (doors open outwards) for latent fingerprints, found eleven useable prints. Culler stated suspect touched nothing else. Departed crime scene 12:15 a.m.**

On August 13, YR-1, Culler came down to police station, looked through police photos of prior armed robbers, but unable to identify anyone. Culler reported that $260 had been stolen. I returned to Convenience Store to search parking lot area for bullet believed to have passed through office window, but found nothing. I contacted appropriate informants requesting info.

On August 15, I received information from confidential informant JS that the word on the street is that Wayne Walker robbed the store in question. JS had not seen Walker for a few days, did not know Walker's address, but reported that he frequented the Pit Stop Bar. Pulled Walker's arrest record. He has a prior assault and larceny, no current address. Found photograph in police files. I went to Pit Stop and asked around, but no one claimed to know Walker or recognize the photograph. I went by the Nite Owl about 7:30 p.m., showed Culler the photo of Walker along with four similar photos. Culler unable to identify anyone, asked if I had profile photos because he had only seen suspect's profile. Checked gun registration files and discovered that Walker owned a .32 caliber handgun.

(continued next page)

41 OFFICER'S SIGNATURE: *Peter Scott*

August 16: campus police reported they had checked with every male student named Hall, none matched description or admitted to being at convenience store. Compared Walker's fingerprint card to the ulnar loop type prints I had lifted from door. I found one of the eleven prints (from the outside of the door) matched Walker's right middle finger (I found 15 points of concordance). Phoned Culler and said we had a suspect. Staked out Pit Stop from 7:00 to 11:00 p.m. but Walker did not show up.

On August 17, I again staked out the Pit Stop. About 10:15 p.m., I received a radio call about a man with a concealed gun wearing a blue striped shirt at the Pit Stop Bar. I took call, entered bar, saw young man with blue striped shirt at end of bar. I approached, recognized suspect as Wayne Walker from photo. Placed him under arrest, patted him down, recovered .32 H & R revolver #AP-45225 from belt in front of pants. Informed him he was under arrest and read him his rights. Suspect did not request lawyer, made statement, "What are you hassling me for? This gun is registered." I drove to Nite Owl, Culler identified suspect as robber.

Suspect booked and gave address as 214 Fairview. I proceeded to house. A woman identified as Nancy Walker, mother of Wayne Walker, gave consent to search suspect's room. She stated Wayne was a good boy and wouldn't do something like this. She stated she had been visiting her sister out of town from August 10 to 14, but that Wayne was in town during that period. Search of suspect's room was negative for money, but turned up a red bandana. Returned to station, repeated warnings, took statement from suspect in which he denied involvement as expected. However, his nervousness suggested he was lying and trying to hide something.

Case cleared by the arrest of Walker on August 17.

BAYSHORE POLICE DEPARTMENT SUPPLEMENTAL REPORT

1 DATE OF REPORT: **8/20/YR-1**
2 OFFICER'S NAME: **Peter Scott**
3 DEFENDANT NAME: **Wayne Brooks Walker**

4 NARRATIVE: **On August 19, I received a telephone call from a person claiming to be the missing witness. The person said he had been in the convenience store on August 12 when it was robbed. The caller declined to give his real name, because he said he used a phony I.D. in the name of Steven Hall to buy beer and did not want to get into trouble. He said he had seen Walker's photograph in the paper, and that we had the wrong guy. He said the real robber was shorter and more stocky with very bushy eyebrows. I believed the call was probably from a friend of Walker's and that it warranted no further investigation. I asked the caller to come see me in person to give a statement but he refused.**

Also on August 19, I checked the distances from Walker home to convenience store. By odometer in patrol vehicle, it is 0.7 miles from 214 Fairview to Nite Owl. I am familiar with the area, and the Nite Owl is the closest convenience store to Walker's home, making it a logical target for Walker. The next closest store is a 7-11 at 1145 West 2nd Street, 1.0 miles from 214 Fairview. That convenience store also was recently robbed (June 22, YR-1) by a man in a red bandana, but witnesses unable to identify Walker in photo. This area is all within the city limits and subject to 30 mph speed limit.

5 OFFICER'S SIGNATURE *Peter Scott*

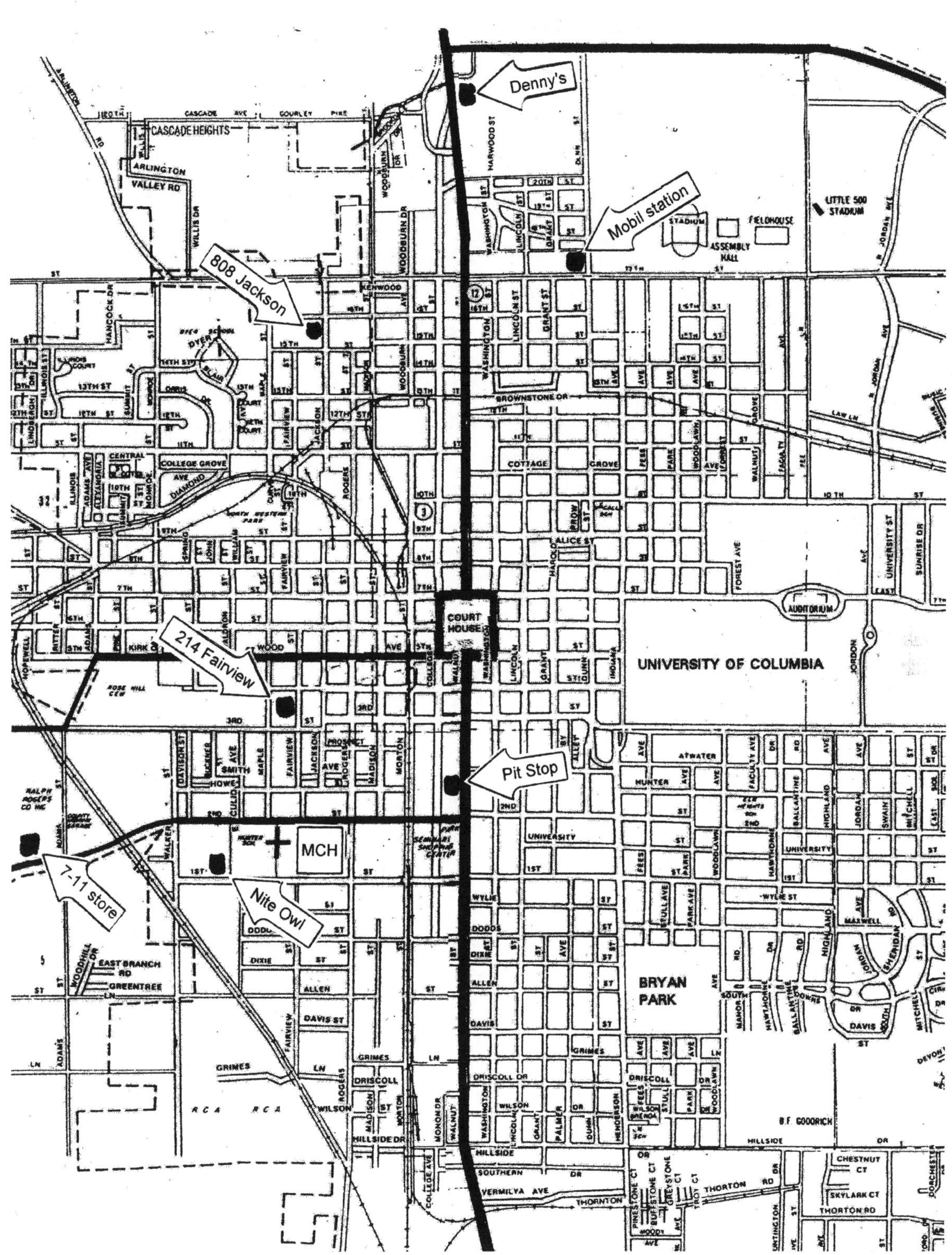

BAYSHORE

SCALE: 1" = 0.4 miles

LOCATION OF FINGERPRINTS
NITE OWL DOORS

Drawn by Det. Peter Scott

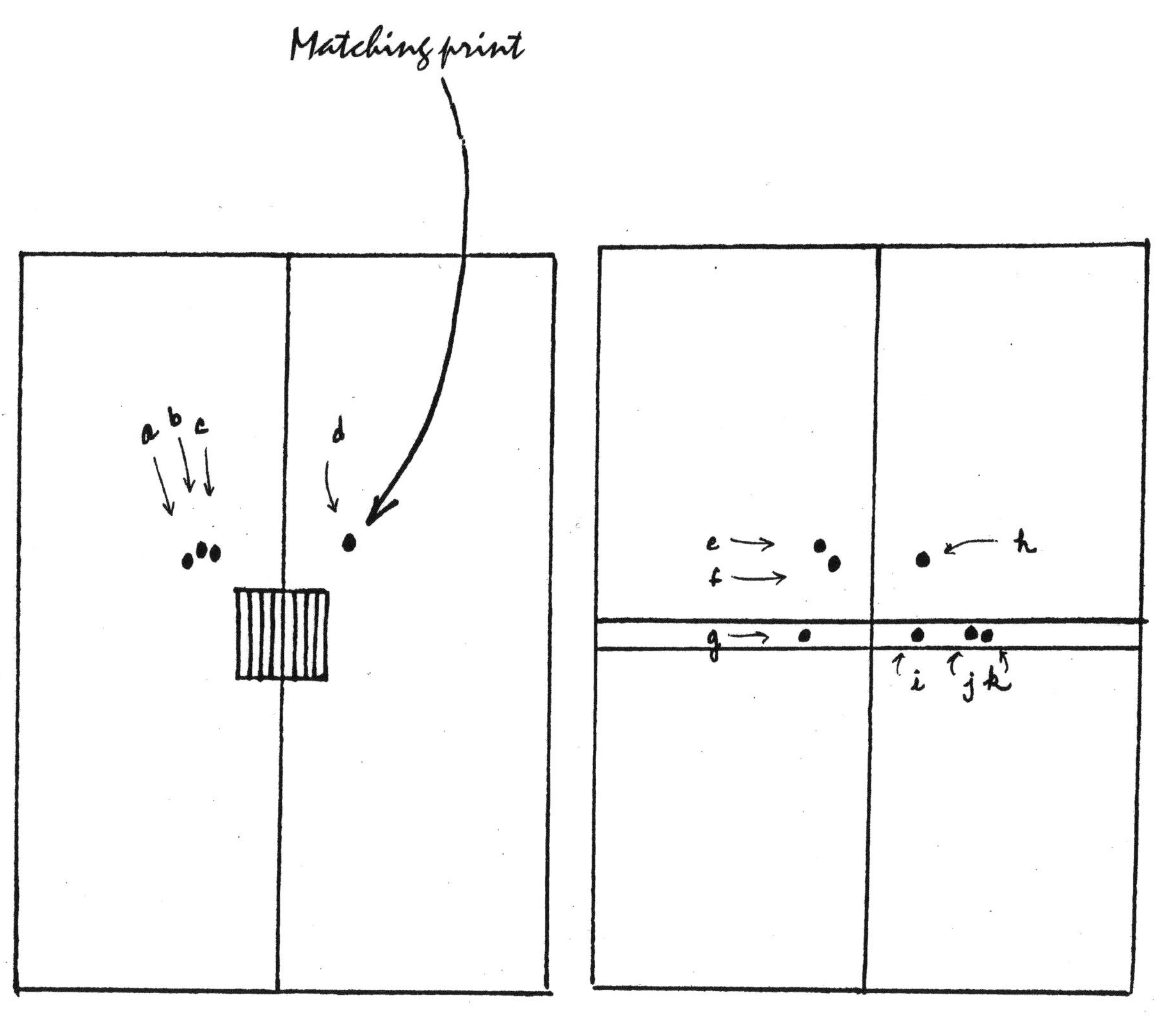

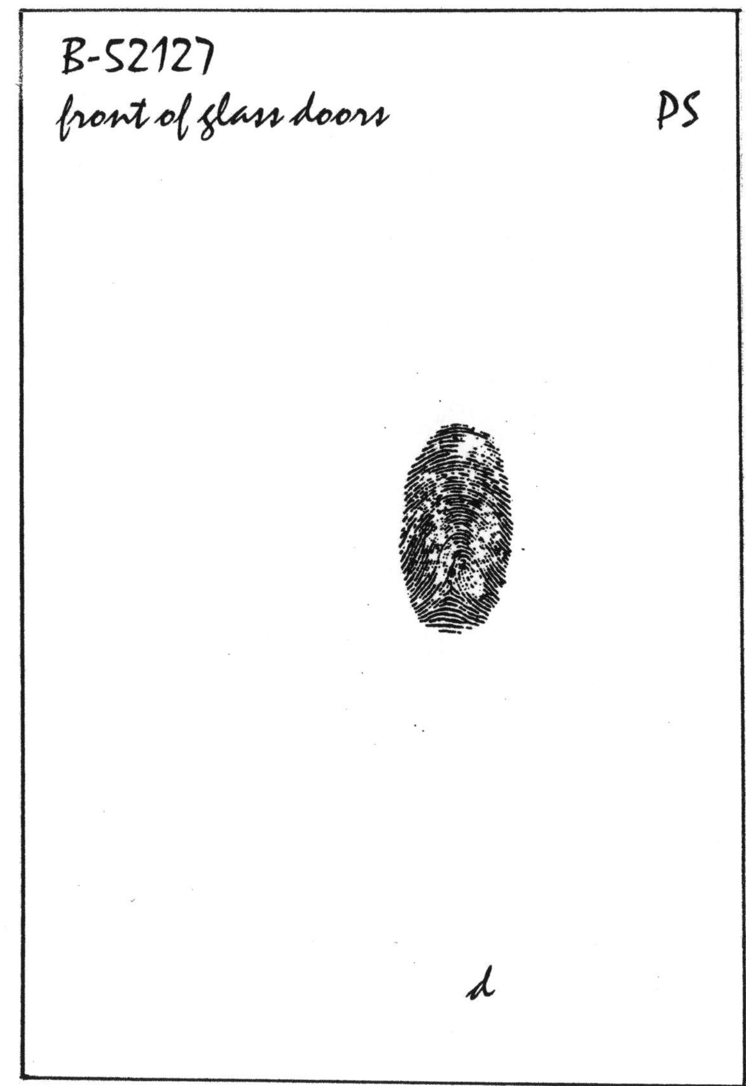
B-52127
front of glass doors
PS
d

NO.		LAST NAME	FIRST NAME	MIDDLE NAME	SEX	
056722F	LOCAL	Walker	Wayne	Brooks	M	
					HT. (Inches) 72	WT. 180
					HAIR BR	EYES BR

SIGNATURE OF PERSON FINGERPRINTED: Wayne B Walker

RESIDENCE OF PERSON FINGERPRINTED: 1032 Maxwell Lane, Bayshore

CITY OF BAYSHORE
POLICE DEPARTMENT
CRIME LABORATORY

DATE OF BIRTH: 6/21/YR-25

PLACE OF BIRTH: Raleigh, NC

SIGNATURE OF OFFICIAL TAKING FINGERPRINTS: Darla Brown

DATE: 11/4 YR-5

ALIASES: Slick

AMPUTATIONS: none

CITIZENSHIP: US

CLASS. ____________

REF. ____________

REASON FINGERPRINTED: Arrested for Assault

1. RIGHT THUMB	2. RIGHT INDEX	3. RIGHT MIDDLE	4. RIGHT RING	5. RIGHT LITTLE
6. LEFT THUMB	7. LEFT INDEX	8. LEFT MIDDLE	9. LEFT RING	10. LEFT LITTLE

LEFT FOUR FINGERS TAKEN SIMULTANEOUSLY	LEFT THUMB	RIGHT THUMB	RIGHT FOUR FINGERS TAKEN SIMULTANEOUSLY

STATE BUREAU OF INVESTIGATION
100 Capitol Street
Jefferson City, Columbia

FIREARM REGISTRATION

Name Wayne Walker | Date of Birth 6/21/YR-25

Address 214 S. Fairview St. | Telephone 286-3121

Bayshore, Col. | Occupation Construction

DESCRIPTION OF FIREARM

Make Harrington + Richardson | Caliber 32

Serial number AP 45225 | Color Black

Date of purchase 5/5/YR-4

Place of purchase Colonial Gun Shop, Hillsborough

I hereby swear that the foregoing information is true and accurate.

Date May 6, YR-4 Registrant Wayne B Walker

Sworn to before me, this the 6th day of May, Yr-4.

Linda Bridgewater-Foster
Clerk of the Circuit Court

LICENSE TO CARRY FIREARM

The person whose name appears on this registration form is hereby licensed by the State of Columbia to possess, transport and carry that firearm on his or her person or in a vehicle, as long as the firearm is in plain sight. This license does not permit the licensee to carry a concealed weapon or to carry this firearm on any public transportation.

Date: 5-11-Yr-4 Approved by: Chip Davis

KEEP THIS FORM WITH YOU AT ALL TIMES.
IT IS YOUR LICENSE TO CARRY A FIREARM

FLOOR PLAN, NITE OWL CONVENIENCE STORE

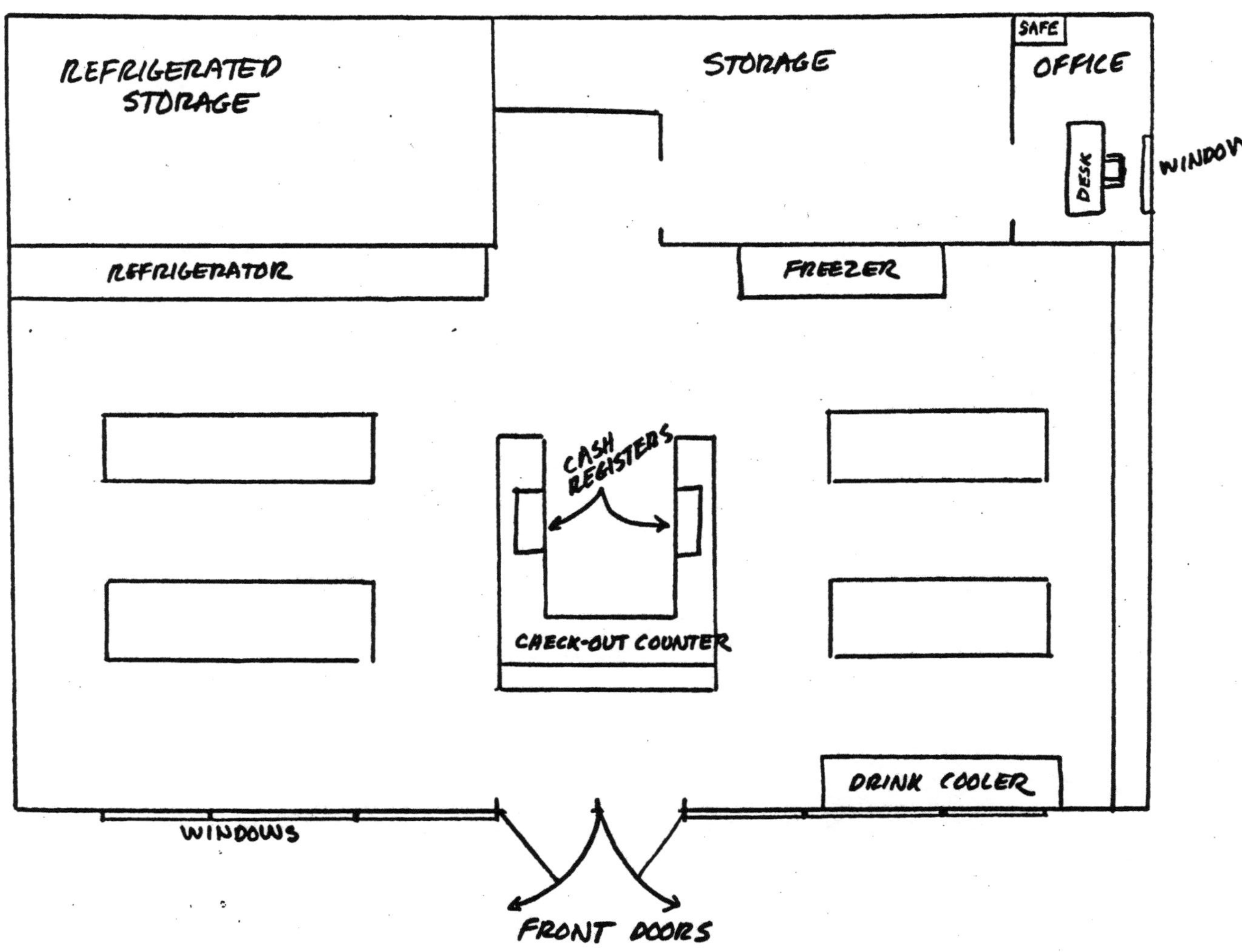

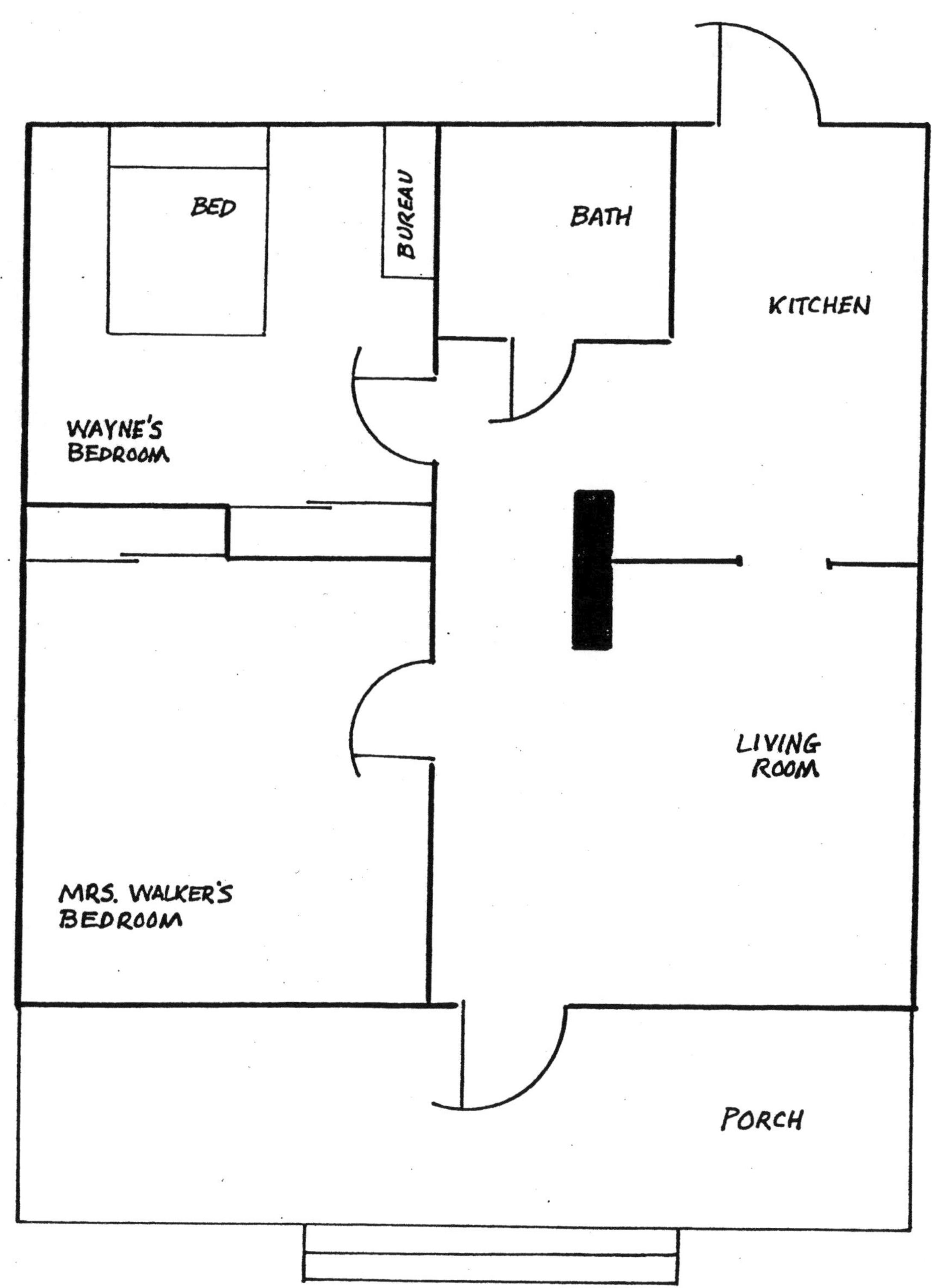

FLOOR PLAN, 214 FAIRVIEW

CITY OF BAYSHORE

✪ POLICE DEPARTMENT "TO SERVE AND PROTECT"

LEGAL RIGHTS ADVICE FORM

Before we ask you any questions, you must understand your rights.

1. You have the right to remain silent.
2. Anything you say can and will be used against you in court.
3. You have the right to consult with a lawyer before we ask you any questions, and to have the lawyer present with you during questioning.
4. If you cannot afford a lawyer, one will be appointed for you before any questioning if you wish.
5. If you decide to answer questions now without a lawyer present, you will still have the right to stop answering at any time.

WAIVER

I have read this statement of my rights and I understand what my rights are. I understand that I may ask for clarification and explanation of my rights if I do not understand them. I am willing to make a statement and answer questions. I do not want a lawyer at this time. I understand and know what I am doing. No promises or threats have been made to me, and no pressure or coercion of any kind has been used against me.

Date: Aug. 17, YR-1 Signature: Wayne B. Walker

Witness: Peter Scott Witness: ______________

Time: 10:30 Place: Bayshore PD Bldg

STATEMENT OF WAYNE B. WALKER
to Detective Peter Scott, B.P.D.
Transcribed from taped interrogation

My full name is Wayne Brooks Walker. I am 24 years old and live with my mother at 214 Fairview St. in Bayshore, Columbia. I was born in Raleigh, North Carolina, but have lived here in Bayshore since I was a year old. I lived at 1032 Maxwell Lane from YR-7 to YR-4, but moved back home when my father died, to take care of my mother. She was afraid to live alone. I purchased a .32 caliber handgun when I moved home because it made my mother feel more secure. I graduated from Bayshore High School in YR-7. I work sometimes for Poe Construction Company as a laborer when jobs are available. I earn $11.00 an hour when I work, and have made about $7000 so far this year. In July I fell playing basketball and injured my foot, and I have not been able to work since. I went to Monroe County Hospital to get it looked at. I was just able to walk without limping and was ready to go back to work the day I was arrested. I am right-handed.

I have a prior record. Six years ago or so I was arrested for a fight at the Pit Stop bar, but the other guy didn't show up to press charges, so the case was dropped. He started it anyway. Four years ago I pleaded guilty to assault. I had hit my girlfriend and knocked her down when I was drunk. Her name is Ellen Lewis. Just before Christmas that same year I was caught for shoplifting a bottle of perfume. I offered to pay for it when they caught me, but the store pressed charges. I pleaded guilty to cover for a friend of mine, Donnie Moore. He was on probation at the time. It was really Donnie who took the perfume, but they would have sent him back to jail for it, so I said I did it. Two years ago I was convicted of assault but the sentence was suspended. I was at a party and got into a fight with a woman who pulled a knife on me. She had me arrested but that charge was dropped. I have never been arrested for driving under the influence no matter what my record says.

On August 12, YR-1, I was at the Pit Stop Bar where I go often. About 10:00 p.m. I started out to Denny's Restaurant on North Walnut to get something to eat. My friend Albert Moore (Donnie's brother) was with me. We'd been shooting pool together. There are three pool tables in the back room at the Pit Stop. I know it was 10:00 because we were listening to a local talk show on the radio called the Jay Meisenhelder Hour where the announcer insults people and tells jokes. It comes on every Saturday night at 10:00 and I usually listen to it. The show had just started.

My car kept stalling. It's a 1972 Oldsmobile Cutlass that I'm restoring. We went to the Mobil Station where Albert works as a mechanic. It took him about an hour to find the trouble. He had to put a new part in the carburetor. So it must have been about 11:00 or so when I left. I don't know the exact time. It could have been a few minutes after 11:00. I didn't have any cash, so I charged the work to my credit card. I'd been out of work for a couple of weeks, so cash was pretty scarce. But I was not worried. My mom was out of town but would be back in a few days. Either she or Al Moore could have loaned me money if I needed it. I dropped Al off at home and then went on to Denny's. I ate a hamburger and then went home about midnight and went to bed.

I left early next morning to drive to Clinton to spend a few days with an old friend of mine from high school named Mike Butler. I was there for four days. We did some drinking and went fishing.

I came back on August 17. I went to the Pit Stop about 5:30 p.m. Some of the guys told me that the police were looking for me. They also said that Pat Riggins was looking to beat my ass because I had said his girlfriend was a whore. I went home and got my gun for protection and then went back to the Pit Stop. I had a chiliburger and a couple of beers. Then some guy came up to me and asked me if I was Wayne Walker. I said yes, and he put a gun to my back and said, "I'll blow you away if you move." He made me put my hands on my head, reached around and took my gun, threw me up against the wall. He handcuffed me and forced me out of the bar and into a black car. He put me in the back seat and drove away. That person was Detective Scott, although he never identified himself to me or read me my rights. I told him I had a permit for the gun, but he just laughed and said to sit tight. I asked what was going on. He said, "It's payback time."

We drove to the parking lot of the Nite Owl Convenience Store. The detective went inside, and came out a minute later with a clerk. I could tell because he was wearing one of those red striped jackets they always have on. The car window was rolled down. I saw the detective point to me and I heard him say, "That's the guy, isn't it?", and I saw the clerk nod his head yes. The detective then got in the car and took me downtown.

At the station, they read me my rights and Detective Scott told me I was being charged with robbing the Nite Owl. I had nothing to do with any robbery and I don't know anything about it. I agreed to give them a statement since I have nothing to hide. In fact, I know who really robbed the store. I heard some of the guys at the Pit Stop talking about it, and they said that Mike Kearny was the one who did it. Mike's a biker who has done this kind of thing before. He's a big, stocky guy with bushy hair and a moustache.

I am familiar with the Nite Owl Convenience Store. It's only a few blocks from where I live. I go there sometimes to buy cigarettes and beer. I don't remember whether I went there August 12 or not, but I stop by once a week or so.

I have read the foregoing and it is complete, true and accurate.

Wayne B. Walker

Wayne Brooks Walker

BAYSHORE POLICE DEPARTMENT
ARREST HISTORY

LAST NAME: **WALKER**
FIRST NAME: **WAYNE** MIDDLE NAME: **BROOKS**
ALIAS: **SLICK**
DATE OF BIRTH: **6/21/YR-25** PLACE OF BIRTH: **RALEIGH NC**
ADDRESS: **1032 MAXWELL LN, BAYSHORE, COL**

HAIR: **BRN** EYES: **BRN** SEX: **M** MARKS/SCARS:
HT: **6'1"** WT: **180**
OCCUPATION: **CONSTRUCTION**

DATE	OFFICER	CIT NO.	CHARGE	DISPOSITION
7/19/-7	LANG	C19008	ASSAULT (MISD)	DISMISSED
11/4/-5	PIATT	W25557	ASSLT ON FEMALE (FEL)	CONVICTED FEL ASSLT 2 YRS, SUSPENDED
12/8/-5	DAVIS	D30122	LARCENY (MISD) FORGERY (MISD)	CONVICTED $250 FINE
4/27/-4	FRICK	L10739	DUI	CONVICTED $600 FINE
6/3/-3	LEE	Y00934	ASSAULT (FEL)	PLED GUILTY MISD ASSAULT 30 DAYS, SUSPENDED
8/17/-1	SCOTT	Y20476	ARMED ROBBERY (FEL) ATT MURDER (FEL)	

DATE PRINTED: 8/19/YR-1

CERTIFIED TRUE AND ACCURATE COPY OF A RECORD
OF THE BAYSHORE POLICE DEPARTMENT
By: Leslie Morse
DESK SERGEANT

DISTRICT ATTORNEY
OF MONROE COUNTY
155 WEST 6TH STREET
BAYSHORE, COLUMBIA

FELONY DIVISION (811) 332-7305

MEMO TO: Robert Hartwell
Public Defender's Office

FROM: Marian Jacobi
District Attorney's Office

RE: Detective Peter Scott

In response to your request to interview Detective Peter Scott, he is involved in an undercover operation at the moment and cannot be contacted directly. We will, of course, make him available before trial if you would like to interview him. In the meantime, I can supply the following additional information about him.

He is 28 years old, graduated from Bayshore High School, and has two years of college in police science. He is married with two children. He has been on the Bayshore Police Department for eight years: five as a public safety officer and three as a detective. He spent six weeks at the state police academy and has attended week-long seminars at both the SBI and FBI schools on investigation techniques including ballistics and fingerprint identification. He has investigated approximately 300 cases as a detective, of which probably 100 were cleared by arrest. Fingerprint identification has played a role in approximately 20 of those cases, and Detective Scott has testified as a fingerprint expert in five previous trials.

Scott also informs me that he has had prior contact with the Walker family. As I am sure you know, Walker's father (James Walker) is currently serving a twenty-year sentence for drug trafficking. Walker was arrested after a six-month investigation by Scott into drugs in the local high schools. I am sure by now you have seen the newspaper article from April 18, YR-4, quoting Scott as saying one day he would get the son, too. Scott informs me that the quotation was taken out of context by a reporter who interviewed him when he was tired, and that it does not mean that he has any grudge against Wayne Walker.

MEMORANDUM

TO: FILE

FROM: ED MOOR, PARALEGAL

RE: STATE V. WALKER

(1) A check of court records indicates that James Walker, the father of Wayne Walker, is currently serving a 20-year sentence for drug trafficking. James was convicted on July 2, YR-4. Mrs. Nancy Walker states that Wayne always tells people his father is dead because he is too embarrassed to admit he is in prison. The record is attached.

(2) A copy of a newspaper story about James Walker's drug charges has been found. It is attached.

(3) Michael Kearny has a prior record for armed robbery, convicted March 18, YR-11, and served seven years. His current whereabouts are unknown. His arrest record is attached.

(4) Detective Scott has a prior administrative action noted in his record. He was accused of lying to a grand jury during an investigation into a police shooting. He was one of several police officers who claimed that a fellow officer fired his weapon in self-defense when that officer killed an unarmed African-American male. Scott was reprimanded and returned to duty after a review board determined that Scott "exercised bad judgment."

Monroe County Circuit Court
Criminal Division
State of Columbia

CERTIFICATE OF DISPOSITION

Court Number: 90327 CR 4

Judge: Guthrie

Case: State v. James Elwood Walker

Original Offense(s): 260.2 Felony Drug Trafficking

Disposition: 260.2 Felony Drug Trafficking

Guilty Plea:

Trial: Convicted 07/02/YR-4

Appeal: Affirmed 05/11/YR-3

Final Judgment Entered: DOC 20 years

Date: 08/23/YR-4

I hereby certify that this is a true excerpt from the records of the Monroe County Circuit Court, Criminal Division, State of Columbia.

Camille Johnson, Clerk of the Circuit Court

By: *Robert Hamilton*, Deputy Clerk

Date: *October 14, Yr-1*

Excerpt from the BAYSHORE HERALD, April 18, YR-4, page 1.

High school drug ring cracked

By Tamara Rossman
Bayshore Herald

BAYSHORE -- The Bayshore Police Depart-ment yesterday announced the arrest of a prime suspect in a six-month investigation into allega-tions of drug trafficking at Bayshore High School. The arrest of James E. Walker, age 48, of 214 South Fairview, Bayshore, culminated a lengthy undercover operation designed to stem the flow of illicit drugs into Bayshore High School. Officers from the Bayshore Police Department, assisted by federal agents from the Drug Enforcement Agency, had been responding to growing concerns by parents' groups about drug abuse in the schools.

David Ewing, deputy administrator of the Monroe County Schools Corporation, said, "What good is a lot of advertising urging students to say 'No' to drugs if we sit back and close a blind eye to the problems of drugs in our schools? It was time we took decisive action."

The suspect, James Walker, was arrested by Detective Peter Scott at a small cabin near Lazy Lake in northeastern Monroe County. Police also seized approximately twenty pounds of marijuana, several ounces of cocaine, and a wide variety of pills which were found on the premises.

At a press conference following the arrest, Det. Scott said, "Walker is the leader of a drug distribution ring that has targeted our high schools. This investigation was personal for me. I think anyone who sells drugs to school children should be hunted down and shot. We've been after this scum for a long time."

Scott said that the investigation would continue. "We've got the head of the snake, but we're still going after the other people in his drug distribution network. We suspect that his son, Wayne Walker, was the main salesman who actually peddled the junk to children in the schools, but we haven't been able to prove it yet. I promise you that I will see him behind bars soon." Wayne Walker's whereabouts are currently unknown.

UNITED STATES DEPARTMENT OF JUSTICE

FEDERAL BUREAU OF INVESTIGATION
IDENTIFICATION DIVISION
WASHINGTON, D.C. 20537

The following FBI record, NUMBER 27 049 522 T32 , is furnished for OFFICIAL USE ONLY. Information shown on this Identification Record represents data furnished FBI by fingerprint contributors. WHERE DISPOSITION DATA IS NOT SHOWN OR FURTHER EXPLANATION OF CHARGE OR DISPOSITION IS DESIRED, COMMUNICATE WITH AGENCY CONTRIBUTING THOSE FINGERPRINTS.

CONTRIBUTOR: IDENTIFIER (ORI) NAME CASE NUMBER (OCA)	SUBJECT: NAME STATE NUMBER	ARRESTED OR RECEIVED	C - CHARGE D - DISPOSITION
CO203010 PD BAYSHORE COL 32115	KEARNY, MICHAEL JOHN CO1630202N	06/17/-14	C - CCC 222.1 ARMED ROBBERY CCC 213.1 RAPE D - 07/12/-14 DISMISSED
CO203010 PD BAYSHORE COL 49772	KEARNY, MICHAEL JOHN CO1630202N	12/21/-12	C - CCC 222.1 ARMED ROBBERY D - 03/18/-11 GUILTY 10 YRS
CO2148 DEPT CORRECTIONS JEFF CITY COL	KEARNY, MICHAEL JOHN CO1630202N	09/02/-4	D - RELEASED SENTENCE SERVED

State of Columbia)
)
vs.)
)
Wayne Walker)

Y20476CR

District Court
Monroe County

PROBABLE CAUSE HEARING

September 14, YR-1

Before Judge Mary Kay Wallace

Court Reporter: Dodie Bowman

Appearances: For the State: Marian Jacobi
For the Defense: Robert Hartwell

Court was convened at 10:35 a.m., whereupon the following proceedings were had:

COURT: Case number Y20476, State versus Walker, on for a probable cause hearing pursuant to Rule 5.2 of the criminal procedure code. The defendant is charged with armed robbery in violation of section 222.1 of the Criminal code and with attempted murder in violation of section 210.2 of the Criminal code. Defendant pleads not guilty. Will counsel approach the bench, please?
Is there any possibility of a plea? We're really backlogged.
MS. JACOBI: We tried, your honor. We offered unarmed robbery and five years.
MR. HARTWELL: The defendant says he didn't do it, your honor. I can't take a plea.
COURT: All right. Step back. The state may call its first witness.
MS. JACOBI: We have only one witness, your honor, Gerald Culler.
BAILIFF: Do you swear or affirm the testimony you are about to give will be the truth, the whole truth, and nothing but the truth?
MR. CULLER: I do.

Q: State your name, address, and occupation.
A: Gerald Culler, 415 West Hill Street, Bayshore. I'm the night manager of the Nite Owl Convenience Store, 609 West First Street, here in the city.
Q: Are you married?
A: Yes. We have no children.
Q: How old are you?
A: 25 years old.
Q: Any prior criminal record?
A: No.
Q: Were you working at the Nite Owl on August twelfth of last year?
A: Yes. I came on at 6:00 and was still working when we were robbed around 11:00 p.m.
Q: Was anyone else there?
A: At the time of the robbery?
Q: At any time.
A: Another clerk, Carol Crow, worked until 10:00. I let her go home then because it was a slow night.
Q: What happened about five minutes before eleven?
A: That man sitting over there, came in with a gun and robbed the place. He got away with $260.00.
Q: You mean the defendant, Wayne Walker?
A: Yes.
Q: Was anyone else in the store at the time?
A: Yes, a customer. I think he was a college student. He had come in and bought a six-pack of beer.
Q: A six-pack of beer?
A: Yeah.
Q: What happened next?
A: Well, I was talking to the customer, just to be pleasant, you know, when the defendant came through the door with a red and white bandana around his face and holding a gun in his hand, like some outlaw holding up a train.
Q: Which way do the doors open?
A: Outwards.
Q: How much of the defendant could you see?
A: I could tell he was a young man, tall, thin, and with brown hair. I could

see his eyes, eyebrows and forehead. Oh yes, and his ears.
Q: Did he have gun?
A: Yes, he was waving around a small black revolver, probably a .32. I'm not sure which hand.
Q: How was he dressed?
A: White T-shirt with a pocket, jeans, black shoes, Addidas I think.
Q: Tell us in your own words what happened.
A: The man pointed his gun at me and told me to stand still or he'd shoot. He told the customer to stand over by the counter so he could watch both of us. He raised the gun up to chest level, pointed it at me, and said, "Give me all the money in the register or I'll splatter your brains from here to White Plains." I opened one register and took out the bills, and put them in a small brown paper sack, like a lunch bag. He then pointed at the other cash register, and I opened it and gave him the money. I mean, I put the money in the bag and handed the bag to him. The robber looked in the bag, and said he wanted the money from the safe.
Q: Would you recognize the voice again if you heard it?
A: Probably not. The guy was trying to disguise his voice by talking in a fake southern accent.
Q: Did you open the safe?
A: No. There is a safe back in the office in the storeroom that had the day's receipts in it, well over a thousand dollars. I told him there wasn't any safe, that all the money was in the register. I decided to bluff him, and I said he was free to look around the store for a safe if he wanted. He sort of glanced around. He was starting to get nervous, I could tell. As he turned his head to the side, his bandana slipped down and I could see the side of his face. He froze for a moment or two, with his face in profile, then turned his back and pulled the mask back up.
Q: What happened next?
A: Now I got scared. I was afraid he would kill me because I had seen his face. I've seen that sort of thing on those true cop stories on television. He ordered us into the storeroom. He followed. When we got there, he told me to turn around. He said, "I ought to kill you right now." He was holding the gun down at his side at about waist level. He fired it, and I fell backwards over the desk.
Q: Did he intentionally shoot the gun at you?

A: Yes, I'd say so.

Q: What happened next?

A: To tell the truth, the gunshot startled me. I would have expected him to bring the gun up before shooting at me, or make some movement. When the gun fired, I was startled, jumped back, and fell over the desk. When I hit the floor, I lay there motionless, figuring he'd think I was dead. A few minutes later I got up. The defendant was gone and so was the customer. I called the cops from the office. I noticed that the window behind the desk was broken, presumably from the gunshot. It definitely had not been broke before.

Q: Did the defendant have an accomplice with him?

A: It looked like he approached the store with another guy who acted as the lookout, but the other guy never got close enough to the store for me to get a good look at him.

Q: What happened next?

A: A few minutes later, Detective Scott arrived from the police station. I told him what happened and gave him a description of the robber.

Q: What about the customer?

A: I told the officer I thought his name was Hall, a college student. Blond hair, medium height. I'd seen his name on a driver's license he used to prove his age when he bought the beer.

Q: What else happened?

A: Well, I told Detective Scott I thought about $200 had been taken, but that I would have to check the receipts to be sure. Scott dusted the doors for fingerprints because that's the only thing I remembered the defendant touching. Scott left about 12:30, and asked me to come to the police station to look through mug shots the next day. I checked the cash register tapes, determined that $261 had been taken, telephoned the manager, and then went home.

Q: Did you look at police photos?

A: Yes, twice. Next day, August 13, I went to the police station and looked through some books of photographs but I didn't recognize anyone. I also told Detective Scott that exactly $261 had been taken. A few days later, I believe on the 16th, Scott came by the store and showed me six photos. I couldn't recognize anyone. I figured he must have had a suspect, because he seemed disappointed when I couldn't pick the guy out.

I reminded him that I'd seen a profile and all the photos were of the full face. I was pretty sure I could recognize him if I saw him again, and I told this to Scott.

Q: Did you see the defendant again?

A: Yes, on August 17. Scott came by the store about 9:30 pm, bringing the suspect he'd picked up. I saw him in the back seat of the patrol car with his profile toward me. I recognized him at once as the defendant. Scott looked pleased and said he'd be in touch.

Q: Did anything else happen?

A: Yes. Over the next week, I received a number of anonymous telephone calls at work from a man who told me to drop the charges or I'd get into big trouble.

MS. JACOBI: That's all. Your witness.

MR. HARTWELL: Mr. Culler, how did you know the man in the police car was a suspect?

A: On the 17th?

Q: Yes.

A: Detective Scott had told me over the phone earlier in the day that he had a suspect in custody who had been identified by police informants as a probable suspect.

Q: On the night of the twelfth, did the robber have a limp?

A: Not that I recall.

Q: But you did see him walk from the front door to the check-out counter, didn't you?

A: Yes.

Q: Did you see him limp?

A: No. But I was looking at the gun.

Q: Isn't it possible you remember the face of my client, Wayne Walker, because he's a frequent customer?

A: I don't remember everyone who comes into the store, but I don't think I'd ever seen him before. If he had been a real frequent customer, I would know.

Q: Which door did the robber enter?

A: I don't recall.

Q: How often are the doors cleaned?

A: They're supposed to be washed every day, during the day shift.

Q: Are they in fact washed every day?
A: No. But they never go more than two or three days.
Q: How do you know this, if you work the night shift?
A: I used to work days as a day clerk before I got promoted to night manager. I also fill in sometimes if the day manager is out of town.
Q: How long have you been the night manager?
A: One year. I worked there three years as a clerk before that.
Q: Has the store ever been robbed before?
A: Yes, but not while I was on duty.
Q: Where did you work before that?
A: Monroe County Hospital in the pharmacy.
Q: Why did you leave that job?
A: I was fired.
Q: You were fired for theft of hospital property, correct?
A: I borrowed a box of adhesive tape for my softball team, to wrap bat handles and stuff.
Q: Borrowed?
A: Well, I took it. They found out and fired me. It was no big deal. I never denied it. People took stuff all the time, so I figured no one would care.
Q: Now, you said the robber's gun was a .32 caliber?
A: Yes.
Q: How could you tell?
A: I've seen a lot of guns on television. I watch all the true police stories, and they often show different types of guns. This one was too small to be a .38, but too big to be a .22.
Q: When the robber's mask slipped off, how long was it off?
A: A second or two.
Q: Where was the gun at this time?
A: Still pointed at me.
Q: How can you be sure?
A: Look, when a guy holds a gun on you, you pay attention. I was thinking of jumping him if he put the gun down.
Q: How could you look at his face and the gun at the same time?
A: I sort of looked from one to the other.
Q: Exactly what description did you give to Detective Scott?
A: Tall young man, dark brown hair and eyes, white T-shirt, jeans,

no facial hair.
Q: Did you tell the Detective whether he was black or white?
A: No, I don't think so. I don't think I said anything about his race. I don't think he asked.
Q: Will you describe in more detail the incident on August 17th, when Detective Scott brought a suspect for you to identify?
A: Sure. About 9:30, Detective Scott came into the store and asked me to step outside for a minute. I turned the cash register over to another clerk and went out in the parking lot with Scott. He pointed to what looked like an unmarked police car, parked at an angle about fifteen feet away.
Q: How could you tell it was a police car?
A: You know, it sat low to the ground, had no markings on it, big tires, and lots of antennas.
Q: Go on.
A: Scott asked me to look at a man in the back seat by the window. I figured he had brought the suspect. I took a few steps toward the car. The interior light was on and I could see clearly into the back seat. As I approached, the defendant turned his head in my direction. When I saw his face, I could tell it was the robber. I told Scott, "that's the guy."
Q: Did you see his profile?
A: Yes.
MR. HARTWELL: Nothing further.
MS JACOBI: One further question. Did anything Detective Scott say or do anything that influenced you in any way in identifying the defendant?
A: No. If he hadn't been the robber, I wouldn't have said he was.
MS. JACOBI: That's all. We move that the defendant be bound over for trial on the charges of armed robbery and attempted murder.
MR. HARTWELL: Oppose the motion.
COURT: The court determines that probable cause has been established. The defendant is remanded to custody and bail is continued in the amount of $20,000.
MR. HARTWELL: If your honor permits and the state will waive the filing of a brief, we would move at this time to suppress all identification procedures because the process used was impermissibly suggestive and therefore violates due process.

MS. JACOBI: We have no objection to arguing that motion at this time. The witness testified he saw the robber's face and was not influenced by what the Detective did. The identification should not be suppressed.

COURT: I'm going to deny the suppression motion at this time.

Certified as a true and accurate transcription of the record of proceedings.

Dodie Bowman

Dodie Bowman, Court Reporter

OFFICE OF THE PUBLIC DEFENDER

309 West Washington Street, Suite 1200
Bayshore, Columbia Phone 232-2475

STATEMENT OF ALBERT MOORE

Made to: Robert Hartwell
Place: Public Defender's Office
Date: Sept. 19, YR-1

My name is Albert Ephraim Moore. I am 23 years old. I graduated from Bayshore High School's vocational program. I then entered the Air Force for three years. I went to auto mechanic school and worked at the Edwards Air Force Base motor pool. Then I returned to Bayshore and got a job at R.B. Smith's Mobil Station as a mechanic. I am single and I live in my own apartment, 808 Jackson Avenue, number 3-B. My family also lives here in town. I have one brother, Donnie. He's just turned 18 and he lives at home. Donnie has been on juvenile court probation for a burglary for the last four years. When he was 13, he and some other kids broke into a house near my parents' home and kind of vandalized it. Donnie was the youngest, and I'm sure he just went along because the older kids were going.

I work for R.B. Smith at his Mobil Station, at the intersection of Dunn and 17th Streets. I am acquainted with Wayne Walker. I have done some work on his car, and have run into him at the Pit Stop. We are friends, and have a fairly good relationship. On weekend evenings, R.B. lets me use the lift and garage at the station to work on my own car, a red '55 Chevy Bel Air Bubbletop into which I have dropped a 427 Chevy "Rat" engine out of a wrecked Corvette. I guess you could say I'm a car nut. I have run my car at some of the local racetracks, modified class. The engine has a high rise Offenhouser intake manifold, a 3/4 race Erikson camshaft, Thrush headers and exhaust, and a four-barrel 980 cubic-foot-per-minute double pump Holley carburetor, all of which I put in myself. The gas mileage is terrible.

On August 12, YR-1, I went to the Pit Stop at 8:00 p.m. when I got off work. I met Wayne there. It was not prearranged; that's where we both go most nights. We shot pool for about two hours, mostly nine-ball. Wayne shoots pool right-handed, so I assume he is right-handed. Wayne was still limping pretty badly on the twelfth. He'd been limping for a couple of weeks after some accident on the job. He works construction but he'd been out of work because of his foot injury.

About 10:00, Wayne asked me if I wanted to go get something to eat at Denny's. I said yes, and we left in his car. I remember looking at a clock on the wall of the pool hall. Wayne drives a 1972 Olds Cutlass with the 350 Rocket engine with a 2-barrel carburetor. One of the reasons we're good friends is that we both love old muscle cars. The Cutlass kept stalling out, and Wayne asked me if I would take a look at it. We pulled into the gas station where I work. When the car idled it ran fine, but when the gas was applied, it coughed and stalled. I checked the spark plugs and wires, which all seemed to be all right. I decided that the problem had to be in the fuel system. I took out the fuel filter, which was not clogged. I then disconnected the various fuel lines, but could not find any blockage. In old cars, the fuel lines get clogged with rust pretty easily. I finally put the compressed air hose on the main fuel line and blew it out and reconnected everything. The car seemed to run okay, so I told Wayne to drive it around the block and see if it was working. He did so and returned in a few minutes, saying the problem was still there. He could have been gone as long as five minutes, but I think it was only a minute or two. I looked at the carburetor, and found that the butterfly valve was stuck. That's the part that regulates how much air gets into the carburetor. The 2-barrel carb used on the 350 was a standard in GM cars in the 70s and 80s.

Since we regularly work on old cars at the station, we had a carburetor rebuilding kit in stock for that engine. I put in a new valve-spring assembly and Wayne charged the kit on his credit card because he said he didn't have any money. There will not be a record of the charge in the computer. It was after hours, so the computers were turned off and I don't know how to turn them on, so we used the old manual credit card machine that slides back and forth over the card. We keep it so we can charge stuff if the power goes out or the computer crashes. We keep copies of every charge slip that is not in the computer, and I can get a copy of it if you want.

The car then ran pretty well, and we left about 11:00 or a little before. I'm pretty sure it was close to eleven, although it could have been 10:45 or as late as 11:15. There are clocks at the station, but I do not wear a watch when working on cars. I did not charge him for labor, but the kit came out of stock. I told him he owed me a couple of beers next time I saw him. He dropped me off back at the Pit Stop and drove off south on Walnut Street. I was tired, so we did not go out to eat. I got my car and drove straight home. The speed limit is 30, but I often go a little faster. It takes me about 5 minutes to get home from the Pit Stop. I got home about 11:10. I am reasonably certain of the time because I switched the television on when I got in after I made a sandwich. I wanted to watch the sports news. I switched over to channel 9, the station I always watch. They were just starting to give the weather report, which they always do about eight to ten minutes into the news.

I know Wayne quite well and I go over to his house quite often. We've sometimes gone fishing together, and we hang out together. I like him and I don't want him to get into trouble. He would never do something like rob a convenience store. He's basically a decent, law-abiding guy. Maybe he's a little wild at times, but not like a criminal. Apart from getting into fights, he's never done anything criminal as far as I know. He doesn't do drugs. I know he was convicted of shoplifting once, but Wayne didn't do it. He told the cops he did to protect my brother Donnie who was on probation at the time. If Wayne hadn't said he did it, my brother would have been sent back to jail.

I am pretty sure I know who did rob the Nite Owl. A guy at the Pit Stop named Carl Dawson told me that a biker named Kearney did the robbery. Dawson's a good guy, and he's usually reliable. It probably won't do you any good to talk to Dawson. I'm sure he'll deny knowing anything about it. Dawson said that anyone who tried to pin it on Kearney was dead meat. I've seen Kearney before, and I'm sure he would kill anyone who turned him in. I would never testify against him.

I have one prior arrest. When I was fifteen they arrested me for stealing a car and forging a fake driver's license. They had me charged with two felonies, but then the judge sent the whole thing over to juvenile court. There they convicted me and put me on probation for three years until I turned eighteen.

This statement is true and accurate to the best of my recollection.

Albert E. Moore

Albert Moore

5410 2866 7309 0021 04405

DO NOT WRITE ABOVE THIS LINE

SOLD TO

WAYNE B WALKER

DRIVERS LICENSE NO.	STATE

	AUTHORIZATION
LICENSE NO. PJZ 223	STATE CL / CLERK AM
FOLIO/CHECK NO.	

Mobil MOBIL OIL CREDIT CORPORATION

DEALER ACCOUNT NUMBER 659 873 4 DATE 08 12 -1

SOLD BY

R B SMITH
740 E 17TH ST
BAYSHORE CL

QTY	DESCRIPTION	AMOUNT	
	W.O. 32-159	41	95
SALES SLIP	TAX	2	10
	MISC.		
	TOTAL	44	05

MERCHANT COPY

PURCHASER SIGN HERE

X Wayne Walker

The issuer of the card identified on this item is authorized to pay the amount shown as TOTAL upon proper presentation. I promise to pay such TOTAL (together with any other charges due thereon) subject to and in accordance with the Agreement governing the use of such card.

THIS FORM TO BE USED WITH MasterCard OR VISA

MERCHANT: RETAIN THIS COPY FOR YOUR RECORDS

5022134

OFFICE OF THE PUBLIC DEFENDER
309 West Washington Street, Suite 1200
Bayshore, Columbia Phone 232-2475

Statement of Michael Tilton Butler

Made to: Robert Hartwell

Statement made on September 15, YR-1

Place: Butler's home, Route 2, Clinton, Columbia

My name is Michael Tilton Butler. I live on Route 2 in Clinton when I am here in Columbia. I live by myself in a cabin on Yellow Lake. I used to live in Bayshore, where I went to high school with Wayne Walker. He's a good friend, and we still see each other often.

In early August, I called Wayne and invited him up for a few days of fishing. I knew he was not working because he had hurt his foot. Wayne arrived Sunday morning, August 13th, and stayed for four days. We mostly went fishing. During that time Wayne said nothing about a robbery, and he did not seem nervous or different in any way. He had very little money with him, and I had to loan him $20.

I work for Texas Gulf Oil Company on an offshore oil rig. I have to leave next week for Venezuela for a long job. We will be working out of the country for two years or so, so there's no way I can come back to testify.

I have read this prepared statement, and it is true and accurate.

Michael T. Butler

Michael T. Butler

September 16, YR-1

✣ Monroe County Hospital

Medical Records Department
684-3583

To: Attorneys

Enclosed is a copy of Wayne Walker's records from his visit to the hospital on July 27, YR-1. This is a regular record filled out for every patient who obtains treatment in the emergency room. It is a printout of the permanent file from the computer system in our medical records department. All entries are promptly dictated by the physician or other person who provides the treatment and a clerk enters them into the computer.

If you need a witness to attest to the report, please call our office to make the necessary arrangements.

Sincerely,

Elizabeth Knoll

Director, Medical Records

✣ Monroe County Hospital

EMERGENCY ROOM REPORT

PATIENT'S NAME AND ADDRESS
WALKER, WAYNE B.
214 FAIRVIEW
BAYSHORE, COL

ACCOUNT NUMBER
11 44 65245 N/N

INSURANCE INFORMATION
NONE

DATE ADMITTED
07/27/YR-1

DATE DISCHARGED
07/27/YR-1

POSTING DATE	PHYSICIAN	DESCRIPTION	TOTAL CHARGES
07 27	LIBERMANN ER	PATIENT FELL ON RIGHT ANKLE PLAYING BASKETBALL. COMPLAINS OF TENDERNESS AND PAIN, DIFFICULTY WALKING. EXAMINATION REVEALED TENDERNESS, DIFFUSE SWELLING OVER TIP OF LATERAL MALLEOUS, ECCHYMOSIS. LATERAL MOVEMENT OF FOOT ACCOMPANIED BY SHARP PAIN. X-RAYS NEGATIVE. DIAGNOSIS MILD TO MODERATE RUPTURE OF TALOFIBULAR LIGAMENT. ADHESIVE STRAPPING PROVIDED.	85.00
07 27	RADIOLOGY	X-RAY ANKLE SERIES	65.00

OFFICE OF THE PUBLIC DEFENDER
309 West Washington Street, Suite 1200
Bayshore, Columbia Phone 232-2475

Interview with Carl Dawson:
Conducted by Robert Hartwell

I located Carl Dawson, age 22, at the Broad Street Pool Hall, at 9:30 p.m., September 20, YR-1. He stated he knew nothing about the robbery and had never heard of anyone named Kearney. He stated he knew Albert Moore, but had not talked to him recently, and had never talked to him about the Nite Owl robbery. He would not tell me his home address nor his telephone number, and he stated he would not sign any kind of statement.

BACKGROUND INFORMATION ON FINGERPRINT IDENTIFICATION

1. Types of prints

Invisible latent print: A latent print is one which is left unintentionally. It does not mean that it is necessarily hidden from sight. An invisible latent print is the kind that needs to be dusted in order to make it stand out. It is left by a deposit of oils, sweat and dirt that accumulates on the finger.

Visible latent print: This kind of print is left because there was sufficient dirt, blood, ink or other substance on the finger so that the latent print is visible without dusting.

Inked print: This type of fingerprint is the formal kind taken by law enforcement personnel with indelible ink and a fingerprint card. An inked print is carefully rolled from fingernail to fingernail so that all of the surface of the finger will show up. They appear square on the fingerprint card.

Plastic print: This is an unusual kind that is left in wax, clay, etc., and can last for a very long time.

2. Background on fingerprints

Fingerprints are a deposit mostly of oils. Since oil is not water soluble, prints on a hard surface can last a long time (up to six months in good conditions). They are not washed away by water nor dried out by heat or sunlight. Prints do begin to fade with time, since the other substances (dirt, sweat) will disappear. Also, since they are oil based, prints can smear fairly easily if other fingers touch the same surface. Detergents and grease cutters will eradicate fingerprints.

"Dusting" for prints is simply the process of carefully brushing a fine powder (like talcum powder) over a surface. Dark powder is used on light colored surfaces, and a light powder on dark surfaces. The powder will stick to the oil and the print will become visible. A piece of clear tape is then placed over the print, and the print is "lifted". This just removes the powder which has stuck to the tape in the shape of the fingerprint. The piece of tape is then put on a card, and this is the print which is used for comparison purposes. In addition, the visible print is usually digitally photographed.

3. Ridge characteristics

To establish identification, it must be shown that a sufficient number of ridge characteristics are found in the same position on both a lifted print and a known sample. The lines that make up a fingerprint are known as ridges, or friction lines.

There are five principal ridge characteristics:

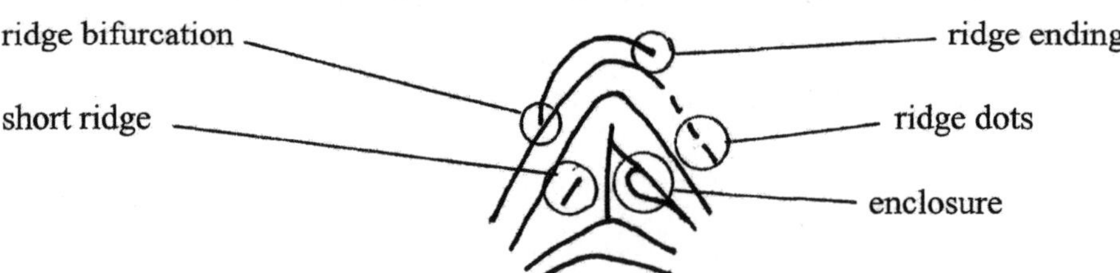

4. Identification process

<u>Step one:</u> Determine the pattern type of the unknown print and the known print, and make sure they are the same.

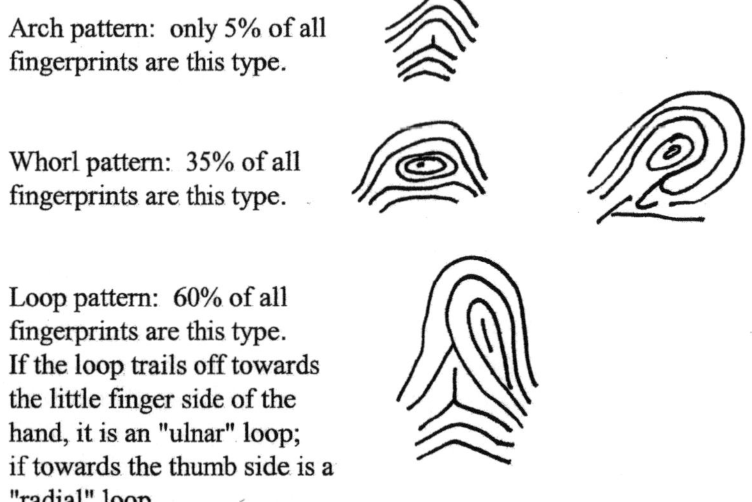

Arch pattern: only 5% of all fingerprints are this type.

Whorl pattern: 35% of all fingerprints are this type.

Loop pattern: 60% of all fingerprints are this type. If the loop trails off towards the little finger side of the hand, it is an "ulnar" loop; if towards the thumb side is a "radial" loop.

<u>Step two:</u> To make sure that the prints are of approximately the same kind, the next step is ridge counting, if it is a loop pattern. This involves drawing a line between the "delta" and the "core", and counting the number of friction lines that intersect it.

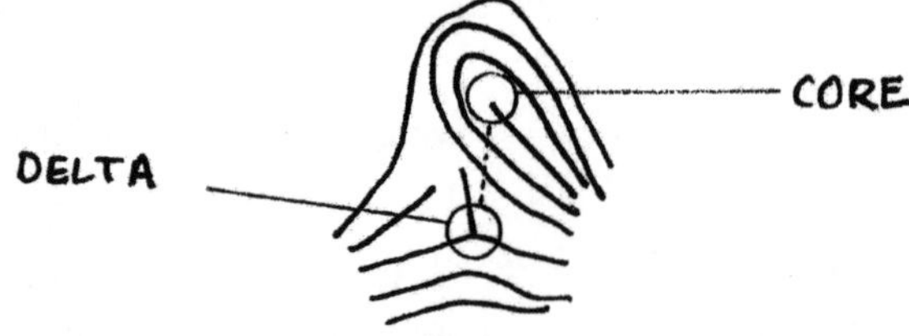

<u>Step three:</u> Identify ridge characteristics on one sample, and look at the other to see if they appear in the same location. If ridge characteristics match, this is a "point of concordance". Most experts agree that 10-12 concordance points are necessary for a perfect match; 8 is certainly the minimum. Note that if a characteristic does NOT match, it is of no importance. The problem can be that there was dirt on a print, or the dusting powder did not stick, and so on.

SELECTED COLUMBIA PATTERN JURY INSTRUCTIONS

Standard Preliminary Instruction Before Trial

Members of the Jury, before we begin the trial, I want to describe how the trial will be conducted and explain what we will be doing -- you, the lawyers for both sides, and I. At the end of the trial I will give you more detailed guidance on how you are to go about reaching your decision. But now I simply want to explain how the trial will proceed.

This is a criminal case. The defendant has been charged with armed robbery and attempted murder. The state is represented at this trial by an assistant prosecutor, __________. The defendant, Wayne Walker, is represented by his lawyer, ___________. The defendant has pleaded not guilty to the charges and denies committing the offenses. He is presumed innocent and may not be found guilty by you unless all of you unanimously find that the state has proved his guilt beyond a reasonable doubt.

The first step in the trial will be the opening statements. The attorneys will tell you about the evidence which they intend to put before you, so that you will have an idea of what the case is going to be. However, what the attorneys say is not evidence. The actual evidence will come from witnesses and exhibits that are offered during trial.

After opening statements, you will hear and see the evidence. The state will present its evidence first. When the state is finished, the defendant will have the opportunity to present evidence, but he does not have to. The witnesses are first examined by the lawyer who calls them and may then be cross-examined by the lawyer for the other side. There may be objections, and you must not consider any evidence that is stricken or that you are told to disregard.

After you have heard all the evidence on both sides, the attorneys will each be given time for their final arguments. In their closing arguments the lawyers will summarize their cases and help you understand the evidence that was presented. Again, however, what the lawyers say is not evidence.

The final part of the trial occurs when I instruct you about the rules of law which you are to use in reaching your verdict. After hearing my instructions, you will leave the courtroom together to make your decision.

There will be occasional recesses during the trial. During these recesses you must not discuss the case with anyone, not even your friends. Nor may you look things up on the Internet. Please keep your cell phones turned off.

All people in this trial are fictional, and the events take place in an imaginary city called Bayshore, in the state of Columbia.

Concluding Instructions: The Final Charge

Members of the Jury:

You will soon leave the courtroom and begin discussing this case in the jury room.

As I told you earlier, the state has accused the defendant, Wayne Walker, of committing the crimes of armed robbery and attempted murder. In order for you to find him guilty, you must be convinced, beyond a reasonable doubt, that he committed these crimes as charged. If you are not convinced beyond a reasonable doubt that he committed these crimes as charged, you must find him not guilty.

Your job is to decide the facts and what happened. The only evidence you may consider is the evidence that was properly admitted at trial. You may not consider any matter that was rejected or stricken by the Court. You may not consider anything you read in the paper or hear from your friends about this case, nor may you do your own investigation or look anything up on the Internet.

It is my job to decide what rules of law apply to the case. You must follow all of the rules as I explain them to you. You may not follow some and ignore others. Even if you disagree or don't understand the reasons for some of the rules, you are bound to follow them.

Proof beyond a reasonable doubt is proof that leaves you firmly convinced of the defendant's guilt. There are very few things in this world that we know with absolute certainty, and in criminal cases the law does not require proof that overcomes every possible doubt. If, based on your consideration of the evidence, you are firmly convinced that the defendant is guilty of the crime charged, you must find him guilty. If on the other hand, you think there is a real possibility that he is not guilty, you must give him the benefit of the doubt and find him not guilty.

An important part of your job will be making judgments about the testimony of the several witnesses including the defendant who testified in this case. You should decide whether you believe what each person had to say, and how important that testimony was. In making that decision I suggest that you ask yourself a few questions: Did the person impress you as honest? Did he or she have any particular reason not to tell the truth? Did he or she have a personal interest in the outcome of the case? Did the witness seem to have a good memory? Did the witness have the opportunity and ability to observe accurately the things he or she testified about? Did he or she appear to understand the questions clearly and answer them directly? Did the witness's testimony differ from the testimony of other witnesses? These are a few of the considerations that will help you determine the accuracy of what each witness said.

Obviously, the state must prove, beyond a reasonable doubt, that the defendant, Wayne Walker, committed that crime. Therefore the identification of Walker by Gerald Culler is an important part of their case. As with any other witness, you must first decide whether Culler is telling the truth as he understands it. But you must do more than that. You must also decide how accurate the identification was and whether the witness saw what he thought he saw. You should consider:

(1) Whether the witness knew the defendant before the crime took place.
(2) Whether the witness had a good opportunity to see the person.
(3) Whether the witness seemed as though he was paying careful attention to what was going on.
(4) Whether the description given by the witness was close to the way the defendant actually looked.
(5) How much time had passed between the crime and the first identification by the witness.
(6) Whether, at the time of the first identification by the witness, the conditions were such that the witness was likely to make a mistake, that is, the witness was not asked to pick out the person he saw from a group of people.
(7) Whether, at an earlier time, the witness failed to identify the defendant.
(8) Whether the witness seemed certain at the time of the first identification and again when he testified here in court.

The state has charged the defendant with armed robbery. To convict the defendant of this crime, the state must prove the following four elements beyond a reasonable doubt:

(1) That the defendant took and carried away property belonging to another;
(2) That the defendant intended to permanently deprive the true owner of that property;
(3) That in the course of taking the property, the defendant threatened another person with immediate serious bodily injury from a deadly weapon, and
(4) That the defendant's purpose was to put that person in fear of immediate serious bodily injury in order to facilitate the taking of the property.

The state also has charged the defendant with attempted murder. To convict the defendant of this crime, the state must prove the following four elements beyond a reasonable doubt:

(1) That the defendant purposely or knowingly committed an act designed to cause the death of another human being;
(2) That the act constituted a substantial step in a course of conduct planned by the defendant to culminate in the death of another human being;
(3) That in the normal course of events, such an act and the consequences logically flowing from it were likely to cause the death of another human being; but
(4) The intended victim does not die.

I submit this case to you with confidence that you will faithfully discharge your duties to be fair and impartial jurors.

Your verdict must be unanimous.

District Court of Monroe County
State of Columbia

State of Columbia	)	
	)	No. Y20476
vs.	)	
	)	**VERDICT FORM**
Wayne Walker	)	

We, the jurors for Monroe County, Columbia, find the defendant:

(1) _____ Guilty

of armed robbery.

_____ Not Guilty

(2) _________ Guilty

of attempted murder.

_____ Not Guilty

____

Jury Foreperson

CASE FILE D:

DAVID C. MARCH

v.

BROWN JUG TAVERN

WRONGFUL DEATH
DRAM SHOP ACT

MARCH V. BROWN JUG TAVERN
CONTENTS OF FILE

GENERAL INSTRUCTIONS

This is a civil wrongful death case, brought by the estate of Helen Gallagher against the Brown Jug Tavern under a Commercial-Server Liability (Dram Shop) Act. Plaintiff alleges that the Tavern served liquor to a visibly intoxicated patron, Oscar Bradley, who later struck Gallagher with his SUV as she crossed the street. Gallagher died after several days in the hospital. The defendant denies knowledge that the patron was intoxicated and alleges contributory negligence on the part of Gallagher. Plaintiff seeks damages for medical expenses, pain and suffering and lost income. The events took place in November two years ago in a fictional city called Bayshore, Columbia (population 150,000).

Potential Witnesses

Oscar T. Bradley -- intoxicated driver who killed Gallagher
Virginia Wagner -- eyewitness, Bradley's companion
Kathi Johnson -- tavern employee who served Bradley
Karen Tucker -- eyewitness
David March -- Gallagher's life partner and administrator of her estate
Jane Moore -- professor of business, University of Columbia
Gerald Adams -- Bayshore police officer

Instructions for use as a full trial (without experts)

1. Plaintiff must call Oscar Bradley and Virginia Wagner as witnesses in his case-in-chief. He may call Gerald Adams or David March.

2. Defendant must call Kathi Johnson and Karen Tucker as witnesses in its case-in-chief. It may call Gerald Adams or David March.

3. The parties have stipulated:
   a. The results of the breath test performed by Gerald Adams are admissible.
   b. The value to Helen Gallagher's estate of her lost earning capacity is $30,000 per year in which she would have worked full time, and $0 for any year in which she would not have worked or would have worked only part-time.

4. Oscar Bradley has settled with David March for $50,000 paid by Bradley's automobile insurance company. Under Columbia law, the judge, not the jury, will handle reducing the final damage award to prevent double recovery by March.

5. The original attorneys have withdrawn from this case, citing conflicts of interest.

Instructions for use as a full trial (with experts)

1. Plaintiff must call Oscar Bradley, Virginia Wagner, and Gerald Adams as witnesses in his case-in-chief. He may call David March, but may call other witnesses only with the approval of the court.

2. Defendant must call Kathi Johnson, Karen Tucker, and Jane Moore as witnesses in its case-in-chief, and may call other witnesses only with the approval of the court.

3. The stipulations on page D-3, paragraph 3, do not apply.

4. The original attorneys have withdrawn from this case, citing conflicts of interest.

Note on Dates

All years in these materials are designated as follows: YR-0 refers to the present year, YR-1 refers to one year ago, YR-2 (the year in which the events happened) refers to two years ago, etc.

In the Monroe County Circuit Court
State of Columbia

DAVID C. MARCH, Administrator of the estate of Helen Gallagher, Plaintiff	)	Civil No. 42449
vs.	)	
Darlene McCormick, d/b/a THE BROWN JUG TAVERN Defendant	)	**COMPLAINT**

Plaintiff for his claim for relief alleges and says that:

1. Plaintiff is the lawfully appointed administrator of the estate of Helen Gallagher, said appointment being made by the Monroe County Probate Court.

2. At the time of the accident described herein, plaintiff was a resident of Monroe County, State of Columbia.

3. At all times mentioned herein, the defendant, Darlene McCormick, was a resident of Monroe County, State of Columbia.

4. At all times mentioned herein, the defendant Darlene McCormick owned and operated a tavern in Monroe County, State of Columbia, known as the Brown Jug Tavern and was duly licensed by the State of Columbia to sell intoxicating alcoholic beverages to the general public at that location.

5. At all times mentioned herein, Darlene McCormick d/b/a The Brown Jug Tavern ("Brown Jug Tavern"), acted through its agents, servants and employees.

6. On November 8, YR-2, The Brown Jug Tavern sold and dispensed intoxicating alcoholic beverages to Oscar Thomas Bradley thereby causing Mr. Bradley to become intoxicated.

7. Once Mr. Bradley became intoxicated, the Brown Jug Tavern carelessly and negligently continued to sell and dispense to Mr. Bradley intoxicating alcoholic beverages in violation of Columbia State Statute §7-5-15.

8. On November 8, YR-2, after Mr. Bradley had become intoxicated, the Brown Jug Tavern carelessly and negligently evicted Mr. Bradley from the premises, which are ten miles from the nearest town, leaving Mr. Bradley with no transportation except to drive his own vehicle.

9. On November 8, YR-2, at approximately 11:30 p.m., Oscar Thomas Bradley was driving his automobile through the intersection of Washington and Kirkwood Streets in Bayshore, State of Columbia, while intoxicated, and struck Helen Gallagher who was crossing Washington Street within a marked crosswalk.

10. The intoxicated state of Oscar Thomas Bradley was a direct and proximate cause of the accident.

11. As a direct and proximate result of the negligent acts of the defendant, Helen Gallagher was killed.

12. As a direct result of the negligence of the defendant, Helen Gallagher was hospitalized for injuries and required to engage the services of doctors for treatment, medication and X-rays and by reason thereof, has incurred medical bills in the amount of $16,095.00.

13. As a result of her death, Helen Gallagher's estate has been deprived of the amount she would have earned during her lifetime, which amount is reasonably worth $3,300,000.

14. As a direct and proximate result of the negligence of the defendant, Helen Gallagher was in great pain and suffered for four days following the accident until her death, which is reasonably worth $200,000.

WHEREFORE, the plaintiff David C. March prays for judgment against the defendant in an amount commensurate with her injuries, for the costs of this action, for trial by jury and for all other just and proper relief.

LERNER LAW OFFICE

By Stanley Lerner

Stanley Lerner
Attorney for Plaintiff

LERNER LAW OFFICE
3131 E. Third Street
Bayshore, Columbia
(811) 587-8423

In the Monroe County Circuit Court
State of Columbia

DAVID C. MARCH, administrator of the estate of Helen Gallagher *Plaintiff* vs. Darlene McCormick, d/b/a "THE BROWN JUG TAVERN", *Defendant*	)))))))))	 Civil No. 42449 **ANSWER**

---

1. Defendant admits paragraph 1.

2. Defendant admits paragraph 2.

3. Defendant admits paragraph 3.

4. Defendant admits paragraph 4.

5. Defendant admits paragraph 5.

6. Defendant denies the allegations contained in paragraph 6.

7. Defendant denies the allegations contained in paragraph 7.

8. Defendant denies the allegations contained in paragraph 8.

9. Defendant denies the allegations contained in paragraph 9.

10. Defendant denies the allegations contained in paragraph 10.

11. Defendant denies the allegations contained in paragraph 11.

12. Defendant denies the allegations contained in paragraph 12.

13. Defendant denies the allegations contained in paragraph 13.

14. Defendant denies the allegations contained in paragraph 14.

First Defense

15. Defendant says that if she should be found to be negligent in any of the respects set forth in the complaint, which she specifically denies, then Helen Gallagher was also negligent which proximately contributed to her death and the damages complained of in the complaint, in that Helen Gallagher was crossing Washington Street in a negligent manner and failed to yield to a motor vehicle as required in section 9-4-88 of the Columbia Code.

Second Defense

16. Defendant says that if Helen Gallagher's negligence did not cause the accident that resulted in her death, then the sole proximate cause of the accident was the negligent driving of Oscar Thomas Bradley and is not the fault of defendant.

WHEREFORE, defendant prays that the court dismiss plaintiff's complaint and award defendant costs and expenses incurred herein.

Lynda Mitchell
Lynda A. Mitchell
Attorney for Defendant
HOUSTON MINNICK & DOS SANTOS
100 North Walnut
Bayshore, Columbia

CERTIFICATE OF SERVICE

I hereby certify that a true copy of the foregoing Answer was mailed, postage prepaid, to Stanley Lerner, 3131 E. Third Street, Bayshore, Columbia, attorney for plaintiff; this *12* day of *January*, YR-1.

Lynda Mitchell
Lynda A. Mitchell

EXCERPTS FROM COLUMBIA STATUTES

§ 34-1-2. Action for wrongful death.-- When the death of a person is caused by the wrongful act or omission of another, the personal representative of the former may maintain an action therefore against the latter, and the damages shall be in such an amount as may be determined by the court or jury, including, but not limited to, reasonable medical, hospital, funeral and burial expenses, such lost earnings as can reasonably be expected to accrue to the estate, and reasonable compensation for the decedent's pain and suffering not to exceed $200,000.

§ 7-5-15. Liability for Furnishing Alcohol. -- A person who furnishes an alcoholic beverage to a person is liable in a civil action for damages caused by the impairment or intoxication of the person who was furnished the alcoholic beverage if:

(a) The person furnishing the alcoholic beverage had knowledge that the person to whom the alcoholic beverage was furnished was visibly intoxicated at the time the alcoholic beverage was furnished; and,

(b) The intoxication of the person to whom the alcoholic beverage was furnished was a proximate cause of the death, injury, or damage alleged in the complaint.

§ 9-4-87. Pedestrian's right-of-way at crosswalks. -- (a) When traffic control signals are not in place or not in operation, the driver of a vehicle shall yield the right-of-way, slowing down or stopping if need be to so yield, to a pedestrian crossing the roadway within a crosswalk when the pedestrian is upon the half of the roadway upon which the vehicle is traveling, or when the pedestrian is approaching so closely from the opposite half of the roadway as to be in danger.

(b) No pedestrian shall suddenly leave a curb or other place of safety and walk or run into the path of a vehicle which is so close as to constitute an immediate hazard.

§ 9-4-88. Crossing at other than crosswalks. Every pedestrian crossing a roadway at any point other than within a marked crosswalk shall yield the right-of-way to all vehicles upon the roadway.

§ 9-4-180. Stopping Distances -- Judicial Notice. All courts of general jurisdiction in this state may take judicial notice of the following table:

Table of Average Speed and Stopping Distances (in feet)

For vehicles with brakes and tires in good condition on dry level pavement free from loose material. For wet pavement add 10% for all-season tires and ABS, 20% for all-season tires and no ABS, 30% for high-performance tires, and 40% for tires with visibly worn tread.

SPEED IN:		AVERAGE STOPPING DISTANCES				TOTAL STOPPING DISTANCES		
Miles per hour	Feet per second	Cars	Vans, SUVs & pickups	Trucks to 36 feet	Driver reaction time	Cars	Vans etc	Trucks
10	14.7	5	5	6	22	27	27	28
15	22.0	11	12	14	33	44	45	47
20	29.3	19	21	25	44	63	65	69
25	36.6	30	33	40	55	85	88	95
30	44.0	43	48	57	66	109	114	123
35	51.3	58	65	78	77	135	142	155
40	58.7	76	85	102	88	164	173	190
45	66.0	96	107	129	99	195	243	228
50	73.3	119	133	159	110	229	207	242
55	80.7	144	161	192	121	265	282	288
60	88.0	171	191	229	132	303	323	336
65	95.3	201	224	268	143	344	367	387
70	102.6	233	259	311	154	387	413	444
75	109.9	268	298	357	165	433	463	504
80	117.2	305	339	406	176	481	481	568
85	124.7	344	384	459	187	531	565	646
90	132.0	386	430	514	198	584	628	706

§ 34-2-67. Present value -- Judicial notice. In all cases in the courts of this state, judicial notice may be taken of the following present value table:

Present value of $1.00 per year over a period of years

Number of years	Rate of return on investment 5%	6%	7%	8%
1	0.95	0.94	0.93	0.92
2	1.86	1.83	1.80	1.77
3	2.72	2.67	2.62	2.57
4	3.55	3.47	3.39	3.31
5	4.33	4.21	4.10	3.98
6	5.08	4.92	4.77	4.62
7	5.79	5.58	5.39	5.21
8	6.46	6.21	5.97	5.74
9	7.11	6.80	6.52	6.26
10	7.72	7.36	7.02	6.70
11	8.31	7.89	7.50	7.11
12	8.86	8.38	7.94	7.50
13	9.39	8.85	8.36	7.87
14	9.90	9.29	8.75	8.26
15	10.38	9.71	9.11	8.58
16	10.84	10.11	9.45	8.87
17	11.27	10.48	9.76	9.11
18	11.69	10.83	10.06	9.38
19	12.09	11.16	10.34	9.62
20	12.46	11.47	10.59	9.82
21	12.82	11.76	10.84	10.02
22	13.16	12.04	11.06	10.21
23	13.49	12.30	11.27	10.39
24	13.80	12.55	11.47	10.56
25	14.09	12.78	11.65	10.72
26	14.38	13.00	11.83	10.87
27	14.64	13.21	11.99	11.01
28	14.90	13.41	12.14	11.13
29	15.14	13.59	12.28	11.25
30	15.37	13.76	12.41	11.36
31	15.59	13.93	12.53	11.46
32	15.80	14.08	12.65	11.55
33	16.00	14.23	12.75	11.64
34	16.19	14.37	12.85	11.72
35	16.37	14.50	12.95	11.79
36	16.55	14.62	13.04	11.86
37	16.71	14.74	13.12	11.93
38	16.87	14.85	13.19	11.99
39	17.02	14.95	13.26	12.05
40	17.16	15.05	13.33	12.11

EXCERPT FROM THE DECISIONS OF THE COLUMBIA SUPREME COURT

Robin HICKMAN, Appellant
(Plaintiff below)

v.

BUD'S TRUCK STOP, Appellee
(Defendant below)

No. 487T4539

Supreme Court of Columbia

June 12, YR-4

DAUBER, Associate Justice

This action was brought under Columbia's new Commercial Server Liability Act, § 7-5-15, to recover damages from a restaurant for the off-premises actions of one of its patrons who had become intoxicated. The basic facts are: one Joseph Franklin spent several hours at the defendant's restaurant drinking beer. He left in a state of intoxication, got into his truck, and drove off. Several minutes later, he crossed the center line and hit plaintiff's car coming the other direction, causing serious injury to the driver. Franklin's blood alcohol level was 0.21 percent. Plaintiff sued Bud's Truck Stop under the Commercial Server Liability Act.

At the close of plaintiff's case, the trial judge directed a verdict for the defendant on the ground that the plaintiff had not shown that Bud's Truck Stop had knowledge that Franklin was intoxicated when it served him. Taken in the light most favorable to plaintiff, her evidence showed that although one waiter served Franklin throughout his stay, that person had no specific recollection of how many beers Franklin drank, nor was there any evidence that Franklin was visibly intoxicated. Plaintiff appeals from this ruling. This is our first opportunity to review this new legislation.

Plaintiff first argues that she should be entitled to a presumption that defendant had knowledge of Franklin's intoxication based on his high blood alcohol level. Plaintiff's expert testified that a person with a blood alcohol concentration of 0.21% would be "very intoxicated," would have difficulty walking a straight line, and their speech would be slow and slurred. Based on this evidence, plaintiff argues that she should have been entitled to a presumption that Franklin would have been visibly intoxicated and that defendant's employees would have been aware of it. We disagree. The statute clearly states that defendants are liable only if they serve liquor to a person they know to be *visibly* intoxicated. This requires affirmative evidence from plaintiffs.

Plaintiff next argues that the evidence was sufficient to establish constructive knowledge on defendant's part. Defendant argues that the plaintiff must prove *actual* knowledge of Franklin's intoxication.

This is a case of first impression in Columbia. No consistent pattern appears in other states. Some require proof of actual, subjective knowledge (citations omitted). Others permit recovery upon proof merely of constructive knowledge, although precise definitions of constructive knowledge vary (citations omitted). An emerging middle ground appears to be the use of an "objective knowledge" standard -- whether a reasonable server of alcoholic beverage would have known the patron was intoxicated, or that there was a high probability of intoxication, based on all the circumstances of the case. See Ronald S. Beitman, Practitioners' Guide to Liquor Liability Litigation 1-23 (2006). We adopt the middle ground as the one most consistent with tort law's reasonable person standard.

Now we turn to the question whether plaintiff in the case before us introduced enough evidence to show that a reasonable server in the position of the defendant's employee would have known that Franklin was intoxicated at the time he was served additional alcohol. All the plaintiff proved was that Franklin was in fact intoxicated. No proof was offered that Franklin displayed any visible signs of intoxication, nor that he was served such a large quantity of alcohol in a short time so that intoxication was inevitable. Judgment affirmed.

B. P. D. AND M. C. S. D. OFFICER FIELD REPORT

DATE OF ACCIDENT Nov. 9, YR-2 (Month Day Year) DAY OF WEEK Thurs TIME ____ A.M. 11:30 P.M.

____ OUTSIDE CITY LIMITS COUNTY Monroe CITY OR TOWN Bayshore

x INSIDE CITY LIMITS TOWNSHIP ____

SPECIFIC LOCATION South Washington Street at Kirkwood intersection

VEHICLE NO. 1		VEHICLE NO. 2	
YEAR	YR-3 MAKE CHEV TYPE VAN	YEAR	____ MAKE ____ TYPE ____
LICENSE NO.	52471 ST. COL YR. -2	LICENSE NO.	____ ST. ____ YR. ____
DRIVER	Oscar T. Bradley	DRIVER	
ADDRESS	701 S. Washington	ADDRESS	
	Bayshore, COL PHONE 336-8973		PHONE
DRIVER'S LIC. NO.	276998660/COL	DRIVER'S LIC. NO.	
D.O.B.	7/14/YR-33 AGE 31 SEX M	D.O.B.	____ AGE ____ SEX ____
OWNER	same	OWNER	
ADDRESS		ADDRESS	
VEHICLE DAMAGE		VEHICLE DAMAGE	
INS. CO. OR AGENT	Boston Casualty	INS. CO. OR AGENT	
ADDRESS	Ron Remak, Bill Brown Ins. Co.	ADDRESS	

PERSONAL INJURIES

NAME	DESCRIPTION OF INJURY
Helen Gallagher, 1012 S. Mitchell St.	Serious condition, unconscious

DESCRIPTION OF ACCIDENT Van struck pedestrian, Helen Gallagher, as she crossed Washington Street. Driver intoxicated.

INVESTIGATING OFFICER Gerald Adams DEPT. BPD

WITNESSES: Karen Tucker -- 4626 Sunset Avenue, Bayshore, Col. 333-0112
Virginia Wagner -- 2505 Rock Creek Rd., Bayshore, Col. 824-8241

PREPARE DIAGRAM OF ACCIDENT ON BACK OF THIS FORM

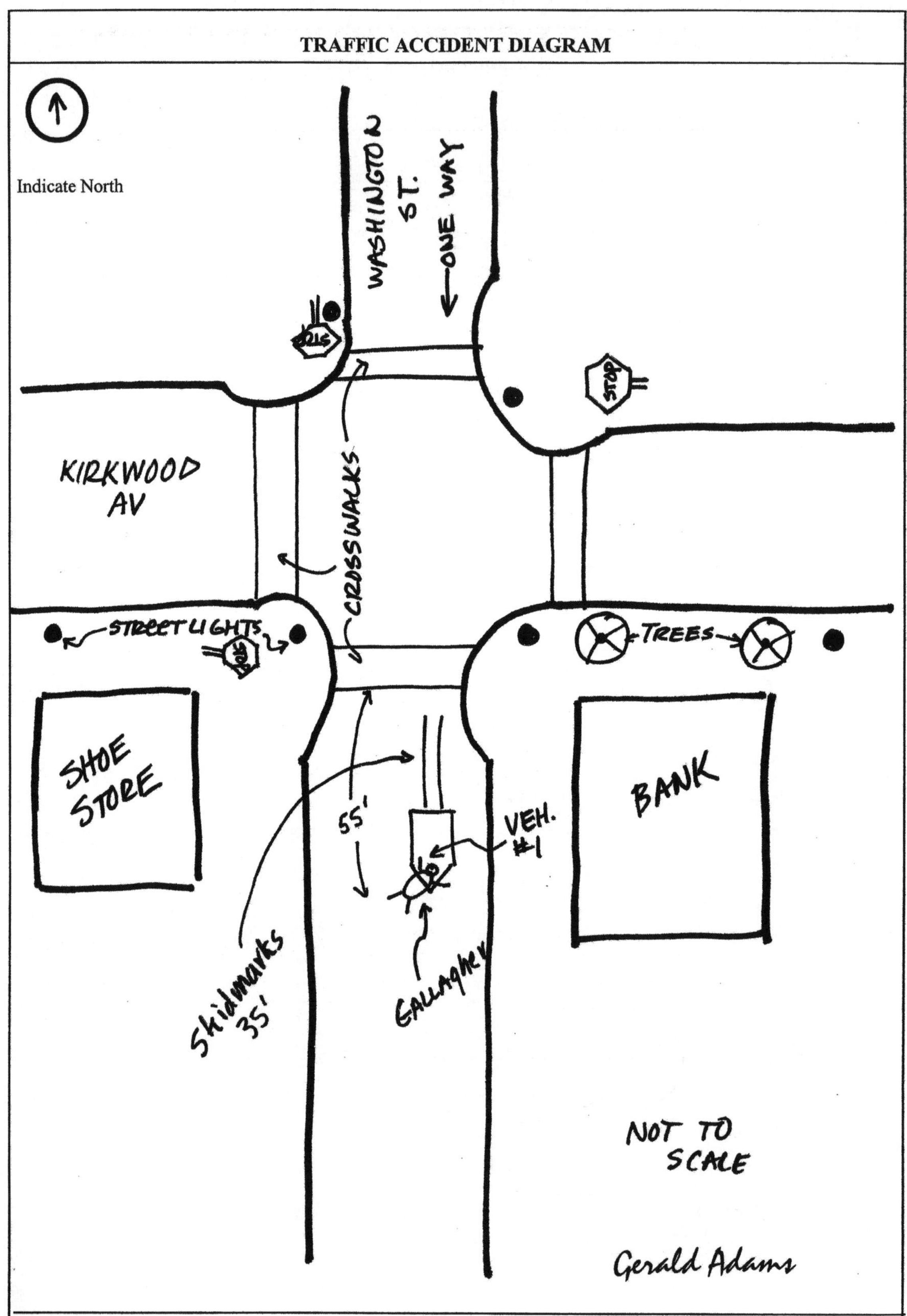
TRAFFIC ACCIDENT DIAGRAM
Indicate North
WASHINGTON ST.
ONE WAY
STOP
STOP
KIRKWOOD AV
CROSSWALKS
STREET LIGHTS
STOP
TREES
SHOE STORE
BANK
55'
VEH. #1
Skidmarks 35'
Gallagher
NOT TO SCALE
Gerald Adams

B. P. D. AND M. C. S. D. OFFICER NARRATIVE REPORT

DATE OF ACCIDENT 11/9/YR-2 DATE OF REPORT 11/10/Yr-2

SPECIFIC LOCATION Kirkwood and Washington Streets

NAME(S) OF PARTIES Oscar T. Bradley

NAME OF OFFICER Gerald Adams DEPARTMENT BPD

NARRATIVE DESCRIPTION OF ACCIDENT:

Responded to call at 11:30 p.m. that there had been a traffic accident at Kirkwood and Washington Street. Proceeded to scene, arrived 11:31 p.m. Chevrolet SUV had struck pedestrian identified from drivers license as Helen Gallagher, Female age 28, 1012 S. Mitchell, Bayshore. Gallagher bleeding and unconscious, positioned under SUV with feet north and head south, approx. 55 feet south of crosswalk. Gallagher taken to Monroe County Hospital.

Driver of Vehicle No. 1 identified as Oscar Thomas Bradley, 701 S. Washington St., Bayshore, said that Gallagher had run out in front of him and that he had not seen her. Appeared intoxicated. Observed several empty beer cans inside vehicle.

Woman identified as Karen Tucker, 4626 Sunset Ave., Bayshore, said she had witnessed accident. She stated that Gallagher was talking on a cell phone and walked into Washington Street right in front of Bradley's vehicle which had just turned left from Kirkwood to Washington.

Measured skidmarks to be 35 feet which started approximately 20 feet south of crosswalk. ?

Passenger in Vehicle No. 1, Virginia Wagner, 2505 Rock Creek Drive, Bayshore, said Gallagher crossing street from west to east when hit, not sure if in or out of crosswalk. Said she and Bradley had been drinking at the Brown Jug.

Administered NHTSA field sobriety tests following standard procedure. Also administered new Horizontal Gaze Nystagmus test. Suspect's eyes began to jerk at about 35 degrees, with jerking at maximum angle very distinct.

Bradley arrested for DUI. Intoximeter administered. BAC 0.17%. ✓

BAYSHORE POLICE DEPARTMENT

SOBRIETY EXAMINATION

DR No. 91-12345

1. DATE AND TIME EXAMINATION STARTED: NOV. 9 YR-2 11:45 PM
2. DRIVER: ☒ YES ☐ NO
3. ACCIDENT: ☒ YES ☐ NO
4. REPORTING DISTRICT 22.01
5. NAME (Last, first middle): BRADLEY OSCAR T.
6. RESIDENCE ADDRESS: 701 S. WASHINGTON — CITY: BAYSHORE
7. OCCUPATION: MECHANIC
8. BOOKING NO.: B361
9. WHERE WERE YOU GOING? HOME
10. WHERE HAVE YOU BEEN? BROWN JUG
11. WHEN DID YOU LEAVE? 15 MINUTES AGO — A.M. / P.M.

12. ALCOHOLIC BREATH	13. FACE	14. EYES	15. SPEECH	16. ATTITUDE	17. CLOTHING	18. COORDINATION	19. BALANCE
Yes – strong	Flushed	red + watery	slow + slurred	cooperative	Normal	Fair	Fair

20. WALKING LINE TEST. ○ RIGHT FOOT △ LEFT FOOT — stopped — 3'

21. REACTION OF PUPILS: SLOW — RIGHT EYE 35° — LEFT EYE 35° — GAZE TEST

22. FINGER TO NOSE TEST: ○ RIGHT INDEX △ LEFT INDEX — 1, 2, 3, 4

DESCRIBE SURFACING AT LOCATION. (Smooth concrete, rough dirt, grass.) SMOOTH CONCRETE

23. UNUSUAL ACTIONS (driving, fumbling in wallet, dropping articles, etc.) WHICH CAUSED OFFICER TO SUSPECT ALCOHOLIC INFLUENCE. ALSO DESCRIBE ANY LIQUOR CONTAINERS FOUND IN DEFENDANT'S POSSESSION. OPEN BEER CANS IN CAR. SEARCHED WALLET FOR 2 MINUTES TO FIND LICENSE. WHEN ASKED IF HE KNEW WHAT HAD HAPPENED, BRADLEY RESPONDED "I WAS FRAMED"

EVIDENCE TAGGED YES (NO) — LOCKER #
VEHICLE LIC.# 52471 — MODEL CHEV — YEAR YR-3 — COLOR BLUE

24. ARE YOU INJURED OR SICK? NO — IF SO, WHERE OR HOW? N/A — ARE YOU TAKING MEDICINE OR DRUGS? NO
25. ARE YOU BEING TREATED BY A DOCTOR OR DENTIST? NO — IF SO, WHO AND FOR WHAT? N/A. — DATE AND TIME LAST TREATED? N/A — A.M. / P.M.
26. ARE YOU EPILEPTIC OR DIABETIC? NO — DO YOU TAKE INSULIN? NO — DATE AND TIME LAST TAKEN? N/A — A.M. / P.M.
27. DO YOU HAVE ANY PHYSICAL DEFECT? NO — IF SO, WHAT? N/A — DOES IT IMPAIR YOU? N/A
28. WHERE ARE YOU NOW? "UP SHIT CREEK" — 29. ACTUAL LOCATION: c/o Washington + Kirkwood — 30. WHAT TIME IS IT? "About midnight" A.M. / P.M. — 31. ACTUAL TIME: 1155 pm
32. WHAT HAVE YOU BEEN DRINKING? HOW MUCH? TIME STARTED? BEER – DON'T KNOW – 8:30 pm — WITH WHOM? Ginny — WHERE DID YOU LAST DRINK? Brown Jug — WHEN? Don't know
33. WHAT HAVE YOU EATEN TODAY? DINNER, BEEF STEW — WITH WHOM? Ginny — WHERE? Her house — WHEN? 7:00 pm
34. WHEN DID YOU LAST SLEEP? LAST NIGHT — HOW MANY HOURS? 7 — WHERE? Home — AWOKE? Don't know
35. CONCLUSION OF OFFICER(S): ☒ UNDER INFLUENCE OF ALCOHOL ☐ NOT UNDER INFLUENCE OF ALCOHOL
36. ADMINISTERING OFFICER (Name—Serial No.—Division): Gerald Adams 314 BPD
37. WITNESSING OFFICER (Name—Serial No.—Division):
38. CHEMICAL TEST: BREATHALYZER (No. & Percent) ☒ — BLOOD ☐ — INTOXIMETER (No. & Seconds Color Reaction) ☒ #289 .17 – .17 — SUBJECT'S WGT. 170
39. APPROVED BY: J.R. Miller 2123

BAYSHORE POLICE DEPARTMENT GAS CHROMATOGRAPH INTOXIMETER CHECK LIST	BLOOD ALCOHOL .17-.17	INSTRUMENT NO. 289	NALCO SAMPLE NO. —
	LOCATION Bayshore PD		DATE TESTED Nov. 10 Yr-2
NAME OF SUBJECT BRADLEY Oscar T.			TIME TESTED 0105 am
WEIGHT 170	VIOLATION Traffic accident	FILE NUMBER YO-12491	

PREPARING FOR THE TEST

1. (✓) Wait at least fifteen minutes after last drink, eating, regurgitation, or smoking before giving test.
2. (✓) Check that main gas valve is fully open (counter-clockwise).
   (NOTE: DO NOT TOUCH CARRIER GAS FLOW VALVE)
3. (✓) Check that orange light is on.
4. (✓) Deflate waste bag. (Waste bag should be connected to instrument)
5. (✓) Switch STANDBY-OPERATE switch to OPERATE.
6. (✓) Depress green button below STANDBY-OPERATE switch until green READY light comes on.

BLANK

7. (✓) SELECT LEVER in BLANK position.
8. (✓) Recorder turned on.
9. (✓) Press ANALYZE button.
10. (✓) When green READY light *remains* on, record Blank result. .00 %
    If Blank result is greater than .00%, repeat steps 9 ( ) and 10 ( ) ______ %

TEST

11. (✓) SELECT LEVER moved to SAMPLE position.
12. (✓) Attach new mouthpiece.
13. (✓) Take breath sample and press ANALYZE button while whistle has been sounding for 3 to 5 seconds.
14. (✓) When green READY light *remains* on, record Test result. .17 %
15. (✓) Deflate waste bag.
16. (✓) Take breath sample and press ANALYZE button while whistle has been sounding for 3 to 5 seconds.
17. (✓) When green READY light *remains* on, record Test result. .17 %
    If the results of the two samples of the subject's breath vary by more than .02% repeat steps 15 ( ), 16 ( ), and 17 ( ) ______ %

BLANK

18. (✓) SELECT LEVER moved to BLANK position.
19. (✓) Press ANALYZE button.
20. (✓) When green READY light *remains* on, record Blank result. .00 %
    If Blank result is greater than .00%, repeat steps 19 ( ) and 20 ( ) ______ %

Operator (Name, Badge, Agency)	Witnessing Officer (If any) (Name, Badge, Agency)
Gerald Adams 1314 BPD	OFC BOLTON 1984B

Remarks:

MONROE COUNTY

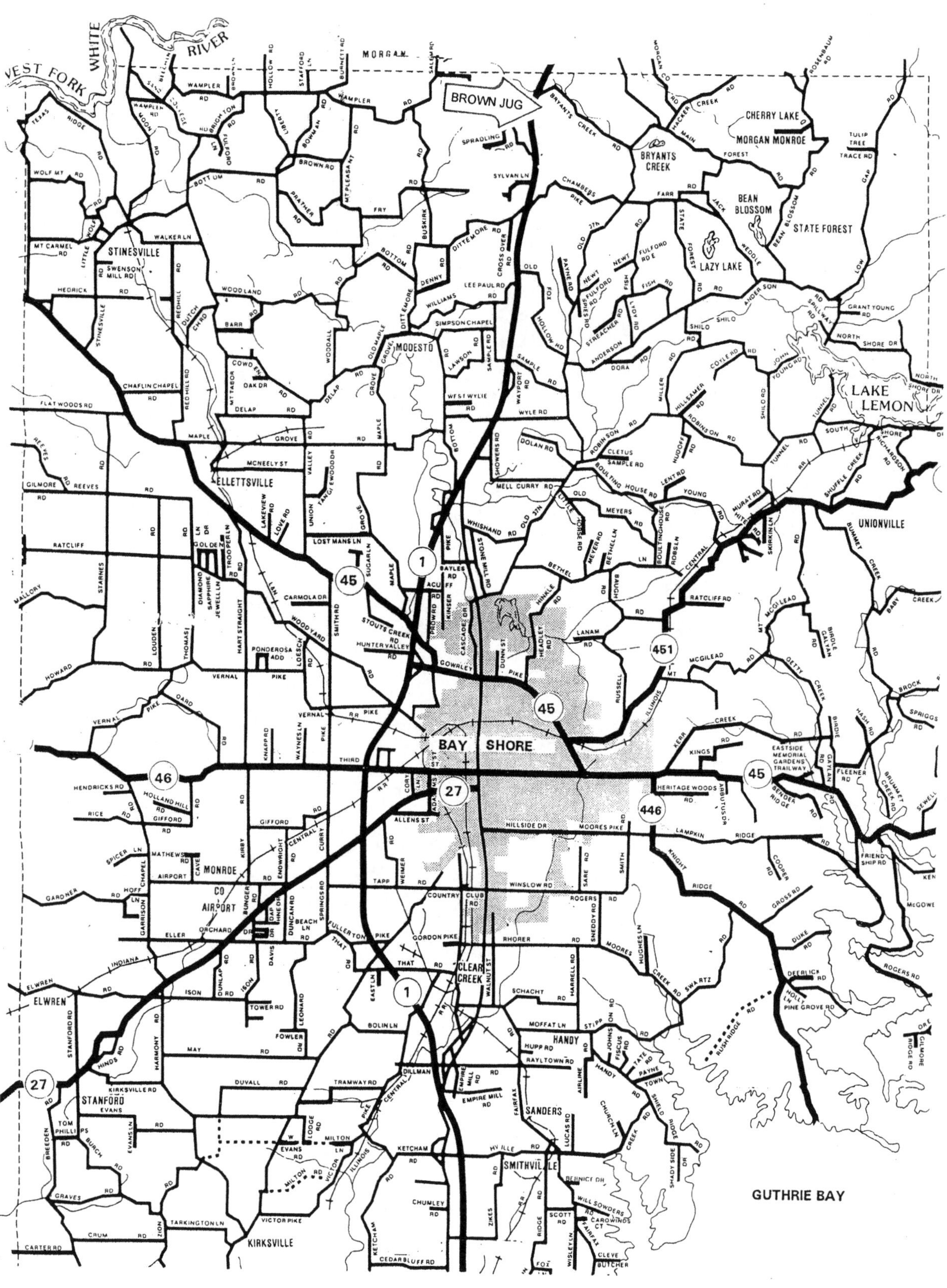

David March)
)
vs.)
)
Brown Jug Tavern)

DEPOSITION OF OSCAR T. BRADLEY

DATE : April 18, YR-1

PLACE : Offices of Houston, Minnick & Dos Santos
100 North Walnut Street
Bayshore, Columbia

TIME BEGAN : 10:05 A.M.

APPEARANCES : For the Plaintiff, appears Stanley Lerner, Esq.
For the Defendant, appears Lynda A. Mitchell, Esq.

STENOGRAPHER : Dodie Bowman

TRANSCRIBED : Dodie Bowman

WHEREUPON THE WITNESS OSCAR T. BRADLEY WAS SWORN BY DODIE BOWMAN, NOTARY PUBLIC

EXAMINATION BY MR. LERNER

Q: Would you please state your name, age and address.
A: Sure. I'm Oscar T. Bradley. I live at 701 South Washington Street, Bayshore, Columbia. I'm thirty-one years old.
Q: Are you married? Children?
A: I am separated. We have two children.
Q: What is your occupation?
A: I'm the assistant service manager for Rogers' Chevrolet.
Q: And, is that all you do? Is it your only job?
A: Yes.

Q: Do you have a criminal record?
A: No, absolutely not.
Q: Any prior traffic tickets?
A: Yes. Two stop sign violations when I was sixteen, and a couple of speeding tickets and D.W.I.'s in the last few years.
Q: Did you plead guilty to all of them?
A: Yes.
Q: Were you ever sentenced to any jail time?
A: No.
Q: Did you go to college?
A: No. Just high school. I was in the auto mechanic's vocational program.
Q: Were you in the service?
A: Yes, the army for four years. I was stationed in Texas.
Q: When were you discharged?
A: Eight years ago this summer.
Q: Turning to November 9, YR-2, what time did you arrive at work?
A: Eight o'clock.
Q: Is that your usual starting time?
A: Yes.
Q: How long had you worked the day before?
A: My usual day -- 8:00 a.m. to 5:00 p.m.
Q: Were you taking any medication of any kind that day?
A: No.
Q: Do you have any health or eyesight restrictions on your drivers license?
A: No. I'm in good health.
Q: Tell me, please, in your own words, what you did on November 9 after work.
A: I went home and changed. Then I went over to my girlfriend's house -- Virginia Wagner. She lives on Rock Creek Road. I got there about 7:00 p.m. We ate dinner and washed the dishes. Then we drank a few beers and watched T.V.
Q: What time did you have the first beer?
A: I don't know. Maybe 8:30 or so.
Q: How many beers did you drink?
A: Four.
Q: How many did Ms. Wagner drink?

A: Maybe two or three. I'm not sure.
Q: When did you leave her house?
A: About 9:15.
Q: What did you do then?
A: We went to the Brown Jug Tavern.
Q: Where is that located?
A: Ten miles north of town on Route 1.
Q: How close is that to Bryant's Creek Road?
A: I'm not sure.
Q: What did you do?
A: We arrived about 9:30. We had a beer or two, then left to go home.
Q: Exactly how many beers did you have at the Brown Jug?
A: I think I had six.
Q: Regular 12-ounce beers?
A: Yeah.
Q: What time did you leave the bar?
A: I'm not sure. I would say about 11:15 p.m.
Q: Did you go directly from there to the intersection of Washington Street and Kirkwood?
A: Yes.
Q: What were you driving?
A: My SUV.
Q: Was anyone in the SUV with you?
A: Yes. Ginny was.
Q: Who was driving?
A: I was.
Q: Were you drunk?
A: I'd say I was tipsy but not real drunk.
Q: How did you approach the intersection of Kirkwood and Washington?
A: From Kirkwood, going east-to-west.
Q: All right. You were going west on Kirkwood and you got to Washington, do you recall a stop sign?
A: Yes, there's a stop sign at the corner.
Q: Did you come to a complete stop before you entered the intersection?
A: No, not exactly. I made, you know, a rolling stop.
Q: How was the traffic?

A: Pretty light. As I approached the corner, I think I remember a car went across Kirkwood from north to south and another car came through the intersection going east, then I turned left.
Q: What kind of vehicle was it that went by just before you turned?
A: A sedan of some sort, I'm not sure what kind.
Q: What were the weather conditions?
A: Cool and dry, a clear night.
Q: Was the intersection well lit?
A: Yeah.
Q: Did you turn left immediately after the car passed?
A: Yes.
Q: Did you make a gradual turn or sharp turn or what?
A: I made a sort of sharp turn onto Washington Street.
Q: Okay. Did you observe any people near the intersection?
A: Yes, I believe I remember seeing three people on the southwest corner where the shoe store is.
Q: What were they doing?
A: Standing on the corner. I guess they were waiting to cross the street.
Q: Do you know for sure what direction they were facing?
A: No.
Q: Did you observe any other people on foot at that time?
A: No.
Q: Did you see a young woman in her twenties anywhere near the intersection?
A: No.
Q: Did you see anyone crossing the street?
A: No.
Q: Mr. Bradley, will you describe in your own words what happened, starting from the time you approached the intersection.
A: Well, I approached the intersection, slowed to almost a complete stop, made the turn, glanced to my right at the people on the corner, and then there was the sound of the impact, and I slammed on the brakes.
Q: Where was your vehicle when you heard the impact?
A: I'm not exactly sure. I'd finished the turn, so I would say about at the crosswalk or a few feet beyond it, that is, south of it.
Q: Did you see Ms. Gallagher crossing the street?

A: No, I did not. She must have run out in front of me.
Q: Did you have your brakes on prior to the impact?
A: No, sir. Well, I had them on as I approached the intersection, but then I accelerated, so my foot was off the brake when the impact happened.
Q: What was the condition of your vehicle?
A: Very good. I keep it in good shape.
Q: What shape were the tires in?
A: They were relatively new, purchased in July, I think. They had less than three thousand miles on them by my best guess.
Q: Had the brakes been adjusted within the preceding six months?
A: I adjusted them myself.
Q: What was the condition of the pavement?
A: I don't know.
Q: All right. Immediately after the impact what did you do?
A: Slammed on the brakes.
Q: What did you see in front of you?
A: Nothing -- just the street and parked cars.
Q: Did you see whether Ms. Gallagher was thrown into the air?
A: No. I didn't see it.
Q: Do you know your speed as you were making the turn?
A: Around fifteen miles an hour. I'm not sure.
Q: And your speed at the time of impact?
A: I don't know exactly. Maybe fifteen miles an hour.
Q: What's the speed limit?
A: 30 miles an hour.
Q: Had you had anything to drink since you left the tavern?
A: No.
Q: On November 9, YR-2, were you covered by liability insurance?
A: Yes, through Allstate.
Q: Do you know what the policy coverage was?
A: Um, no. The minimum required.
Q: Have you complied with all the conditions required by the policy, like filing a report?
A: Yes.
Q: What was the first indication you had of Ms. Gallagher's presence?
A: The sound of the impact.

Q: At the impact, how far from the east curb were you?
A: I would say about ten feet from it or maybe a little more.
Q: As best you can tell, where on your SUV was the point of impact?
A: Left front, about one-third of the way across. By left, I mean the driver's side.
Q: When you said you slammed on the brakes, will you describe that in more detail?
A: I put force on the brake pedal as quickly and hard as I could, using my left foot. The SUV has automatic transmission.
Q: What did you do next?
A: I jumped out and ran around to the front to see what I had hit.
Q: What did you see?
A: I saw the body of Ms. Gallagher, lying partly under the truck. She was on her back, with her head and chest in the street and her legs under the truck.
Q: What was she wearing?
A: I don't remember. I was pretty shook up. I'd never seen her coming. I don't know where she came from.
Q: All right. Were there any marks on the front of your SUV?
A: There was a dent above the grill. I don't think it was there before. Sort of level with the headlights.
Q: Can you draw a diagram for me?
A: I'll try. Here.
Q: Attach this as deposition exhibit one. Is this x-mark the point of the dent?
A: Yes.
Q: What did you do after you saw Ms. Gallagher?
A: I yelled to some people who had gathered to call the police. Then I knelt down to see if she was still alive.
Q: Was she?
A: Yes.
Q: Was she conscious?
A: Yes.
Q: Did you say anything to her?
A: I said, "Where did you come from?"
Q: Did she say anything to you?
A: After a minute, she said something that sounded like, "Oh, God, oh, God

David always told me to be more careful, that someday my carelessness would get me killed." Then she asked me to call Dave, to get Dave for her. I did not know then who she was talking about.
Q: Do you remember speaking to any bystanders after the accident?
A: I was very shaken. I don't remember talking to anyone until the police officer questioned me.
Q: Do you know for sure if you said anything to anyone?
A: No, I have no idea.
Q: There were bystanders around after the accident?
A: Yes, there were people around.
Q: Let's go back for a minute, to the Brown Jug Tavern. You said you had six beers. Were you at the bar or a table?
A: A table.
Q: Who served you?
A: Kathi. I don't know here last name. She's always there.
Q: Will you draw a diagram of the bar, indicating with a "B" where you were sitting?
A: Sure.
BY MS. MITCHELL: Attach this diagram as deposition exhibit two.
Q: Does this wall in the center of the Tavern go all the way to the ceiling?
A: No. It has railings like a fence. It's solid up to about five feet, and then has vertical slats of wood up to the ceiling.
Q: Can you see through it?
A: Sure. The slats are about two inches wide with about one inch of space between them. Of course, it gets pretty dark and smoky some nights.
Q: Did Kathi say anything to you about your drinking?
A: Nope.
Q: In your opinion, did you become intoxicated while you were at the Brown Jug?
A: Yeah, after about the fourth beer.
Q: Did you continue to drink after that?
A: Yeah, I ordered two more.
Q: Were you visibly intoxicated?
A: Probably -- I tend to get loud and rowdy.
Q: Why did you leave?
A: Kathi wouldn't serve me another beer. She said I was too drunk. I was

yelling at her to bring me another goddam beer. Then the bouncer came over and told me to pay up and get out. He followed me to the door and waited to make sure I left.

Q: Do you know this bouncer's name?
A: No. He doesn't work there anymore, either.
Q: Are you a regular patron of the Brown Jug?
A: Yep. I've been going there for years.
Q: Why go to a bar so far out of town?
A: Because they let you smoke. They're not under -- there's some city ordinance that you can't smoke in bars, but they're in the county.
Q: Do you think you were at fault in Helen Gallagher's death?
A: Yes. I was driving drunk and my reflexes were slow. It was those last couple of beers that put me over the limit.
Q: Were you arrested?
A: Yeah. They put me in jail overnight because I blew a .165 on the breathalyzer.
Q: Has the criminal case gone to trial?
A: No.
Q: Has your drivers license been suspended because of this incident?
A: Yes. It was suspended for one year but I have it back now.
Q: Did the police ask you to perform various field sobriety tests?
A: Yeah, walking a straight line and touching my nose, standing on one foot and looking at a penlight.
Q: How did you perform?
A: I don't remember.

MR. LERNER: I have no further questions.

WHEREUPON IT WAS STIPULATED THAT READING AND SIGNING BY THE WITNESS IS HEREBY WAIVED PURSUANT TO RULE 30(e).

Bradley deposition
Exhibit One

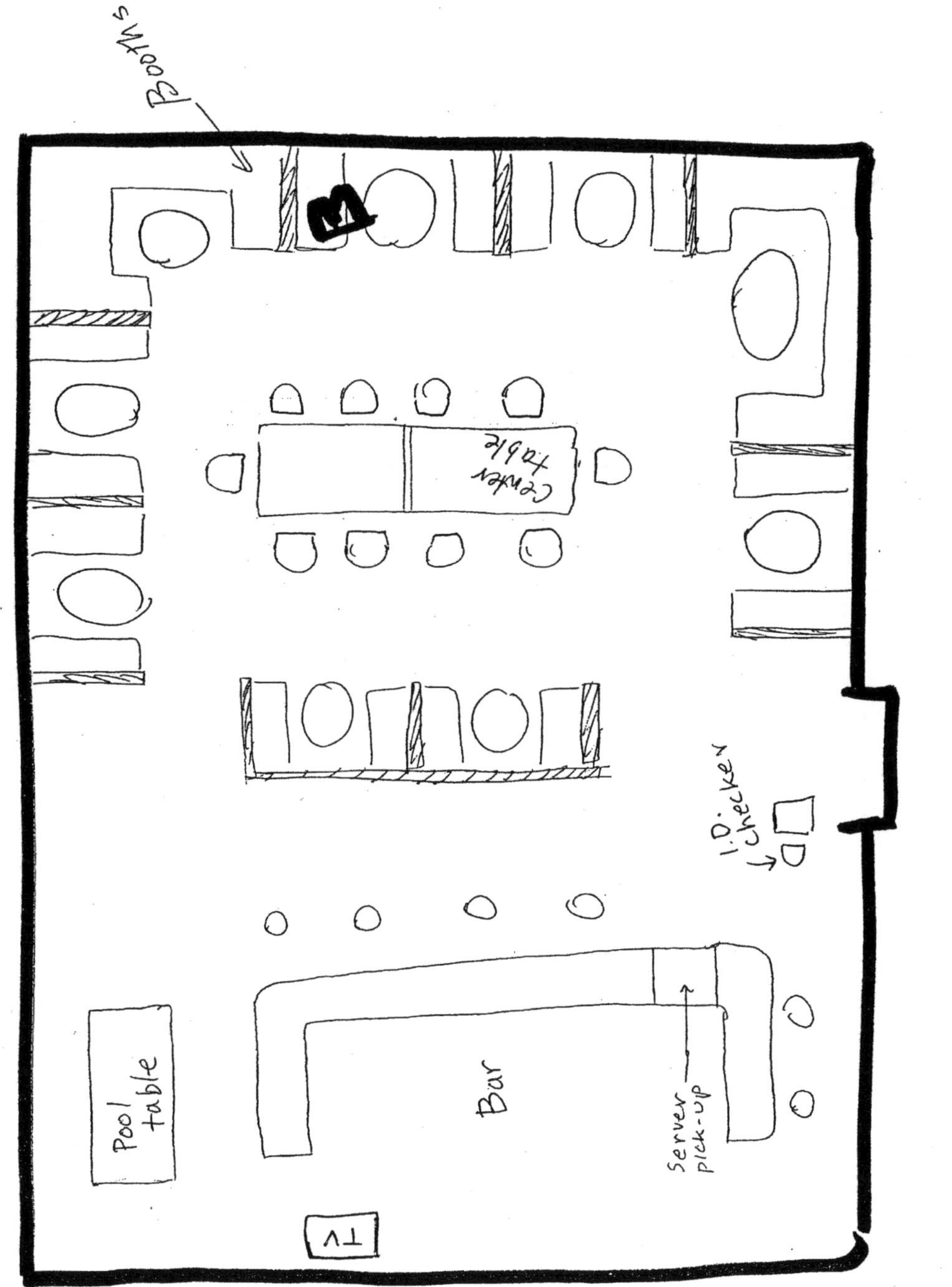

Bradley deposition Exhibit Two

STATE OF COLUMBIA
DEPARTMENT OF MOTOR VEHICLES

STATE OFFICE BUILDING
JEFFERSON CITY, COLUMBIA

DRIVING RECORD OF

BRADLEY, OSCAR T.
DL 276998660 EXP 07 14 +1
701 S WASHINGTON ST. BAYSHORE, COL

DATE OF ARREST	LOCATION	DMV CODE	DISPOSITION
08 15 -17 BAYSHORE PD	BAYSHORE, COL VIOL STOP SIGN	245	DISMISSED
10 09 -17 BAYSHORE PD	BAYSHORE, COL VIOL STOP SIGN	245	GUILTY
06 02 -14 COL STATE POL	BROWNSBURG, COL SPEEDING 65/55	110	GUILTY
12 18 -9 COL STATE POL	CHESTER, COL SPEEDING 70/55	112	GUILTY
07 15 -6 PENN STATE POL	PHILADELPHIA, PA SPEEDING 70/55	912	UNKNOWN
09 20 -5 BAYSHORE PD	BAYSHORE, COL DWI	501	GUILTY RECKLESS DR
05 09 -4 COL STATE POL	BAYSHORE, COL DWI	501	GUILTY
12 06 -3 MONROE CSD	BAYSHORE, COL DWI	501	GUILTY
11 09 -2 BAYSHORE PD	BAYSHORE, COL DWI	501	

THIS COPY OF THE RECORDS OF THE COLUMBIA DEPARTMENT OF MOTOR VEHICLES IS CERTIFIED AS AN ACCURATE COPY OF DEPARTMENT RECORDS.

DATE 1/6/Yr-0 SIGNED: Russell Carlberg

TITLE: Deputy Administrator

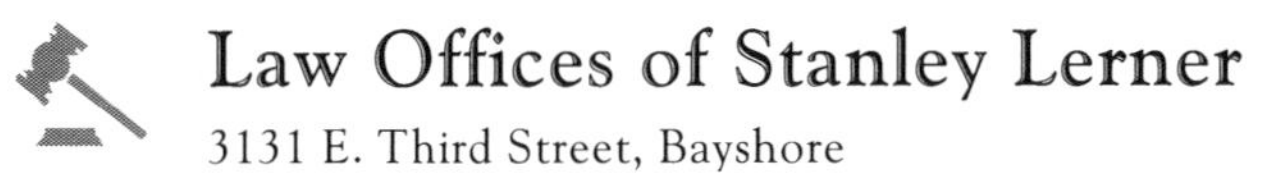
Law Offices of Stanley Lerner
3131 E. Third Street, Bayshore

Phone 811-JUSTICE
Your Attorneys in the College Mall

SETTLEMENT AGREEMENT AND RELEASE

David March, being the lawfully appointed administrator of the Estate of Helen Gallagher, having received sufficient and valuable consideration, does hereby release and waive all pending and future claims against Oscar Thomas Bradley and the Allstate Insurance Company as his liability insurance carrier, arising out of the accident of November 9, YR-2, in which Helen Gallagher was killed.

It is an integral part of this agreement that the terms of the settlement and the amount of the consideration shall not be disclosed.

Signed:

David March ______________________ Date: January 15, YR-0
David March
Administrator, Estate of Helen Gallagher

Oscar T. Bradley ______________________ Date: Jan. 15, YR-0
Oscar Thomas Bradley

Lynn F. Foltz ______________________ Date: Jan. 15, YR-0
Lynn F. Foltz
Allstate Insurance Company

DAVID MARCH)
)
vs)
)
BROWN JUG TAVERN)

DEPOSITION OF VIRGINIA WAGNER

DATE : May 6, YR-1
PLACE : Offices of Houston, Minnick & Dos Santos
100 N. Walnut Street
Bayshore, Columbia

TIME BEGAN : 2:20 p.m.

APPEARANCES : For the Plaintiff, appears Stanley Lerner, Esq.

For the Defendant, Lynda A. Mitchell, Esq.

STENOGRAPHER : Dodie Bowman

TRANSCRIBED : Dodie Bowman

WHEREUPON THE WITNESS VIRGINIA WAGNER WAS SWORN BY DODIE BOWMAN, NOTARY PUBLIC

EXAMINATION BY MS. MITCHELL

Q: State your name and address, please.
A: Virginia Wagner, 2505 Rock Creek Road, Bayshore.
Q: Are you employed?
A: Yes, I work part-time at Walgreen's, running a cash register.
Q: Are you married?
A: Divorced. I have two small children.
Q: Do they go to school?
A: No, they are too young.
Q: How old are you, Ms. Wagner.

A: 25 years old.
Q: Have you lived in Bayshore long?
A: All my life. I went to Bayshore High School.
Q: Did you go to college?
A: No.
Q: Ms. Wagner, were you in the company of Oscar Thomas Bradley on November 9, YR-2, from approximately 7:00 p.m. to midnight?
A: Is that the day the accident happened, Thursday?
Q: Yes. Were you with Mr. Bradley?
A: Yes.
Q: Tell us, please, in your own words, what happened that day.
A: Oscar came over about 7:00 and we had dinner together. He's my boyfriend. Then we went to the Brown Jug Tavern. We sat in one of the back booths and had several more beers. I think I had four and Oscar had six or seven, but I'm not sure. About 11:00, Oscar got pretty rowdy. Some friends of his were sitting in another booth across the room, and he started shouting to them. The waitress came over and told him twice to be quiet. Oscar said he'd be quiet if she would bring him another beer. She did.
Q: Was Oscar drunk at this time?
A: Yes.
Q: Visibly drunk?
A: Not falling down or anything, but definitely loud and rowdy and beginning to slur his words.
Q: Go on.
A: He drank his beer and started calling over to his friends again, and shouting "goddam" this and "goddam" that, and the bouncer came over and threw us out. We drove back into town. About 11:30, we got to Kirkwood and Washington Street. Oscar ran through a stop sign, just missed a car, turned left and hit a woman crossing the street. She was thrown up into the air and down the street, then landed on the ground in front of the SUV. She rolled over a few times and came to rest so that the truck almost completely covered her body. There was blood all over the road, and it was horrible. An ambulance came. They took her to the hospital, but she looked dead to me. They arrested Oscar for drunk driving and I drove the SUV home.
Q: Where were you when the SUV struck the woman? Tell us first whether

you knew her or recognized her.
A: No, I'd never seen her before that I know of. I read in the paper that her name was Helen Gallagher, but the name didn't mean anything to me.
Q: Where were you exactly at the moment of impact?
A: I was in the front passenger seat of Oscar's SUV. We had just turned south onto Washington Street into the left lane. We were a few feet from the curb and maybe 10 feet south of the crosswalk.
Q: Was anyone else around.
A: A couple of people.
Q: Do you know what the speed limits are on Washington and Kirkwood?
A: Yeah, I think it's thirty-five.
Q: Sorry to interrupt. Please describe exactly what you saw as Oscar made the turn onto Washington. Start before he turned.
A: I was looking down Kirkwood toward the intersection, just sort of watching the traffic. I saw a man cross the street from right to left, that is, going south toward the shoe store. Well, two cars crossed Kirkwood headed south. The second one almost hit us because Oscar ran the stop sign. He slowed down, and then started turning.
Q: Did you see Ms. Gallagher? Which way was Ms. Gallagher going?
A: From east to west across Washington. She was on my left.
Q: Can you describe her?
A: Sure, she was a young woman, wearing a blue jacket and dark slacks, light colored blouse, and red shoes. The jacket was buttoned because it was a bit a chilly that night. Oh, and the blouse had a bow on it, I think. I have a blouse like that which I wear a lot. Oh, and dark hair, but no coat.
Q: Glasses?
A: No, I don't think so.
Q: Was she carrying any purse or packages?
A: I don't remember anything but I can't be sure.
Q: Describe exactly how she crossed the street.
A: Well, she didn't cross it because she was hit by Oscar's SUV.
Q: Describe what you saw.
A: I first saw her standing on the corner by the bank talking on her cell phone. Then I looked away because that's when that car almost hit us. When I looked back, she was half way across Washington Street, right in the path of Oscar's SUV. She looked up at us, startled, and then ran down

Washington like she was trying to get out of the way. Then Oscar just ran her down. He must have been still looking at the car that almost hit us, which was in the right lane. He hit Ms. Gallagher and she flew up in the air and was thrown down the street, you know, towards the south. As I looked, she fell back down and landed on the street and rolled over a few times. I could feel that Oscar hit his brakes -- the rear end of the SUV rose up and I could hear the brakes shrieking. The SUV came to rest so that it just covered her body completely. You could only see her head.
Q: Was she still using her cell phone when she was crossing the street?
A: I don't know.
Q: Was she in the crosswalk before she started running down the street?
A: I think so, but I'm not sure, it all happened real fast.
Q: All right. What happened next?
A: A police car drove up, followed by an ambulance. They put the woman on a stretcher and she was taken to the hospital. Then they made Oscar walk a straight line and touch his fingers to his nose, and they took him downtown. They told me to come get him in the morning, so I went home.
Q: Did Oscar drink at your house before you went out?
A: Yes. He had a couple of beers. I'm not exactly sure how many. We both had a couple of beers.
Q: Was Oscar driving the whole time?
A: Yes.
Q: Did his driving scare you at all?
A: Not until we left the Brown Jug. That was a pretty wild ride back into town. He was all over the road. I thought we'd both be killed for sure. He had dropped the car keys about four times before he could even get the SUV started.
Q: Did he drink anything after he left the Brown Jug?
A: Yes. He opened a beer, drank about half of it, and then threw it out the window because it was warm.
Q: Had you been drinking?
A: Yeah. I'd probably had six beers that night. But I wasn't drunk.
Q: Which happened first, the impact or the sound of brakes?
A: I don't know. They happened about the same time.
Q: Do you know how fast Oscar was going?
A: No idea, but he didn't appear to be speeding, though.

Q: While you were at the scene of the accident, did you hear Ms. Gallagher say anything?
A: No, and she didn't look like she was in any condition to say anything. I thought she was dead.
Q: Did you hear Mr. Bradley say anything?
A: Yes. He kept repeating, "I never saw her, I never saw her, why did I have that last beer?"
Q: Are you and Mr. Bradley still dating?
A: Yes.
Q: Has the fact that he killed someone affected your relationship?
A: Look, it was a tragedy and all that, and Oscar was drunk, but it was still just an accident. I'm real sorry Mrs. Gallagher got killed, but it was night-time and Oscar was distracted by the other cars and stuff, and she stepped out in front of him. It was just an accident.
Q: That's all.

WHEREUPON IT WAS STIPULATED THAT READING AND SIGNING BY THE WITNESS IS HEREBY WAIVED PURSUANT TO RULE 30(e).

David March)
)
v.)
)
The Brown Jug Tavern)

DEPOSITION OF KATHI GENEVA JOHNSON

DATE	:	April 24, YR-2
PLACE	:	Law Office of Stanley Lerner 3131 East Third Street Bayshore, Columbia
TIME	:	1:15 p.m.
PRESENT	:	Stanley Lerner, attorney for plaintiff Lynda A. Mitchell, attorney for defendant Diana Watts, certified stenographic recorder

---

THE WITNESS WAS FIRST DULY SWORN BY DIANA WATTS, WHEREUPON THE FOLLOWING PROCEEDINGS WERE HAD:

Q: (By Mr. Lerner): State your name, address and occupation, please.
A: Kathi Geneva Johnson, 1033 Maxwell Lane, Bayshore. I am a waitress at the Brown Jug Tavern.
Q: Were you at work on November 9, YR-2?
A: On the advice of my lawyer, I refuse to answer any more questions because the answers might incriminate me.
Q: Lynda, is she going to assert the fifth to every question?
A (By Ms. Mitchell): Yes. If you'll agree to voluntarily terminate this deposition and not seek any further discovery from Ms. Johnson, we will supply you with a prepared statement; otherwise, you get nothing.
(By Mr. Lerner): Don't you have a conflict of interest? You represent the tavern.
(By Ms. Mitchell): Take it or leave it.
(By Mr. Lerner): Okay, we'll take it.

END OF DEPOSITION.

LAW OFFICES
HOUSTON, MINNICK & DOS SANTOS
A PROFESSIONAL CORPORATION

DONALD L. HOUSTON
MEGAN STONE MINNICK
ROBERTO X. DOS SANTOS*
LYNDA A. MITCHELL
BARRY J. GREENBERG
*Also admitted in Florida

100 NORTH WALNUT
BAYSHORE

(811) 520-2020
FAX (811) 520-3477

NORTHSIDE OFFICE
4755 NORTH COLLEGE
(811) 639-3333

STATEMENT OF KATHI GENEVA JOHNSON

My name is Kathi Geneva Johnson, 1033 Maxwell Lane, Bayshore, Columbia. My date of birth is March 3, Yr-29. I am a waitress employed at the Brown Jug Tavern.

This statement concerns the events of November 9, Yr-2, in Monroe County, Columbia, occurring during the evening hours at the Brown Jug Tavern, located at the corner of State Highway number 1 and Bryants Creek Road. The statement is being prepared on May 2, Yr-1, at the offices of Houston, Minnick and Dos Santos, with advice of counsel, Lynda A. Mitchell. Lynda A. Mitchell has explained to me that she represents Darlene McCormick, owner of the Brown Jug Tavern, and that this raises the possibility of a conflict of interest. She has suggested to me that I seek the advice of independent counsel before preparing this statement, but I have decided to waive the conflict of interest and proceed on her advice.

I was born and raised in Wichita Falls, Kansas. When I was eighteen, I moved to Los Angeles to try to become either an actor or a model. I lived there for four years, during which I worked as a tour guide at Universal Studios and as a waitress. When I realized I was not going to break into the movies, I decided to return to school. I applied to several state universities, and got in to the University of Columbia. I am going to school part time and working at the Brown Jug Tavern to support myself. I rent a small house on Maxwell Lane and have a roommate, Becky DeWitte, who is also a student. I am currently classified as a junior, majoring in English. I would like to be a school teacher when I finish.

I was hired to work at the Brown Jug Tavern in the spring of YR-4. I do not recall who hired and trained me. I remember that they wanted to know if I had experience waitressing at a place that served liquor, and I said that I had. The first couple of nights that I worked, they had me team up with an experienced server and work a busy night -- St. Patrick's Day, I believe. They showed me how to recognize the kind of fake drivers licenses carried by college students. They also told me not to serve obviously intoxicated patrons. If I had any questions about whether a patron was intoxicated, I was to consult either the bartender or one of the bouncers. I asked if we had to keep track of the precise numbers of drinks a customer had and if there was a set limit to the number of drinks I could serve, because we had done it that way at the Baked Potato where I worked at in North

Hollywood. I was told no, that the important question was whether the person was visibly intoxicated.

The Brown Jug is one large room divided by a half wall in the middle. The half wall is like a large picket fence. From the bar, you can see sort of half images of the booth area. But from the corner of the bar where servers pick up their drink orders, you have a clear view into the booth area. The lighting is dim, but there is enough to see by. People want a little atmosphere, but they have to be able to read the menus. Each booth has a 40-watt bulb light.

I was working the evening shift at the Brown Jug Tavern on November 9, Yr-2. It was a Thursday night, and was moderately busy. I don't specifically remember who else was working that night. There would have been a bartender, a bouncer to check ID's at the door, a second server and a cook and busboy back in the kitchen. I was assigned the booths; the other server had the bar and the center table, but we'd help each other out if it got busy. From 9:00 pm until 11:15 p.m., most of the booths were full, with little turnover. I cannot recall specifically what anyone had to eat or drink, because we do not let our customers run tabs. You bring them a drink and they pay for it on the spot.

I am acquainted with Oscar Bradley and his girlfriend Ginny. Oscar is a regular. He's probably in the Brown Jug five nights a week. He's asked me out a few times, but I have always refused. Frankly, I am not interested in dating a drunk auto mechanic. Oscar drinks quite a lot, mostly beer, but he's a pretty big guy and does not usually show much effect from the beer. I assume he is probably an alcoholic, and everyone knows that they can tolerate a high level of alcohol without becoming impaired.

On November 9, Yr-2, Oscar and Ginny were at the Brown Jug. I think they arrived about 9:00 pm, but I'm not sure. I judge time by when the bar fills up and when it begins to empty out. It's usually pretty full by 9:00 pm. Oscar and Ginny got the last empty booth. I served them several beers over the next few hours, but I don't know how many. Oscar may have had as many as seven or eight. They did not order any food. They were there until a little after 11:00, when they left.

At no time did Oscar Bradley appear visibly intoxicated to me. I would not have served him if he had. That's company policy. I remember that his eyes looked a little red and watery, but it can get pretty smoky in there. Oscar stayed seated the whole time as far as I remember. He didn't stumble or break anything, or start a fight or do anything that drunks do. He did get boisterous at one point, shouting back and forth to a friend of his who was playing pool. I said something jokingly to him about the shouting, and he said he was just shouting for better service. He's always kidding around like that. At about 11:15, he ordered another beer. I told him I thought he had had enough, and he said "Yeah, I guess it's time to go home. I've got more beer in the SUV anyway." He asked how much he owed, and I told him he had already paid me. Then he and Ginny left, and I heard Ginny ask him if he wanted her to drive, and he said no, he thought he could make it home. I watched them walk out and thought Oscar looked a little wobbly, but not real drunk. I've seen lots of guys in worse shape leave here and drive home.

Oscar Bradley has not been back to the Brown Jug much since the accident. I guess killing that woman must have shaken him up, so that he is drinking less.

I have read the foregoing statement carefully, and it is true and accurate to the best of my recollection.

Kathi G. Johnson

Kathi G. Johnson

STATEMENT OF WITNESS
KAREN TUCKER

My name is Karen Tucker. I live at 4626 Sunset Avenue, Apartment 15, Bayshore. I live with my daughter, Sally. I am 27 years old and divorced. I work from 7:30 a.m. to 4:30 p.m. at Crescent Donuts on South Walnut Street. I grew up here in Bayshore.

On Thursday, November 9, YR-2, I left work a little after four o'clock, and went to pick Sally up at the Southside day care center on Rogers Street. I dropped her off with my ex-husband who was taking her to visit her grandmother, so I had the whole weekend free. My ex-husband's name is Jason Tucker. He works for U-Haul as some kind of manager.

Thursday night, I went to Rocky's with two of my girlfriends, Erica Goodman and Donna May. We've known each other since high school. We had a few drinks and did some serious dancing. It's a great club for dancing. About 11:30 p.m. we left. Rocky's is on the corner of Fourth and Walnut Streets. We walked up to Kirkwood, and then east toward the Olde English Pub for a nightcap. We were on the south side of Kirkwood. We had just crossed Washington Street and gone about a half-block, when I realized I'd left my coat at Rocky's.

I told Erica and Donna I would meet them at the Pub, turned around and headed back. They walked on ahead. When I turned around, I was next to the Federal Savings Bank. It was just 11:35. I'm certain of the time because I looked at the time and temperature sign outside Federal Savings Bank. As I turned around, I saw Oscar Bradley in a SUV across the street. He was stopped at the stop sign on Kirkwood, waiting to turn left. His left turn signal was on. I recognized him because he was an auto mechanic who had done some work on our car before my husband and I got divorced. I think it was in September, YR-8. There was other traffic, but I didn't pay a lot of attention to it. A car drove through the intersection on Kirkwood, going west to east, and then Mr. Bradley turned left. There was nothing usual about his driving. His SUV passed in front of me. I had gone about two steps at this point, and was pretty much right in front of the bank about 50 feet from the intersection.

I did not see the actual accident because my view was blocked by the corner of the bank building. However, I am sure of two things. Ms. Gallagher was not in the crosswalk or anywhere near it, because I was looking right at because I was about to cross it myself. Also, Mr. Bradley was not speeding. He was going maybe fifteen miles per hour. There was plenty of light at the corner. He was driving carefully and looked like he was in control of his SUV. how sure?

I was on the south side of Kirkwood, in front of the bank. I looked north and saw the SUV as I was walking toward Washington Street. The SUV turned left and drove south on Washington. I was looking at the intersection to see if any cars were coming. Then I looked straight ahead across the empty crosswalk. The SUV had just disappeared out of my so my view was blocked by the corner of the bank building. At this time I heard a thump and a screech of tires that must have been Mr. Bradley hitting Ms. Gallagher.

I heard a scream and jumped forward a few steps. I saw Ms. Gallagher's purse fly into the air, and the back end of the SUV Mr. Bradley was driving screech to a stop. I do not remember seeing Ms. Gallagher's body at that time, but it may already have been under the SUV. I immediately ran over to the accident. Ms. Gallagher was lying partly under the SUV, and Mr. Bradley was trying to help her. He was obviously upset, and was saying she had stepped right out into his path, that he never saw her until it was too late. He said a couple of times that he should not have kept drinking after he left the bar. The comment was odd, because he did not seem drunk to me, but I was paying more attention to Ms. Gallagher.

I waited until the police officer arrived a few minutes later, and told him what I had seen. While we were talking an ambulance arrived and took her to the hospital. After I talked to the policeman, I went back to Rocky's and got my coat. Then I went to the Pub to join my friends.

I had never seen Miss Gallagher before, as far as I know. When I was at the scene, she appeared to be unconscious the whole time. I never heard her say anything.

December 6, YR-2 *Karen Tucker*

Karen Tucker

Statement taken by Griff Parry, investigator for Boston Casualty Insurance Company, at 4626 Sunset Avenue, Apartment 15, Bayshore, Columbia, on December 5, YR-2. Read and signed by witness on December 6, YR-2.

DAVID MARCH)
)
vs)
)
BROWN JUG TAVERN)

DEPOSITION OF DAVID MARCH

DATE : May 6, YR-1

PLACE : Offices of Houston, Minnick & Dos Santos
100 North Walnut Street
Bayshore, Columbia

TIME BEGAN : 1:00 p.m.
APPEARANCES : For the Plaintiff, appears Stanley Lerner, Esq.
For the Defendant, appears Lynda A. Mitchell, Esq.

STENOGRAPHER: Dodie Bowman

TRANSCRIBED : Dodie Bowman

WHEREUPON THE WITNESS DAVID MARCH WAS SWORN BY DODIE BOWMAN, NOTARY PUBLIC

EXAMINATION BY MS. MITCHELL

Q: State your name and address.
A: David March, 1012 South Mitchell Street.
Q: Are you employed?
A: I am an associate professor of business economics at the University of Columbia.
Q: Are you married?
A: No.
Q: How old are you?
A: 32.
Q: Where did you go to school?

A: Harvard undergraduate and Michigan graduate school. I have an M.B.A. and a Masters in economics, both from Michigan.
Q: What was the nature of your relationship to Helen Gallagher?
A: She was my life partner. She was a graduate student at the university. We had lived together for three years before she died.
Q: Not married?
A: No.
Q: Any children?
A: No.
Q: All right. Tell me what you know about the accident on November 9, YR-2, in which Ms. Gallagher was killed.
A: Not much. Helen was going out with some graduate student friends.
Q: Do you know where she would have gone?
A: No.
Q: Do you know why she was in the middle of Washington Street at 11:30 p.m.?
A: No.
Q: Did she have a history of mental problems?
A: No.
Q: Later that evening, did the police call to tell you she had been taken to the hospital?
A: Yes. She was in intensive care. I rushed over to Monroe County Hospital.
Q: Did you talk to Officer Adams there?
A: I don't really remember. I know he was there, but I don't remember if I talked to him. I was pretty upset.
Q: What happened at the hospital?
A: They let me in to see Helen for a few minutes.
Q: Was she conscious?
A: Yes, for a little while anyway.
Q: Did she say anything to you?
A: Yes.
Q: Please tell me everything you recall.
A: I held her hand and asked her how she felt. She said she was numb. I asked her what happened. She said a van had run the stop sign, that she had tried to get out of the way but had slipped. The rest was personal.
Q: Did she say where she had been when she was hit?

A: No. She just said she was crossing the street.
Q: I'm sorry, but I'll have to ask what else she said to you.
A: I tried to be brave and told her she would be all right. She shook her head and said that she knew how badly she was hurt. She said she was sorry that she hadn't been more careful, because now we were going to be robbed of a life together. Then she closed her eyes and the nurse asked me to leave. She never regained consciousness.
Q: What time was this?
A: I don't know.
Q: What happened next?
A: I cancelled my Friday classes, and pretty much stayed at the hospital until she died on Sunday.
Q: Did you receive a bill from the hospital?
A: Yes.
Q: Yes. Is this bill the only one?
A: Yes.
Q: It indicates that $12,876 was paid by insurance, and $3219 is due?
A: Yes.
Q: How did you arrive at the figure of $3.3 million for Gallagher's lost earnings? Helen was not working.
A: She was a year away from her Ph.D. in economics. She planned to teach in a university. Here at the University of Columbia, average salaries in the economics department are around $95,000 a year. She would have started at age 29 or 30, giving her about forty years of employment to age 70. That's about $3,800,000. Most universities also provide about 15-20% fringe benefits and retirement, so I added another $700,000. If it costs about $30,000 a year for food, clothing, and shelter, you have to reduce the total value to the estate by $1.2 million. That leaves around $3.3 million lost to her estate.
Q: She did not have a job offer, did she?
A: No.
Q: Aren't jobs in universities hard to get?
A: Not in business and economics. Besides, she was one of the best graduate students in the department.
Q: You're not in the economics department are you?
A: No, the business school.

Q: You said $95,000 was the average salary. That's not a starting salary, is it?
A: No. Starting salaries are around 50,000. But senior salaries can be $150,000 or more, so it averages out. That's what an average is.
Q: Who was the beneficiary in Ms. Gallagher's will?
A: I was. I am.
Q: So you will inherit everything that ends up in Gallagher's estate?
A: Yes.
Q: Oh, one more quick item. Can you explain the statement she made that said "Dave always told me my carelessness would get me killed"?
A: She didn't say that to me, but she was probably referring to the fact that she was a little absent-minded. I used to kid her about not paying attention to stoplights and things like that, mostly when she was driving.
Q: What about when she was walking?
A: Well, she'd get absorbed in discussions about her work sometimes and not pay attention. One time she walked into a mailbox when we were in the midst of an argument about the proper way to calculate inflation for cost-of-living increases.
Q: Did Helen call you on her cell phone the night of the ninth?
A: Yes, around 11:30. She called to say she would be home in half an hour.
Q: What is her cell phone number?
A: 811-325-7373.
Q: What is your home phone? I assume she called you at home?
A: Yes. It's 811-269-4602.
Q: Anything else you wish to say?
A: No.
Q: No further questions.

WHEREUPON IT WAS STIPULATED THAT READING AND SIGNING BY THE WITNESS IS HEREBY WAIVED PURSUANT TO RULE 30(e).

✥ Monroe County Hospital

STATEMENT

PATIENT'S NAME AND ADDRESS
HELEN S GALLAGHER
1012 S MITCHELL ST
BAYSHORE COLUMBIA

ACCOUNT NUMBER
56 10294 D

INSURANCE INFORMATION
ANTHEM 5108883266

DATE ADMITTED
11/09/YR-2

DATE DISCHARGED
11/13/YR-2

POSTING DATE	PHYSICIAN	DESCRIPTION	TOTAL CHARGES
11 09		AMBULANCE SERVICE	235.00
11 09		ICU DAILY CHARGE	1320.00
11 09	LESTER	RADIOLOGICAL SERVICES	380.00
11 09		WHOLE BLOOD UNITS	410.00
11 10		ICU DAILY CHARGE	1320.00
11 10	STEPANOVICH	SURGERY	4000.00
11 10		OPERATING ROOM CHARGE	4070.00
11 11		ICU DAILY CHARGE	1320.00
11 12		ICU DAILY CHARGE	1320.00
11 13		ICU DAILY CHARGE	1320.00
11 13	STEPANOVICH	ICU HOSP VISITS	400.00
12 08		INS PAYMENT	12,876.00 CREDIT
		BALANCE DUE	3219.00

COPY 1
FOR STATE VITAL RECORDS

REGISTRATION DISTRICT NO. 5 LOCAL NO. 53

DIVISION OF HEALTH SERVICES - VITAL RECORDS BRANCH

MEDICAL EXAMINER'S CERTIFICATE OF DEATH

DECEASED

1. NAME OF DECEASED — FIRST: Helen — MIDDLE: Susan — LAST: Gallagher
2. DATE OF DEATH (MONTH, DAY, YEAR): 11/13/YR-2
3. SEX: F
4. COLOR or RACE: Wh
5. STATE OF BIRTH (IF NOT IS U.S.A. NAME COUNTRY): Wisconsin
6. DATE OF BIRTH: 4/23/YR-31
7. AGE (IN YEARS LAST BIRTHDAY): 28 — IF UNDER 1 YEAR: MONTHS / DAYS — IF UNDER 24 HOURS: HOURS / MIN.

8a. PLACE OF DEATH COUNTY: Monroe
8b. CITY OR TOWN: Bayshore
8c. NAME OF HOSPITAL OR INSTITUTION (IF NOT IN EITHER, GIVE STREET AND NUMBER): Monroe County Hospital
8d. INSIDE CITY LIMITS (SPECIFY YES OR NO): Yes

USUAL RESIDENCE (WHERE DECEASED LIVED)
9a. STATE: Columbia
9b. COUNTY: Monroe
9c. CITY OR TOWN: Bayshore
9d. STREET ADDRESS OR R.F.D. NO.: 1012 S. Mitchell Street
9e. INSIDE CITY LIMITS (SPECIFY YES OR NO): Yes

10. MARRIED, NEVER MARRIED, WIDOWED, DIVORCED (SPECIFY): Never married
11. SURVIVING SPOUSE (IF WIFE, GIVE MAIDEN NAME): na
12. CITIZEN OF WHAT COUNTRY?: USA
13. SOCIAL SECURITY NUMBER: unk.
14a. USUAL OCCUPATION (KIND OF WORK DONE DURING MOST OF WORKING LIFE, EVEN IF RETIRED): student
14b. KIND OF BUSINESS OR INDUSTRY:
15. FATHER'S NAME: Jason Gallagher
16. MOTHER'S MAIDEN NAME: unk.
17a. INFORMANT'S NAME AND ADDRESS: David March, 1012 S. Mitchell Street, Bayshore
17b. RELATION TO DECEASED: lives with

CAUSE

PART 1. DEATH CAUSED BY: ENTER ONLY ONE CAUSE PER LINE FOR (A), (B), (C) — APPROXIMATE INTERVAL BETWEEN ONSET AND DEATH

18. CONDITIONS, IF ANY, WHICH GAVE RISE TO IMMEDIATE CAUSE (a), STATING THE UNDERLYING CAUSE LAST

(a) IMMEDIATE CAUSE: Shock due to loss of blood

(b) DUE TO, OR AS A CONSEQUENCE OF: Traffic accident — 4 days

(c) DUE TO, OR AS A CONSEQUENCE OF:

PART II. OTHER SIGNIFICANT CONDITIONS CONTRIBUTING TO DEATH BUT NOT RELATED TO CAUSE GIVEN IN PART I (a)

19a. Multiple internal injuries

19b. AUTOPSY (SPECIFY) YES OR NO: No — M.E. OR OTHER

19c. IF YES WERE FINDINGS CONSIDERED IN DETERMINING CAUSE OF DEATH:

20a. ACCIDENT, SUICIDE, HOMICIDE, UNDETERMINED, NATURAL CAUSES, OR PENDING (SPECIFY): Accident

20b. DESCRIBE HOW INJURY OCCURED (ENTER NATURE OF INJURY IN PART I OR PART II): Deceased struck by van while crossing street

20c. TIME OF INJURY — MONTH: Nov. DAY: 9 YEAR: -2 HOUR: 4:50p

20d. INJURY AT WORK (SPECIFY YES OR NO): no

20e. PLACE OF INJURY AT HOME, FARM, STREET, FACTORY, OFFICE BLDG., ETC. (SPECIFY): street near corner

20f. CITY OR R.F.D.: Bayshore — COUNTY: Monroe — STATE: Col.

CERTIFIER

MEDICAL EXAMINER CERTIFICATION: ON THE BASIS OF THE EXAMINATION OF THE BODY AND/OR THE INVESTIGATION, IN MY OPINION, DEATH OCCURRED ON THE DATE AND DUE TO THE CAUSE(S) STATED.

21a. DEATH OCCURRED (HOUR): 5:00 p M

21b. THE DECEDENT WAS PRONOUNCED DEAD — MONTH: 11 DAY: 13 YEAR: -2 HOUR: 5:15 p M

21c. DATE SIGNED (MONTH, DAY, YEAR): 11/13/YR-2

22a. SIGNATURE:

22b. ADDRESS: Municipal building

22c. MEDICAL EXAMINER OF (SPECIFY COUNTY): Monroe

BURIAL

23a. BURIAL, CREMATION, OTHER (SPECIFY): Cremation
23b. DATE:
23c. NAME OF CEMETERY OR CREMATORY: Valhala
23d. LOCATION (CITY, TOWN, OR COUNTY): Bayshore — (STATE) Col.

24. FUNERAL HOME — NAME / ADDRESS: Allen Funeral Home, Third St., Bayshore
25. SIGNATURE OF FUNERAL DIRECTOR: [signature] — LICENSE NO. 12041
26. DATE REC'D BY LOCAL REG.: 11-15-yr-2
27. SIGNATURE OF REGISTRAR: [signature]
28. SIGNATURE OF EMBALMER (IF EMBALMED): — LICENSE NO.

MEDICAL EXAMINER: After you have initiated the Certificate of Death, give copies 1 & 3 to funeral director when body is released, and route copy 2 to Chief Medical Examiner. If cause of death is pending, file Supplemental Report of Cause of Death (Form VS 8A) when the additional information has been obtained.
FUNERAL DIRECTOR: Copy 1 must be completed and filed with the Local Registrar within 5 days after Death. Copy 3, when signed by the medical examiner is your authorization for final disposition.

DHS FORM 2164
REV. 1/75

Paul Swain Investigations

809 W 6th Street, Bayshore, Columbia

(811) 332-8544 sherlockswain@zipper.net

RE: MARCH V. BROWN JUG TAVERN
FROM: PAUL SWAIN
SUBJECT: Results of Investigation

As a result of investigation, the following information has come to light:

(1) Karen Tucker has two bad check convictions. She pleaded guilty to a violation of §224.5 on January 15, YR-5; and to a second charge on May 6, YR-5. In both cases she was fined $50 and agreed to pay off the checks. There is a note in the court file on both cases that she admitted knowing she had insufficient funds when she wrote the checks. The January conviction was for $25.86 check to Kroger's Grocery Store; the June conviction was for $88.45 check to Tom Cherry Mufflers. Certified copies attached.

(2) Karen Tucker was divorced on the grounds of adultery (hers) on December 5, YR-6. Apparently Mr. Tucker claimed that he was not the father of a child, Sally, born in June, YR-7. Ms. Tucker got custody of the child.

(3) Virginia Wagner was convicted of felonious battery, §211.1 on November 5, YR-3. The complaint charges that she wounded a man named David Warren with a handgun. I could not track down Warren, but the arresting officer says that Wagner claimed Warren was trespassing and trying to break into the house when she was home alone. Warren was an old boyfriend and was acquitted of trespassing. The judge suspended sentence. Certified copy attached.

(4) The Brown Jug Tavern previously received a warning from the Columbia Alcoholic Beverages Control Commission for serving alcohol to intoxicated patrons. A copy is attached.

(5) I obtained a copy of Helen Gallagher's cell phone record for November, YR-2. It is attached.

THE STATE OF COLUMBIA
THE ALCOHOLIC BEVERAGES CONTROL COMMISSION
300 CENTER STREET
JEFFERSON CITY, COLUMBIA

William A. Samuel
Commissioner

Tel (811) 722-5400

September 5, Yr-2

Ms. Darlene McCormick
ABC Unrestricted License No. 7465
The Brown Jug Tavern
P.O. Box 3535
Bayshore, Columbia

Dear Licensee:

The Commission has received notice from the Attorney General's Office that during the six month period January 1 to June 30, Yr-2, four adults and one minor who were arrested for Driving While Impaired have stated that they were last served alcoholic beverages at your establishment prior to their violation of the drunk driving laws.

The commission notes that your business has been cited a total of 15 times since we began keeping records in YR-5. We are placing you on notice that if further reports are forwarded, we will conduct an independent investigation of your premises to determine whether you are serving intoxicated persons in violation of Columbia Code § 7-5-15. Such investigation could lead to a hearing to suspend or revoke your license.

Sincerely,

ALCOHOLIC BEVERAGES CONTROL COMMISSION

By: ______________________________________

William A. Samuel

WAS/pmg

CERTIFIED TRUE AND ACCURATE COPY
ALCOHOLIC BEVERAGES COMMISSION
STATE OF COLUMBIA

Date: Dec. 12, YR-1
By: David K. Cox
Title: Deputy Clerk

OFFICIAL DOCUMENT

Monroe County Circuit Court
Criminal Division
State of Columbia

CERTIFICATE OF DISPOSITION

Court Number: 1590-CR-03

Judge: Beatty

Case: State v. Karen Tucker

Original Offense(s): 222.5 Bad check under $500

Disposition: 222.5 Bad check under $500

Guilty Plea: January 15, Yr-5

Trial:

Appeal:

Final Judgment Entered: $50, costs and restitution

Date: January 15, Yr-5

I hereby certify that this is a true excerpt from the records of the Monroe County Circuit Court, Criminal Division, State of Columbia.

Camille Johnson, Clerk of the Circuit Court

By: *Robert Hamilton*, Deputy Clerk

Date: *January 29, YR-0*

Monroe County Circuit Court
Criminal Division
State of Columbia

CERTIFICATE OF DISPOSITION

Court Number: 1185-CR-05

Judge: Guthrie

Case: State v. Karen Tucker

Original Offense(s): 222.5 Bad check under $500

Disposition: 222.5 Bad check under $500

Guilty Plea: June 6, Yr-5

Trial:

Appeal:

Final Judgment Entered: Fine $50, costs and restitution

Date: June 6, YR-5

I hereby certify that this is a true excerpt from the records of the Monroe County Circuit Court, Criminal Division, State of Columbia.

Camille Johnson, Clerk of the Circuit Court

By: *Robert Hamilton*, Deputy Clerk

Date: *January 29, YR-0*

Monroe County Circuit Court
Criminal Division
State of Columbia

CERTIFICATE OF DISPOSITION

Court Number: 31011-CR-13

Judge: Diekhoff

Case: State v. Virginia Wagner

Original Offense(s): 211.1 Felony assault

Disposition: 211.2 Misd assault

Guilty Plea:

Trial: November 7, YR-3

Appeal: No

Final Judgment Entered: Probation 1 year and costs

Date: December 5, YR-3

I hereby certify that this is a true excerpt from the records of the Monroe County Circuit Court, Criminal Division, State of Columbia.

Camille Johnson, Clerk of the Circuit Court

By: *Robert Hamilton*, Deputy Clerk

Date: *January 29, YR-0*

Call Detail November Yr-2 811-325-7373

User Name : HELEN GALLAGHER

Rate Code: RM70=Rollover FM 700, ESM1=Unlimited Expd M2M, UNW9=Unlimited N&W
Rate Period (PD): DT=Daytime, NW=Nwknd
Feature: M2MC=Expanded Mobile To Mobile, VM=VoiceMail

Item	Day	Date	Time	Number Called	Min	Rate Code	Rate Pd	Feature
41	MON	11/06	11:18AM	717-507-8896	7	RM70	DT	
42	MON	11/06	2:28PM	316-269-4603	2	RM70	DT	
43	TUE	11/07	10:07AM	316-269-4607	7	RM70	DT	
44	TUE	11/07	10:47AM	316-269-4607	12	RM70	DT	
45	TUE	11/07	11:03AM	316-269-4603	2	RM70	DT	
46	TUE	11/07	11:28AM	316-269-4603	1	RM70	DT	
47	TUE	11/07	3:14PM	811-369-0134	8	ESM1	DT	M2MC
48	WED	11/08	3:16PM	316-269-4607	3	RM70	DT	
49	WED	11/08	3:29PM	316-269-4607	2	RM70	DT	
50	WED	11/08	4:12PM	811-855-7360	1	RM70	DT	
51	THU	11/09	7:19PM	811-361-8862	2	ESM1	DT	M2MC
52	THU	11/09	11:34PM	811-269-4602	1	RM70	NW	

UNIVERSITY OF COLUMBIA
DEPARTMENT OF ECONOMICS
Maxwell Hall 300
Bayshore, Columbia
811-855-2301

REPORT OF JANE S. MOORE, Ph.D.

Associate Professor
Department of Economics
University of Columbia

I am an associate professor with tenure in the economics department at the University of Columbia. I have a Ph.D. in economics from U.C.L.A., and I specialize in the areas of personal and family income and investments. I have written a basic textbook and published half a dozen articles. I have been asked by David March, a colleague in the business school, to calculate the present value to the estate of lost future earnings for an academic economist who would have worked for forty years. I calculate it to be $996,636.

The hypothetical economist probably would earn $7,384,144 in nominal dollars over the next forty-year period.

Current salaries for entry level assistant professors in economics departments range from $40,000 to $60,000 with a mean of $47,800. Average salaries for tenured professors range from $54,000 to $85,000 with a mean of $70,180. Final salaries the year before retirement range from $70,000 to $170,000 with a mean of $106,120. Contributions to retirement plans by universities range from 7.6% to 15.0% of salary, with a mean of 9.0%.

The worse case scenario is that the hypothetical economist would start with compensation worth $43,040 ($40,000 salary plus 7.6% retirement contribution), average $59,180 ($55,000 plus 7.6%) and retire at $75,320 ($70,000 plus 7.6%). Under this scenario, he or she would average $43,040 for the first six years (untenured) and $59,190 for the next thirty-four years, for a total lifetime income in YR-O dollars of $258,240 plus $2,012,460, which equals $2,270,700.

The best case scenario, assuming a $60,000 starting salary, $85,000 average, $170,000 final, and 15% retirement, yields a total lifetime income in YR-O dollars of $3,737,500.

The most likely scenario, using average compensation figures, yields a total lifetime income in YR-O dollars of $2,913,483. Our hypothetical professor would earn $47,800 plus 9% retirement contribution to start, which amount would not increase in real dollars until tenure six years later. After tenure, he or she would receive an average of $70,180 plus 9% retirement. In his or her final year, he or she would receive $106,120 plus 9%.

However, this figure must be corrected for inflation. Over the last forty years, inflation as calculated by the Consumer Price Index has averaged 5.0%, so salaries could be expected to increase in nominal terms by 5.0% a year. That would make the total lifetime compensation amounts of $6,857,496 (worst case), $11,287,220 (best case) and $8,798,695 (average case).

According to the Federal Bureau of Labor Statistics, for two-income two-person families employing domestic help, each wage earner expends an average of 66% of their income on taxes, joint housing expenses, and personal consumption, and has 34% of his or her income for gifts, savings, and investments. Thus, the net loss to the person's estate is actually 34% of his or her lifetime income, or $2,991,556 (average case).

This amount must be reduced to present value. This can be calculated by assuming that a lump-sum award is invested in a low-risk account, that an amount equal to 34% of the deceased's predicted income is withdrawn each year, and the balance is reinvested. At the end of the fortieth year, the account should contain exactly enough to withdraw the amount for that year leaving a balance of zero. Historically, low-risk investment could be expected to return about two percent more than inflation. Thus, since I used a five percent inflation rate, I would calculate the discount rate expecting the investment to yield a seven percent return.

Over forty years, the amount withdrawn each year adjusted for inflation would average $74,789 ($2,991,556 ÷ 40). Using a standard present value table, it would require a lump sum of $996,636 ($74,789 x 13.33) to compensate the estate for the loss of the deceased's income.

Jane S. Moore

Dr. Jane S. Moore

01/15/YR-0

SELECTED COLUMBIA PATTERN JURY INSTRUCTIONS

Preliminary Instructions

Members of the jury. This is a civil lawsuit brought on behalf of Helen Gallagher against the Brown Jug Tavern. It is based on a statute that prohibits commercial servers of alcoholic beverages from giving additional alcohol to visibly intoxicated patrons, and makes them liable for the subsequent conduct of those patrons if they violate this provision. Plaintiff alleges that the Tavern served alcohol to a visibily intoxicated Oscar Bradley whose SUV later struck and killed Helen Gallagher. Defendants allege that Bradley did not become visibily intoxicated until after he left the Tavern, and that Helen Gallagher was contributorily negligent in her own death.

Your function in this case is to decide, after considering all the evidence presented, what happened -- what the facts are -- and you are to apply the facts you find to the instructions of law I give you. You should use your common sense in considering the evidence, and you may draw reasonable inferences from the evidence.

My function as Judge is to preside over the trial: to rule on points of law and to instruct you on the law. It is our responsibility to see that this case is decided in accord with the facts and the law.

To begin the case the lawyers will make opening statements in which they tell you what they expect the evidence to be. This should help you to understand the evidence as it is presented through the witnesses later and make you aware of conflicts and differences that may arise in the testimony. After opening statements, you will hear and see the evidence. The witnesses are first examined by the lawyer who calls them and may then be cross-examined by the lawyer for the other side. There may be objections, and you must not consider any evidence that is stricken or that you are told to disregard. After all the evidence has been presented, the lawyers make their closing arguments.

There will be occasional recesses during the trial. During these recesses you must not discuss the case with anyone, not even your friends. Nor may you look things up on the Internet. Please keep your cell phones turned off.

Please keep an open mind as the evidence is presented. Remember that your job is to reach your verdict only after you have heard and considered all the evidence, the instructions of law, and the final arguments of the lawyers

All people in this trial are fictional, and the events take place in an imaginary city called Bayshore, in the state of Columbia.

Concluding Instructions and Charge to the Jury

Members of the Jury:

It is now my duty as judge to instruct you in the law that applies to this case. It is your duty as jurors to follow these instructions and to apply the rules of law to the facts as you find them from the evidence.

Your job is to determine the facts and decide what happened. The only evidence you may consider is the evidence that was properly admitted at trial in the form of the testimony of the witnesses, the exhibits, and any facts admitted or agreed to by counsel. Statements, arguments and opinions of counsel are not evidence in the case. You must disregard any evidence to which an objection was sustained by the court and any evidence ordered stricken by the court. You may not consider anything you read in the paper or hear from your friends about this case, nor may you do your own investigation or look anything up on the Internet.

Although you are to consider only the evidence in the case in reaching a verdict, you must bring to the consideration of the evidence your everyday common sense and judgment as reasonable men and women. Thus, you are not limited solely to what you see and hear as the witnesses testify. You may draw reasonable inferences from the evidence which you feel are justified in the light of common experience, keeping in mind that such inferences should not be based on speculation or guess.

A verdict may never be influenced by sympathy, prejudice or public opinion. Your decision should be the product of sincere judgment and sound discretion in accordance with these rules of law.

The plaintiff has the burden to prove that Helen Gallagher died, that the defendant knowingly served liquor to an already intoxicated patron, and that such act was a proximate cause of the death of Helen Gallagher.

The defendant has the burden of proving, as an affirmative defense, that some contributory negligence on the part of Helen Gallagher was a proximate cause of her death.

In a civil case, whenever a party must prove something, they must prove it is true by a preponderance of the evidence. The term "preponderance of the evidence" means such evidence as, when weighed with that opposed to it, has more convincing force, and from which it appears that the greater probability of truth lies therein.

A proximate cause of injury is a cause which, in natural and continuous sequence, is a significant factor in producing the injury, and without which the injury would not have occurred.

The plaintiff, David March, seeks to establish that the Brown Jug Tavern violated the law that holds commercial servers of alcoholic beverages responsible for the actions of its intoxicated patrons. To prove his case, the plaintiff must prove the following propositions by a preponderance of the evidence:

1. A patron or guest on the defendant's premises was served intoxicating liquor;
2. The person was intoxicated when served;
3. The defendant knew or under the circumstances reasonably should have known that the person was intoxicated;
4. That patron or guest, while intoxicated, operated a motor vehicle;
5. The operation of a motor vehicle by the impaired person was reasonably foreseeable by the defendant; and
6. The operation of the automobile by the intoxicated person caused the plaintiff's death or injury within the scope of the foreseeable risk.

If you find for the plaintiff on the question of liability, you then must determine the amount of money which will fairly compensate for those damages which were proved by the evidence. You may consider:

1. The value of lost earnings and loss of earning capacity, considering the age, health and life expectancy of the deceased;
2. The reasonable expenses of medical care; and
3. The reasonable value of any pain and suffering experienced by the deceased before her death.

In calculating reasonable damages for future lost earnings, you may take into account the effects of inflation and you may assume that plaintiff will invest the lump sum you award so that normal interest dividends will accrue. Bear in mind that you are to award damages for future earnings that have been lost by Helen Gallagher's estate. David March is here only as Helen Gallagher's representative. He does not seek to recover any money that he personally has lost because of Gallagher's death.

The defendant Brown Jug Tavern seeks to establish that Helen Gallagher was contributorily negligent. To prove its case, the defendant must prove the following propositions by a preponderance of the evidence:

1. Helen Gallagher was contributorily negligent by failing to exercise ordinary care in crossing the street; and
2. Her own actions were a proximate cause of her death.

If you find that Helen Gallagher was contributorily negligent, you should reduce the damage award by an amount commensurate with her portion of responsibility for the accident.

It is now your turn to retire to the jury room to start your deliberations. Your verdict must be unanimous.

In the Circuit Court of Monroe County
State of Columbia

David C. March,	)	
Plaintiff	)	Civil Number 42449
	)	
vs.	)	**VERDICT**
	)	
The Brown Jug Tavern,	)	
Defendant	)	

We the jurors of Monroe County find as follows:

1. Was the defendant liable? Yes ___ No ___

2. If so, what are the total damages? ________________

3. Was Helen Gallagher contributorily negligent? Yes ___ No ___

4. If so, by what percentage must the damages be reduced? _____%

5. What are the total damages defendant must pay to plaintiff? ______________

____
Jury Foreperson

CASE FILE E:

STATE OF COLUMBIA

v.

BARBARA W. TOWNSLEY

ATTEMPTED MURDER
BATTERED WOMAN DEFENSE

STATE V. TOWNSLEY
CONTENTS OF FILE

GENERAL INSTRUCTIONS

This is a criminal case in which the defendant shot and wounded her husband. The state alleges that she attempted to kill her husband out of anger and jealousy because he was having an affair. The defendant claims self defense and that she was a battered spouse. The incident occurred in July of last year, in a fictional city called Bayshore, Columbia (population 150,000).

Potential witnesses

Nicholas B. Townsley -- victim (husband)
Barbara Williams Townsley -- defendant (wife)
Tina Dawn Moran -- Nick Townsley's girlfriend
James W. Lane -- a neighbor
Patrick McCardle -- police detective
Dr. Jordan S. Fox -- emergency room physician
Dr. Linda C. Cochran -- psychologist

Instructions for use as a full trial (without experts)

1. The state must call Nicholas Townsley and Tina Moran as witnesses in its case-in-chief, and may call Dr. Fox. Other witnesses may be called only with the approval of the court.

2. The defense must call Barbara Townsley and James Lane as witnesses in her case-in-chief, and may call Dr. Cochran. Other witnesses may be called only with the approval of the court.

3. Dr. Fox need not be called. The parties have entered into the following stipulation: "Dr. Jordan S. Fox examined and treated Nicholas Townsley in the Emergency Room. Mr. Townsley had two bullet wounds, one in his right wrist, and one entering from his lower back, perforating the liver, and exiting from his upper chest. His wrist was broken. There were two cuts on his scalp. His blood alcohol content was .05%. There was no evidence of other drugs. He required surgery and remained in the hospital for one week."

4. Dr. Cochran need not be called. The parties have stipulated: "Dr. Linda C. Cochran is a clinical psychologist who has examined Barbara Townsley and reviewed the case file. In her opinion, Ms. Townsley was suffering from Battered Woman Syndrome at the time of the shooting brought on by a pattern of physical abuse over several years. She lived in a constant state of fear of her husband, had low self-esteem, and felt helpless and isolated. It is common for women suffering this syndrome to be unable to leave their husbands. She felt her life was in constant danger, and that killing her husband was necessary to save her own life. There is considerable controversy among psychologists over the legitimacy of Battered Woman Syndrome as a unique mental state."

5. The original attorneys have withdrawn from this case, citing conflicts of interest.

Instructions for use as a full trial with experts

1. The state must call Nicholas Townsley, Tina Moran, and Dr. Fox as witnesses in its case-in-chief, and may call other witnesses only with the approval of the court.

2. The defense must call Barbara Townsley, James Lane, and Dr. Cochran as witnesses in her case-in-chief, and may call other witnesses only with the approval of the court.

3. The original attorneys have withdrawn from this case, citing conflicts of interest.

Stipulation

Any criminal offense listed as a misdemeanor is one for which the maximum statutory penalty is one year or less. Any offense listed as a felony is one for which the maximum penalty is more than one year.

Note on Dates

YR-0 refers to the present year, YR-1 refers to one year ago (the year in which the events took place), YR-2 refers to two years ago, etc.

Acknowledgments

I am grateful to Prof. Lynne Henderson of UNLV for her assistance in the preparation of this file. My understanding of battering and drafting of the defendant's narrative have been greatly improved by reading Martha Mahoney, *Legal Images of Battered Women: Redefining the Issue of Separation,* 90 MICH. L. REV. 1 (1991) and Karen McKinnie, *The Use of Expert Testimony in the Defense of Battered Women*, 52 U. COLO. L. REV. 587 (1981).

STATE OF COLUMBIA
County of Monroe

FILE # 08606

THE STATE OF COLUMBIA	)	
	)	
vs.	)	**INDICTMENT**
	)	
BARBARA W. TOWNSLEY, Defendant	))	

THE GRAND JURORS FOR THE STATE UPON THEIR OATH PRESENT:

That on or about the 6th day of July, YR-1, at or about 7:30 p.m., in Monroe County, BARBARA W. TOWNSLEY unlawfully and willfully did feloniously:

Count I: Attempt to murder Nicholas B. Townsley by shooting him with a handgun with the intent to kill him therewith, in violation of Columbia Criminal Code § 210.2.

Count II: Assault Nicholas B. Townsley with the intent and purpose to cause him bodily harm, and did cause him serious bodily injury by shooting him with a handgun and inflicting wounds upon him, in violation of Columbia Criminal Code § 211.2.

George Bell
Assistant District Attorney

WITNESSES:
Nicholas B. Townsley
James W. Lane
Dr. Jordan S. Fox
Det. Patrick McCardle, BPD ✘

The witnesses marked with an X were sworn by the undersigned foreperson of the Grand Jury, and this bill was found to be ✘ a True Bill/__ not a True Bill.

This the *15th* of *July*, YR-1

Michelle Davis
Grand Jury Foreperson

EXCERPTS FROM COLUMBIA CRIMINAL CODE

§ 100.2 DEFINITIONS. Throughout this Article, the following definitions apply:

(1) "Purposely:" A person acts purposely when it is his or her conscious object to engage in conduct. A person purposely causes a particular result when the person purposely engages in conduct and the result is within the contemplation of the actor, or is different only in the seriousness or extensiveness of the harm caused.

§ 103.4 USE OF FORCE IN SELF-DEFENSE. (a) The use of force toward or upon another person is justifiable when the actor reasonably believes that such force is immediately necessary for the purpose of protecting the actor against the use of unlawful force by another person on the present occasion.

(b) The use of deadly force is not justified unless the actor reasonably believes that such force is necessary to protect the actor from death, serious physical injury, kidnapping or rape; nor is it justifiable if:

(1) the actor provoked the use of force in the same encounter; or

(2) the actor knows that the use of deadly force can be avoided by retreat or withdrawal from the encounter, except that the actor is not obliged to retreat from the actor's own dwelling.

(c) In all instances, the defendant shall have the burden of proving self-defense by a preponderance of the evidence.

§ 105.1 CRIMINAL ATTEMPT. A person is guilty of an attempt to commit a crime if, acting with the kind of culpability otherwise required for commission of the crime, the actor purposely does anything which, under the circumstances as the actor believes them to be, is an act constituting a substantial step in a course of conduct planned to culminate in the actor's commission of the crime. An attempt to commit a crime constitutes an offense of the grade and degree one step lower than the most serious offense which is attempted.

§ 210.2 MURDER. A person is guilty of murder if the actor purposely causes the death of another human being. Murder is a felony of the first degree.

§ 210.3 MANSLAUGHTER. (a) A person is guilty of manslaughter when:

(1) The actor recklessly causes the death of another human being; or

(2) The actor commits a homicide that would otherwise be murder under the influence of extreme mental or emotional disturbance for which there is reasonable explanation or excuse. The reasonableness of such explanation or excuse shall be determined from the viewpoint of a person in the actor's situation under the circumstances as the actor believes them to be.

(b) Manslaughter is a felony of the second degree.

§211.2 AGGRAVATED ASSAULT. A person is guilty of aggravated assault if the actor:

(a) Attempts to cause serious bodily injury to another, or causes such injury purposely; or

(b) Attempts to cause or purposely causes bodily injury to another with a deadly weapon.

Aggravated assault under subparagraph (a) is a felony of the second degree; aggravated assault under subparagraph (b) is a felony of the third degree.

Cynthia SMITH

v.

The STATE of Columbia

No. 37071

Supreme Court of Columbia

May 13, YR-2

The defendant was charged with killing her live-in boyfriend. She claimed self-defense. The case is before us to consider whether an expert's opinion regarding "battered woman syndrome" was admissible at trial.

The testimony showed that the defendant and the victim had been living together on and off for several years. On the night of the shooting, the defendant went to bed early. The boyfriend came upstairs and started rubbing her shoulders. The defendant asked him to stop because she was tired. The defendant shook her and said, "You don't tell me when to touch you." The defendant started to go downstairs, but the boyfriend balled his fist and told her she was not going anywhere. Then he kicked her in the back, hit her in the head with his fist, choked her, threw her against the door, and hit her with a lamp. He announced he was leaving to get a six-pack, but would be back later and she better be there. When he left the house, the defendant tried to call her mother but the boyfriend had pulled the telephone out of the wall. After a few minutes, the defendant heard the boyfriend returning. She got a gun out of a chest of drawers and shot him as he came through the front door.

The evidence also showed that the boyfriend had beaten the defendant periodically over the six years they were together. She was scared to stop seeing him because he made threats. After the beatings he would apologize and say he loved her. She never called the police or told her friends because she believed him when he said he would not hit her anymore.

The defendant offered the expert testimony of a clinical psychologist that this behavior is consistent with "battered woman syndrome" in which the victim lives in constant fear of the man who beats her. The expert also would have testified that women suffering this syndrome often do not report the beatings. The expert was not permitted to testify.

Most courts that have considered the question of the admissibility of "battered woman syndrome" have held it to be admissible (Citations omitted).... They hold that the testimony is relevant because it helps the jury evaluate the truthfulness of the defendant's claim that she perceived herself to be in imminent danger and thus acted in self defense.

Our law of self-defense is that a person who is not the aggressor in an encounter is justified in using reasonable force against an adversary when she reasonably believes she is in imminent danger of bodily harm and must use force to protect herself. This is neither a subjective nor an objective standard, but asks the jury to look at the encounter from the standpoint of a reasonable person in defendant's position. When a battered woman strikes back she may not be in what most people would consider immediate danger at the time she kills her abuser. Evidence of battered woman syndrome is offered to try to convince a jury that from the defendant's perspective, she was in a situation where deadly force was necessary to protect herself from serious injury or death. Such testimony is minimally relevant, and it is then up to the jury to decide whether her perception was reasonable.

The trial court's judgment is reversed.

BAYSHORE POLICE DEPARTMENT ARREST REPORT

1 DATE OF REPORT: **7/06/YR-1**
2 TIME: **10:45 pm**
3 ARRESTING OFFICER'S NAME: **Patrick McCardle**
4 RANK: **Det**
5 BADGE: **3111**

6 DEFENDANT NAME: **Barbara W Townsley**
7 ADDRESS: **2412 Rockport Rd #9-B, Bayshore**
8 CRIMES: **210.2 Att murder, 211.2 Assault**

9 VICTIM NAME: **Nicholas B. Townsley**
10 SEX: **M**
11 AGE: **29**
12 ADDRESS: **2412 Rockport Rd #9-B, Bayshore**
13 CONTACT INFORMATION: **244-0316**
14 EMPLOYER: **Stone Electric**

15 DATE OF CRIME: **7/06/YR-1**
16 TIME: **7:30 pm**
17 LOCATION: **Knightridge Apartments, Rockport Rd.**
18 TYPE OF PREMISES: **Parking lot**
19 WEATHER: **hot, dry**
20 HOW ATTACKED OR COMMITTED: **Defendant shot husband during domestic altercation**
21 WEAPON/TOOLS: **.32 H & R revolver, serial # AP-45225**
22 PERSON REPORTING CRIME: **James W. Lane**
23 ADDRESS: **2412 Rockport Rd Apt. 7-B**
24 CONTACT INFORMATION: **244-2886**
25 TIME/DATE OF REPORT: **7:40 pm 7/06/YR-1**
26 TOTAL VALUE STOLEN:
27 TOTAL VALUE RECOVERED:
28 CURRENCY:
29 JEWELRY:
30 AUTOS:
31 COMPUTERS/TV ETC:
32 FIREARMS:
33 OTHER:

34 TOTAL PERSONS INVOLVED: **1**
35 TOTAL ARRESTED: **1**
36 ADULTS ARRESTED: **1**
37 JUVENILES ARRESTED: **0**
38 TOTAL AT LARGE: **0**

39 OTHER BPD OFFICERS INVOLVED:

40 NARRATIVE: **At about 7:40 pm, I responded to a 911 report of a shooting in a parking lot in front of Building B at Knightridge Apartments, 2412 Rockport Road. Victim was Nicholas Townsley, apartment 9-B. Perpetrator was Barbara W. Townsley, same address, wife of victim. Neighbors on scene reported that suspect shot her husband with handgun during domestic altercation. James W. Lane who called in the incident said he heard gunshots but did not know details. Victim unconscious, removed to Monroe County Hospital by EMT. I recovered a .32 caliber revolver at the scene belonging to suspect containing 6 empty cartridges and smelling like it had just been fired. Suspect was at scene, appeared to be in state of shock, but did not appear hurt. Several recent bruises on suspect corroborated domestic altercation explanation. Suspect taken to police station and booked on preliminary assault charge. After warnings, suspect gave voluntary statements that was recorded and transcribed.**

Cleared by arrest.

41 OFFICER'S SIGNATURE: *Patrick McCardle*

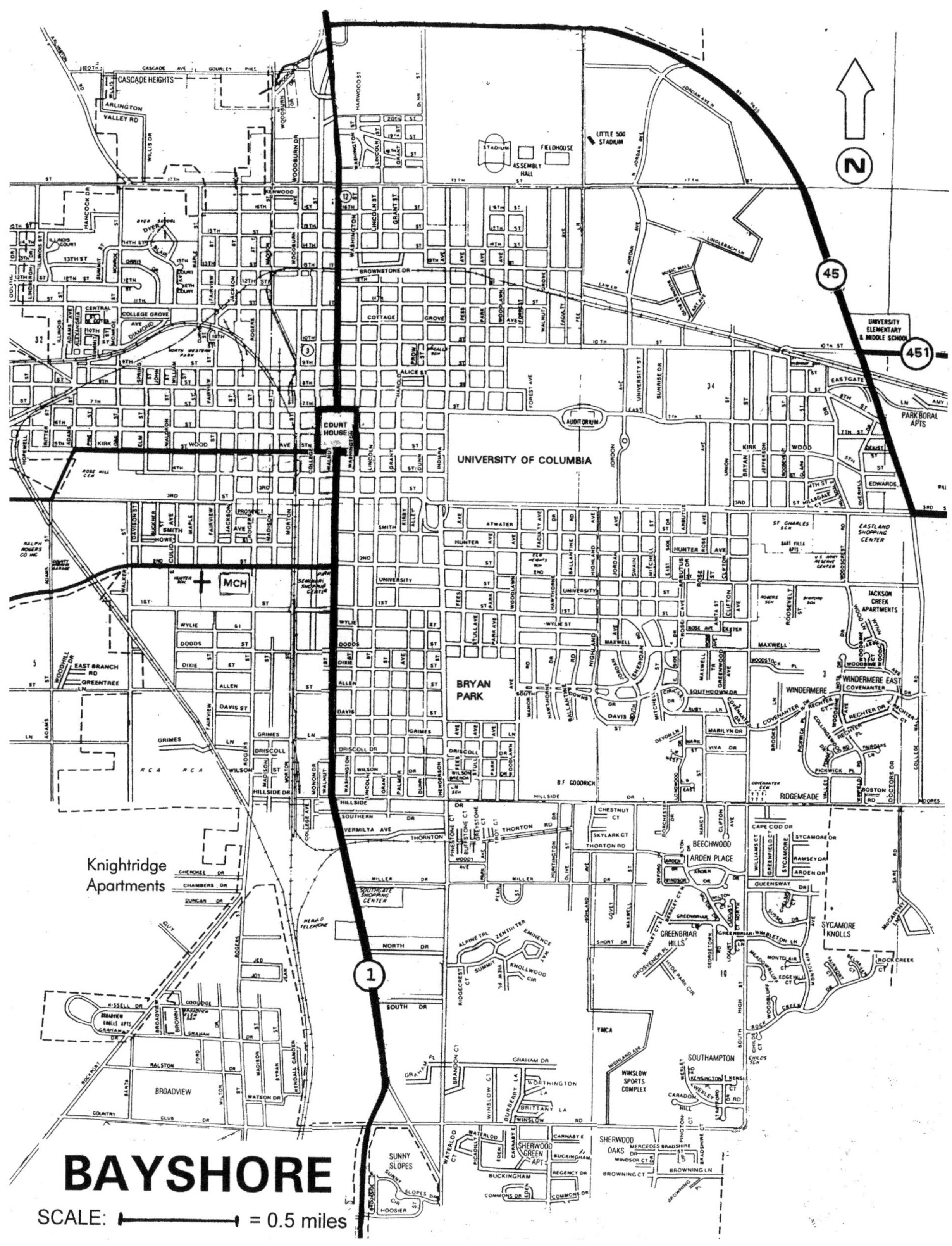

BAYSHORE
SCALE: = 0.5 miles
N
45
451
1
UNIVERSITY OF COLUMBIA
COURT HOUSE
BRYAN PARK
MCH
Knightridge Apartments
CASCADE HEIGHTS
ARLINGTON VALLEY RD
STADIUM
FIELDHOUSE
ASSEMBLY HALL
LITTLE 500 STADIUM
AUDITORIUM
UNIVERSITY ELEMENTARY & MIDDLE SCHOOL
PARK BORAL APTS
EASTGATE
WINDERMERE
WINDERMERE EAST
JACKSON CREEK APARTMENTS
EASTLAND SHOPPING CENTER
BEECHWOOD
ARDEN PLACE
SYCAMORE KNOLLS
GREENBRIAR HILLS
SOUTHAMPTON
WINSLOW SPORTS COMPLEX
YMCA
SHERWOOD OAKS
SHERWOOD GREEN APT
SUNNY SLOPES
BROADVIEW
COLLEGE GROVE
EAST BRANCH RD
GREENTREE
RIDGEMEADE
BOSTON

E

D

C

F

Clubhouse

B

A

Guard House

ROCKPORT RD.

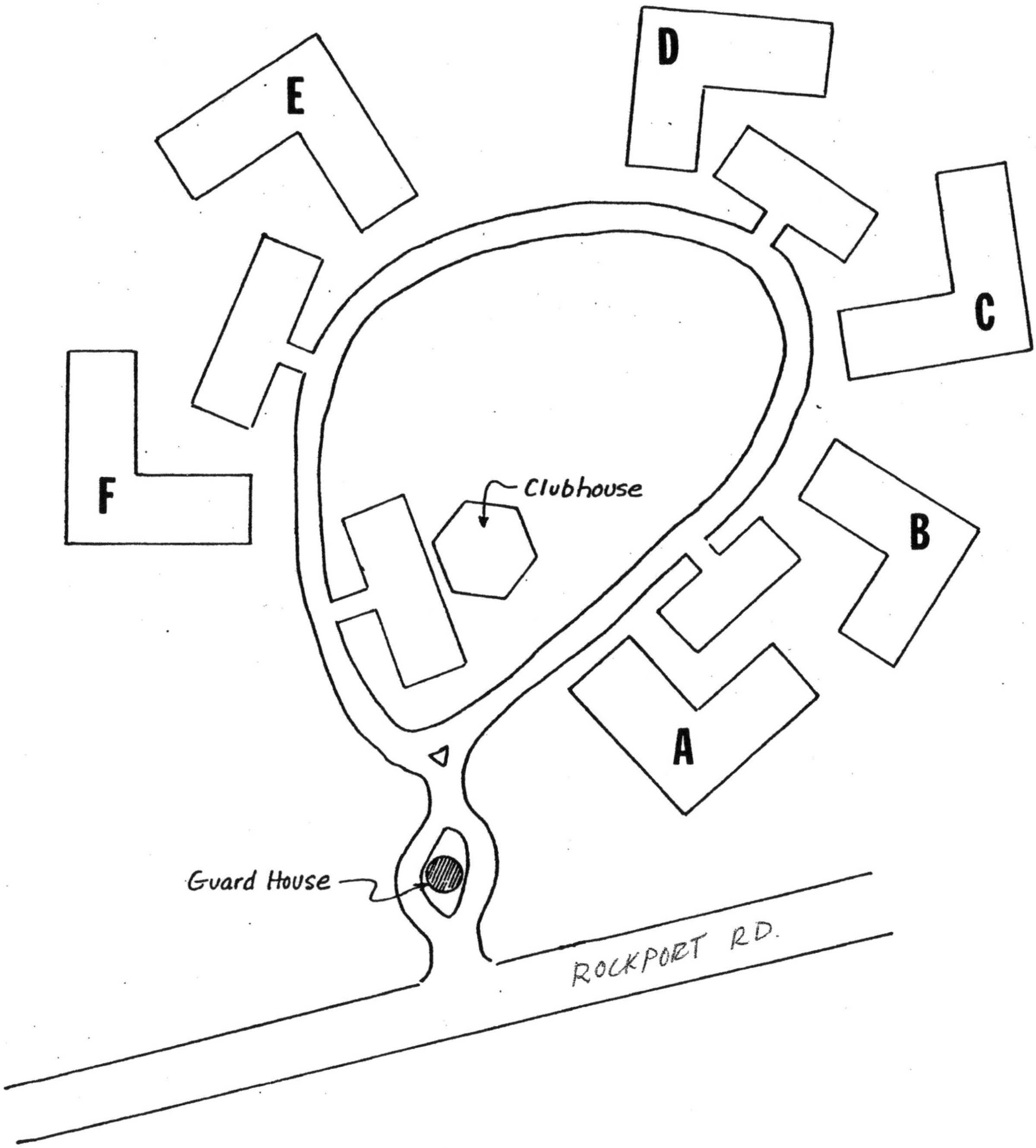

CITY OF BAYSHORE

"TO SERVE AND PROTECT"

LEGAL RIGHTS ADVICE FORM

Before we ask you any questions, you must understand your rights.

1. You have the right to remain silent.

2. Anything you say can and will be used against you in court.

3. You have the right to consult with a lawyer before we ask you any questions, and to have the lawyer present with you during questioning.

4. If you cannot afford a lawyer, one will be appointed for you before any questioning if you wish.

5. If you decide to answer questions now without a lawyer present, you will still have the right to stop answering at any time.

WAIVER

I have read this statement of my rights and I understand what my rights are. I understand that I may ask for clarification and explanation of my rights if I do not understand them. I am willing to make a statement and answer questions. I do not want a lawyer at this time. I understand and know what I am doing. No promises or threats have been made to me, and no pressure or coercion of any kind has been used against me.

Date: *July 6, Yr-1* Signature: *Barbara W. Townsley*

Witness: *Patrick McCardle* Witness: ______________

Time: *9:30 pm* Place: *Bayshore PD Bldg*

STATEMENT OF BARBARA W. TOWNSLEY

Date:	July 6, YR-1
Place:	Bayshore Police Department 105 Main Street, Bayshore, Columbia
Time Began:	9:30 p.m.
Present:	Det. Patrick McCardle, Lt. Kevin Delong Barbara W. Townsley Dodie Bowman, stenographer and notary public

Ms. Bowman: Ms. Townsley, do you swear to answer truthfully all questions asked?
Ms. Townsley: Yes.
Det. McCardle: Will you state your full name, home address and place of employment?
A: Barbara Williams Townsley, Apartment 9B, 2412 Rockport Road, Columbia. I don't work.
Q: Is that the Knightridge Apartment complex?
A: Yes.
Q: How long have you lived there?
A: Five years.
Q: With your husband?
A: Yes.
Q: Did you shoot your husband this evening?
A: Yes.
Q: Are you currently on drugs, medication or alcohol?
A: No.
Q: Do you require medical attention?
A: No.
Q: Why did you shoot your husband?
A: I don't know exactly. I thought he would kill me.
Q: Please tell me about your personal and family background.
A: I am 28 years old, born January 23, YR-29. I went to Bayshore High School. My mother has passed away. I met Nick in Yr-8. We dated for two years and then got married. I have no children. I worked at Kroger's supermarket for four years, but Nick made me stop working when we got married.
Q: What was your maiden name?
A: Williams. I wanted to keep my name when I got married, but Nick insisted that I take his name.
Q: Do you have a criminal record of any kind?
A: No.
Q: Have you ever been disciplined by an employer, teacher, or other person of authority?

A: No, wait, yes I was once. Junior year of high school I was suspended from school for a week for cheating on a test.
Q: Any other such incidents?
A: No.
Q: Tell me about your marriage to Nicholas Townsley.
A: Well, we've known each other since high school. We started dating in YR-8 when we met at a party. It was casual at first, but gradually got more serious. I guess Nick got serious first. He would get real jealous if I went out with anyone else. I was a little scared of his anger -- he could just explode. But it would blow over quickly.

We got married six years ago on June 19. I guess it was a pretty ordinary marriage, except we had no children. I quit work and tried to make Nick happy and keep a good home for him. I'm not all that good a cook, and I guess he was kind of disappointed. After the first year, the marriage got kind of unhappy. We couldn't have kids, and Nick wanted some, and he blamed me. It got so I just couldn't please him. I remember our first anniversary, I cooked a special dinner but it didn't come out right. Nick yelled at me that I was trying to poison him and he dumped out his food, so I said I'd make him something else. I went to heat some casserole in the microwave and he pushed me and I fell into the door of the microwave and split open my forehead. It started to bleed and Nick started screaming incoherently and stormed out to his car and left.

There were several incidents after that where Nick hit me. I don't remember specific dates or anything. Something would happen. He would blow up about inconsequential things. Sometimes he broke furniture or dishes. Once about three years ago, he pulled a kitchen knife and slammed it into the butcher block and the blade snapped. The police came but didn't do anything. One of the worst days was in the spring, YR-3, when I wanted to go shopping. He had promised me I could go. I hadn't had any new clothes in a year. I got dressed up on Saturday morning to go, and he said, "Where do you think you're going?" I said, "Shopping." He said, "How are you going to get there -- walk?" I said I was going to drive. He said, "No you're not, I'm using the car." I started to cry and said he'd promised. He stormed out of the house and got in the car. I ran out and stood in front of the car and said this wasn't fair. He drove the car into me, knocking me down. He gunned the engine and said he'd run over me if I didn't get up. I was able to get back into the house. I couldn't get out of bed for a week.
Q: Did you report this to the police?
A: No. I was afraid to.
Q: Did Nick ever threaten you with a gun?
A: No.

Q: Did you ever call the police?
A: Yes, once, when he threatened me with the knife. They told me they couldn't do anything about family matters.
Q: Did you ever seek help from your family?
A: I went to my mother a couple of times in the beginning, but she told me to work things out and not to call the police because it would only make things worse and shame the family. I never really told her how serious it was, because I was too embarrassed.
Q: Why didn't you leave Nick?
A: I don't know. At first, he loved me and needed me, and would always be sorry when he hit me. There were times when he was very loving and tender. When things got bad, I guess I had no place to go and no money. I still thought we could work things out. He still brought me flowers and candy, and we would slow-dance in the living room and he would sing love songs to me. Even when the violence became more frequent over the last year, he still expressed caring and tenderness toward me.
Q: How was your marriage the last few months?
A: Nick started running around with Tina, and things started to get worse at home. We seemed to fight more often and he started staying out all night. In the last few weeks he started talking about divorcing me and moving in with Tina. He said he was tired of me and wanted a real woman.
Q: Did he have any life insurance?
A: I don't know. He handled the finances and wouldn't tell me anything.
Q: Do your consider yourself a battered woman?
A: No. I'm not one of those women who stayed and stayed to be beaten. Nick wasn't like that. He flew off the handle, but he didn't beat me over and over. Up until the last few months I was okay. I wouldn't have stayed around like Farrah Fawcett in "The Burning Bed."
Q: Okay, let me ask about the gun you used to shoot Nick.
A: Okay.
Q: Is this weapon your gun?
A: Yes. I bought it six months ago for protection.
Q: From Nick?
A: Yes.
Q: Have you ever fired your gun at a person?
A: Not before tonight.
Q: Okay. Now, turning to the events of this evening, please tell me in your own words what happened.
A: Nick came home at 4:30 p.m. as usual. I made dinner and we ate and I started washing the dishes. A little before 7:30 p.m. Nick got a phone call and said he had to go out.

I knew it was his girlfriend Tina. He walked out the front door of the apartment. I was in the middle of washing the frying pan. I thought he was leaving me for good, so I ran out after him, still carrying the wet frying pan. When I got to the parking lot, Tina was there with Nick. I heard her telling Nick to calm down, and she had her hand on his arm. He said, "I'm not going to tell you anything." He was very loud and his face was red. The he saw me and screamed, "What do you want? Get out of my face." He pushed Tina hard and she fell down. I asked Nick to be quiet or the police would have him arrested. He shouted at me, "You don't tell me what to do, you bitch." Then he slapped me. Some other tenants had gathered, and someone -- I don't remember who -- said they were going to call the police. I heard Tina tell Nick again to be quiet, and calm down or she was leaving. She opened the door of her car, but Nick pulled her out and hit her. I ran over and begged him to stop and come back inside the apartment. He said, "You're not telling me anything." Then he hit me and knocked me to the ground. He jumped on me, and I hit him with the frying pan, hitting him once on the head. It didn't even phase him. I tried to hit him again, but Nick just jerked the frying pan out of my hand. He hit me once with it and then raised it over his head in a clenched fist. I scrambled away. He threw it at me, but missed. Then Nick started coming at me. I ran back into the apartment and grabbed the gun. I came back outside and Nick came toward me. He said he was going to have to teach me a lesson. He had the frying pan in his hand and he hit me in the face with it. I fell to my knees a little stunned. I saw Nick about ten feet away at the open door of Tina's car. He was reaching under the seat. Then he turned around and started toward me again. I was afraid he might have a gun. I thought he was going to kill me this time. This time he was going to get a weapon and kill me. I pointed my gun at him and fired six times. I emptied the chamber. I was in shock. I don't remember firing all six times, just the sound of the gun clicking after all the bullets were used up. Nick was lying on the ground, bleeding. A few minutes later, the police arrived.

Q: I want to clear up a few details. You say Nick had a gun?
A: I thought he might. I'm not sure.
Q: Did you see a gun in his hand?
A: No.
Q: How far away was he when you fired?
A: About 10 feet.
Q: Please describe exactly where Tina's car was.
A: It was right in the middle --
Q: Could you draw a sketch that we can attach to this statement?
A: Sure. Okay.
Q: When Nick hit you the first time, describe exactly what he did.

A: He slapped the side of my head with his open hand.
Q: Now, just before you fired your gun, could you mark where you were on the drawing?
A: Okay.
Q: Was your back against a parked car?
A: No. I was a few feet away.
Q: Was anything obstructing you to the left or right?
A: No. That's just open parking lot.
Q: Why didn't you just run away?
A: I didn't think about it. It all happened real fast.
Q: Do you know James W. Lane?
A: Yes, he's a neighbor. We're friendly but not friends.
Q: Was Nick drinking this evening?
A: He had four or five beers around supper time.
Q: What is Tina's last name?
A: Moran.
Q: Did you know her personally?
A: Not exactly.
Q: What do you mean?
A: Well, she called the apartment a lot. She had something going with Nick.
Q: Had you ever met her personally?
A: Yes, once, sort of. I went to her home once to ask her to leave Nick alone, to tell her he was married to me. But there was some kind of party going on, so I left. I think I know which one she was, but I left in a hurry. This was a couple of days before the shooting.
Q: Was Nick there also?
A: Yes. I asked him to come home with me, but he just laughed.
Q: How did you get there?
A: I don't remember. Maybe I walked.
Q: Before you fired your gun, did you give Nick any warning?
A: I'm not sure. I don't think so. It all happened fast.
Q: Are you aware you shot him in the back?
A: No, that's not right. He was coming toward me when I pulled the trigger.
Q: Were you seriously injured in any way?
A: No. He hit me a couple of times but I guess I'm okay.
Q: Why did you pull the trigger?
A: I was afraid for my life. I thought he would kill me this time.
Q: Did you consider any other choice?
A: No, there was no alternative.

Q: Why didn't you run away?
A: I was on the ground at the time.
Q: Why didn't you just leave him -- get a divorce?
A: He would have found me and killed me.
Q: Do you have anything you would like to add?
A: No.

END OF STATEMENT

Barbara W. Townsley

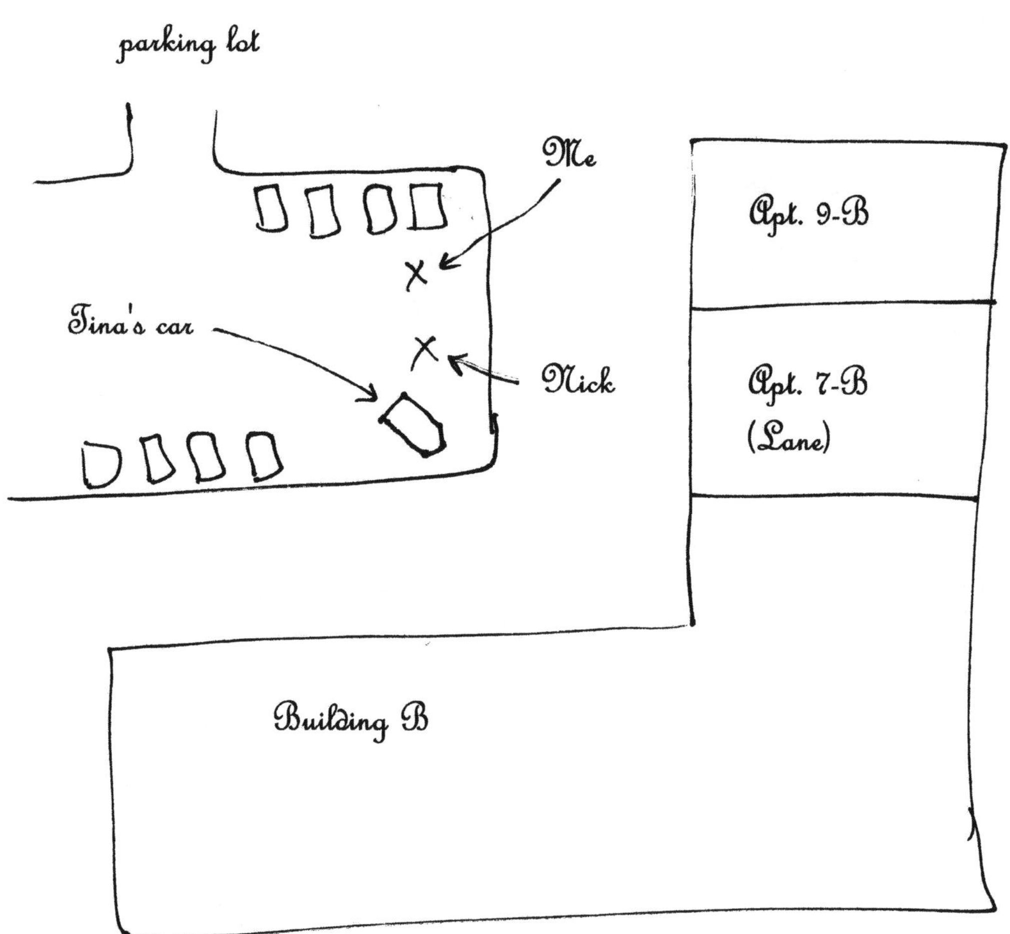

COLUMBIA DEPARTMENT OF HOMELAND SECURITY

100 East Capitol Street 522

Jefferson City, Columbia

FIREARM REGISTRATION AND PERMIT

BARBARA WILLIAMS TOWNSLEY
2412 ROCKPORT RD APT 9B
BAYSHORE, COLUMBIA

Date of Birth: JAN 23, YR-29
Telephone: 811-238-3050
Occupation: UNEMPLOYED

DESCRIPTION OF FIREARM

Make: HARRINGTON & RICHARDSON
Caliber: 32
Serial: AP-45225
Color: BLACK
Date purchased: FEB 12, YR-1
Place purchased: WAYNES WORLD OF GUNS, BAYSHORE, COL.

PERMIT TO CARRY FIREARM

The person whose name appears on this registration form is hereby licensed by the State of Columbia to possess, transport and carry that firearm on his or her person or in a vehicle, as long as the firearm is in plain sight. This license does not permit the licensee to carry a concealed weapon or to carry this firearm on any public transportation.

Date: February 18, YR-1

Not valid unless it bears an official signature: *Mickey Weber*

Title: *Commissioner*

KEEP THIS FORM WITH YOU AT ALL TIMES.
IT IS YOUR PERMIT TO CARRY A FIREARM

CERTIFIED TRUE AND ACCURATE COPY OF A RECORD
OF THE COLUMBIA DEPT OF HOMELAND SECURITY
DATE: *Jan. 25, YR-0* By: *Claire Munger*
Clerk

CITY OF BAYSHORE

POLICE DEPARTMENT "TO SERVE AND PROTECT"

TO: ATTORNEYS

FROM: LT. KEVIN DELONG

DATE: OCT 21, YR-1

RE: BARBARA W. TOWNSLEY

We looked through our files and were able to locate three prior incident reports concerning Barbara W. Townsley and Nicholas Townsley. They are attached. These reports are routinely filled out by our officers who respond to a field call.

BAYSHORE P.D.

Case Report

RE: Nicholas Townsley		Location Home	
Complainant Barbara Townsley		Address 2412 Rockport #9B	Phone
Date committed June 19 Yr-5	Time 9:45 p.m.	Persons Arrested	No.
Reported By neighbor			No.
Address	Phone		No.
Date Reported June 19, Yr-5	Time 9:25 p.m.	Arrested By	Date
Reported To 911		Total Value of Property Stolen - - $	
How Reported telephone		Value of Property Recovered - - $	
Officer Assigned Asher		Recovered By	Date
		Date	

DETAILS OF COMPLAINT:

Called to scene of domestic disturbance. Advised by complainant that her husband had hit her in the face and pushed her into microwave oven. Complainant asked if we could just keep him in jail for a few hours to cool off. Stated she did not want him arrested and she was not hurt. Husband stated he was sorry and had been drinking and would sleep it off. No further action warranted.

I recommend this case be closed

Unfounded ☒

Cleared by Arrest ☐

Exceptionally Cleared ☐

Inactive (Not Cleared) ☐

Signed James Asher Date June 19
Investigating Officer.

Signed TCStah Date June 19 Yr-5
Commanding Officer.

BAYSHORE P.D.

Case Report

RE: Nicholas B. Townsley	Location 2412 Rockport Apt. 9-B
Complainant Barbara W. Townsley	Address .... Phone ....
Date committed Sept. 3 Yr-5 Time 1:15 a.m.	Persons Arrested .... No. ....
Reported By neighbor	.... No. ....
Address .... Phone	.... No. ....
Date Reported same Time 1:05 a.m.	Arrested By .... Date ....
Reported To 9-1-1	Total Value of Property Stolen - - $ ....
How Reported called	Value of Property Recovered - - $ ....
Officer Assigned Houseman, Randy	Recovered By .... Date ....
	Date ....

DETAILS OF COMPLAINT:

Unknown caller reported fight and noise in Apt. 9-B. Undersigned officer responded. C/W reported that she had fallen in the kitchen and hit her head. Husband Nicholas Townsley stated he did not hit her that hard. C/W badly bruised around face, lip cut and bleeding. She refused medical assistance. I asked if she wished to file a complaint against her husband. She said no. Husband promised not to hit her any more.

I recommend this case be closed
Unfounded .... ☐
Cleared by Arrest .... ☐
Exceptionally Cleared .... ☐
Inactive (Not Cleared) .... ☐

Signed Randy Houseman Date Sep 3, Yr-5
Investigating Officer.

Signed [signature] Date 9/3/-5
Commanding Officer.

BAYSHORE P.D.

Case Report

RE: Nicholas B. Townsly	Location Knightridge Apt. 9-B
Complainant Barbara Townsly	Address Rockport Rd. Phone
Date committed May 2, Yr-4 Time 10:45 p.m.	Persons Arrested No.
Reported By Barbara Townsly	No.
Address Knightridge Apt. 9-B Phone	No.
Date Reported same Time 10:45 p.m.	Arrested By Date
Reported To Officer	Total Value of Property Stolen - - $
How Reported In person	Value of Property Recovered - - $
Officer Assigned Daniel Brown	Recovered By Date
	Date

DETAILS OF COMPLAINT:

While on routine patrol through Knightridge Apartments, I was flagged down by a young woman who said her husband had a knife. Went to apartment 9-B. Suspect said it was only a lover's quarrel. I asked complainant if he actually threatened her with a knife. She said no. Suspect also denied having a knife. Complainant expressed willingness to return home and talk things out. No further action seemed warranted. Both parties gave assurances they were alright.

I recommend this case be closed
Unfounded ☐
Cleared by Arrest ☐
Exceptionally Cleared ☐
Inactive (Not Cleared) ☐

Signed D Brown *Investigating Officer.* Date May 3, Yr-4

Signed Franklin Shobba *Commanding Officer.* Date May 3, Yr-4

State of Columbia)
)
-against-)
)
Barbara W. Townsley)

DEPOSITION OF NICHOLAS B. TOWNSLEY

Date: November 10, YR-1
Place: Public Defender's Office
309 West Washington, Room 1209
Bayshore, Columbia
Present: George Baker, for the State
Bonnie Martin, for the defendant
Nicholas B. Townsley
Diana Watts, stenographer and Notary Public

MS. WATTS: Mr. Townsley, do you swear to answer truthfully all questions asked during this deposition?
MR. TOWNSLEY: I do.
MS. MARTIN: State your name and address please.
A: Nicholas B. Townsley, 2412 Rockport Road, Apartment 9-B, Bayshore.
Q: How old are you?
A: Twenty-nine; I was born February 16, Yr-30.
Q: Tell me about yourself, like where you live, if you're married, and so forth.
A: I live in apartment 9-B, Knightridge Apartments. I'm married to Barbara. We've known each other since high school. Let's see, I work at Tom Stone Electrical as an electrician. I went to college for two years here at University of Columbia, but quit and went to work as an electrician.
Q: What were your interests in College?
A: Mostly playing basketball. I was a physical education major.
Q: Have you ever been arrested?
A: Yes, several times for public intoxication, trespassing, that sort of thing.
Q: Were you ever convicted?
A: Yes, I had to pay a fine a couple of times. Most of that was when I was younger. The last one was malicious mischief three years ago. I paid a

$50 fine.

Q: What happened?

A: I got drunk and dumped garbage in the front seat of a guy's car.

Q: Why?

A: He was a bartender at the Brown Jug Tavern where I go sometimes, and he'd thrown me out of the bar for being rowdy a couple of days before. I was mad and wanted to get even, but it was a stupid thing to do.

Q: Tell me about your marriage to Barbara.

A: It was okay. We started dating in Yr-8 and got married in Yr-6. She was very loving at first, but I kind of outgrew her. She stayed home all the time and I wanted to go out and have fun. I would have ideas about going to a movie, or going out boating, or meeting some friends at the Brown Jug Tavern, but she'd never want to go out. I think I just fell out of love with her. She was a whiner and complainer.

Q: Did you ever hit Barbara?

A: A few times, out of frustration. She had a way of needling me that would drive me to the breaking point. She would ask what I wanted for dinner, and when I got home she would have made something I don't like and then she'd claim it was what I said I wanted. She'd agree to go over to my parents' house, and then at the last minute claim she had a headache. Sometimes she would accuse me of not being man enough to get her pregnant. I'd get angry and sometimes I'd hit her.

Q: Did you ever threaten her with a knife?

A: No, absolutely not.

Q: Did you ever threaten her with a gun?

A: No.

Q: Did you ever run into her with the car?

A: Yes, once, but it was an accident. It was in April, Yr-3. I was mad at something and got in the car to leave. I had just started it up when she ran out in front. I couldn't stop and knocked her down.

Q: How many times have you hit Barbara over the last six years?

A: I have no idea.

Q: Too many times to count?

A: That's not what I mean. I'd guess I've hit her maybe ten or twelve times since we got married.

Q: Did you beat Barbara on your first wedding anniversary?

A: No. She fell and hit her head on the door of the microwave oven.

Q: In September, Yr-5, did you hit Barbara?

A: I don't remember.

Q: Do you recall the police being called in the fall of Yr-5?

A: Not specifically. The police came a couple of times to check on noise. We did have fights, mostly shouting, and our neighbor would call the cops. We came to blows a couple of times, but Barbara was never seriously hurt, and the police just left each time.

Q: Who is Tina Moran?

A: I met her about two years ago when I made a service call at her house. She lived alone and all the power had gone out and she thought she heard noises. She was real scared when I got there. I fixed her power -- the main circuit breaker needed to be reset -- and stayed until she calmed down. I ended up staying all night. She was fun to talk to.

Q: Have you seen her since then?

A: Yes, once or twice a week. We've fallen in love.

Q: Have you had sexual intercourse with Ms. Moran?

A: Yeah.

Q: Is your wife aware of this relationship?

A: Not a first. We tried to hide it, but I think Barbara probably knew anyway. Wives figure that stuff out. Over the last few months she must have known because she started to get real jealous. She would always ask where I'd been and whether I was with another woman. In my business I'm on call for electrical emergencies one night a week, and every time I went out, Barb would accuse me of seeing someone else.

Q: Were you seeing Tina during this time?

A: Yes. We were in love. Then on July 4, Tina invited me over to her apartment for a party. Barb got all upset, so I told her I wanted a divorce, that I was tired of her nagging. She put on a real scene, crying and begging me not to leave her. When I started to leave, Barb grabbed me and started pulling at my clothes, and I had to hit her to get free so I could get out the door. A few minutes after I got to Tina's, Barb burst in. I don't know how she knew where I was. She was crying and yelling incoherently about Tina being a tramp and calling her the whore of Babylon and accusing her of breaking up our home.

Q: Did she refer to Tina by name?

A: I'm not sure. Come to think of it, I don't think so. I don't think she knew which woman was Tina. She probably thought she would catch us alone and didn't realize it was a party.
Q: What happened next?
A: Barb looked sort of confused and ran out. I spent the night with Tina because I was still mad at Barb. I returned home on July 5 and told Barb again that I was going to see a lawyer and file for divorce.
Q: How did she react?
A: She said something like she couldn't stand to see me with another woman, that I was being cruel. She seemed sullen and quiet.
Q: Describe in detail what happened on July 6.
A: I got home about 4:30. We ate supper about 6:00. Then I got -- I mean Barb and I ate dinner together, not Tina -- then I got a phone call from Tina about 7:15 saying she was coming over and needed to talk to me. I said not to come to the apartment because Barbara was in one of her moods. She said she had to come over and would meet me in the parking lot in fifteen minutes. At 7:30, I told Barb I was going out for awhile. She said, "So you're going out with that tramp again." I said Tina wasn't a tramp and she could have a divorce any time she wanted it. Barb said, "I'll see you in hell first," and I left. I went out to the parking lot and Tina pulled up. She got out of the car and told me she had gotten a threatening phone call from her brother who wanted Tina to send him money or he would sue to get half of their mother's estate which she had left all for Tina. It made me angry, and I said something like, "Don't give that S.O.B. anything." Tina told me to calm down. About this time, Barbara came up to me, and said, "I thought I told you not to bring your whore back here." She kept crowding me, you know, stepping real close, and then I would step back, and she would crowd in again, yelling at me.
Q: Had you been drinking.
A: I'd had one beer for dinner.
Q: Any other alcohol that day?
A: No, not that I remember.
Q: Had you taken any drugs that day?
A: No.
Q: Have you ever taken drugs illegally?

A: Sure. I've smoked marijuana, and I tried cocaine a couple of times. I took amphetamines during exams when I was in college. So what? Everyone does that sort of thing, even presidential candidates.
Q: What happened next?
A: I was getting real mad. Barb was out of control. I pushed her away and told her to leave me alone. Tina grabbed my arm again and said to forget it, let's get out of here. I pushed her arm away and said, "She can't tell me what to do."
Q: How far away was Barbara?
A: About five feet. She wheeled around and told me to shut up, that she'd had enough. She came toward me, screaming "I've had enough" and I slapped her. She was getting hysterical. At this point Tina said maybe she should leave but I grabbed her arm and said she should stay there.
Q: What happened next?
A: Barb went crazy. She ran up and screamed at me. She jumped on me, grabbed me and started hitting me. I slapped her away, but she came at me with a frying pan. She hit me on the head with it. When she swung a second time, I grabbed her arm and pulled the pan away from her. I held it up and said, "What if I hit you with this, would you like that?" I shook Barbara and she lost her balance and fell.
Q: How were you holding the pan?
A: Out in front of me, raised a little.
Q: Did you threaten Barb with it or try to hit her?
A: No.
Q: Do you know where she got the big bruises on the side of her face?
A: No, maybe she hit her face on the asphalt when she fell down.
Q: What happened next?
A: Barb ran back inside the apartment. I figured the crisis had passed. I leaned over and picked up the frying pan which was lying on the pavement. Barb came back out of the apartment. I raised the frying pan and said, "Just stay there."
Q: How far away were you?
A: Twenty or thirty feet.
Q: Did she have a gun in her hand?
A: Yes, a small black revolver.
Q: Had you ever seen it before?

A: No.
Q: Would you recognize it if you saw it again?
A: Yes, I think so.
Q: What did you do next?
A: I went over to Tina's car, tossed the pan into the back seat, and reached in to slide the seat back so I could get in the driver's side. I wanted to get out of there. I thought I heard a noise, so I turned around quickly. As I turned around, I saw Barb crying and aiming her gun at me, holding it out in both hands. I tried to run but hit the car door. The next thing I remember is waking up in the hospital.
Q: Do you remember being shot?
A: No.
Q: Did you hear a gunshot?
A: No.
Q: You didn't see Barbara shoot you?
A: No.
Q: As best you can, could you sketch a diagram of what happened, where you were and where Barbara was when she shot you?
A: Okay.
MS. MARTIN: Can we include this as exhibit one for this deposition?
MR. BAKER: No problem.
Q: Mark where the earlier struggle took place, please.
A: Right here, sort of. I'm not sure exactly.
Q: Before Barbara fired her gun, did she say anything?
A: Not that I remember.
Q: What happened in the hospital?
A: They put a cast on my right wrist, the one the bullet had broken, put three stitches in my head, and had to operate on me to remove a bullet from my liver. I had tubes coming out of me for drainage for a few days after they operated. And they gave me medication of some kind.
Q: Who was your doctor?
A: Dr. Fox, Jordan Fox.
Q: Have you discussed this case with the district attorney?
A: Yes, of course.
Q: Has he influenced your testimony in any way?
A: No. I am telling the truth.

Q: Have you discussed the case with Tina Moran?
A: Yes.
Q: Have you told her what to say?
A: No.
Q: Are you aware of any other witness to this incident?
A: Well, maybe our neighbor Jim Lane.
Q: Did you start the fight?
A: No, I was trying to get out of there.
Q: How do you feel about Barbara?
A: I think she's crazy and I just want to be rid of her. I certainly don't love her anymore. She tried to kill me.
MS. MARTIN: Nothing further.

WHEREUPON IT WAS STIPULATED THAT READING AND SIGNING BY THE WITNESS IS HEREBY WAIVED PURSUANT TO RULE 30(e).

I certify pursuant to Rule 30(f) that this is a true record of the deposition.

Diana Watts

Diana Watts

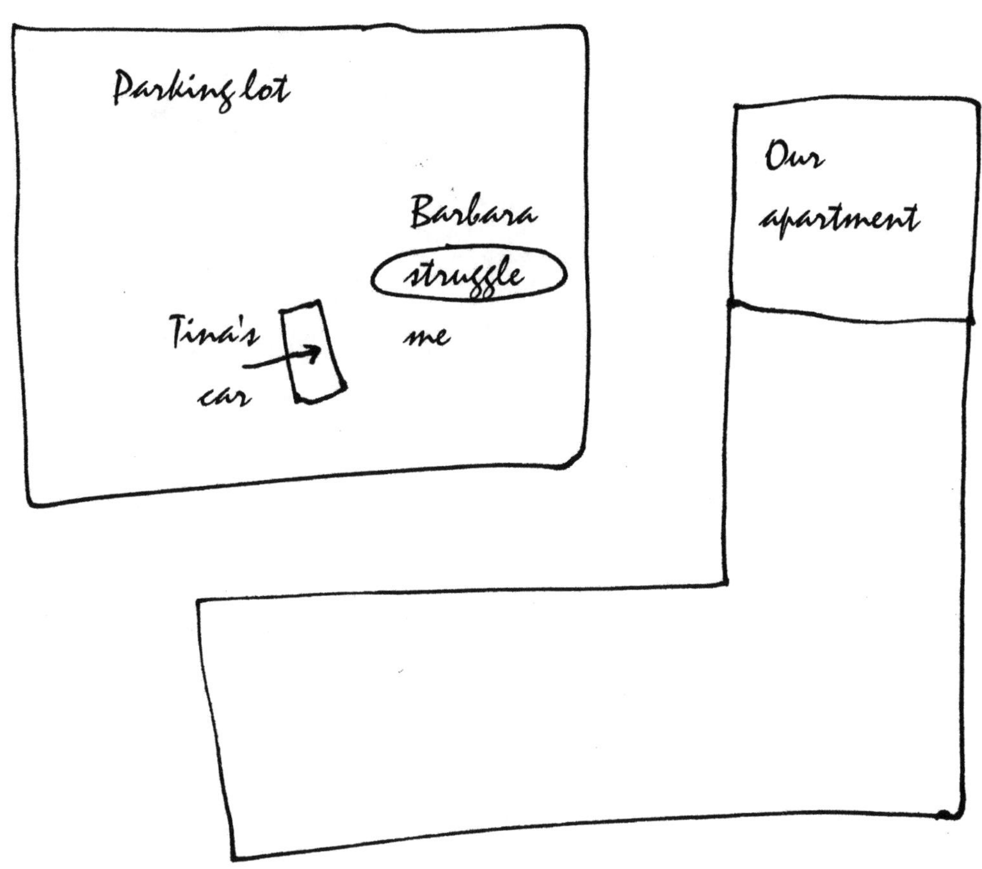

Nick Townsley

BAYSHORE POLICE DEPARTMENT
ARREST HISTORY

LAST NAME: **TOWNSLEY**
FIRST NAME: **NICHOLAS** MIDDLE NAME: **BAKER**
ALIAS:
DATE OF BIRTH: **2/16/YR-30** PLACE OF BIRTH: **SAN DIEGO CA**
ADDRESS: **2412 ROCKPORT RD #9-B, BAYSHORE COL**

HAIR: **BRN** EYES: **BRN** SEX: **M** MARKS/SCARS:
HT: **5'11"** WT: **180**
OCCUPATION: **ELECTRICIAN**

DATE	OFFICER	CIT NO.	CHARGE	DISPOSITION
7/14/-8	MORGAN	Y2123S	ASSAULT, TRESPASS	DISMISSED
4/19/-6	LONG	Y0312U	PUBLIC INTOX	DISMISSED
9/9/-5	MORGAN	Y2190V	TRESPASS, PUB INTOX	GUILTY - $100 FINE
8/6/-4	LONG	B31601	MALICIOUS MISCHIEF	GUILTY - $50 FINE

DATE PRINTED: 11/19/YR-1

CERTIFIED TRUE AND ACCURATE COPY OF A RECORD
OF THE BAYSHORE POLICE DEPARTMENT
By: Leslie Morse
DESK SERGEANT

DISTRICT ATTORNEY
OF MONROE COUNTY
155 WEST 6TH STREET
BAYSHORE, COLUMBIA
CRIMINAL INVESTIGATION DIVISION (811) 332-7305

STATEMENT OF TINA DAWN MORAN

Made To: Pat Enright, Investigator
Place: 155 West 6th St., Room 612, Bayshore, Columbia
Date: November 3, Yr-1
In re: State v. Townsley

My name is Tina Dawn Moran. I was born October 22, Yr-27, in Atlanta, Georgia. My family moved here when I was four. My parents divorced when I was in high school, and my father left town. I have since lost track of him. After high school, I went to St. Martin College and majored in Government. During my third year, my mother got very ill, so I came home in the spring of Yr-6. I got a job as a fitness instructor at the Women's Health Club, which is an exercise center downtown. My mother died shortly after I got back, and I stayed on in our house at 101 Glenwood Avenue, here in Bayshore. I have an older brother, Bruce, who is a pilot in the Navy stationed in Seattle. I am in excellent health, have good hearing, good eyesight, and a good memory.

I have known Nicholas Townsley for two years. I met him when he came over to fix burned-out power switches in my house. The power had gone out in a storm and I called an electrician, and Nick came out. He fixed the power, and stayed and talked. I liked him a lot. He was intelligent and funny, but a little sad and depressed. He was in an unhappy marriage, and I got him to talk about it. His wife, Barbara, had quit her job when they got married, expecting him to support her. She didn't take care of her appearance, didn't do much house cleaning, and didn't even try to cook decent meals. He knew he had made a mistake, but was afraid she couldn't take care of herself, so he was afraid to leave her. He said she nagged him constantly, and accused him of being sexually inadequate, especially compared to her previous boyfriends.

I felt sorry for Nick, so I invited him over a couple of times to parties. We had a good time and he fit in with my friends. He came over for a Christmas party in Yr-2 and we both got too drunk and we slept together. We realized that we were falling in love. We kept dating, on and off.

I met his wife Barbara for the first time on July 4, Yr-1. I was having a party, and Nick was there along with lots of other people. I was out in the kitchen, when Barbara burst in and went over and tried to pull Nick out of the house. They got into a fight. I heard her yelling about something. I came into the living room just as Nick hit her. He didn't hit her hard, just hard enough to quiet her down, like a slap. She left, saying, "I'll get you for this, you son-of-a-bitch." Nick says she's done this kind of thing before. That night was the first time we spent all night together.

On July 6, Yr-2, I got a call from my brother, Bruce. He's a Navy pilot in Seattle. He said he needed money, and wanted his half of my mother's estate. I told him that she had died years ago, and what little money she had left was all gone. He asked about the house, and I said I was living in it. He said half of it was rightly his, and if I didn't send him $10,000, he'd get a court order to sell the house so he could get his half of the money. Obviously, I was very upset. I worried about it and finally decided I had to talk to Nick. He knows a lot about finances and courts. I called at 7:15. He said he couldn't talk on the phone because Barbara was in one of her jealous moods. He said I should come over and he would meet me in the parking lot at 7:30 p.m.

I got to the parking lot of Knightridge Apartments and Nick was waiting for me. I got out of the car and told him about the phone call. He got real angry, and I told him to calm down and let me finish the story. I think Nick was even angrier than I was.

About that time Barbara came up to Nick and accused him of being a liar and then turned her back and walked away. I tried to calm Nick down. He yelled something at Barbara about she couldn't tell him what to do. I could tell he was still pretty agitated. I figured I ought to leave, so I started to walk back to my car, but Nick stopped me.

Then I saw Barbara go over to Nick and say something. Nick pushed her away and she fell backwards. I could not tell whether Nick actually hit her or she just fell down. Then they got into a real fight. Barbara was hitting at Nick and he hit her with his fists. Then she hit Nick with a frying pan a couple of times on the head. I ran over and screamed at them to stop fighting. Then I ran over to some people standing at the edge of the parking lot and screamed for someone to break up the fight and call the police.

When I looked up again, Barbara was going inside the apartment. I heard Nick say something about teaching her a lesson. I got in the passenger side of my car and said, "Come on Nick, let's go." I figured things were over. I flipped down the visor mirror to check my make-up. A minute had passed. Then I heard a lot of gunshots. I ducked down, and then I thought she must have shot him. I jumped out and saw Nick lying next to the car, bleeding.

Soon after that, the police came. I went with Nick to the hospital. They rushed him into surgery. He was in the hospital for two weeks. He had a cast on his right arm and tubes sticking out of his side. He told me he had been shot in the wrist and in the back. He complained a lot about headaches and that his wrist hurt when I saw him in the hospital.

Now that Barbara has tried to kill Nick, he will be able to get a quick divorce as soon as she goes to jail. There's some special provision in the law for that. He'll finally be rid of her so we can get married.

I have given this statement voluntarily and it is true and accurate to the best of my recollection.

Tina D. Moran

Tina D. Moran

OFFICE OF THE PUBLIC DEFENDER
309 West Washington Street, Suite 1200
Bayshore, Columbia Phone 232-2475

STATEMENT BY JAMES W. LANE

Date: September 30, Yr-1
Made to: Bonnie Martin, Deputy Public Defender
Place: Public Defender's Office

I am giving this statement voluntarily in response to a request from Bonnie Martin, an attorney representing my neighbor, Barbara Townsley. Barbara has been charged with assault for shooting her husband, Nicholas. I was a witness to that shooting.

I am 39 years old, born June 6, Yr-40. I am an X-ray technician at Monroe County Hospital. I got that job over ten years ago after I got out of the Navy. I was a medic in the Navy, stationed first in San Diego and then at the base hospital in Naples, Italy. I live in apartment 7-B, Knightridge Apartments, 2412 Rockport Road, with my wife, Nancy Newton. She teaches third grade. We have no children. We live at Knightridge because I am often at the hospital at odd hours, and Knightridge has security guards patrolling in the evening in case Nancy has to be home alone.

I am acquainted with the Townsleys. They live next to me in apartment 9-B. The walls are not very thick, and we can hear them sometimes. I feel sorry for Barbara. They have frequent fights, and it always sounds like Nick starts them. He is a violent person and he beats Barbara frequently. I cannot understand why she stays with him. I would estimate that they have one shouting match a week, and at least one physical fight per month. This has been going on for the full five years they have lived next to us. I have often seen Barbara with bruises or a black eye.

Nick is a violent person. He has threatened or menaced me a couple of times. The first couple of times when I heard them fighting and heard the sound of things breaking, I ran next door to see if everyone was okay. Nick would appear at the door and tell me to get the hell away and leave them alone or he'd "beat my ass." This happened two or three times in the first few months they lived next door. On at least one occasion I could see past Nick into the apartment, and saw Barbara on the floor crying with blood in her face. I was scared of Nick, so I stopped trying to intervene.

The next few times that the fighting sounded really bad, I called the police. I don't remember the exact dates, but it was several years ago. The police would come but not do anything. Then little things would start happening to me. My car tires were flat one morning, and the headlights were broken one day after I had called the police. After one incident, Nick came over and told me to keep my nose out of their business or he'd break it. I asked Barbara one day if she wanted me to do anything, and she said she wanted me to keep out of it, that they could work out their problems themselves. She asked me not to call the police again, so I did not.

On July 4th, YR-2, Barbara asked me if I would drive her to a house on Glenwood Avenue for a few minutes. She said it was important and that Nick had the car. There was nothing unusual about her appearance. I drove her there. There were several cars parked in front like for a party. She went in for maybe two minutes, and then came out. Her eyes were red like she had been crying, but she said she was okay and I drove her home. She did not say anything about why she went or what happened, but i figured it had to do with nick.

On July 6, YR-2, I left the apartment about 7:30 p.m. to run an errand. I backed my car out of its parking place. As I was looking over my shoulder, I saw Nick, Barbara and a woman I don't know arguing in the parking lot. He was upset and appeared slightly intoxicated. Nick said something like he wasn't going to tell Barbara anything. The young woman, whom I understand to be Tina Moran, went over to Nick and I heard her tell him to be quiet and calm down. He pushed her away, almost knocking her down. I had walked over and was standing on the curb nearby. Nick did not look normal. His face was red and his muscles were tense and his movements were very fast and jerky. He was agitated. I did not get close enough to see his eyes so I cannot be sure, but he looked like he might be having a drug reaction, probably to cocaine. I saw a lot of that in the Navy.

Then Nick hit Barbara and knocked her down. He jumped on her and started pummeling her with his fists. I looked away for a moment to see if anyone else was going to call the police. I saw the couple from 5-B going inside the apartment building and figured they were going to call. I looked back, and Barbara and Nick were struggling together. Barbara had a frying pan in her hand, but Nick got it away from her and raised it over his head as if to hit her. He threw it at her but missed. Barbara ran inside the apartment and came out with a gun. I decided to get in my car for protection in case they started shooting. I got in and looked out through the back window and saw Nick hit Barbara with the frying pan, then turn and walk away. Barbara was on the ground. I decided to pull the car back into its parking place. I'm not sure why.

I turned away and reached for the ignition. I heard Nick shout he was going to teach her a lesson, and then I heard the sounds of gunshots. I did not see what happened, because I ducked. I then looked out and saw Barbara standing up with the gun in her hand. I couldn't see Nick so I got out. I saw him lying next to his car, bleeding heavily from the abdomen. He was unconscious but alive. He did not have a weapon in his hands, and I don't know what happened to the frying pan. A few minutes later the police arrived. They put Nick in the police car and took him to the hospital.

I have read the foregoing and it is true and accurate to the best of my ability.

James W. Lane

✣ Monroe County Hospital

Emergency Care Department
684-3597

October 15, Yr-1

Mr. George Baker
Prosecuting Attorney
155 West 6th Street
Bayshore, Columbia

Dear Mr. Baker:

At your request, I am sending you in writing my recollection of my treatment of Nicholas Townsley for gunshot wounds.

Mr. Townsley was admitted via the Emergency Room on July 6, Yr-1.

I performed an exploratory laparotomy and cleaned and set a wound to his right wrist. Townsley had been hit by two bullets, one hit the right wrist breaking some bones, and the other entered his lower back on the right side and exited from the front. It is impossible to tell which bullet hit first. Neither did any permanent damage. Mr. Townsley had a blood alcohol level of .05 percent, the equivalent of about 3 glasses of wine or 3 twelve-ounce beers. At that level he would have been uninhibited but not yet seriously drunk. We did not test for other drugs in his blood because of the emergency nature of the case.

I have instructed Medical Records to send a copy of Mr. Townsley's Admission and Discharge Reports.

Sincerely,

JSFox

Jordan S. Fox, M.D.

✣ Monroe County Hospital

Medical Records Department
684-3583

October 16,Yr-1

Mr. George Baker
Assistant District Attorney
155 West 6th Street
Bayshore, Columbia

Re: Nicholas B. Townsley

Dear Mr. Baker:

At the request of Dr. Jordan Fox, I enclose the two summary reports on Nicholas B. Townsley.

The two reports are computer print-outs. All our medical records are stored on computer. Physicians and authorized nurses dictate their reports, and clerks enter them into the computer. While each physician is free to follow whatever form he or she thinks appropriate, hospital policy requires them to file an admission report and a discharge report on every patient in their care.

Sincerely,

Elizbeth Knoll

Elizabeth Knoll
Director, Medical Records

MONROE COUNTY HOSPITAL Bayshore, Columbia

NAME: Townsley, Nicholas Baker Patient #: 5612811

DATE ADMITTED: 7/6/YR-1

PHYSICIAN: Jordan S. Fox

ADMISSION REPORT

This approximately 28-year-old male was admitted to the ER following a shooting. Examination in the ER revealed a missile wound with point of entry and point of exit at about the level of the ninth rib and the lateral lower chest wall. There was also a missile wound involving the right wrist. X-rays revealed some lead fragments along the course of the missile tract overlying the liver. There was no evidence of entry into the pleural space on the x-rays. X-rays of the wrist revealed a fracture in the site of the styloid process of the radius.

PAST HISTORY AND REVIEW OF SYSTEMS: Taken under emergency conditions. The patient was unconscious on admission.

PHYSICAL EXAMINATION: HEENT: Laceration on the head.

NECK: Was supple.

CHEST AND ABDOMEN: There are two wounds involving the lateral aspect of the right lower chest at the level of the 9th rib; one is in the posterior axillary line and one is in the anterior axillary line, slightly more medial than the anterior axillary line. The anterior one is the larger one, and is assumed for that reason to be the point of exit. There is a recent abrasion in the midline between the xyphoid and the umbilicus.

ALCOHOL BLOOD CONTENT: 0.05 percent.

GENITALIA AND RECTAL: Unremarkable.

LOW EXTREMITIES: Unremarkable.

ADMITTING DIAGNOSIS: Gunshot wound, right lower chest wall with laceration of the liver. Gunshot wound involving the right wrist. Lacerations on the scalp.

Jordan S. Fox, M.D.

DICTATED: 7/7/YR-1 ENTERED: 7/7/YR-1 ktb
THIS COPY PRINTED: 10/16/YR-1

MONROE COUNTY HOSPITAL Bayshore, Columbia

NAME: Townsley, Nicholas Baker Patient #: 5612811

ADMITTED: 7-6-YR-1

DISCHARGED: 7-1-YR-1

PHYSICIAN: Jordan S. Fox

DISCHARGE REPORT

PRESENT ILLNESS: This 28-year-old male was admitted via the ER following a gunshot wound. X-rays revealed fractures of the 7th and 8th ribs anteriorly with metallic and bone fragments within the hepatic substance adjacent to the rib fracture sites. X-rays of the right wrist revealed a fracture which involved the articulate surfaces of the radius at the wrist joint. Lacerations on the head.

PHYSICAL EXAMINATION: Revealed a well developed, well nourished male appearing the stated age. Positive physical findings revealed a missile injury with the apparent entrance site in the posterior axillary line at the level of the 9th rib with an apparent exit site in the anterior axillary line at the level of the 9th rib. Lungs were clear and well expanded. The abdomen revealed some guarding in the right upper quadrant, otherwise was unremarkable. Extremities were within normal limits, with the exception of the right wrist where there was a missile injury involving the area of the styloid process of the radius. At admission, there was a heavy odor of alcohol on his breath and the patient was unconscious.

ACCESSORY CLINICAL FINDINGS: On admission the hematocrit was 41, urinalysis revealed 2+ sugar; on July 7, serum electrolytes were within normal limits on several occasions. Hematocrit on July 9 was 39 and on July 11 was 35. Drainage from the lower chest wall wound on July 9th revealed no bacterial growth in 48 hours. On July 12, white blood cell count was within normal limits, as was the urinalysis and the hematocrit was 36.5%. Chest x-rays on several occasions were negative.

COURSE IN HOSPITAL: The patient was taken immediately to the operating room from the ER where an exploratory laparotomy was done through upper paramedian incision. There was a laceration involving the lateral surface of the right lobe of the liver at the level of 8th or 9th rib. No active bleeding was noted from it. As it was inaccessible for suturing it was elected to drain the area with two Penrose drains at a lateral stab wound. This was done and the entry and exit site of the chest wall were debrided and drained. The postoperative course was uneventful. The patient was initially treated with Achromycin and Bupronex for three days, and later changed to Keflex. All wounds healed and were clean at the time of discharge. The patient was afebrile for three days prior to discharge. At the time of the exploratory laparotomy the right wrist was debrided and the wound drained and placed in an appropriate cast. This was dressed at periodic intervals and will be followed by removal of the cast, four weeks from the time of the original injury. The lacerations on the scalp were stitched closed.

FINAL DIAGNOSIS: Gunshot wound of the lower chest wall and upper abdomen with laceration of the liver. Gunshot wound of the right wrist with comminuted fracture of the articulate surface of the radius. Lacerations on the head.

OPERATIONS: Exploratory laparotomy with drainage of liver and debridement of wound and repair of left wrist gunshot wound.

DISCHARGE MEDICATION: Keftab 250 mg. every 6 hours for 7 days.

Jordan S. Fox, M.D.

DICTATED: 7/1/YR-1 ENTERED: 7/1/YR-1 ktb
THIS COPY PRINTED: 10/16/YR-1

BAYSHORE WOMEN'S COUNSELING CENTER
709 West First Street
Bayshore, Columbia

Dr. Mary M. O'Donnell
Director
Dr. Linda C. Cochran
Dr. Elvia Bishop
Staff Psychologists
Melissa Curtis, ACSW
Counselor

Telephone (811) 328-4666

REPORT ON BARBARA W. TOWNSLEY
October 11, YR-1

My name is Dr. Linda C. Cochran. I am a clinical psychologist. I have my own private practice in Bayshore. Much of my practice is taken up with counseling women in abusive and codependent relationships. I am an adjunct professor of psychology at the University of Columbia and teach a course on the Psychology of Women. I am the staff psychologist at Crocus House, a shelter for abused women. My resume is attached to this statement. At the request of attorney Bonnie Martin, I have talked extensively with Barbara Townsley. We had six sessions together over a three week period in August YR-1, shortly after she had been charged with the attempted murder of her husband. In addition, I have reviewed the police and court records and talked to friends and family members. It is my conclusion, based on all available information, that Ms. Townsley was suffering from Battered Woman Syndrome at the time she shot her husband.

Battered Woman Syndrome is a condition induced in some women by a pattern of physical abuse within an intimate interpersonal relationship with someone the victim trusts. It is characterized by a state of mental distortion in which the woman believes she is helpless, isolated, and dependent on the abuser. In extreme cases, the victim believes her options are reduced to killing or being killed. Battered Woman Syndrome is a concept that was developed primarily by Dr. Lenore Walker in the 1970s, and described in her book *Battered Women.* At the time, it was ridiculed by the men who dominated the psychology profession, and many still refuse to admit that it exists. The syndrome explains the characteristics that many physically abused women display, and the psychological effects that regular beatings have on them. Not all women who are subject to physical abuse suffer from Battered Woman Syndrome, however. Some are able to break the cycle of abuse (often with the help of counseling) and leave the abusive environment before the onset of the syndrome.

One common pattern of battering is a cycle that follows three distinct stages that vary in duration and intensity. The first stage is "tension-building," in which minor batterings, verbal abuse, and threats occur. During this stage, the victim denies the reality of the situation and becomes passive and submissive in an attempt to avoid any escalation in the level of violence. The second stage is "violence," in which a serious battering incident occurs, often involving dangerous weapons, and during which the victim is often seriously injured. The third stage is "contrition and forgiveness." In this phase, the abuser becomes loving and contrite, and promises to reform or get help. He may become almost childlike in his attempts to win forgiveness. He vows never to hit the victim again. The victim forgives him, and a period of intense, peaceful intimacy follows. The experience of the victim in this loving stage may be so intense that she will subconsciously initiate the next violent episode in order to experience the emotional "high" of the contrition-forgiveness stage.

Although some escape, many women are unable to extricate themselves from this cycle of violence. The victim may be isolated from the outside world by her abuser, who has all property, cars and financial matters in his name and under his control. She often has no marketable skills, abilities or job experience that would enable her to support herself, nowhere to go, no money of her own, and little self-esteem. She has learned that the police and courts will not help her. Previous complaints to the police have gone unanswered, prosecutors may have declined to prosecute, and she may have faced hostile questioning about prior incidents in which she "dropped charges." Some battered women deny they are being battered and try to distance themselves from the stereotype of the battered woman. At the beginning of the relationship, the victim may have attempted to resist the battering or leave the abuser, but was unable to do so because the police and family members told her to return home and work things out, and the abuser retaliated with violence and threats to kill her if she tried to leave again. The victim comes to believe that if she does not submit, she will be killed.

From the victim's perspective, the most disturbing aspect of Battered Woman Syndrome may be "learned helplessness." The victim is beaten even when she has done nothing bad. The abuser finds fault with completely inconsequential actions by the woman. She cannot avoid the battering by being submissive and doing what the abuser demands. Thus, she learns there is nothing she can do to reduce the chances of being beaten, nor can she predict when she will be beaten. She learns she is helpless to control outcomes.

In some cases, the level of violence begins to increase. The victim comes to believe that she will be killed by the abuser. She perceives that if she tries to escape, she will be caught and killed. If she stays, she will be killed. Her only option is to kill her attacker, but she is likely to perceive him as being nearly omnipotent. Therefore, few women ever find the courage to strike back. Those few victims who eventually do strike back at their abusers usually do so when he is sleeping, unarmed, and/or has his back turned. Even in that condition, the abuser is seen by his victim as immensely powerful and an imminent threat to her safety.

In Barbara Townsley's case, she fits closely the profile of the battered woman who has been subject to the three-stage cycle of abuse with escalating violence. Her husband beat and abused her over the years. He put the house, the cars, and the checking account in his name only. He insisted she give up her name and take his when they were married. He also insisted that she give up her job. She reported his attacks a couple of times, but the police and courts did nothing, and her husband punished her for her "betrayal" by physical violence, so she learned it was safer to put up with the violence than try to stop it. In recent months, the violence was increasing.

On July 6, Barbara shot her husband after a particularly violent attack. Although she is somewhat unclear about the details, she apparently shot him twice. The first time, he appeared to be unhurt, which only reinforced her impression about how powerful he was. The second time she shot him in the back as he was walking away. Although this is not self-defense in the usual sense, I believe that she felt her husband was still an imminent danger to her when she fired at him.

Linda C. Cochran

DR. LINDA C. COCHRAN

Bayshore Women's Counseling Center
709 West First Street
Bayshore, Columbia
(811) 328-4666

AREAS OF PRACTICE

Women's Issues. Individual, Marital and Family Therapy. Eating Disorders. Weight Control. Stress/Anxiety Therapy. Sexual Abuse Counseling.

EDUCATIONAL BACKGROUND

Ph.D. in Clinical Psychology, YR-5; University of Columbia.
B.A. in Psychology, YR-10; Univ. of California - Santa Cruz

HONORS AND DISTINCTIONS

Appointed Senior Research Fellow, Women's Health Institute, YR-2.
Special Service Award, United Way of Columbia, YR-2.
Rebecca S. Bradway Fellowship, Univ. of Columbia, YR-7 to YR-5.

PROFESSIONAL AFFILIATIONS

Adjunct Professor of Psychology, University of Columbia since YR-3.
Staff Psychologist, Crocus House (Shelter for Abused Women).
Advisory Committee on Battered Women, National Organization for Women.
Consultant, Monroe County Juvenile Court

PUBLICATIONS

"Representing Women Who Defend Themselves Against Violence," Women's Rights Law Reporter 4:17 (YR-1) (co-authored with attorney Valerie Heinz-Johnson).

"Clinical Diagnosis of Battered Woman Syndrome: Two Cases," Midwest Counseling Journal 23:322 (YR-2).

"Battered Woman Syndrome and Premenstrual Syndrome: A Comparison and Critique," Women's Health Quarterly 44:32 (YR-3).

OTHER

Columbia Civil Liberties Union Mental Health Committee
Consultant, Columbia State Public Defender's Office
Member, NOW
Member, Pro-Choice Feminist Coalition of Bayshore

SELECTED COLUMBIA PATTERN JURY INSTRUCTIONS

Preliminary Instructions:

Members of the jury: This is a criminal case brought by the State of Columbia against Barbara Townsley. She is charged with attempted murder and assault for shooting her husband. She has pleaded not guilty to the charge. The fact that she has been charged is not evidence of guilt. The State must prove beyond a reasonable doubt each element of the offenses charged. Until then, the defendant is presumed to be innocent of the charges against her.

The trial will proceed in the following order: First, the attorneys will make their opening statements, in which they explain to you the evidence they will introduce and the issues they will address.

Second, the state will present its evidence through witnesses and exhibits. During this stage, the law requires the State to introduce enough evidence to convince you beyond a reasonable doubt that the defendant is guilty of the crimes charged. When the State has finished, the defense has the opportunity to present evidence of innocence. The defendant may offer evidence or may not. She has no obligation to prove her innocence. She is presumed innocent, and the burden of proof is on the state to prove otherwise. During the evidence phase, the witnesses are first examined by the lawyer who calls them and may then be cross-examined by the lawyer for the other side. There may be objections, and you must not consider any evidence that is stricken or that you are told to disregard.

At the end of the trial, the attorneys will present their closing arguments, in which they summarize evidence and discuss the case. What the lawyers say is not evidence, however. After closing arguments, I will give you some further instructions about the law and you will retire o deliberate.

It is your duty throughout the trial to be fair and impartial, and keep an open mind. You should not form or express an opinion during the trial and should reach no conclusion in this case until you have heard all of the evidence, the arguments of counsel, and the final instructions as to the law.

There will be occasional recesses during the trial. During these recesses you must not discuss the case with anyone, not even your friends. Nor may you look things up on the Internet. Please keep your cell phones turned off.

All people in this trial are fictional, and the events take place in an imaginary city called Bayshore, in the state of Columbia.

Concluding Instructions:

Members of the jury. You have now heard the evidence and the arguments of counsel. It is my duty to instruct you on the law, which you are obliged to follow.

It is your duty to determine the facts and decide what happened. The only evidence you may consider is the evidence that was properly admitted at trial. You may not consider any matter that was rejected or stricken by the Court. You may not consider anything you read in the paper or hear from your friends about this case, nor may you do your own investigation or look anything up on the Internet.

You are the sole judges of the weight of the evidence and of the credibility of witnesses. In determining the credibility of any witness and the weight to be given to the testimony of any witness, you may take into account any interest the witness has in the result, and any bias or prejudices the witness disclosed. You may consider the opportunity or lack of opportunity of the witness to observe the events, and the reasonableness of the testimony in light of all the evidence in the case. You are not required to set aside your common knowledge, but may consider the evidence in light of your own experiences in the affairs of life.

Do not let bias, prejudice, or sympathy play any part in your deliberations.

The State must prove beyond a reasonable doubt each element of the offenses charged. There is a presumption of the defendant's innocence in a criminal case. That presumption of innocence should continue and prevail in your minds unless you are convinced of her guilt beyond a reasonable doubt.

Reasonable doubt is not a mere possible doubt, it is a doubt that arises from your consideration of the evidence and one that would cause a careful person to pause and hesitate in the graver transactions of life.

Barbara Townsley is charged with attempted murder. This charge includes the lesser offense of attempted manslaughter. You may find the defendant guilty of one of these offenses or not guilty of either, but you may not convict her of both.

The defendant also is charged with aggravated assault. This is a separate offense, and you should convict or acquit the defendant of assault independently of your decision concerning her guilt of attempted murder.

The first charge is attempted murder. To sustain this charge, the State must prove beyond a reasonable doubt that Barbara Townsley purposely committed an act constituting a substantial step in a course of conduct whose purpose was to cause the death of Nicholas Townsley. A person acts purposely when she has the conscious object to cause death and she formed that intention before acting.

If you have a reasonable doubt of the defendant's guilt on the charge of attempted murder, you should consider whether she is guilty of attempted manslaughter. To sustain this charge, the State must prove beyond a reasonable doubt that Barbara Townsley attempted to cause the death of Nicholas Townsley under circumstances that would be murder except that she acted under the influence of extreme emotional disturbance for which there was a reasonable excuse. You should determine the reasonableness of the excuse from the viewpoint of a person in her situation under the circumstances as she believed them to be.

The second charge is aggravated assault. To sustain this charge, the State must prove beyond a reasonable doubt that Barbara Townsley, with the purpose of causing bodily injury to Nicholas Townsley, caused bodily injury to him by means of a deadly weapon.

The defendant asserts the affirmative defense of self-defense to all charges. To establish this defense, she must prove that she reasonably believed Nicholas Townsley was using or about to use unlawful physical force upon her and that she used only such force which she reasonably believed to be necessary. A person is not justified in using deadly force if she knows that the use of deadly force can be avoided with complete safety by retreating. The defendant has the burden of proving self-defense by a preponderance of the evidence. "Preponderance of the evidence" means the greater weight of evidence. If she proves self-defense to you, it is a complete defense to both charges.

Your verdict must be unanimous.

MONROE COUNTY DISTRICT COURT
STATE OF COLUMBIA

State of Columbia Plaintiff vs. Barbara W. Townsley Defendant	)))))))	08608 **VERDICT**

We the jurors of Monroe County find the defendant:

A. As to Count I of the indictment:

__ Not guilty of either Attempted Murder or Attempted Manslaughter.

__ Not guilty of Attempted Murder but guilty of Attempted Manslaughter.

__ Guilty of Attempted Murder.

B. As to Count II of the indictment:

__ Not guilty of Aggravated Assault.

__ Guilty of Aggravated Assault.

____
Jury Foreperson

CASE FILE F:

LARRY JAMES KANE

v.

MICHAEL LOWELL BOND and THE CITY OF BAYSHORE

CIVIL RIGHTS ACT
POLICE BRUTALITY

KANE v. BOND & CITY OF BAYSHORE
CONTENTS OF FILE

GENERAL INSTRUCTIONS

This is a civil rights action brought in federal court under 42 U.S.C. § 1983, based on a police officer shooting a young man during the course of a routine traffic accident investigation. The victim of the shooting is suing the police officer for using excessive force, and the city for having policies that condoned the use of force by its officers. He seeks compensatory and punitive damages. The police officer claims he only used reasonably necessary force in self-defense. The city claims the officer was acting outside his authority and against city policies. The events took place in July two years ago, at an apartment complex in a fictional city called Bayshore, Columbia (population 150,000).

Potential Witnesses

Larry Kane -- plaintiff
Victoria Curtin -- Kane's girlfriend
Michael Bond -- defendant police officer
Alexandra Spiro -- eyewitness
Robert Sullivan -- chief of police
Dr. Gordon Linton -- doctor who operated on Kane

Instructions concerning exhibits

1. Any party may use a gun, nightstick (or reasonable approximation thereof), or set of keys as an exhibit. No objections may be made on grounds that an exhibit does not precisely match its description in the file. For example, if a toy gun is used, no objections may be made that it is the wrong size, wrong manufacturer, lacks the correct serial number, etc.

2. The hospital records and the bill for services (pages F-55 to F-59) are all true and accurate copies of business records of Monroe County Hospital.

Instructions for use as a three-party trial

1. Plaintiff must call Larry Kane and Victoria Curtin, and may either call Dr. Linton as an expert witness or use the alternative medical stipulation described below. Plaintiff may call other witnesses only with the approval of the court. Plaintiff must cross-examine Michael Bond and Alexandra Spiro. Cross-examination of Robert Sullivan is optional.

2. Defendant Bond must call Michael Bond and Alexandra Spiro as witnesses in his case-in-chief, and may call other witnesses only with the approval of the court. Bond must cross-examine Victoria Curtin and Robert Sullivan. Cross-examinations of Dr. Linton and Larry Kane are optional.

3. Defendant City of Bayshore must call Robert Sullivan as a witness in its case-in-chief, and may call other witnesses only with the approval of the court. The City must cross-examine Larry Kane. Cross-examination of Michael Bond is optional.

Instructions for use as a two-party trial

1. The trial judge granted a motion to dismiss the case against the City of Bayshore on the ground of immunity (do not be concerned with whether this ruling is correct). Bond is the only defendant remaining in the case.

2. Plaintiff must call Larry Kane and Victoria Curtin, and may either call Dr. Linton as an expert witness or use the alternative medical stipulation described below. Plaintiff may call other witnesses only with the approval of the court. Plaintiff may not call Robert Sullivan.

3. Defendant Bond must call Michael Bond and Alexandra Spiro as witnesses in his case-in-chief, and may call other witnesses only with the approval of the court. Bond may not call Robert Sullivan.

Alternative medical stipulation

In lieu of calling Dr. Gordon Linton as a witness, the parties have stipulated to the following:

> "Dr. Gordon Linton is the surgeon who operated on Larry Kane at the Monroe County Hospital Emergency Room, July 6, YR-2. Mr. Kane had been hit by two bullets. One hit his right wrist and broke some bones. The other entered his lower back on the right side, and exited from his mid-chest area. Neither bullet did any permanent damage. It is impossible to tell which bullet hit him first. Dr. Linton cleaned the wounds and set the wrist in a plaster case. Mr. Kane spent one week in the hospital. At the time he was admitted, Mr. Kane had a blood-alcohol level of 0.05%, the equivalent of about four beers. At that level, most men would be uninhibited but not seriously intoxicated, and there would have been no significant impairment of physical coordination. In Dr. Linton's opinion, Mr. Kane would have been in extreme pain for two to three days, then moderate pain for a week, and then mild discomfort in the wrist for a month. Dr. Linton removed Mr. Kane's cast on August 14, YR-2, at which time the wrist appeared to be healing normally and Mr. Kane said he felt fine."

Stipulations

1. Any criminal offense listed as a misdemeanor is one for which the maximum statutory penalty is one year or less. Any offense listed as a felony is one for which the maximum penalty is more than one year.

2. The original attorneys have withdrawn from this case, citing conflicts of interest.

Note on Dates

All years are designated as follows: YR-0 refers to the present year, YR-1 refers to one year ago, YR-2 (the year in which the events took place) refers to two years ago, etc.

UNITED STATES DISTRICT COURT
EASTERN DISTRICT OF COLUMBIA

Larry James Kane, *Plaintiff*	)	
vs.	)	Civil No. 1:05-cv-0359
Michael Lowell Bond and City of Bayshore, *Defendants*	)	

AMENDED COMPLAINT

1. This is an action for damages sustained by a citizen of the United States against a police officer and the Bayshore Police Department based on the use of unnecessary and excessive force.

2. This action is brought pursuant to 42 U.S.C. § 1983 and the Fourth and Fourteenth Amendments to the Constitution of the United States.

3. This court has jurisdiction pursuant to 28 U.S.C. §§ 1331, 1332, and 1343.

4. Plaintiff Larry J. Kane is a resident of Monroe County, state of Columbia, and a citizen of the United States.

5. At all times relevant hereto, defendant Michael Bond was a police officer cadet employed by the Bayshore Police Department, a public agency, and was acting within the scope of his authority as a police officer under color of state law.

6. The defendant City of Bayshore is a municipal corporation in the state of Columbia and operates the Bayshore Police Department. At all times relevant, it employed defendant Bond and had the responsibility for training and supervising him.

7. On July 6, YR-2, at or about 7:30 p.m., at or near the Knightridge Apartments, 2412 Rockport Road, plaintiff was detained by defendant Michael Bond for questioning concerning a traffic accident.

8. Michael Bond intentionally and without provocation, struck plaintiff on the head with a "nightstick" and the butt of a handgun, causing injury.

9. Without warning or justification, Michael Bond intentionally shot plaintiff in the back and wrist, causing serious injury.

10. While plaintiff was in the hospital, defendants arrested him for Resisting Arrest, which charge was subsequently dismissed by the Monroe County Circuit Court.

11. As a result of the conduct described above, plaintiff experienced humiliation, emotional distress, pain and suffering, incurred expenses including legal fees and medical expenses, was physically injured requiring hospitalization, and was otherwise damaged.

12. On information and belief, defendant Michael Bond was acting in accordance with official policies and practices of the Bayshore Police Department which permitted untrained police officer cadets to carry and use guns without adequate training or supervision.

FIRST CAUSE OF ACTION

13. At all times relevant to this cause of action, Michael Bond was acting under color of state law and pursuant to his authority as a police officer employed by the City of Bayshore and with knowledge that excessive force by law enforcement personnel was a violation of prevailing constitutional law.

14. Michael Bond intentionally and maliciously caused plaintiff to be deprived of his civil and constitutional rights by using an excessive degree of force that was unreasonable under the circumstances in violation of plaintiff's rights under the Fourth and Fourteenth Amendments to be free from unreasonable seizure.

SECOND CAUSE OF ACTION

15. Acting under color of state law, the City of Bayshore through its Police Department, with reckless disregard for plaintiff's rights, created a policy of training inexperienced cadets in the field and allowing them to carry loaded firearms prior to completing police training, which policies were a significant cause of the injuries to Plaintiff and the deprivation of his Fourth and Fourteenth Amendment rights.

RELIEF REQUESTED

WHEREFORE, Plaintiff demands relief jointly and severally against all defendants as follows:

A. Compensatory damages in the amount of $14,920.

B. Compensatory damages in the amount of $500,000 for pain and suffering.

C. Punitive damages in the amount of $5,000,000.

D. Reasonable attorneys fees pursuant to 42 U.S.C. §1988.

E. Such other relief as the court deems just and proper.

DEMAND FOR JURY TRIAL

Pursuant to Rule 38(b), Federal Rules of Civil Procedure, plaintiff hereby demands trial by jury on all issues in this action.

s/ George L. Baker
George L. Baker
Attorney for Plaintiff
Lerner Law Office
3131 E. Third St.
Bayshore, Columbia

UNITED STATES DISTRICT COURT
EASTERN DISTRICT OF COLUMBIA

Larry James Kane, Plaintiff	)	Civil No. 1:05 cv 0359
vs.	)	
Michael Lowell Bond and City of Bayshore, Defendants	)	**ANSWER OF DEFENDANT MICHAEL L. BOND**

Defendant Michael Bond answers Plaintiff's allegations as follows:

1. The allegations in paragraph 1 are denied.

2. Defendant is without knowledge or information sufficient to form a belief as to the truth of the allegations in paragraph 2.

3. Defendant is without knowledge or information sufficient to form a belief as to the truth of the allegations in paragraph 3.

4. Defendant is without knowledge or information sufficient to form a belief as to the truth of the allegations in paragraph 4.

5. With respect to the allegations in paragraph 5, Defendant admits that Bond was a cadet employed by the police department, and denies the rest of the paragraph.

6. Defendant is without knowledge or information sufficient to form a belief as to the truth of the allegations in paragraph 6.

7. Admitted.

8. The allegations in paragraph 8 are denied.

9. The allegations in paragraph 9 are denied.

10. The allegations in paragraph 10 are denied.

11. The allegations in paragraph 11 are denied.

12. The allegations in paragraph 12 are denied.

13. The allegations in paragraph 13 are denied.

14. The allegations in paragraph 14 are denied.

15. The allegations in paragraph 15 are denied.

First Defense

16. If defendant Michael Lowell Bond did the acts alleged in paragraphs 8 through 12 of the complaint, he did so in self-defense of his person, using no greater force than was reasonable and necessary to protect himself from imminent serious bodily harm.

Second Defense

17. If defendant Michael Lowell Bond did the acts alleged in paragraphs 8 through 12 of the complaint, he did so believing his actions were justified and within his statutory authorization as a police officer of the State of Columbia in the course of an attempt to lawfully apprehend plaintiff.

WHEREFORE, defendants pray that the complaint be dismissed and they recover their costs and expenses incurred herein.

s/ Megan S. Minnick
Megan S. Minnick
Attorney for Defendant Bond
HOUSTON, MINNICK & DOS SANTOS
100 N. Walnut Street
Bayshore, Columbia

CERTIFICATE OF SERVICE

I hereby certify that on September 13, YR-1,a copy of the foregoing was filed with the Clerk of Court electronically using the CM/ECF system, which sent notice to counsel for plaintiff George L. Baker.

September 13, YR-1

s/ Megan S. Minnick
Megan S. Minnick
Attorney for Defendant Bond

UNITED STATES DISTRICT COURT
EASTERN DISTRICT OF COLUMBIA

Larry James Kane, Plaintiff vs. Michael Lowell Bond and City of Bayshore, Defendants	))))))))	 Civil No. 1:05cv-0359 **ANSWER OF DEFENDANT** **CITY OF BAYSHORE**

---

1. Defendant is without knowledge or information sufficient to form a belief as to the truth of the allegations in paragraph 1.

2. Defendant is without knowledge or information sufficient to form a belief as to the truth of the allegations in paragraph 2.

3. Defendant is without knowledge or information sufficient to form a belief as to the truth of the allegations in paragraph 3.

4. Defendant is without knowledge or information sufficient to form a belief as to the truth of the allegations in paragraph 4.

5. Defendant admits Bond was a police cadet employed by the city, but denies the remainder of paragraph 5.

6. Defendant admits paragraph 6.

7. Defendant is without knowledge or information sufficient to form a belief as to the truth of the allegations in paragraph 7.

8. Defendant is without knowledge or information sufficient to form a belief as to the truth of the allegations in paragraph 8.

9. Defendant is without knowledge or information sufficient to form a belief as to the truth of the allegations in paragraph 9.

10. Defendant is without knowledge or information sufficient to form a belief as to the truth of the allegations in paragraph 10.

11. Defendant is without knowledge or information sufficient to form a belief as to the truth of the allegations in paragraph 11.

12. Defendant denies paragraph 12.

13. Defendant is without knowledge or information sufficient to form a belief as to the truth of the allegations in paragraph 13.

14. Defendant is without knowledge or information sufficient to form a belief as to the truth of the allegations in paragraph 14.

15. Defendant denies paragraph 15.

FIRST DEFENSE

The complaint fails to state a claim upon which relief can be granted because defendant is a municipality entitled to sovereign immunity.

SECOND DEFENSE

If defendant Michael Lowell Bond did the acts alleged in paragraphs 8 through 12 of the complaint, he did so in his personal capacity for personal reasons, and not acting as a police officer, and therefore not acting under color of state law.

THIRD DEFENSE

If defendant Michael Lowell Bond did the acts alleged in paragraphs 7 through 12 of the complaint, he did so contrary to the policies and practices of the City of Bayshore Police Department and without authorization.

WHEREFORE, defendant City of Bayshore prays that the complaint be dismissed as to it and they recover their costs and expenses incurred herein.

s/ Vivian Tucker
Vivian Tucker
Bayshore City Attorney's Office
201 E. 4th Street, Bayshore, Columbia

CERTIFICATE OF SERVICE

The undersigned certifies that on September 14, YR-1, she filed a copy of this Answer with the Court using the CM/ECF system, which has served notice on counsel for all parties.

September 14, YR-1

s/ Vivian Tucker
Vivian Tucker
Columbia Attorney No. 26534

SUMMARY OF THE LAW OF CIVIL RIGHTS ACTIONS

1. *42 U.S.C. §1983 (The Civil Rights Act of 1871)*: "Every person who, under color of any statute, ordinance, regulation, custom or usage, of any State or Territory or the District of Columbia, subjects, or causes to be subjected, any citizen of the United States ... to the deprivation of any rights, privileges, or immunities secured by the Constitution and laws, shall be liable to the party injured in an action at law, suit in equity, or other proper proceeding for redress."

2. *Graham v. Connor*, 490 U.S. 386 (1989), is the leading case on section 1983 claims involving allegations of excessive force or police brutality. It held that an excessive force claim in the context of an investigative stop or arrest of a free citizen is properly classified as a fourth amendment claim. Whether the force used was unconstitutionally excessive is a question of objective reasonableness under the specific facts and circumstances of the case. Courts must balance the nature, quality and extent of the intrusion on the plaintiff's right to be free from unreasonable seizures against the governmental interest. The courts should consider the severity of the crime at issue, whether the plaintiff posed an immediate threat to the officers involved or to others, and whether the plaintiff actively resisted arrest or attempted to flee. These circumstances must be judged from the "perspective of the reasonable officer on the scene." The intent or motivation of the particular officer is irrelevant.

3. In *Tennessee v. Garner*, 471 U.S. 1 (1985), the Supreme Court applied a fourth amendment analysis to the shooting of a fleeing suspect. The Court held that it was unreasonable, and therefore actionable under §1983, for an officer to use deadly force to prevent the escape of a fleeing suspect who did not pose an immediate threat to the safety of the officers or others. Deadly force may only be used where there is probable cause to believe the suspect may cause physical harm to the officers or others because he threatens someone with a gun or is believed to have committed a crime involving serious physical injury, threatened serious physical injury, or the use of a deadly weapon.

4. In *City of Canton v. Harris*, 489 U.S. 378 (1989), the Supreme Court held that a municipality is not jointly liable for an officer's civil rights violations on a *respondeat superior* theory. To make a case against a city, the plaintiff normally must show recurring use of excessive force, coupled with "deliberate indifference" to the rights of the municipality's inhabitants. Deliberate indifference can be shown by failure to train officers or refusal to discipline officers who use excessive force.

5. The essential elements of a §1983 action against an individual police officer are:

a. The plaintiff is a citizen of the United States.

b. The plaintiff was deprived of some right, privilege or immunity secured by the Constitution of the United States. The use of excessive force by the police in apprehending a criminal suspect is a violation of the Fourth Amendment right to be free from unreasonable seizures, which is applicable to the states through the Due Process clause of the Fourteenth Amendment. Whether the force used is excessive is an *objective* standard (the subjective intent of the officer is irrelevant). Given the circumstances as they appeared to be, how much force would a reasonable police officer have used, considering:

1. the severity of crime for which the suspect was being arrested.
2. whether plaintiff posed an immediate threat to the police or others.
3. whether plaintiff resisted arrest or tried to flee.

The use of deadly force is reasonable only if the officer has probable cause to believe that serious physical harm to himself or others is imminent. Usually a warning must be given before deadly force is used, if feasible.

c. Plaintiff was injured.

d. The deprivation of rights proximately caused the injuries.

e. Defendant acted under color of state law (within the apparent authority of a statute, ordinance, custom, usage or regulation). Employees and agents of the state are presumed to be acting under color of law if they are engaged in activities within the scope of their apparent authority.

f. The defendant acted intentionally.

6. The essential elements of a §1983 action against a municipality are slightly different. In addition to proving the elements listed above, plaintiff must prove that the city has either an implicit or explicit policy or practice of depriving persons like plaintiff of their rights. In excessive force cases, city policy has been shown in several ways:

a. The police department has a custom or policy condoning excessive force.

b. The police department has a specific policy, practice or regulation that caused the use of force.

c. Failure to train or discipline officers, demonstrating deliberate indifference to their use of force against citizens.

d. Failure to act on previous reports of excessive force.

Cities are *not* liable under a theory of *respondeat superior.* Plaintiff must prove that a police department policy led to the use of excessive force.

7. It is a defense to a §1983 action that the police officer was acting wholly outside his or her official duties. Under such circumstances, the officer is not operating under color of state law, so the basis in federal jurisdiction is lacking. Such a case would have to be brought in state court as an ordinary intentional tort. However, it is not a defense that the officer was acting without specific authorization.

8. It is a defense that the force used was reasonable and necessary under the circumstances, either to protect the officer, protect the public, prevent the escape of a criminal suspect, or apprehend a person when the officer has probable cause to believe they have committed a crime.

9. A helpful summary of the law of police misconduct can be found in Joseph G. Cook and John L. Sobieski's treatise, CIVIL RIGHTS ACTIONS, volume 7, chapter F9 (2009).

State of Columbia
County of Monroe

State of Columbia	)	No. Y21902
	)	
vs.	)	Assault, Resisting Arrest
	)	
Larry J. Kane	)	
	)	

Before Hon. Velda Hall
Monroe County District Court
July 28, YR-2

Appearances: for the State: A.D.A. Nancy May
for Mr. Kane: Robert Hartwell, P.D.
Court Reporter: Dodie Bowman

TRANSCRIPT OF CRIMINAL PROCEEDINGS

Court convened at 2:05 p.m., whereupon the following proceedings were had:
COURT: Call case number Y21902, Larry Kane, charged with assault and resisting arrest. Is this case ready for trial?
MS. MAY: No your honor, this is the defendant who was shot by the police during a traffic stop. Each side accuses the other of assault.
COURT: What do you wish to do, Ms. May?
MS. MAY: Your honor, after an investigation of this situation the state does not feel it can determine who was at fault or who started it nor obtain a conviction against either the defendant or the officer. Therefore, we move pursuant to Rule 48 to dismiss the complaint against Kane, and we do not intend to file charges against officer Bond.
COURT: All right, case . . .
MR. HARTWELL: May I be heard?
COURT: All right.
MR. HARTWELL: Your honor, we object to the dismissal. I would point out that Mr. Kane was shot in the back and hospitalized.

COURT: I don't believe Rule 48 requires your consent, counsel. Case number Y21902 is dismissed on motion of the state. Formal filing of a written dismissal is dispensed with.

Certified as accurate: *Dodie Bowman*

Dodie Bowman
Court Reporter

September 19, YR-2

Larry James Kane	)
	)
-against-	)
	)
Michael L. Bond and	)
City of Bayshore	)

DEPOSITION OF MICHAEL L. BOND

Date: November 10, YR-2
Place: Offices of Stanley Lerner
3131 E. Third St.
Bayshore, Columbia
Time Began: 9:30 a.m.
Present: George Baker, for plaintiff
Vivian Tucker, for defendants
Michael Bond
Dodie Bowman, stenographer and notary public

MS. BOWMAN: Mr. Bond, do you swear to answer truthfully all questions asked during this deposition?
MR. BOND: Yes.
MR. BAKER: Will you state your full name, address and place of employment?
A: Michael Lowell Bond, 1752 South Walnut Street, Bayshore, Columbia. I work as a patrol officer for the Bayshore Police Department.
Q: How long have you worked there?
A: Since April 16, Yr-2.
Q: What are your duties?
A: I am assigned to a radio car and I patrol Bayshore. I handle routine complaints, make traffic stops, and investigate traffic accidents. From April 16, Yr-2 to October 15, I was a police officer cadet undergoing training in addition to my field assignments.
Q: Please tell me about your personal and family background.
A: I was born January 23, YR-26. I went to Bayshore High School. My mother has passed away, but my father still lives here. I am not married. I was married but I got divorced after only a year. I have one child that I send support to. I worked at a Grand Union Supermarket for two years,

doing stock work and patrolling the aisles for people who eat food, and then got a job as a security guard at Knightridge. I worked there for four years and finally got a job here. I always wanted to be a police officer.

Q. Did you receive any law enforcement training?

A: Well, I had on-the-job training as a private security guard . . .

Q: No, I mean at the Bayshore Police Department.

A: Yes. The Department hires you as a cadet and you receive six months of training before you become a full patrol officer. For the first two weeks, you read a training manual that contains a lot of stuff in it on traffic laws and how to fill out a ticket, and basic procedures like reading suspects their rights. You have to pass a written multiple-choice test. Then you are assigned to work with an experienced officer so you learn the routine, go to court, learn how to take fingerprints, preserve evidence, and so on. Then after a couple of months they put you out in the field by yourself. It's like flying solo when you're taking flying lessons.

Q: Did you attend the Columbia Police Academy?

A: No. With the budget cuts, the Department couldn't afford it. They have to pay tuition, you know. So the Department instituted the on-the-job training program instead.

Q: Prior to July 6, YR-2, had you received any training in the use of firearms?

A: Yes. We had to put in 20 hours at the pistol range with the instructor. We had to pass a proficiency test.

Q: Did you receive any training specifically in when to use your firearm in a confrontation with a suspect?

A: No live training, but there was a written policy in the training manual which I read.

Q: Do you think the Department adequately prepared you for the confrontation with Larry Kane on July 6?

A: No, but other officers say that nothing prepares you for your first life-and-death situation.

Q: Did you know Larry Kane prior to July 6, YR-2?

A: Yes.

Q: Will you explain that acquaintance in detail?

A: I first encountered Kane on July 4, YR-2. I responded to a call from a resident of the Knightridge apartments to investigate excessive noise at a party. I went to apartment 3-B which belongs to Victoria Curtin where a

Fourth of July party was in progress. I asked them to please keep the noise down. Larry Kane followed me out of the apartment, shouting obscenities. I told him to be quiet or I would arrest him. He picked up a stick and said, "Just try it, bozo." I pulled my revolver and ordered him to put down the weapon or I would arrest him as drunk and disorderly. He said, "Fuck, you," but he put down the stick. Then he got into his car and drove away.

Q: Was this at the apartments where you used to work as a security guard?

A: Yes.

Q: Was this gun issued by the Bayshore Police Department?

A: No, it was my personal gun. Cadet officers are not issued guns by the Department until they are promoted to patrol officer status.

Q: Did the Department know you were carrying your own gun?

A: Sure. Everyone carried them.

Q: Did you report this incident?

A: Not officially because there was no arrest, but I told my supervisor, Lt. Patrick McCardle about the incident. He criticized my handling of the incident and said I had to control the situation whenever a suspect had a weapon because they pose a danger to the public.

Q: Did you tell Lt. McCardle that you were carrying a personal firearm?

A: Sure -- he knew about it anyway. He didn't say anything to me about not carrying it. In fact, all the experienced officers tell you to carry an extra firearm because you're a target whenever you're out in the field in a police uniform.

Q: Were you by yourself on July 4?

A: Yes. At that time it was customary for cadets in their third month of training to go out solo.

Q: Is that policy still in effect, to your knowledge?

A: No. Chief Sullivan put a new guy in charge of cadets shortly after this incident and he required that all cadet officers be accompanied by an experienced officer in the field.

Q: Okay. Turning to July 6, please describe what happened.

A: I went on duty at 4:00 p.m., and was assigned to patrol the area on the southwest side of Bayshore. Things were uneventful until a little before 7:30 when I got a radio run to investigate a vehicular accident at building B, Knightridge Apartments. I proceeded to the scene and saw two vehicles had run into each other. It appeared that a YR-4 Ford Mustang had backed into a Mercedes. I recognized Larry Kane who was arguing with a woman identified as Alexandra Spiro. As I approached, I also recognized Victoria Curtin from apartment 3-B. I heard her telling Kane to calm down, and she had her hand on his arm. I asked him if he was Larry Kane and he said, "I'm not going to tell you anything." He was very loud and his face was red and it smelled like he had been drinking. I turned to ask Ms. Spiro her name and to tell me about the accident when I heard Kane scream, "Get out of my face." I turned and saw him push Ms. Curtin away.

I then told Kane to be quiet or I would hold him for disorderly conduct. Kane said, "You ain't gonna hold me any goddam place." Some other tenants had gathered, so I went back to my car and radioed for a back-up unit. At this time my back was to Kane, but I heard Ms. Curtin tell him again to be quiet, and he was shouting something like, "I'm not going to shut up and that kindergarten cop can't arrest me. I know my rights. I'm going home." I turned around and Kane was getting in his car. I ran over and told him he was being detained and could not leave until I had completed my investigation. I was standing beside the door to his car. He said, "You're not arresting me." I put my hand on the car door. Kane suddenly opened the door and pushed it into me, knocking me to the ground. I jumped up and grabbed his arm before he could close the door. I reached over and snatched his keys out of the ignition and stepped back. I pulled my nightstick and ordered him out of the car. He jumped at me, and I swung with the nightstick, hitting him once on the head. It didn't even phase him. I began to wonder if maybe he was on drugs, like angel dust.

We struggled and Kane pulled the nightstick out of my hand. He raised it over his head in a clenched fist. I pulled my revolver and pointed it at him and told him to put it down. He threw it at me, but missed. I jumped out of the way. Kane rushed at me again, and grabbed me in a bear hug. I hit him several times on the head with my gun, and then scrambled free. I put the gun back in its holster. Kane jumped me again and tried to get my gun. I pulled free but he knocked me down.

I got up on one knee, a little stunned. I saw Kane about ten feet away at the open door of his car. He was reaching under the seat. I thought he was going for a weapon, and I saw something metal in his left hand, and

I drew my revolver and fired six times. I emptied the chamber. I was in shock. I don't remember firing all six times, just the sound of the gun clicking after all the bullets were used up. Kane was lying on the ground, bleeding. A few minutes later, the back-up unit arrived.

Q: Please describe exactly the positions of the Mustang and the Mercedes when you first arrived.

A: They were right in the middle --

Q: Could you draw a sketch that we can attach to the deposition?

A: Sure.

MR. BAKER: Can we attach this as exhibit one?

MS. TUCKER: Of course.

Q: Is this the correct angle of the cars and the direction in which they pointed?

A: To the best of my memory.

Q: In other words, both cars appeared to have been backing out of parking places when they collided?

A: Ms. Spiro was backing out. Kane's car was already out.

Q: Was Spiro's car the last one in her row?

A: I'm not certain, either last or next to last.

Q: How could you tell Kane and Spiro were arguing?

A: I could hear them yelling and see them pointing at cars and making angry gestures.

Q: How close were you to Kane when you first confronted him?

A: Two or three feet away.

Q: When Kane pushed Victoria Curtin, did she fall down?

A: No.

Q: Did she ask for your help?

A: No.

Q: Can you mark on exhibit one where Kane and Spiro were arguing?

A: Sure.

Q: When Kane jumped at you the first time, describe exactly what he did.

A: He got out of the car fast, put his feet on the ground, and then lunged at me with him arms out like he was going to grab me around the waist.

Q: What did you mean when you said Kane was trying to pull your gun out of its holster?

A: His hand was on the gun and my hand was on his. I could feel him trying

to pull upwards when I was pushing downwards.
Q: Now, just before you fired your gun, could you mark exhibit one with your location?
A: Okay.
Q: Was your back against a parked car?
A: No. I was a few feet away.
Q: Was anything obstructing you to the left or right?
A: No. That's just open parking lot.
Q: As far as you know, you followed Police Department practice and custom in this encounter?
A: Yes, sir.
Q: At the point at which you first pulled your gun and pointed it at Mr. Kane, was he under arrest or a suspect in any crime?
A: No. Well, maybe trying to leave the scene of an accident.
Q: Were you aware that Larry Kane was dating Victoria Curtin?
A: Yes.
Q: And you knew Victoria, didn't you?
A: Yes.
Q: What kind of relationship do you have with Victoria Curtin?
A: What do you mean?
Q: Did you have a social or personal relationship with her?
A: Not exactly.
Q: What do you mean?
A: Well, I liked her. I met her when I worked as the apartment security guard. She was good-looking. I talked to her sometimes. I asked her out a couple of times but she said no.
Q: Were you jealous of Larry Kane?
A: Sure, a little. But that had nothing to do with the shooting.
Q: Before you fired your gun, did you give Mr. Kane any warning?
A: No. It all happened fast.
Q: Are you aware you shot him in the back?
A: No, I don't believe that's right. He was looking at me when I shot.
Q: Were you injured in any way?
A: No.
MR. BAKER: No further questions.
MS. TUCKER: Mr. Bond, did you hold any malice toward Mr. Kane?

A: No. I didn't like him much, but I wouldn't say I had any strong feelings about him.
Q: Why did you pull the trigger?
A: I was afraid for my life. I thought he was pulling out a gun.
Q: Did you think you had any other choice?
A: No, there was no alternative.
MS. TUCKER: That's all I have.

WHEREUPON IT WAS STIPULATED THAT READING AND SIGNING BY THE WITNESS IS HEREBY WAIVED PURSUANT TO RULE 30(e).

I certify pursuant to Rule 30(f) that this is a true record of the deposition.

Certified as accurate: *Dodie Bowman*

Dodie Bowman
Notary Public

BOND DEPOSITION
EXHIBIT ONE

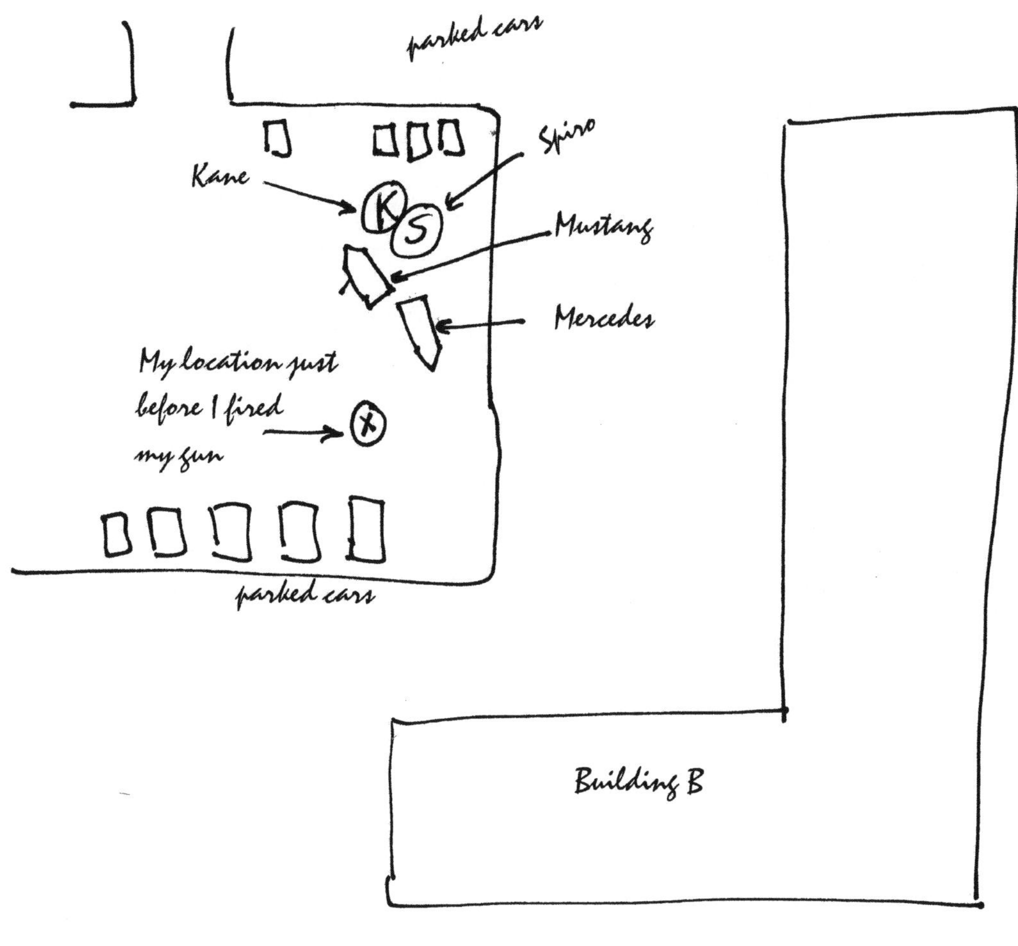

Michael Bond

CITY OF BAYSHORE

"TO SERVE AND PROTECT"

ROBERT SULLIVAN, CHIEF OF POLICE (811) 339-1584

STATEMENT OF ROBERT SULLIVAN
December 19, YR-2

The following statement has been prepared by Robert Sullivan, Chief of Police, City of Bayshore, in consultation with Vivian Tucker, attorney for the City of Bayshore.

My name is Robert C. Sullivan. I am 48 years old, married, with two children in high school. I have lived in Bayshore since YR-11. I have worked for the Bayshore Police Department ever since I arrived here. I started out in YR-26 working for the New York City Police Department, 12th precinct in Manhattan. I was trained at the New York City Police Academy, took night classes in criminal justice at Pace University, attended three summer sessions at the FBI Academy in criminal investigation techniques, and passed my sergeant's exam on the first try in YR-16.

In YR-12, my wife was assaulted and seriously injured by three male juveniles on the street in front of our apartment building. We decided that it was time to leave New York. I sent letters and resumes to all the police departments in medium and small cities that had relatively low crime rates. I got several responses, including one from Bayshore, which was looking for a Chief of Detectives. I accepted the Bayshore job. I was Chief of Detectives from YR-11 to YR-7. I was selected by the police commission to replace Chief Donaldson when he retired in June, YR-7, and I have been in that position ever since.

I was Chief of Police for Bayshore at the time of the altercation between Larry Kane and one of my cadets, Mike Bond. I was in charge of Police Department policy, including the hiring and training of cadets. I report to the civilian police commission which is appointed by the mayor of Bayshore. Our annual budget is set by the Bayshore City Council based upon my recommendation. I have no personal knowledge of any of the events that occurred around the fourth of July weekend, YR-2. I was out of town with my family. I found out about the shooting on July 7. I have never talked to Mr. Kane about the incident, and I have no idea who he is.

I understand from the police reports and my interview with Officer Mike Bond that Kane was injured but that it was as much Kane's own fault as Bond's. I was satisfied at the time that Bond acted in self-defense and the shooting was justified, so I approved Bond to continue working for the police department. Shortly thereafter, he qualified to become a regular patrol officer. He was reprimanded for carrying a personal weapon.

According to our records, Michael Bond was hired as a police officer cadet on April 16, YR-2. I am responsible for the cadet program, although Lt. Patrick McCardle was the immediate supervisor. The program was instituted in YR-3 in response to budget cuts made by the City Council. We used to send rookie police officers to a six-week training program at the state police academy, but it cost us $8500 per person. Under the two-year budget approved by the Council in YR-3, we had to trim almost $100,000 a year out of our expenses. We could make part of the amount by not purchasing new patrol vehicles for two years, but the remaining amount could only be met by either reducing the number of officers or eliminating the training program. I recommended to the mayor, and he agreed, that we could provide adequate training here in Bayshore, so that eliminating the training program was preferable to reducing the size of the police force.

To make up for the absence of a formal training program, I instituted a new policy that gave preference in hiring new officers to applicants with prior law enforcement or security experience, and then put them on a six-month on-the-job training program as a cadet. Bond was one of the applicants we hired because he said he had experience in private security work. I do not recall who he worked for. I have no specific memory of running a background check on him, but it is my practice to run such a check on every person we hire to verify prior employment and see if he has a criminal record. There is nothing in Bond's personnel file to indicate a prior criminal record or a problem with verifying his prior employment.

In lieu of sending new cadets to the academy, we provide on-the-job training by assigning them to experienced police officers for six months. They spend most of their time working with patrol officers, because that is where they will start out. We make sure they spend at least a little time with the detective squad, so that they can be trained in crime scene and evidence preservation. During this time cadets are in uniform and are issued all standard police department gear except a service revolver. They have to complete twenty hours of firearm instruction before the end of their six-month training in order to be hired permanently as a patrol officer. It has always been official policy that no officer may carry a personal firearm or any weapon that is not issued by the Department. However, it is well known that many officers violate the policy and carry a back-up gun. If we find out about it, we enter a disciplinary warning in their file, which can result in loss of seniority points and can delay promotion. I had no specific knowledge prior to the shooting incident that Bond was carrying a personal firearm and he was not given permission to do so. After this incident, I strengthened the policy against personal weapons and instituted a mandatory two-day suspension without pay for any officer caught with a personal firearm while on duty.

As I had envisioned the cadet program, our trainee officers would always be teamed with experienced officers in the field. Apparently Lt. McCardle decided to send the cadets into the field in relatively safe areas by themselves occasionally to give them confidence they could handle the job. These "solo days" were his idea and I never approved them, although they had apparently been going on for several months without incident under McCardle's supervision. Bond was unsupervised on the day of the incident. After the shooting, I fired McCardle, took over direct supervision of the training program myself, and have eliminated the "solo days". If an experienced officer had been accompanying Bond on July 6, this whole regrettable incident might not have happened. Bond could have watched someone defuse a tense situation and learned from it. McCardle has left town, and I do not know his current whereabouts. I do not remember the exact date he was terminated.

On the day of the shooting, it was official Police Department policy that cadet officers were not to carry weapons, were to go into the field only when accompanied by a senior officer, and were not to become involved in citizen confrontations without the approval of a supervisor. All these policies were explained to cadets and well known to them. Bond violated these policies and therefore was acting outside the scope of his official duties when he confronted and shot Larry Kane.

I have read the foregoing statement, and it is true and accurate to the best of my recollection.

Signed: *Robt C Sullivan*
Robert C. Sullivan
Chief of Police

CITY OF BAYSHORE

✪ POLICE DEPARTMENT "TO SERVE AND PROTECT"

ROBERT SULLIVAN, CHIEF OF POLICE (811) 339-1584

TO ALL OFFICERS:

As of this day, no personal firearms of any kind are to be worn or carried by officers in the field. Violation of this policy will result in immediate two-day suspension without pay. Officers on special assignments may continue to seek permission to carry non-standard firearms on a case-by-case basis.

July 10, YR-2

Robert Sullivan
Chief of Police

D

E

C

F

Clubhouse

B

A

Guard House

ROCKPORT RD.

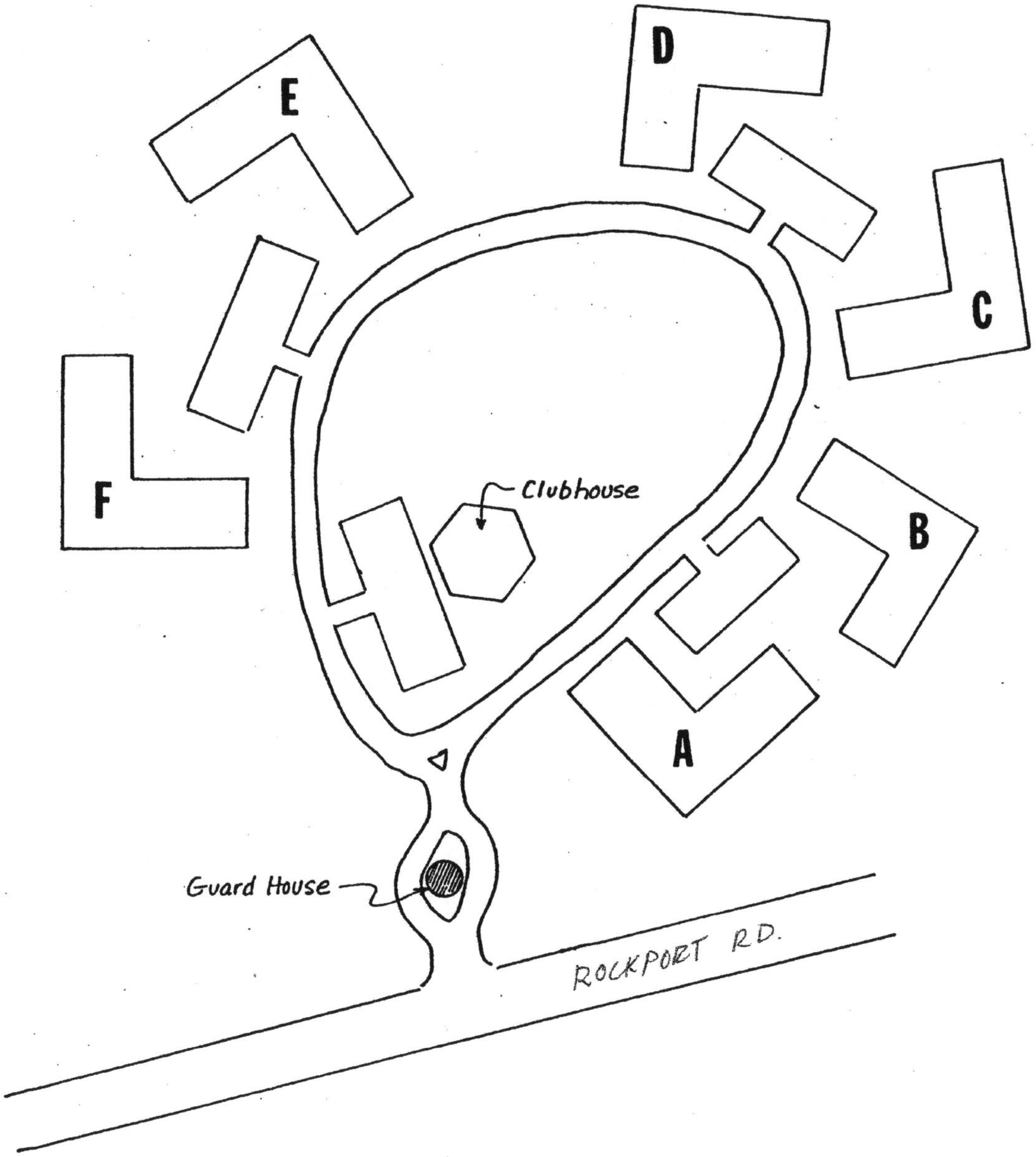

Larry James Kane	)	
	)	
-against-	)	**DEPOSITION OF LARRY J. KANE**
	)	
Michael L. Bond and	)	
The City of Bayshore	)	

Date: November 10, YR-2
Place: Offices of Stanley Lerner
3131 E. Third St.
Bayshore, Columbia
Time Began: 11:00 a.m.
Present: George Baker, for plaintiff
Vivian Tucker, for defendants
Larry James Kane
Dodie Bowman, stenographer and Notary Public

MS. BOWMAN: Mr. Kane, do you swear to answer truthfully all questions asked during this deposition?
MR. KANE: I do.
MS. TUCKER: State your name and address please.
A: Larry Kane, 1711 Miller Drive, Bayshore.
Q: What is your date of birth?
A: February 16, YR-27.
Q: When did you decide to bring suit against the city?
A: As I was recovering in the hospital. I talked to a lawyer after I got out.
Q: Why did you decide to bring a lawsuit?
A: Because that son of a bitch trigger-happy cop shot me for no reason.
Q: Tell me about yourself, like where you live, if you're married, and so forth.
A: I live by myself in an apartment. I'm single. I moved here three years ago after college at Humboldt State. I got a job working part-time with a marine biologist collecting sea animals. It brings in enough money to live on. I'm working out in the open and around the ocean.
Q: What were your interests in college?
A: I was a biology major, and I was active in the Humboldt Environmental Society. I also was involved for awhile in the California Nonviolent Peace

Coalition.

Q: What's that?

A: A group that used nonviolent civil disobedience to fight for environmental issues, like interfering with whale fishing or blocking the entrance to nuclear power plants under construction.

Q: In the course of that, did you break any laws like trespassing on private property or interfering with law enforcement officers?

A: Yes, it was necessary some times.

Q: Were you ever convicted?

A: No.

Q: Do you generally like the police?

A: Not really. I think they are violent and dangerous.

Q: Tell me about your current social life. Do you have a girlfriend?

A: Sort of. Victoria Curtin and I see each other sometimes. It's not a steady thing.

Q: Do you sleep together?

A: Sometimes.

Q: How often?

MR. BAKER: Note an objection.

Q: Please answer the question.

A: Maybe once a week.

Q: Was this relationship ongoing in July?

A: Yes. We'd been seeing each other for a year or so.

Q: Do you have a criminal record?

A: I was convicted for malicious mischief three years ago. I paid a $50 fine.

Q: What happened?

A: I got drunk and dumped garbage in the front seat of a guy's car.

Q: Why?

A: He was a bartender at Jason's Pub where I go sometimes, and he'd thrown me out of the bar for being rowdy a couple of days before. I was angry and wanted to get even. It was a pretty stupid thing to do.

Q: Let's start with the July fourth incident. In your own words, what happened on July 4, YR-2?

A: I was at a party at Vicki Curtin's apartment. She lives in apartment 3-B at the Knightridge Apartments on Rockport Road. It was a Fourth of July party and there had been a lot of drinking going on, and so I guess we were being pretty noisy. Bond, in his police uniform, came in and pulled the plug on the stereo. Then he said, "All right, kids, the party's over. You've got to quiet down or I'll run you all in for disorderly conduct." Then he turned and left. I followed him outside and said we were guests on private property and we were entitled to have a good time on the fourth of July. I think he was just mad because he had to work. He turned on me and said he'd run me in to the station any damn time he pleased. I was a little drunk and feeling tough, so I said, "Try it any time, bozo." He pulled out his gun and pointed it at me telling me, "Don't fuck with the cops. Just get in your car and leave." He said he never wanted to see me at Vickie's apartment again. I explained that she had invited me, but he didn't look like he wanted to hear it. I got in my car and drove off. I may have shouted an obscenity at him as I drove off.

Q: What exactly did you say?

A: I said, "I'll get you for this, you son of a bitch."

Q: What did you mean by that?

A: That I would report him, or file a complaint or something. But I never did.

Q: Do you know how Bond knew Victoria Curtin?

A: Yes. I called Vickie and explained what had happened. She said "I'm not surprised. That guy's a creep. He used to work here as a security guard and he was always hanging around, watching me and trying to look in my windows at night." Then she asked if I wanted to come over on July 6 to go swimming and eat dinner. I said yes.

Q: Please describe in detail what happened on July 6, YR-2.

A: I went over to Vickie's about 2:00. We swam and laid out in the sun until about 5:00. Then we set up a charcoal grill and cooked a steak and ate dinner. I cooked the steak and Vickie made a salad. I started to leave about 7:30, after Vickie said she had something to do that evening.

Q: Did you and Vickie have sex on that occasion?

A: It's none of your business.

MR. BAKER: Go ahead and answer, Larry.

A: No, we didn't.

Q: Were you disappointed or angry when you left?

A: I guess maybe a little disappointed, but not angry.

Q: What happened next?

A: I went outside, got in my car, started it up, and backed out. Then my car stalled, and as I was restarting it, some woman in a Mercedes backed into me.

Q: What kind of car do you have?

A: A YR-4 Ford Mustang.

Q: What happened next?

A: I got out of my car. The woman, named Alexandra Spiro, I think, got out and came toward me. She accused me of backing into her, but I pointed out that she was the one who ran into me. We argued about it for a few minutes. Vickie came out of her apartment and told me to calm down. About this time, Bond arrived in his big police car, came up to me, and said, "I'll bet this is your fault. I thought I told you not to come back here." He kept crowding me, you know, stepping real close, and then I would step back, and he would crowd in again.

Q: Had you been drinking?

A: I'd had one beer for dinner.

Q: Any other alcohol that day?

A: No, not that I remember.

Q: Had you taken any drugs that day?

A: No.

Q: Have you ever taken drugs illegally?

A: Sure. I've smoked marijuana, and I tried cocaine a couple of times. I took amphetamines during exams when I was in college. So what? Everyone does that sort of thing.

Q: What happened after Mr. Bond started crowding you?

A: He backed me all the way up to my car. Then he sort of smiled, and turned to Ms. Spiro and said, "I'm sorry this kid ran into you. He's been trouble here before." I stepped forward and said, "It wasn't my fault." Vickie grabbed my arm and said to forget it. I pushed her arm away and said, "I won't forget it. This is an outrage."

Q: How far away was Bond?

A: About five feet. He wheeled around and told me to shut up or he'd shut me up. I was starting to get mad. I told him the police weren't supposed to take sides and asked him to call another police car. Bond said he could arrest me and lock me up if I didn't shut up. Then he walked away. I asked Vickie to call 9-1-1, but he said I should just calm down and forget it. I said I was not going to forget it, that this was a free country and we had laws, and that the police couldn't just harass people. I went to sit in my car.

Q: Did you tell anyone what you were doing?

A: No. I was mad, and not thinking too clearly.

Q: So it could have appeared to Bond that you were trying to leave the scene?

A: I don't know.

Q: What happened next?

A: Bond came over and yelled at me to get out of my car. He ran up and yanked open my car door, screaming that I was under arrest. He pulled the door so hard that he fell over backwards. I started to laugh. He jumped up and he was red in the face. He said, "Get out of the car or I'll come in and get you." I said, "Hey, let's not get personal about this." He pushed me toward the passenger seat and pulled the keys out of the ignition. He pulled out his nightstick, held it out, and told me to get out of the car. When I did, he hit me on the head with it for no reason. I said, "If you weren't a cop I'd take that stick away from you and shove it up your ass." Bond took his badge off, tossed it aside, and said, "Just try it, tough guy." Then he swung a second time and I grabbed his arm and pulled the stick away from him. Then he pulled out his gun and told me to throw down the stick. I tossed it aside.

Q: How were you holding it?

A: Down at my side.

Q: Did you threaten Bond with it or try to hit him?

A: No.

Q: Did you raise the nightstick over your head or throw it at him?

A: No, I didn't do either of those things.

Q: What direction did you toss it?

A: I don't remember. I wasn't going to argue with a madman holding a gun.

Q: What happened next?

A: Bond put the gun back into its holster. No, wait, first, I took a step forward to get clear of the car door in case I had to run. I turned to see where Vickie was. I was going to ask her again to call 9-1-1. I couldn't tell what hit me because my back was turned, but I think Bond hit me twice on the head with his gun butt. I fell to my knees. I was stunned and it's all a little blurry after this. Bond put the gun back in his holster and stepped up to me. I raised my arms to protect my head because I thought he was

going to hit me again. He reached for his gun. I grabbed him around the waist and put my hand over his so he couldn't pull the gun out. I was sure he was going to kill me. There was a wild, crazy look in his eyes. I pushed him back.
Q: Did he say anything?
A: Not that I remember.
Q: What did you do next?
A: I went over to my car and reached under the seat with my left hand for the extra set of car keys I keep there. I wanted to get out of there. I thought I heard a noise, so I turned around quickly. As I turned around, I saw Bond on one knee aiming his gun at me. I tried to run but hit the car door. The next thing I remember is waking up in the hospital.
Q: Do you remember being shot?
A: No.
Q: Did you hear a gunshot?
A: No.
Q: You didn't see Bond shoot you?
A: No.
Q: As best you can, could you sketch a diagram of what happened, where you were and where Bond was?
A: Okay.
MS. TUCKER: Can we include this as exhibit one for this deposition?
MR. BAKER: No problem.
Q: Mark where the struggle took place, please.
A: Right here, sort of. I'm not sure exactly.
Q: Before Bond fired his gun, did he say anything?
A: Not that I remember?
Q: What happened in the hospital?
A: They put a cast on my right wrist, the one the bullet had broken, put three stitches in my head, and had to operate on me to remove a bullet from my liver. I had tubes coming out of me for drainage for a few days after they operated. And they gave me medication of some kind.
Q: How do you know?
A: I could see the cast. The doctor told me about the other stuff. He said I had been shot in the back.
Q: Who was your doctor?

A: Dr. Linton.
Q: When was the operation?
A: I guess immediately when I got to the hospital, because it was all over by the time I woke up. I was in the hospital for a week while they checked on me and then I was released. Dr. Linton removed the cast three weeks later.
Q: Did you and Dr. Linton talk about the incident?
A: Not really. He'd just bustle in and spend two minutes with me, and then leave.
Q: Are you right or left-handed?
A: Right handed.
Q: How's your wrist?
A: It still hurts and it's real stiff. It doesn't hurt as bad as it did at first. For the first six weeks or so, it was always painful, sort of a dull throbbing. I still can't use it much or play sports or anything, but the doctors say it should be healed by Christmas. When the cast was on, it used to itch all the time.
Q: How's your abdomen?
A: Okay, I guess. It hurt for a week or so, but that's gone away and I don't seem to have any real problems with it. You can still see the scar on my stomach, though.
Q: How about your head?
A: Well, I was pretty embarrassed for awhile because they had to shave the top of my head to put in stitches, but that's grown back now. I had real bad headaches for two weeks. But they've gone away. I had a pretty bad time in the hospital, what with the headaches and my wrist throbbing and itching. I didn't sleep well -- I kept waking up. The first two days were really bad because they strapped me down so I wouldn't tear open the surgery. But I was pretty drugged up those first two days and don't remember much.
Q: Do you have hospital and doctor's bills?
A: Mr. Baker has them.
MR. BAKER: I'll get you copies. The total was $11,980.00
Q: Have they been paid by anyone?
A: Only my insurance.
Q: Have you discussed this case with your attorney?

A: Yes, of course.
Q: Has he influenced your testimony in any way?
A: No. I am telling the truth.
Q: Have you discussed the case with Victoria Curtin?
A: Yes.
Q: Have you told her what to say?
A: No.
Q: Are you aware of any other witness to this incident?
A: Well, Vickie said that one of her neighbors told her she had seen part of the incident and agreed that Bond started it for no reason, but I don't know the person's name.
MS. TUCKER: That's all I have.
MR. BAKER: Larry, did you start the fight?
A: No, sir.
Q: Did you ever attack Michael Bond?
A: No.
MR. BAKER: Nothing further.

WHEREUPON IT WAS STIPULATED THAT READING AND SIGNING BY THE WITNESS IS HEREBY WAIVED PURSUANT TO RULE 30(e).

I certify pursuant to Rule 30(f) that this is a true record of the deposition.

Certified as accurate: *Dodie Bowman*

Dodie Bowman
Notary Public

Larry Kane Deposition
Exhibit ONE

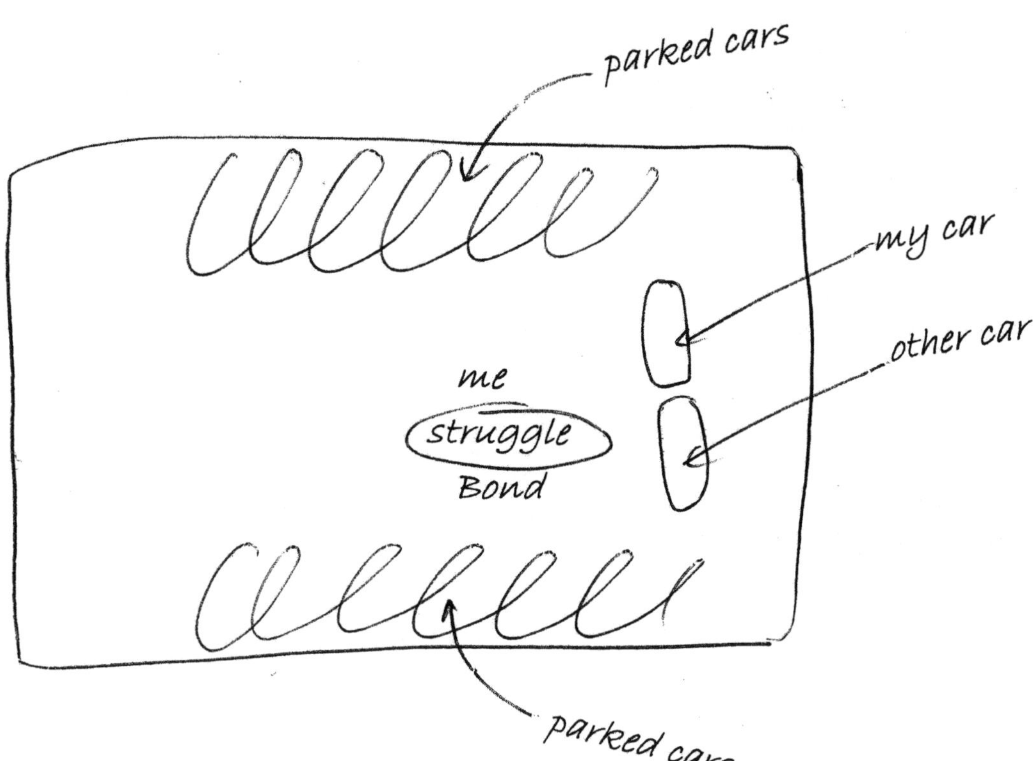

Larry Kane

BAYSHORE POLICE DEPARTMENT
ARREST HISTORY

LAST NAME: **KANE**
FIRST NAME: **LARRY** MIDDLE NAME: **JAMES**
ALIAS: **WILD MAN**
DATE OF BIRTH: **2/16/YR-27** PLACE OF BIRTH: **SAN DIEGO CA**
ADDRESS: **1711 MILLER DR, BAYSHORE COL**

HAIR: **BRN** EYES: **BRN** SEX: **M** MARKS/SCARS: **SCARS ON LEFT HAND**
HT: **5'11"** WT: **170**
OCCUPATION: **MARINE BIOLOGIST**

DATE	OFFICER	CIT NO.	CHARGE	DISPOSITION
8/6/-5	LONG	B3160	MALICIOUS MISCHIEF	GUILTY - $50
7/6/-2	BOND	Y2190Z	ASSAULT, TRESPASS	DISMISSED

DATE PRINTED: 11/14/YR-1

CERTIFIED TRUE AND ACCURATE COPY OF A RECORD
OF THE BAYSHORE POLICE DEPARTMENT
By: *Leslie Morse*
DESK SERGEANT

STATEMENT OF VICTORIA LEIGH CURTIN

Made to: George Baker, Esq.
Place: 3131 E. Third Street
Bayshore, Columbia
Date: November 3, YR-2

My name is Victoria Leigh Curtin. I am 25 years old. I was born in YR-27 in Atlanta, Georgia, but moved here when I was four years old. I was an economics and business major at Ohio State University, graduating with my B.A. in YR-4. After college, I travelled around Europe for six months and then got a job as an assistant manager at Citibank in New York City. Two years ago my mother became quite ill, so I returned to Bayshore. I got a job a few weeks after I got here as the business manager of the downtown Women's Health Club, an exercise center and figure salon for women. I am in excellent health, have good hearing and eyesight, and a good memory. I currently live at 2412 Rockport Road, the Knightridge Apartments number 3-B, here in Bayshore. I have one older brother, Bruce, who is a pilot in the Navy. My parents have just retired.

On July 4, YR-2, I had a Fourth of July party at my apartment. There were a lot of people there, including Larry Kane. I have known Larry for about a year and a half. I like him but he is not my only male friend. Larry and I have occasionally had sexual relations, but not on a regular basis. My sex life is my own business. I am not promiscuous, but I will say that Larry is not my only sexual partner. The party on the Fourth of July got a little wild. Apparently Michael Bond, a police officer, had to come over and quiet things down. I was in the swimming pool when this happened, so all I know is what I was told. Later that night Larry called and said that Mr. Bond had run him off the property after they had gotten into a tussle. He asked me out for July 6th, but I already had a date that evening. It was my day off, so I invited him over for the afternoon to go swimming.

I am personally acquainted with Michael Bond. He used to work as a security guard at Knightridge Apartments. I had a lot of problems with him when he worked here. I am not the only single woman in the apartments who he has bothered. Some of my friends have had similar experiences. Bond was always hanging around the pool and ogling the women in bathing suits. He came by my apartment sometimes and he called me up about every two weeks to ask me out. I told him I was not interested, but he kept calling me. He also tried to look in my bedroom window. I used to see him outside my apartment at night, close to my windows. I think a man who goes around peeping in windows like that is sick. He also has hassled other men I've gone out with.

On July 6, YR-2, Larry came over about 2:00 p.m. We went swimming and ate dinner. As I recall we grilled a steak, but I am not certain. Larry had consumed four or five beers while we cooked and ate, but was certainly not drunk. This was between 5:00 and 7:30 p.m. Larry left about 7:30 because I had another date at 8:00. I think this made Larry mad. He is sort of possessive, which drives me crazy. It's too bad, because I think I could get serious about him if he were more mature. We had an argument about our relationship just before he left.

A few minutes later, I heard a crash, and looked out my window. Larry had crashed into another car. I do not know the other person. I went outside. Larry looked really mad and all tense. He was arguing with the other driver. I went up to Larry and told him to calm down and tell me what happened. He said something like, "Look at that mess. That woman backed right into me." About that time Bond arrived. He came up to Larry and accused him of being at fault. Larry said that it was not his fault, but Bond turned his back and walked away. I tried to calm Larry down. He yelled something at Bond and Bond told him to shut his mouth or he would shut it for him. Larry said something about the police and got into his car. I could tell he was still pretty agitated, but it looked like things were over, so I started to walk back to my apartment.

I'd only taken three or four steps when I saw Bond run over to Larry's car. I was now about 15 feet from the car. Bond pulled open the door and fell backwards. I could not tell whether Bond pulled the door or Larry pushed it open. But I could definitely see Bond's hand on the door handle. Then they got into a real fight. Bond was grabbing at Larry and pulled him out of the car. Then Bond hit Larry with his nightstick a couple of times on the head for no reason. I ran over and screamed at them to stop fighting. Then I ran over to some people who had gathered at the edge of the parking lot and screamed for someone to break up the fight and call the police, that Bond was beating Larry up.

When I looked up again, Bond had his gun out. I heard him call Larry a son of a bitch. Larry took a step forward and then turned away from Bond and leaned forward like he was about to run, but Bond hit him on the head with his gun before Larry could get away. Larry fell down, and Bond put the gun back in its holster. Then they went at it again. I can't remember exactly who did what. I ran to my apartment to call the police. When I was inside I heard what sounded like a lot of gunshots. I ran back out and saw Larry lying next to his car, bleeding. Bond was in his police uniform the whole time. No other police were on the scene until after the shooting was over.

I went with Larry to the hospital. They rushed him into surgery. Larry was in the hospital for two weeks. He had a cast on his right arm and tubes sticking out of his side. Larry told me he had been shot in the wrist and in the back. He complained a lot about headaches and that his wrist hurt when I saw him in the hospital. I've seen him since then, and he still complains that his wrist hurts. He was over at my apartment once that I remember in late August and picked up a beer in his right hand. As he started to drink it he cried out in pain and dropped the beer. He said his wrist still hurt if he moved it the wrong way. There were a couple of similar incidents in August and September, and then his wrist seemed to get better.

I have read this statement and it is true and accurate.

Victoria L. Curtin

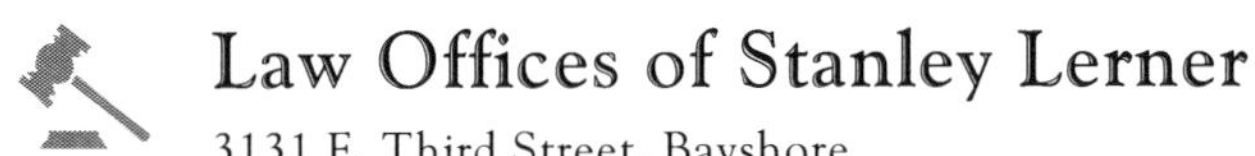

Law Offices of Stanley Lerner

3131 E. Third Street, Bayshore

Phone 811-JUSTICE

Your Attorneys in the College Mall

MEMO TO: Vivian Tucker

FROM: George Baker

RE: Victoria Curtin

This is a supplemental disclosure pursuant to your earlier discovery request that we produce documents relating to Ms. Curtin's credibility. She has no criminal record or college disciplinary record of which I am aware, although her sorority was placed on suspension after allegations that some members prepared term papers for others. I have no indication she was involved. However, one incident has come to my attention for which I have no documentation:

Ms. Curtin was asked to resign from Citibank. Her former supervisor, Mark Senak, (212) 386-2987, reports that she was asked to resign after an audit showed a $150,000 shortage in her department. While Senak says that Curtin was not personally responsible, she discovered the shortage and tried to hide it by falsifying a quarterly report. Curtin said at the time that she thought she could discover who embezzled the money and convince them to return it before the audit. She admitted it had been an error of judgment, but she did not want the shortage on her record.

CITY OF BAYSHORE

City Attorney's Office
Municipal Building
201 East 4th Street
Bayshore, Columbia

Vivian Marie Tucker, *City Attorney*
Riley J. Berman, *Staff Attorney*
(811) 633-6045

STATEMENT OF ALEXANDRA SPIRO

Date: September 30, YR-2

Made to: Vivian Tucker, Attorney, City of Bayshore

Place: Municipal Building, room 301
201 East 4th Street, Bayshore

I am giving this statement of my own free will in response to a request from Vivian Tucker, an attorney representing the City of Bayshore in litigation concerning a police shooting incident that I witnessed. The shooting took place on July 6, YR-2, at approximately 7:30 pm, in the parking lot of my apartment building at the Knightridge Apartments, 2412 Rockport Road, Bayshore.

I am 34 years old, born June 9, YR-36. I am an X-ray technician at Monroe County Hospital. I am single and live in apartment 15-B of the Knightridge Apartments. When I graduated from high school, I went to one year of college and didn't like it, so I enlisted in the Navy. I served as a medical technician for six years. I was stationed in San Diego, Guam, and Naples. In YR-11, I was arrested by military police for possession of marijuana. Because it was my third offense, I was given 30 days in the brig and a medical discharge. I moved to Bayshore and got a job in the radiology department at Monroe County Hospital. I have worked there continuously since then and have had no further problems with drugs. While working at the hospital, I completed the medical technician program at Monroe Community and Technical College, and am now a certified X-ray technician.

I am vaguely acquainted with Michael Bond. He worked as a security guard at the Knightridge Apartments for several years. He always seemed pleasant, professional, and even-tempered. He always talked to me when he saw me. I do not recall him ever being violent or angry. I heard several residents of the apartment complex express similar surprise at this shooting incident because they also remembered him as a nice, even-tempered guy. He ran a few errands for me and let service people into my apartment when I was working. He also has helped me move furniture on a couple of occasions.

On July 6, YR-2, I left the house at 7:30 to get groceries. I backed my Mercedes out of its parking place at the very end of the lot. As I was looking over my shoulder, I saw a Ford Mustang back out of a parking place across the lot very quickly. He backed about twenty feet, then slammed on the brakes. His car skidded backwards into mine. I got out to look and the damage was very minor. The driver of the other car ran over to me and started yelling that it was my fault. I had never seen him before, but I now know him to be Larry Kane. Mr. Kane was upset and appeared slightly intoxicated. I let him yell and then suggested that we let our insurance companies settle it.

A few minutes after the accident, Michael Bond showed up in a police car. He went up to Mr. Kane and asked him something. I think he asked to see his driver's license. Mr. Kane responded that he wasn't going to tell Bond anything. So, Mr. Bond came over to me and I explained what happened, showed him the damage, and told him it was no big deal. A young woman, whom I understand to be Victoria Curtin, went over to Mr. Kane and I heard her tell him to be quiet and calm down. Mr. Kane pushed her away, almost knocking her down. I had walked over and was standing by the door of my car. Mr. Kane and Ms. Curtin were by the front end of his car. Mr. Kane did not look normal. His face was red and his muscles were tense and his movements were very fast and jerky. He was agitated. I did not get close enough to see his eyes so I cannot be sure, but he looked like he might be having a drug reaction, probably to cocaine. I saw a lot of that in the Navy.

Mr. Kane then got into his car and shut the door. Bond walked over and I heard him ask Kane to step out of his car. He said something about arresting Kane, but I didn't hear it all. He was about a foot from the car and his hands were at his side. Bond did not appear angry to me. Kane then pushed open the car door and it hit Bond and knocked him down. Bond stood up and pulled out his nightstick. He told Kane to get out of the car. I moved to get well out of the way. I walked to my car. I looked back, and Kane and Bond were struggling together. I did not see who started it. Kane got the nightstick away from Bond and raised it over his head as if to hit Bond. Bond pulled his gun, pointed it at Kane, and told him to drop it. Kane threw the nightstick off to one side. I decided to get in my car for protection in case they started shooting. I got in and looked out through the back window and saw that Kane and Bond were wrestling again, but at least Bond had put his gun away. I decided to move my car back into its parking place and out of the way of the fight. I have no idea why moving my car seemed important at that moment.

I turned away and reached for the ignition and heard the sounds of gunshots. I did not see what caused it, because I ducked. I then looked out and saw Bond standing up with the gun in his hand. I couldn't see Kane, so I got out. I saw him lying next to his car, bleeding heavily from the abdomen. He was unconscious but alive. Kane did not have a weapon in his hands as far as I could tell.

A few minutes later, more police arrived. They put Kane in a police car and took him to the hospital.

In my opinion, Kane had several opportunities to stop the fight. All he had to do was stop struggling and trying to get away. If he had just done what Bond wanted, or if he had just stood quietly with his arms at his side, none of this would have happened.

I have read this statement carefully and it is true and accurate.

Alexandra Spiro

✣ Monroe County Hospital

Emergency Care Department
684-3597

September 30, YR-2

Mr. George Baker, Esq.
3131 East Third Street
Bayshore, Columbia

Dear Mr. Baker:

This letter is in response to your telephone inquiry of last week regarding Larry Kane. I received Mr. Kane's release today allowing me to disclose his medical information.

I am the surgeon who attended Mr. Kane when he was brought to the Monroe County Hospital Emergency Room on July 6, YR-2. I am on the staff at Monroe County Hospital.

I performed an exploratory laparotomy and cleaned and set a wound to his right wrist. Kane had been hit by two bullets, one hit the right wrist breaking some bones, and the other entered his lower back on the right side and exited from the front. It is impossible to tell which bullet hit first. Neither did any permanent damage. Mr. Kane had a blood alcohol level of .05 percent, the equivalent of 3 to 4 glasses of wine or twelve-ounce beers. At that level he would be uninhibited but not yet seriously drunk. In my opinion, Mr. Kane would have been in extreme pain for two or three days, moderate pain for a week, and only occasional mild pain in the wrist from ten days to a month after that.

I saw Mr. Kane only three times briefly after the operation; twice in the hospital to verify that he was making satisfactory progress, and once to remove the cast in mid-August. We did not discuss the shooting incident.

The complete medical record is attached. Call me if I can be of further assistance.

Sincerely,

GPLinton

Gordon P. Linton, M.D.

NAME: Kane, Larry   Patient #: 5612811
DATE ADMITTED: 7-6-YR-2
PHYSICIAN: Gordon Linton

ADMISSION REPORT

This approximately 25-year-old male was admitted to the ER following a shooting. Examination in the ER revealed a missile wound with point of entry and point of exit at about the level of the ninth rib and lateral lower chest wall. There was also a missle wound involving the right wrist. X-rays revealed some lead fragments along the course of the missle tract overlying the liver. There was no evidence of entry into the pleural space on the x-rays. X-rays of the wrist revealed a fracture in the site of the styloid process of the radius.

PAST HISTORY AND REVIEW OF SYSTEMS: Taken under emergency conditions. The patient was unconscious on admission.

PHYSICAL EXAMINATION: HEENT: Laceration on the head.

NECK: Supple.

CHEST AND ABDOMEN: There are two wounds involving the lateral aspect of the right lower chest at the level of the 9th rib; one is in the posterior axillary line and one is in the anterior axillary line, slightly more medial than the anterior axillary line. The anterior one is the larger one, and is assumed for that reason to be the point of exit. There is a recent abrasion in the midline between the xyphoid and the umbilicus.

ALCOHOL BLOOD CONTENT: .05 percent.

GENITALIA AND RECTAL: Unremarkable.

LOW EXTREMITIES: Unremarkable.

ADMITTING DIAGNOSIS: Gunshot wound, right lower chest wall with laceration of the liver. Gunshot wound involving the right wrist. Lacerations on the scalp.

Gordon P. Linton, M.D.

DICTATED: 7/7/YR-2

ENTERED: 7/7/YR-2 ktb

THIS COPY PRINTED: 10/16/YR-1

NAME: Kane, Larry
ADMITTED: 7-6-YR-2
DISCHARGED: 7-22-YR-2
PHYSICIAN: Gordon Linton

Patient #: 5612811

DISCHARGE REPORT

PRESENT ILLNESS: This 25-year-old male was admitted via the ER following a gunshot wound. X-rays revealed fracture of the 7th and 8th rib anteriorly with metallic and bone fragments within the hepatic substance adjacent to the rib fracture sites. X-rays of the right wrist revealed a fracture which involved the articulate surfaces of the radius at the wrist joint. Lacerations on the head.

PHYSICAL EXAMINATION: Revealed a well-developed, well-nourished male appearing the stated age. Positive physical findings revealed a missile injury with the apparent entrance site in the posterior axillary line at the level of the 9th rib with an apparent exit site in the anterior axillary line at the level of the 9th rib. Lungs were clear and well expanded. The abdomen revealed some guarding in the right upper quadrant, otherwise was unremarkable. Extremities were within normal limits, with the exception of the right wrist where there was a missile injury involving the area of the styloid process of the radius. There was a heavy odor of alcohol on his breath. The patient was unconscious.

ACCESSORY CLINICAL FINDINGS: On admission the hematocrit was 41, urinalysis revealed 2+ sugar; on July 7, serum electrolytes were within normal limits on several occasions. Hematocrit on July 9 was 29 and on July 11, 35. Drainage from the lower chest wall wound on July 10th revealed no growth in 48 hours. On July 18, white blood cell count was within normal limits, as was the urinalysis and the hematocrit was 36.5%. Chest x-rays on several occasions were negative.

COURSE IN HOSPITAL: The patient was taken immediately to the operating room from the ER where an exploratory laparotomy was done through upper paramedian incision. There was a laceration involving the lateral surface of the right lobe of the liver at the level of the 8th or 9th rib. No active bleeding was noted from it. As it was inaccessible for suturing it was elected to drain the area with two Penrose drains at a lateral stab wound. The was done and the entry and exit site of the chest wall were debrided and drained. The postoperative course was uneventful. The patient was initially treated with Achromycin and Bupronex for three days, and later changed to Keflex. At the time of discharge he was given Keftabs. All wounds healed and were clean at the time of discharge. The patient was afebrile for three days prior to discharge.

At the time of the exploratory laparotomy the right wrist was debrided and the wound drained and placed in appropriate cast. This was dressed at periodic intervals and will be followed by removal of the cast, four weeks from the time of the original injury. The lacerations of the scalp were stitched closed.

FINAL DIAGNOSIS: Gunshot wound of the lower chest wall and upper abdomen with laceration of the liver. Gunshot wound of the right wrist with comminuted fracture of the articulate surface of the radius. Superficial laceration of head.

OPERATION: Exploratory laparotomy with drainage of liver and debridement of wound and repair of left wrist gunshot wound. Stitches in scalp.

DISCHARGE MEDICATION: Keftabs 250 mg. every 6 hours for 7 days.

Gordon P. Linton, M.D.

DICTATED: 7/22/YR-2

ENTERED: 7/22/YR-2 sfn

THIS COPY PRINTED: 10/16/YR-1

✥ Monroe County Hospital

STATEMENT

PATIENT'S NAME AND ADDRESS
LARRY JAMES KANE
1711 MILLER DR
BAYSHORE, COL

ACCOUNT NUMBER
32 1966423 GS

INSURANCE INFORMATION
ANTHEM 133989911

DATE ADMITTED
07/06/YR-2

DATE DISCHARGED
07/20/YR-2

POSTING DATE	PHYSICIAN	DESCRIPTION	TOTAL CHARGES
07 06		EMERGENCY ROOM	590.00
07 06	LINTON	PROF SERVICES	4000.00
07 06		OPERATING ROOM	3200.00
07 06	LESTER	X-RAY SERVICES	920.00
		PROF SERVICES	350.00
07 06	LAB	CLINICAL LAB SERVICES	460.00
07 07	LINTON	HOSP VISIT	45.00
07 08	LINTON	HOSP VISIT	45.00
07 08		PHARMACY	220.00
07 10	LINTON	HOSP VISIT	45.00
07 14	LINTON	HOSP VISIT	45.00
07 20		14 DAYS SEMIPRIVATE ROOM	4900.00
08 11	LINTON	OFFICE VISIT	100.00
08 29		INS PAYMENT	11,936.00 CREDIT
		BALANCE DUE	2984.00

JURY INSTRUCTIONS

Preliminary Instructions

Members of the jury, this is a civil lawsuit brought by Larry Kane against Michael Bond and the City of Bayshore. It is based on a federal civil rights law that says any public servant who deprives a citizen of his or her constitutional rights may be sued for damages. Plaintiff alleges that the defendant Michael Bond exceeded his authority as a police officer and used excessive force against him. Defendants assert that the force used by Michael Bond was reasonably necessary under the circumstances.

It will be your duty to determine the facts and decide what happened. The only evidence you may consider is the evidence that will be presented in court. You may not consider anything you read in the paper or hear from your friends about this case. You should use your common sense in considering the evidence, and you may draw reasonable inferences from the evidence.

My function as Judge is to preside over the trial: to rule on points of law and to instruct you on the law. It is our responsibility to see that this case is decided in accord with the facts and the law.

To begin the case the lawyers will make opening statements in which they tell you what they expect the evidence to be. This should help you to understand the evidence as it is presented through the witnesses later and make you aware of conflicts and differences that may arise in the testimony. After opening statements, you will hear and see the evidence. It will come from witnesses and from exhibits. The Plaintiff will present his evidence first, and then the Defendants will present their side of the story. The witnesses are first examined by the lawyer who calls them and may then be cross-examined by the lawyer for the other side. There may be objections, and you must not consider any evidence that is stricken or that you are told to disregard. After all the evidence has been presented, the lawyers make their closing arguments. What the lawyers say is not evidence.

There will be occasional recesses during the trial. During these recesses you must not discuss the case with anyone, not even your friends. Nor may you look things up on the Internet. Please keep your cell phones turned off.

Please keep an open mind as the evidence is presented. Remember that your job is to reach your verdict only after you have heard and considered all the evidence, the instructions of law, and the final arguments of the lawyers.

All people in this trial are fictional, and the events take place in an imaginary city called Bayshore, in the state of Columbia.

Concluding Instructions and Charge to the Jury

Members of the Jury, it is now my duty as judge to instruct you in the law that applies to this case. It is your duty as jurors to follow these instructions and to apply the rules of law to the facts as you find them from the evidence.

It is your duty to determine the facts and decide what happened. The only evidence you may consider is the evidence that was properly admitted at trial through the testimony of the witnesses and the exhibits. You may not consider any matter that was rejected or stricken by the Court. You may not consider anything you read in the paper or heard from your friends about this case, nor may you do your own investigation or look anything up on the Internet.

Statements, arguments and opinions of counsel are not evidence in the case. However, if the attorneys stipulate as to the existence of a fact, you must accept the stipulation as evidence and regard that fact as proved.

Although you are to consider only the evidence in the case in reaching a verdict, you must bring to the consideration of the evidence your everyday common sense and judgment as reasonable men and women. Thus, you are not limited solely to what you see and hear as the witnesses testify. You may draw reasonable inferences from the evidence which you feel are justified in the light of common experience, keeping in mind that such inferences should not be based on speculation or guess.

A verdict may never be influenced by sympathy, prejudice or public opinion. Your decision should be the product of sincere judgment and sound discretion in accordance with these rules of law.

The plaintiff has the burden to prove that he was injured, that the defendant deprived him of a constitutional right under color of state law, and that such act was a proximate cause of his injuries.

The defendant has the burden of proving, as an affirmative defense, that he had a reasonable belief that the force he used was necessary and lawful.

In a civil case, whenever a party must prove something, they must prove it is true by a preponderance of the evidence. The term "preponderance of the evidence" means such evidence as, when weighed with that opposed to it, has more convincing force, and from which it appears that the greater probability of truth lies therein.

A proximate cause of injury is a cause which, in natural and continuous sequence, is a significant factor in producing the injury, and without which the injury would not have occurred.

The plaintiff, Larry Kane, seeks to establish that the defendant Michael Bond violated his civil rights. To prove his case, plaintiff must prove the following propositions by a preponderance of the evidence:

1. That Plaintiff is a citizen of the United States.
2. That the defendant deprived plaintiff of his constitutional right to be free from unreasonable seizures by using excessive force in apprehending him. In considering whether excessive force was used, you may consider the following factors:
    a. the severity of the crime
    b. whether plaintiff posed an immediate threat
    c. whether plaintiff resisted or tried to flee
    d. what a reasonable police officer would have done
3. That Plaintiff was injured as a proximate result of defendant's conduct.
4. That Defendant acted under the apparent authority of a state statute, ordinance, custom, usage or regulation, within the scope of his official duties.
5. That Defendant acted intentionally

If the evidence convinces you that the defendants deprived plaintiff of his civil rights, you should return a verdict for the plaintiff.

[Optional instruction for three-party trial]. The plaintiff, Larry Kane, also seeks to establish that the defendant City of Bayshore violated his civil rights. To prove his case, plaintiff must prove the following propositions by a preponderance of the evidence:

1. That Plaintiff is a citizen of the United States.
2. That the City deprived plaintiff of his constitutional right to be free from unreasonable seizures by establishing, maintaining, or condoning a pattern, practice or policy of deliberate indifference to the rights of inhabitants similarly situated to plaintiff.
3. That Plaintiff was injured as a proximate result of conduct by a police officer that resulted from the pattern or practice of the defendant municipality.

The defendant Michael Bond claims that any force he used was justified. To prove his case, the defendant Michael Bond must establish by a preponderance of the evidence that the force used was necessary for self-defense or part of his lawful duties. Any person who reasonably believes he is under attack may use such force in self-defense as reasonably appears necessary under the circumstances, but may not use excessive force.

A police officer is lawfully entitled to use force to apprehend a person if the officer has probable cause to believe the person has committed a crime, is an imminent threat to the safety of any person, or is attempting to resist arrest or flee from custody, but an officer may not use excessive force.

If the evidence convinces you that Bond's actions were justified, you should return a verdict for the defendants.

In this case, defendant Bond used deadly force, which is permitted only if he had probable cause to believe that serious physical harm to himself or others was imminent and gave a warning to plaintiff if feasible.

[Optional instruction for three-party trial]. The defendant City of Bayshore claims that the acts of Michael Bond were wholly outside his official duties and therefore were not done under color of state law. To prove its case, the defendant City of Bayshore must establish by a preponderance of the evidence that the conduct of Michael Bond was outside the scope of his authority and that at the time of the conduct complained of, Bond was acting as a private citizen and not as a police officer. If the evidence convinces you of this fact, you should return a verdict in favor of the City of Bayshore.

If you find for the plaintiff, you must award Larry Kane damages in an amount that will reasonably compensate him for all injuries or harms proximately caused by the acts of the defendants. The award shall include the reasonable value of medical and hospital care and reasonable compensation for any pain, discomfort, fears, anxiety, and other mental or emotional distress suffered by the plaintiff. No definite standard is prescribed by law by which to fix reasonable compensation for pain and suffering, nor are the arguments of counsel evidence of the proper amount. You should use your own calm and reasonable judgment to fix the damage award in light of the evidence.

If you find for the plaintiff, you may consider whether you should award additional damages against the defendant Bond for the sake of example and punishment. You are not required to award these punitive damages; it is entirely up to you. You may award punitive damages only if you find by a preponderance of the evidence that the defendant deliberately deprived plaintiff of his civil rights, or was guilty of actual malice. Actual malice means the defendant's motives were primarily to harass, annoy or injure plaintiff. The law provides no fixed standard as to the amount of punitive damages, but leaves that to the sound discretion of the jury.

Your verdict must be unanimous.

UNITED STATES DISTRICT COURT
EASTERN DISTRICT OF COLUMBIA
CIVIL DIVISION

Larry James Kane,	)	
Plaintiff	)	Civil Action
	)	Case No. 1:05-cv-0359
vs.	)	
	)	
Michael Lowell Bond and	)	**VERDICT**
The City of Bayshore	)	
Defendants	)	

We the jurors of the Eastern District of Columbia find:

_____ for the defendants.

_____ for the plaintiff in the amount of:

a. Actual damages: ______________________________

b. Punitive damages (if any): ______________________

Signed: ____
Jury foreperson

[alternate verdict form]

UNITED STATES DISTRICT COURT
EASTERN DISTRICT OF COLUMBIA
CIVIL DIVISION

Larry James Kane
Plaintiff

vs.

Civil Action
Number 1:05-cv-0359

Michael Lowell Bond
Defendant

VERDICT

and

The City of Bayshore
Defendant

We the jurors of the Eastern District of Columbia find:

_____ for the defendants.

_____ for the plaintiff.

__ against defendant Bond.

__ against defendant City of Bayshore.

a. Actual damages: ______________________________

b. Punitive damages (if any): ______________________

Signed: _____________________________________
Jury foreperson

CASE FILE G:

STATE OF COLUMBIA

v.

ROBERT MEADOWS

BRIBERY
POSSESSION OF COCAINE

STATE V. MEADOWS
CONTENTS OF FILE

GENERAL INSTRUCTIONS

This is a criminal case brought by the State of Columbia against Robert Meadows, a police officer. The state alleges that Meadows is guilty of bribery and possession of cocaine for coercing Nancy Hatton, a drug dealer, into giving him cocaine in return for not prosecuting her on a drug charge. The defendant has pleaded not guilty to both charges. All events take place in January of this year, in a fictional city called Bayshore, Columbia (population 150,000).

Potential Witnesses:

Nancy Hatton -- complainant.
Sgt. Andrew Sutton -- Bayshore Police Department internal affairs investigator.
Susan Engle -- police chemist.
Robert Meadows -- defendant.
John Summers -- police informant.
Carolyn Smith -- shift supervisor, Special Narcotics Unit, Bayshore Police Department.

Instructions for use as a full trial:

1. The state must call Nancy Hatton and Andrew Sutton, and may call Susan Engle, as witnesses in its case-in-chief. Other witnesses may be called only with the approval of the court.

2. The defendant must call Robert Meadows and John Summers, and may call Carolyn Smith, as witnesses in his case-in-chief. Other witnesses may be called only with the approval of the court.

3. In lieu of calling Susan Engle, the prosecutor may enter the following stipulation: "Susan Engle is a chemist who works for the Bayshore Police Department. She received an envelope of white powder from Sgt. Andrew Sutton on January 19, YR-0, in connection with the case against Robert Meadows. She tested the contents of the bag and determined it contained 1 3/8 oz. plus 4 grains of 10% cocaine. She also tested a substance brought in by Officer Meadows in the Hatton case on January 4th which proved to be lactose."

4. In lieu of calling Carolyn Smith, the defense may enter the following stipulation: "Lieutenant Carolyn Smith is Robert Meadows' shift supervisor in the Special Narcotics Unit. On January 18, at his request, she gave him $5000.00 in department funds to make a drug purchase. She became aware of the internal affairs investigation on January 19, but does not remember discussing it with anyone."

5. The original attorneys have withdrawn from this case, citing conflicts of interest.

Stipulations:

1. The photocopy of the matchbook (page G-71) is a true and accurate reproduction of the original and is admissible to the same extent as the original would be.

2. The telephone number "399-1294" is a pay telephone located at the Sunset Bar at 621 South Woodlawn Street.

3. Robert Meadows' cell phone number is 584-2199. It is unlisted.

4. Any criminal offense listed as a misdemeanor is one for which the maximum statutory penalty is one year or less. Any offense listed as a felony is one for which the maximum penalty is more than one year.

5. The booklet “Drugs of Abuse” (pages G-9 and G-10) is an official publication of the Drug Enforcement Agency, prepared by DEA officials.

Note on dates:

Years in this file are indicated as follows: YR-0 refers to the present year, YR-1 refers to one year ago, YR-2 to two years ago, etc.

STATE OF COLUMBIA
County of Monroe

THE STATE OF COLUMBIA	)	Criminal no. 88396
	)	
vs.	)	**INDICTMENT**
	)	
ROBERT MEADOWS,	)	
Defendant	)	

THE GRAND JURORS FOR THE STATE UPON THEIR OATH PRESENT:

That on or about the dates and times specified below, in Monroe County, ROBERT MEADOWS unlawfully and willfully did feloniously:

Count I: Commit the crime of BRIBERY IN THE FIRST DEGREE, in that on or about January 3 and January 5, YR-0, in the course of his public employment as a police officer, he solicited, accepted and agreed to accept an item of value from Nancy Hatton, to wit, two ounces more or less of cocaine, as consideration for a violation of a known legal duty as a public servant, to wit, in exchange for not prosecuting Nancy Hatton for possession and sale of a controlled substance, in violation of Columbia Criminal Code § 240.1.

Count II: Commit the crime of POSSESSION OF A CONTROLLED SUBSTANCE, in that on or about January 5 and January 18, YR-0, he unlawfully possessed approximately one and three-eighths ounces of cocaine, a Schedule II controlled substance, without a valid prescription therefor, in violation of Columbia Criminal Code § 484.7.

James Byers
Assistant District Attorney

WITNESSES:
Nancy Hatton
Sgt. Andrew Sutton, BPD ✗
Dr. Susan Engle, BPD

The witnesses marked with an X were sworn by the undersigned foreperson of the Grand Jury, and this bill was found to be ✗ a True Bill/__ not a True Bill.

This the 29th of January, YR-0

Ozie Davis Jr.
Grand Jury Foreperson

EXCERPTS FROM COLUMBIA CRIMINAL CODE

§240.1. Bribery in the first degree. (a) A person is guilty of bribery in the first degree if such person offers, confers, or agrees to confer upon another, or solicits, accepts, or agrees to accept from another:

(1) Any benefit, service, or item of value as consideration for the recipient's decision, opinion, recommendation, vote, or other exercise of discretion as a public servant, judicial officer, or public administrator; or

(b) Any benefit, service, or item of value as consideration for a violation of a known legal duty as a public servant, judicial officer, or public administrator.

(b) Bribery in the first degree is a felony of the second degree.

§484.7. Possession of a controlled substance. (a) A person who, without a valid prescription, knowingly or intentionally possesses a controlled substance classified in schedule I, II, III, or IV, commits possession of a controlled substance.

(b) Possession of a controlled substance is a felony of the third degree. However, the offense is a felony of the second degree if the drug involved is classified in schedule I or II and has an aggregate weight of two (2) ounces or more.

§482.6. Schedule II controlled substances. The controlled substances listed in this section are included in schedule II:

(a) Any of the following substances, whether produced directly or indirectly by extraction from substances of vegetable origin, or independently by means of chemical synthesis:

* * *

(4) Coca leaves, and any salt, compound, derivative, or preparation thereof which is chemically equivalent or identical with any of these substances, but not including decocainized coca leaves or extractions which do not contain cocaine or ecgonine.

§483.3. Authorized possession of controlled substances. Notwithstanding any other provision of this chapter, the following persons may lawfully possess controlled substances:

(a) A duly licensed manufacturer, distributor, or dispenser of controlled substances.

(b) A person duly licensed to conduct research with those substances to the extent authorized by the state board of pharmacy.

(c) An agent or employee of a licensed manufacturer, distributor, or dispenser if such person is acting in the usual course of business.

(d) An ultimate user under a duly ordered prescription.

(e) A law enforcement agency or officer acting in the course of legitimate law enforcement duty in order to seize, test, preserve as evidence or destroy controlled substances.

Drug Enforcement Administration, U.S. Department of Justice, Drugs of Abuse 37-40 (1995)

Cocaine

The most potent stimulant of natural origin, cocaine is extracted from the leaves of the coca plant (Erythroxylon coca), which has been grown in the Andean highlands of South America since prehistoric times. The leaves of the plant are chewed in the region for refreshment and relief from fatigue.

Pure cocaine, the principal psychoactive ingredient, was first isolated in the 1880s. It was used as an anesthetic in eye surgery for which no previously known drug had been suitable. It became particularly useful in surgery of the nose and throat because of its ability to anesthetize tissue while simultaneously constricting blood vessels and limiting bleeding. Many of its therapeutic applications are now obsolete because of the development of safer drugs as local anesthetics.

Illicit cocaine is usually distributed as a white crystalline powder, often diluted by a variety of other ingredients, the most common of which are sugars such as lactose, inositol, mannitol, and local anesthetics such as lidocaine. The frequent adulteration is to increase volume and thus to multiply profits.

The drug is most commonly administered by being "snorted" through the nasal passages. Symptoms of repeated use in this manner may resemble the congested nose of a common cold.

The intensity of the psychological effects of cocaine, as with many psychoactive drugs, depends on the rate of entry into the blood. Intravenous injection or smoking produces an almost immediate intense experience. Cocaine hydrochloride, the usual form in which cocaine is sold, while soluble in water and sometimes injected, is fairly insensitive to heat. Conversion of cocaine hydrochloride to cocaine base yields a substance that will become volatile when heated. "Crack," or cocaine base in the form of chips, chunks or "rocks," is usually vaporized in a pipe or smoked with plant material in a cigarette or a "joint". Inhalation of the cocaine fumes produces effects that are very fast in onset, very intense, and are quickly over. These intense effects are often followed within minutes by a dysphoric "crash," leading to frequently repeated doses and rapid addiction.

Because of the intensity of its pleasurable effects, cocaine has the potential for extraordinary psychic dependency. Recurrent users may resort to larger doses at shorter intervals until their lives are largely committed to their drug addiction. Anxiety, restlessness, and extreme irritability may indicate the onset of a toxic psychosis similar to paranoid schizophrenia. Tactile hallucinations so afflict some chronic users that they injure themselves in attempting to remove imaginary insects from under the skin. Others feel persecuted and fear that they are being watched and followed.

Excessive doses of cocaine may cause seizures and death from, for example, respiratory failure, stroke, cerebral hemorrhage, or heart failure. There is no specific treatment for cocaine overdose. Nor does tolerance develop to the toxic effects of cocaine. In fact, there are studies which indicate that repeated use lowers the dose at which toxicity occurs. There is no "safe" dose of cocaine.

BAYSHORE POLICE DEPARTMENT ARREST REPORT

1 DATE OF REPORT: **1/21/YR-0**
2 TIME: **1:45 pm**
3 ARRESTING OFFICER'S NAME: **Andrew Sutton**
4 RANK: **Sgt**
5 BADGE: **86**

6 DEFENDANT NAME: **Robert Meadows**
7 ADDRESS: **1012 N Park St, Bayshore**
8 CRIMES: **240.1 Bribery, 484.7 Possession of controlled substance**

9 VICTIM NAME: **Nancy K. Hatton**
10 SEX: **F**
11 AGE: **26**
12 ADDRESS: **400 E Jackson, Bayshore**
13 CONTACT INFORMATION: **282-3747**
14 EMPLOYER: **none**

15 DATE OF CRIME: **Between Jan 3 and Jan 18, YR-0**
16 TIME:
17 LOCATION: **Bayshore Police Station**
18 TYPE OF PREMISES: **Hallway -- public area**
19 WEATHER: **unknown**
20 HOW ATTACKED OR COMMITTED: **Defendant demanded and received cocaine from victim in exchange for no arrest.**
21 WEAPON/TOOLS:
22 PERSON REPORTING CRIME: **Nancy K. Hatton**
23 ADDRESS: **400 E Jackson**
24 CONTACT INFORMATION: **282-3747**
25 TIME/DATE OF REPORT: **2:40 pm 1/16/YR-0**
26 TOTAL VALUE STOLEN: **$6600 (approx value, 2.2 oz. cocaine)**
27 TOTAL VALUE RECOVERED: **$6600**
28 CURRENCY: **$2500**
29 JEWELRY:
30 AUTOS:
31 COMPUTERS/TV ETC:
32 FIREARMS:
33 OTHER: **1 3/8 oz. cocaine, value $4100 approx**

34 TOTAL PERSONS INVOLVED: **1**
35 TOTAL ARRESTED: **1**
36 ADULTS ARRESTED: **1**
37 JUVENILES ARRESTED: **0**
38 TOTAL AT LARGE: **0**

39 OTHER BPD OFFICERS INVOLVED:

40 NARRATIVE: **Victim Nancy K. Hatton, known drug dealer, informed ADA James Byers on January 16 that a police officer was demanding drugs from her in exchange for not arresting her. Hatton offered to trade name of officer for leniency on felony gun charge pending in court. Matter turned over to Internal Affairs. I interviewed Hatton 11:00 am January 16. She states she was apprehended on January 3, YR-0, by suspect police officer Robert H. Meadows for possession of small amount of powder cocaine. Suspect told Hatton he would let her go if she gave him two ounces of cocaine. Hatton agreed and was released. She met suspect Meadows on January 5, time unknown, in front hallway of police station and gave him 2 ounces of powder cocaine. Check of arrest records corroborates Meadows arrested Hatton for possession on January 3, but charges dropped January 7 when lab report came back negative (lactose only). Hatton says suspect probably switched evidence and sent lactose to lab.**

I obtained search warrant on Jan. 18 for suspect Meadows' apartment, executed it at 3:30 pm. Suspect was at home. I seized 1 3/8 oz. powder cocaine and drug paraphernalia. Lab report verified that substance was cocaine. Suspect Meadows claimed drugs had been delivered to him minutes before by informant John Summers and that Meadows was in process of sending it to the lab and planned to arrest unknown seller who had delivered substance to Summers. Also seized $2500 in cash found in apartment. Suspect claimed money belonged to police department as part of undercover investigation.

Jan. 20, lab confirmed substance was cocaine. After conferring with Capt. Friedman, and on his advice, arrested Meadows at his apartment 7:15 am, January 21.

41 OFFICER SIGNATURE: *Andrew Sutton*

CITY OF BAYSHORE

✪ POLICE DEPARTMENT "TO SERVE AND PROTECT"

REPORT TO: CAPTAIN WILLIAM FRIEDMAN
INTERNAL AFFAIRS, BAYSHORE POLICE DEPT.

FROM : SGT. ANDREW L. SUTTON *ALS*

DATE : JANUARY 22, YR-0

RE : INVESTIGATION OF OFFICER ROBERT H. MEADOWS ON SUSPICION OF BRIBERY AND DRUG USE

On Jan. 16, YR-0, you assigned me to investigate allegations of misconduct on the part of Officer Meadows. That investigation has culminated in the arrest of Officer Meadows on Jan. 21 on charges of bribery and possession of cocaine.

On Jan. 16, I talked to Nancy Hatton, a known drug dealer who claimed to have information relating to misconduct on the part of Officer Meadows. Hatton disclosed Meadows' name only after she struck a deal with the district attorney's office to reduce a pending gun charge to a misdemeanor and a promise of no jail time. Hatton's two written statements, given to me on January 16 and January 17 are attached. In summary, she alleged that she was shaken down by Officer Meadows following a January 3 drug arrest. Meadows demanded drugs in return for dismissing charges. Hatton supplied Meadows with 2 ounces of cocaine, street value $6000 on January 5. On January 7 the drug charges against Hatton were dismissed.

Because of Hatton's record and the plea bargain, I felt this unsubstantiated allegation against Officer Meadows did not amount to probable cause. I set out to see if any of Hatton's charges could be verified. I first pulled the district court file on Hatton's drug charge. It verified that Hatton was arrested for felony possession of cocaine on January 3, YR-0; that she was released without bond upon the recommendation of Officer Meadows; and that the case was dismissed at a preliminary hearing on January 7 because the lab report came back indicating that the substance tested was not cocaine (file attached). When I talked to Hatton again on Jan. 17, she said Meadows must have switched powders, because she is positive he had taken 3 grams of cocaine from her. Other sales had been made from the same batch and no complaints. She refused to give names of persons she sold to. Hatton also said that she cuts cocaine with lidocaine crystals, not lactose.

On the morning of January 18th, I attempted to verify that Hatton met with Meadows at the police station on January 5, YR-0, at 11:00 p.m. The officers' logbook indicated that Meadows checked out for the evening at 10:20 p.m. The visitors' log did not have an entry for Nancy Hatton. Photocopies of these pages are attached. I have been unable to locate either Jeff Thomas or Alvin Johnson who Hatton referred to. Johnson is reported to be a big time dealer. Motor Vehicles has no Mercedes registered to anyone named Thomas.

I spoke to Lt. Carolyn Smith of special narcotics who is Meadows' supervisor without disclosing the nature of my investigation. I told her we needed some lactose to simulate cocaine as part of a training exercise, and asked if there was any available from special narcotics. She said that officially they had none, but I should talk to either Meadows or Dan Powell. She remember that they had purchased some for a lecture on drug abuse they gave at Bayshore High School in early December, YR-1.

Based on this information, I obtained a search warrant for Meadows' home, an apartment at 1012 North Park Street. I executed the warrant on the evening of January 18 at approximately 8:45 p.m., after verifying Meadows' address through department payroll records. At 8:45 p.m. I knocked on Meadows' door. He opened it and I identified myself and showed him the search warrant. He said, "What is this, a joke?" I said that I was serious and that he might be in serious trouble. I stepped into the entrance foyer. As I did so, I could see in plain view on a table in the living room a clear plastic bag containing a white powder. I walked over to it and picked it up. Meadows stated, "Don't take that, you'll break the chain of custody. I just got this a few minutes ago from an informant named Summers as part of an investigation." I asked why he had it on the table and he said Summers had just left and he was getting ready to send it to the lab for testing. I said I had to take it under the warrant. He seemed upset, saying that I was blowing his investigation, but not nervous. I continued to search and Meadows followed me around. He asked me a couple of times why I was searching and I told him I was investigating charges against him but was not at liberty to reveal the details until the investigation was complete. I also found drug paraphernalia: plastic bags in the kitchen and a set of scales.

In a drawer in a desk in another room I found $2500 in cash: twenty-five one-hundred dollar bills. I asked Meadows where it came from and he said, "It's department money, you jerk. I'm in special narcotics, remember? We need cash on hand to make buys." I took it as evidence. Meadows said I would get in trouble for this. I left his home at approximately 10:30 p.m. I put the powder in an evidence bag, put a seal on it, initialed it, and put down the case number. I locked it in my desk overnight.

On January 19, I delivered it to the police lab and personally handed it to the chemist, Susan Engle. On January 20, Ms. Engle called me and said it was cocaine. I picked up the powder and a lab report from her. I discussed the case with Capt. Friedman and, on his advice, arrested Meadows the morning of Jan. 21.

As you already know, I have had dealings with Meadows before and we are not on very good terms. He doesn't like Internal Affairs, and I don't particularly like the way Special Narcotics operates. We got into a physical altercation once at a bachelor party for one of the patrol officers, in August, YR-1. We were both a little drunk. Meadows accused me of being a lousy cop because I worked for Internal Affairs. I responded something to the effect of "Better a lousy cop than a dirty one. Everyone knows that special narcotics officers always have their own personal drugstores." Meadows hit me with his fist and bloodied my nose, and I told him that one day I would catch him on one of his scams. I had no reason at the time to believe he was involved in anything illegal. We apologized to each other when we sobered up and I maintain no ill will toward him. I do not believe that this incident has affected my judgment in this investigation.

I have worked for this department for eleven years, the last five for internal affairs. I have investigated many allegations against officers, maybe 200 or so, and found most to be unfounded. I personally believe that Hatton is lying and that Meadows is telling the truth. This is just the kind of unsubstantiated charge that a clever person with a grudge against the police knows is difficult to disprove. Meadows showed none of the nervousness or desperation that I have seen in guilty police officers, has no history of this kind of thing, and has no motive or exceptional need for money that I can detect. I suggest further investigation into Ms. Hatton's motives.

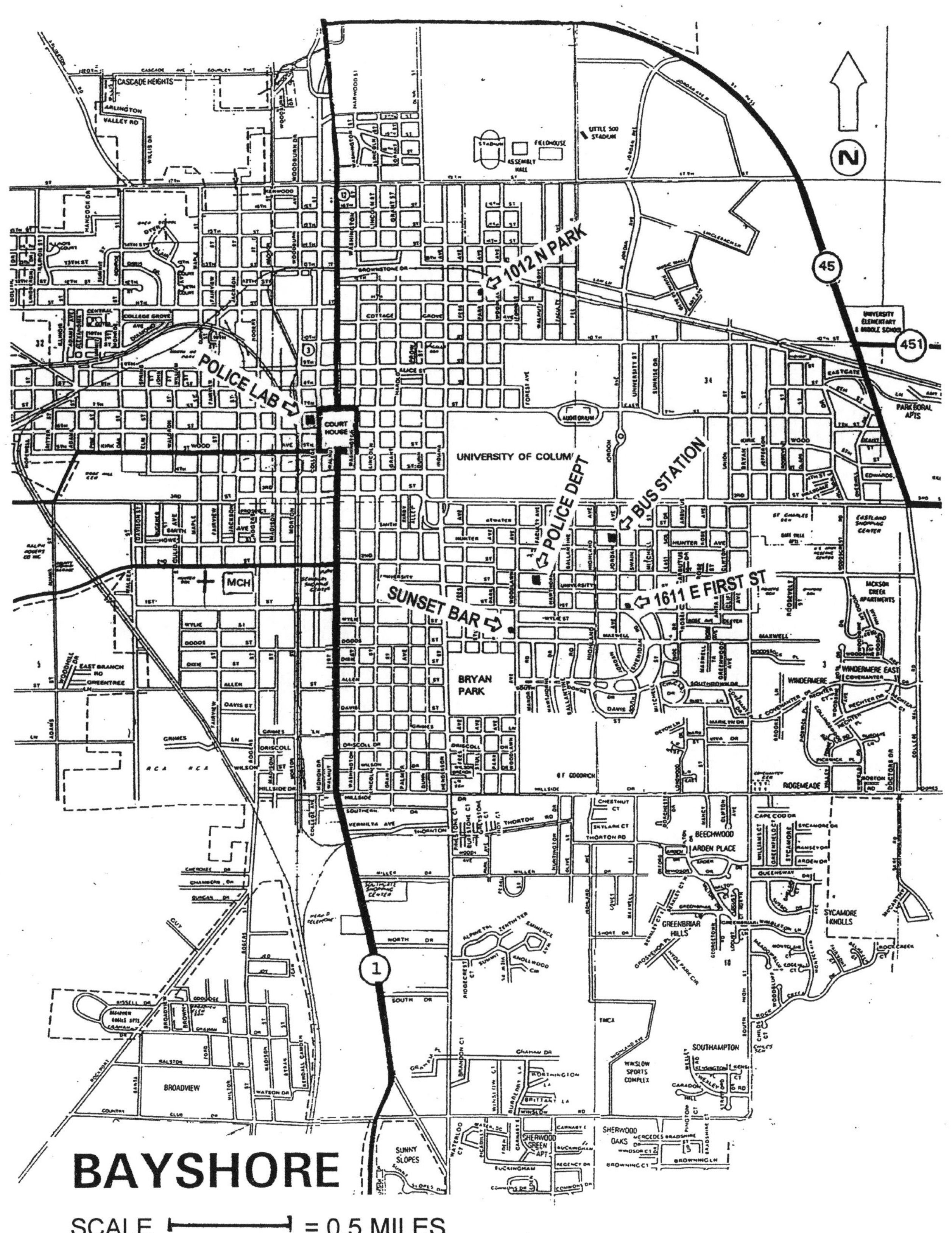

BAYSHORE
SCALE = 0.5 MILES
1012 N PARK
POLICE LAB
COURT HOUSE
UNIVERSITY OF COLUM
POLICE DEPT
BUS STATION
1611 E FIRST ST
SUNSET BAR
MCH
BRYAN PARK
CASCADE HEIGHTS

CITY OF BAYSHORE

"TO SERVE AND PROTECT"

STATEMENT OF NANCY K. HATTON

Made to Sgt. Andrew Sutton
January 16, YR-0, 4:00 p.m.
Transcribed from taped interrogation

My name is Nancy K. Hatton, 400 E Jackson. I am giving this statement voluntarily of my own free will. Under the terms of my plea agreement with the prosecutor, I understand his promise of leniency is good only if I tell the truth and cooperate fully in this investigation.

I am a local resident, 26 years old. I moved here in YR-8 after dropping out of college my freshman year. I am single. I do not have a job, and support myself by selling drugs -- marijuana, crack, and cocaine mostly, and a little ecstasy. I've been in the business eight years. I never handle pills or heroin. I have a criminal record. I've been in prison twice: once for 18 months in YR-5 and YR-4; and once for two years from YR-3 to YR-1. I've been out for about a year. I looked for a job, but no one wants to hire someone with a record. I have to eat, so I took up drug selling again. It's better than prostitution or welfare. I live pretty good. I tried working as a waitress once, at Rico's Supper Club. That was about 6 years ago. But I quit because the owner was a real hard-ass, hassling me and ordering me around. I dumped some ecstasy in the soup to get even and quit. I heard some people got sick, but they never found out who did it.

On January 3, YR-0, I was driving over to my boyfriend's house about 8:00 when that son-of-a-bitch Meadows pulled me over near Bryan Park. I hadn't done anything wrong. Meadows said some bull about a traffic violation, like I ran a stoplight or something. I know that he was lying. I didn't run any stoplights. Meadows put on the flashing light on his unmarked car and I stopped. He came over and said, "I'm glad to see you're finally out of prison," and he sort of laughed. Then he said, "Let's see if you're staying clean this time," and he opened the door, grabbed my hair, and pulled me out of the car. He searched me but didn't find anything, so he searched the car. He found a small bag of cocaine I had stashed under the seat when I saw the flashing light. He opened the bag, tasted the stuff, and then laughed. He held it up and said, "Looks like another felony. That's thirty years as an habitual offender." He handcuffed me and drove to the station. He never read me my rights or anything.

I know that he stopped me just to hassle me because he doesn't like me. He was involved in the two drug busts that I did my time for. Those jerks at special narcotics think they own the world. I even heard that Meadows was telling people I was an informer just to get me in trouble. I hope he gets convicted for shaking me down. He won't live ten minutes in prison.

Meadows took me to the station, booked me and then took me into an interrogation room. He held up the coke and said, "You know this is your third felony and you'll get stuck with the 'bitch' this time." That's street slang for the 30 years extra time you get added to your sentence for being an habitual offender. I could tell he wanted something because he sort of hesitated and stared at me. I thought maybe he wanted me to be an informer, but I'd rather do the 30 years than inform against the guys in the drug business. Then he said, "Maybe we can work something out." That's when it dawned on me that he was looking for a bribe. I asked, "What will it take to work out this beef." Meadows hesitated and then said, "About two ounces of your good stuff." I said okay, but asked how he would arrange to get me off. He said, "Trust me, a lot can happen to this bag on the way to the lab." I said, "Do I have a choice?" He told me I'd have to spend the night in jail to make it look good, but he'd get me released. He told me to bring him the cocaine in a brown mailing envelope to the police station at the end of the evening shift, 11:00 p.m., on January 5. I thought that sounded stupid, but figured it was his neck.

Next day, I went to court. Meadows was there. He told the judge I should be released without bail because he thought the stuff I'd been carrying was not cocaine. That's when I realized how he was going to get me off. He was going to switch the cocaine he'd taken from me with lidocaine or some other powder so the lab report would show no cocaine and the court would dismiss charges. I was released. Sure enough, on January 7 when I went back to court, the District Attorney announced that the lab report showed it wasn't cocaine, and charges were dismissed. Meadows was very clever, because he didn't even look like he had anything to do with it.

On January 5, I went to the police station with two and one-quarter ounces of cocaine. I'd put in the extra so he couldn't say I had shorted him. I could have sold it on the street for $3000 an ounce. I entered the front door of the police station right at 11:00 p.m. Meadows was in the hallway and came toward me. I handed him the envelope and he walked out the front door without saying anything. I turned around and left. No one else was in the hallway at that time. As I had entered, I did see a snitch named Candy Summers outside the police station, just standing around. It's not surprising, because everyone knows he's Meadows' boy, even though he constantly rips off Meadows. He skims a little cash and a few drugs off the top each time he sets up a bust.

On January 15, I was busted on a felony weapon charge for carrying a gun with the serial number defaced. I knew I was in trouble because it would be my third felony so the district attorney could charge me as an habitual offender. So when I saw the D.A. in court on the next morning, I offered to trade testimony against Meadows for a charge reduction. I made them give me the deal in writing, which they did.

Incidentally, I heard that Meadows sold an ounce of coke a few days ago to a guy named Jeff Thomas. I don't know where he lives, but he comes by Bryan Park sometimes in a Mercedes and buys cocaine from me. I know this because another dealer named Alvin Johnson told me that Thomas had mentioned it to him when they were conducting some business a couple of days ago.

Signed: Nancy K. Hatton

CITY OF BAYSHORE

✪ POLICE DEPARTMENT "TO SERVE AND PROTECT"

SUPPLEMENTARY STATEMENT OF
NANCY K. HATTON

Made to Sgt. Andrew Sutton
at Bayshore Police Headquarters
January 17, YR-0, 5:30 p.m.

My name is Nancy K. Hatton, and I am giving this statement voluntarily of my own free will.

When I was arrested by Robert Meadows on January 3, I was definitely carrying cocaine, not lactose. I had used some from the same batch and got high. I also had sold some to about a dozen regular customers over New Year's weekend, and no one called me to complain. In fact, one customer used some and then called me back on January 2 to ask for more, saying it was good stuff. Also, I do not cut my cocaine with lactose. I use lidocaine. It's harder to get, but makes a smoother high than lactose. Lactose can also cause some people to have stomach problems because it's derived from milk.

When I delivered the coke to Meadows on January 5, I did not sign in on the visitors' log. Like I said, I met Meadows as soon as I walked in the door. Anyway, I was there to make a drug deal, so why would I sign my name? The coke was a in a clear plastic bag inside the brown envelope.

Signed: Nancy K. Hatton

UNITED STATES DEPARTMENT OF JUSTICE
FEDERAL BUREAU OF INVESTIGATION
IDENTIFICATION DIVISION
WASHINGTON, D.C. 20537

The following FBI record, NUMBER 3 021 999 T6 , is furnished for OFFICIAL USE ONLY. Information shown on this Identification Record represents data furnished FBI by fingerprint contributors. WHERE DISPOSITION DATA IS NOT SHOWN OR FURTHER EXPLANATION OF CHARGE OR DISPOSITION IS DESIRED, COMMUNICATE WITH AGENCY CONTRIBUTING THOSE FINGERPRINTS.

CONTRIBUTOR: IDENTIFIER (ORI) NAME CASE NUMBER (OCA)	SUBJECT: NAME STATE NUMBER	ARRESTED OR RECEIVED	C - CHARGE D - DISPOSITION
CO203010 PD, BAYSHORE COL 444021	HATTON, NANCY K #107628W	09/12/-8	C - CCC 222.3 MISD THEFT D - 09/19/-8 GUILTY FINE $25
CO203010 PD, BAYSHORE COL 508222	HATTON, NANCY K #107628W	04/12/-7	C - CCC 484.8 MISD POSS DRUGS D - 07/02/-7 GUILTY PROB 1 YR
CO203010 PD, BAYSHORE COL 618957	HATTON, NANCY K #107628W	08/11/-6	C - CCC 484.10 MISD POSS DRUG CCC 242.2 MISD RESIST ARR D - DISMISSED
CO203010 PD, BAYSHORE COL 619583	HATTON, NANCY K #107628W	09/16/-6	C - CCC 484.4 FEL SALE DRUGS CCC 253.2 POSS WEAPON D - 03/21/-5 GUILTY 18 MONTHS
CO203010 PD, BAYSHORE COL 642301	HATTON, NANCY K #107628W	11/11/-4	C - CCC 484.4 FEL SALE DRUGS D - 01/23/-1 GUILTY 2 YRS
CO203010 PD, BAYSHORE COL 700028	HATTON, NANCY K #107628W	01/03/-0	C - CCC 484.6 FEL POSS DRUGS D - 01/07/-0 DISMISSED
CO203010 PD, BAYSHORE COL 700116	HATTON, NANCY K #107628W	01/15/-0	C - CCC 253.4 FEL POSS WEAPON

FELONY COMPLAINT

213-B CR 92
DOCKET NUMBER

CRIMINAL COURT

Part D-4 County Monroe

DEFENDANTS

#1 Nancy K. Hatton — NAME; 26 — AGE
400 E. Jackson St — STREET ADDRESS
Bayshore — CITY; Col. — STATE

#2 ______ NAME ______ AGE
______ STREET ADDRESS
______ CITY ______ STATE

#3 ______ NAME ______ AGE
______ STREET ADDRESS
______ CITY ______ STATE

Defendants are charged with a violation of

CCC 484.7 Possession

R.H. Meadows — OFFICER'S NAME; 921 — SHIELD #; SNU — COMMAND

______ VACATION/LEAVE ______ DUTY CHART

2516
PCT.—ARREST SERIAL # *Complaint prepared by*

Search Warrant # ______ Executed in this case.

ADJOURNMENT

To Part D-4

To Date January 7, Yr-0

Bail Condition

#1 Released on own recognizance per — INS. CO. BAIL BOND OR CASH BAIL
#2 request of officer — INS. CO. BAIL BOND OR CASH BAIL
#3 ______ INS. CO. BAIL BOND OR CASH BAIL

______ The defendant, upon being released on his own recognizance, was directed by the Court pursuant to section 510.40 of the CPL.

ADJ. REQUEST	PRESENT	ABSENT	NOTIFY	EXCUSED
People (circled)	Officer (circled)	Officer	Officer	Officer
Defense	Complainant	Complainant	Complainant	Complainant
Consent	Defendant (circled)	Defendant	Defendant	
Court	Attorney	Attorney	Attorney	

SPEEDY TRIAL

______ Adjournment period to be excluded under 30.30 CPL.

✓ Adjournment period to be charged under 30.30 CPL.

✓ The defendant, being without counsel, consents to this adjournment after having been advised of his rights under the Speedy Trial Rules and the effect of his consent.

______ Psychiatric examination ordered
Custody
Out Patient

______ Narcotic examination ordered.

______ Medical attention required.

1/4/Yr-0 — Date
Guthrie — Judge

DISPOSITION

✓ Hearing waived.

______ Hearing held.

✓ Dismissed – Lab report negative

______ Held for the Grand Jury

Bail Condition

#1 ______

#2 ______

#3 ______

______ The defendant, upon being released on his own recognizance, was directed by the Court pursuant to section 510.40 of the CPL.

Charges reduced to ______

______ Converted to an Information

______ Converted to a Misdemeanor Complaint

1/7/Yr-0 — Date
Guthrie — Judge

Form No. CRC. 1F(Rev. 6-1-73)-100M-531022(74) 346

BAYSHORE POLICE DEPARTMENT ARREST REPORT

1 DATE OF REPORT: **1/04/YR-0**
2 TIME: **1:15 am**
3 ARRESTING OFFICER'S NAME: **Robert H Meadows**
4 RANK: **Det**
5 BADGE: **921**

6 DEFENDANT NAME: **Nancy K Hatton**
7 ADDRESS: **400 E Jackson, Bayshore**
8 CRIMES: **484.7 Possession of controlled substance**

9 VICTIM NAME:
10 SEX:
11 AGE:
12 ADDRESS:
13 CONTACT INFORMATION:
14 EMPLOYER:

15 DATE OF CRIME: **Jan 3, YR-0**
16 TIME: **9:00 pm**
17 LOCATION: **Henderson St between 1st Street and Maxwell Ln**
18 TYPE OF PREMISES: **Public street**
19 WEATHER: **Cold, clear**
20 HOW ATTACKED OR COMMITTED: **Defendant possessed bag of possible cocaine in plain view in car**
21 WEAPON/TOOLS:
22 PERSON REPORTING CRIME: **Officer observed**
23 ADDRESS:
24 CONTACT INFORMATION:
25 TIME/DATE OF REPORT:
26 TOTAL VALUE STOLEN:
27 TOTAL VALUE RECOVERED:
28 CURRENCY:
29 JEWELRY:
30 AUTOS:
31 COMPUTERS/TV ETC:
32 FIREARMS:
33 OTHER:

34 TOTAL PERSONS INVOLVED: **1**
35 TOTAL ARRESTED: **1**
36 ADULTS ARRESTED: **1**
37 JUVENILES ARRESTED: **0**
38 TOTAL AT LARGE: **0**

39 OTHER BPD OFFICERS INVOLVED:

40 NARRATIVE: **Observed Nancy K. Hatton, known drug dealer, run red light without stopping. Stopped her vehicle. Upon approaching suspect vehicle, officer observed bag of white powder in plain view on front seat. Field test for cocaine negative but powder sent to lab for trace analysis and suspect arrested because she is known drug dealer. Probably a bad case -- powder may not be cocaine.**

41 OFFICER SIGNATURE: ***Robert H. Meadows***

STATE OF COLUMBIA
COUNTY OF MONROE

District Court
MONROE COUNTY

PART D-4

THE STATE OF COLUMBIA

Docket #213 B 92

VS

Transcript of Proceedings

NANCY K. HATTON

Date: January 4, YR-0

Present: Brian Taylor, Assistant District Attorney
Nancy K. Hatton, pro se

Judge: P. M. Guthrie

Reporter: Dodie Bowman

Court was convened at 9:30 a.m., whereupon the following proceedings were had:
CLERK: Call case number 213-B 92, State versus Hatton on for a first appearance on a felony drug charge, section 484.7 of the penal code.
COURT: Ms. Hatton, do you have an attorney?
DEFENDANT: No.
COURT: Can you afford to retain counsel?
DEFENDANT: Yes I can, judge.
COURT: All right. Do you want me to read the charges against you and your rights?
DEFENDANT: No. I know them.
COURT: Mr. Taylor, what about bail?
MR. TAYLOR: One moment, your honor. Your honor, Police Officer Robert Meadows is here and he informs me that his field test of the drugs involved was negative and he thinks there's a good chance the lab report will be negative.
COURT: Is that correct, Officer Meadows?

MEADOWS: Yes, your honor. I would suggest that the defendant be released without bail because the case will probably have to be dismissed.
COURT: When can we expect the lab report?
MEADOWS: Three days, your honor.
COURT: All right, I'll adjourn this case until 2:00 p.m., January 7. Is that satisfactory to the state?
MR. TAYLOR: Yes, your honor.
COURT: Can you return at that time, Ms. Hatton?
DEFENDANT: Yes sir.
COURT: Case number 213 B 92 adjourned.

END OF TRANSCRIPT

Certified as accurate: *Dodie Bowman*

Dodie Bowman
Court Reporter

STATE OF COLUMBIA District Court
COUNTY OF MONROE Monroe County

Part D-4

THE STATE OF COLUMBIA Docket #213-B CR 92

VS

NANCY K. HATTON

TRANSCRIPT OF PROCEEDINGS

Date: January 7, YR-0
Present: Brian Taylor, Assistant District Attorney
Nancy K. Hatton, pro se
Judge: P.M. Guthrie
Reporter: Dodie Bowman

Court was convened at 2:00 p.m., and the following proceedings were had:

CLERK: Call case number 213 B 92, State versus Hatton, adjourned from January 3. The defendant is charged with a violation of section 484.7 of the penal code.

COURT: All right. This matter was adjourned pending receipt of the lab report. Do you have the report yet?

MR. TAYLOR: Yes, your honor. The lab report indicated that the defendant possessed lactose which is not a controlled substance. I have a copy for the court file. Since she did not have any cocaine, the State would move to dismiss this charge.

COURT: Motion granted. No written motion is required. You are free to go, Ms. Hatton.

DEFENDANT: Thank you, your honor.

END OF TRANSCRIPT

Certified as accurate: Dodie Bowman

Dodie Bowman
Court Reporter

BAYSHORE POLICE DEPARTMENT
POLICE LABORATORY ANALYSIS REPORT

POLICE LAB NO: 02388
DATE OF REPORT: 01/06/YR-0
CASE NO: 700116M
U.F. 61 NO: 265
ARREST NO: 381
VOUCHER NO: AO31542

LAB CLASSIFICATION: NARCOTICS

RECEIVED FROM: MEADOWS ROBERT
DATE RECEIVED: 01/04/YR-0

BADGE: 921
COMMAND: SPECIAL NARCOTICS UNIT

THE FOLLOWING ITEM(S):

TRACKING NO.	IDENTIFYING MARKS	DESCRIPTION	DEFENDANT(S)
700116	RM	Plastic evidence envelope containing white powder	Hatton Nancy K

RESULTS OF EXAMINATION OR ANALYSIS:

ENVELOPE CONTAINED 1/8 OZ + 4 GRAINS LACTOSE.
NO CONTROLLED SUBSTANCES PRESENT.
POST ANALYSIS WEIGHT 51 GRAINS.

I HEREBY CERTIFY THAT THE FOREGOING REPORT IS A TRUE AND ACCURATE COPY OF THE ORIGINAL REPORT.

Susan Hart Engle

CHEMIST/TECHNICIAN POLICE LAB

DISTRICT ATTORNEY
OF MONROE COUNTY
155 WEST 6TH STREET
BAYSHORE, COLUMBIA

FELONY DIVISION (811) 332-7310

The state of Columbia hereby enters into the following plea agreement with Nancy Hatton:

(1) That the state shall accept a plea of guilty to CCC § 247.4 (misdemeanor possession of a weapon) to satisfy the pending charge under section 247.5, felony possession of an altered weapon;

(2) That Nancy Hatton shall cooperate fully and honestly in the investigation into charges against Robert H. Meadow, including giving honest and truthful testimony;

(3) That no charges will be brought against Nancy Hatton for her part in transactions with Robert H. Meadows in January, YR-0;

(4) That Nancy Hatton shall not assert her privilege against self-incrimination regarding these matters;

(5) That sentencing of Nancy Hatton will be postponed until after the resolution of any charges brought against Robert H. Meadows; and

(6) That if Nancy Hatton cooperates fully and testifies truthfully, the State shall recommend that her sentence be suspended.

Date: 1/16/Yr-0 For the State: James Byers, ADA

Defendant: Nancy K. Hatton

Defense Attorney: waived

VISITORS' LOG

Date: JAN. 5 CONT'D

Name	In	Out
Cary Depel	8:12	8:31
Danier Fogel	8:40	9:12
Laura Goodman	8:40	9:12
Bonnie J. Forest	9:05	10:01
Ben Bergen	10:20	11:05
Steve Walcutt	11:31	11:41

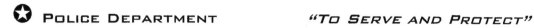

OFFICERS DUTY LOG

SPECIAL NARCOTICS &
CRIME CONTROL UNIT

DATE:

NAME	INITIALS	IN	OUT
CPT. WILLIAM DAY	WD	0730	1630
LT. HARRY HAWKINS			
LT. CAROLYN SMITH	CS	0800	1730
SGT. RICHARD GONZALEZ	RG	0745	1650
SGT. MARK GRUBB	MG	14:05	~~305~~ 23:15
SGT. EDDIE PORTER	EP	1005	1915
OFC. JUDITH BOOKER	JB	0800	1730
OFC. THORNTON DAMON			
OFC. JACK LINDSEY	JL	0900	1810
OFC. ROBERT MEADOWS	RHM	11:15	22:20
OFC. DANIEL POWELL			
OFC. CLARENCE STURGIS	CS	0830	1830

CITY OF BAYSHORE

✪ POLICE DEPARTMENT
CRIME LABORATORY

"TO SERVE AND PROTECT"

Report of Susan Hart Engle

Ref. No. 02414
State v. Robert Meadows

I am a forensic chemist employed by the Bayshore Police Department. My primary duties are to test substances suspected of being narcotics. I have worked at the police laboratory since June, YR-2. The lab is located in the annex just west of the courthouse and is used by several regional law enforcement agencies

I obtained my B.S. degree in chemistry from Purdue University in June, YR-4. I received an M.S. degree in chemistry from the University of Texas in June YR-2. I did not complete my Ph.D., but took the job in Bayshore when my husband got a job here at the university. I have attended two summer courses for police laboratory chemists in Chicago sponsored by the Drug Enforcement Administration. In the course of my work, I have tested approximately 300 substances thought to be narcotics, of which approximately 50 were cocaine. I have testified in court as an expert for the State in approximately 20 cases.

On January 19, YR-0, Sgt. Andrew Sutton, personally known to me, arrived at the police laboratory at 4:45 p.m. and handed me a sealed plastic envelope containing a plastic bag filled with a white powder. The envelope was sealed and the seal marked with Sgt. Sutton's initials and the case number, and a chain of custody form attached. I signed the chain of custody form and I witnessed Sgt. Sutton sign it. I then entered the description and case number in the laboratory inventory log. I locked the sealed envelope by itself in one compartment of the safe in my laboratory. There are only two keys to that safe. I have one, and the director of the laboratory has the other in a sealed envelope.

On January 20, YR-0, I unlocked the safe and removed the evidence. The seal was intact. I broke the seal, removed the plastic bag, and weighed the powder at one and three-eighths ounces plus 4 grains. I then performed standard chemical tests and microscopic examination on a small amount (approx. 10 grains) of the substance, and concluded beyond doubt that the powder contained approximately 10% cocaine. Cocaine crystals that have been treated with dilute hydrochloric acid and 5% gold chloride are readily identifiable under a microscope. The other 90% of powder appeared to be lidocaine, but I did not bother to test it fully as lidocaine is not a controlled substance.

I placed the powder, bag, and envelope into another plastic envelope, sealed it, and marked my initials, the date, and the case number on it. I reattached the chain of custody form, returned it to the safe, and sent Sgt. Sutton an email that I was done. He came by the laboratory about 3:00 p.m. I turned the evidence over to him and we both signed the chain of custody form.

I prepared a standard laboratory analysis report like we fill out in all cases. I gave a copy to Sgt. Sutton and filed a copy in the records department of the police laboratory.

I am also the chemist who tested the substance brought in by Officer Meadows on January 4. That substance turned out to be lactose, a disaccharide sugar, also known as "milk sugar" because it is commonly derived from milk or other diary products. It is harmless and not a controlled substance. I tested it on January 7. Lactose is commonly used by drug dealers to cut cocaine because it superficially resembles cocaine crystals and can be readily purchased in drug stores and from chemical supply companies. I followed the same procedures in that case; however, we threw out the lactose and the chain of custody form instead of giving it back to Officer Meadows because the case was dismissed.

I have read the foregoing and it is true and accurate.

Susan Hart Engle

Susan Hart Engle
Chemist

BAYSHORE POLICE DEPARTMENT
CHAIN OF CUSTODY FORM

Suspect/ Defendant(s)
Name: Meadows, Robert H
Address: 1012 N. Park St
Bayshore Col.
Name:
Address:

Seizing Officer
Name: Andrew Sutton
Command: IA
Badge No: 86
Case No: 701385M
Date/time: Jan 18 Yr-0, 9:00 pm
Location: 1012 N. Park St.
Received from: Personally obtained

Signature: *Andrew Sutton*

Description of Seized Items: Bag of white powder

CHAIN OF CUSTODY				
DATE	TIME	SURRENDERED BY	RECEIVED BY	Comments (purpose, whether seal broken, etc)
Jan 19 Yr-0	4:45 pm	A Sutton	S. Engle	For testing - intact
1/20	3:00 pm	S. Engle	A Sutton	Seal broken, put in new bag, resealed

BAYSHORE POLICE DEPARTMENT
POLICE LABORATORY ANALYSIS REPORT

POLICE LAB NO: 02414
CASE NO: 701385M
U.F. 61 NO: 279
ARREST NO: 395
VOUCHER NO: AO31559

DATE OF REPORT: 01/20/YR-0

LAB CLASSIFICATION: NARCOTICS

RECEIVED FROM: SUTTON ANDREW

DATE RECEIVED: 01/04/YR-0

BADGE: 86

COMMAND: INTERNAL AFFAIRS

THE FOLLOWING ITEM(S):

TRACKING NO.	IDENTIFYING MARKS	DESCRIPTION	DEFENDANT(S)
701385	AS	Plastic evidence envelope containing white powder	Meadows Robert

RESULTS OF EXAMINATION OR ANALYSIS:

ENVELOPE CONTAINED COCAINE
PRE ANALYSIS WEIGHT 1 1/4 OZ + 52 GRAINS
POST ANALYSIS WEIGHT 1 1/4 OZ + 36 GRAINS

I HEREBY CERTIFY THAT THE FOREGOING REPORT IS A TRUE AND ACCURATE COPY OF THE ORIGINAL REPORT.

Susan Hart Engle

CHEMIST/TECHNICIAN POLICE LAB

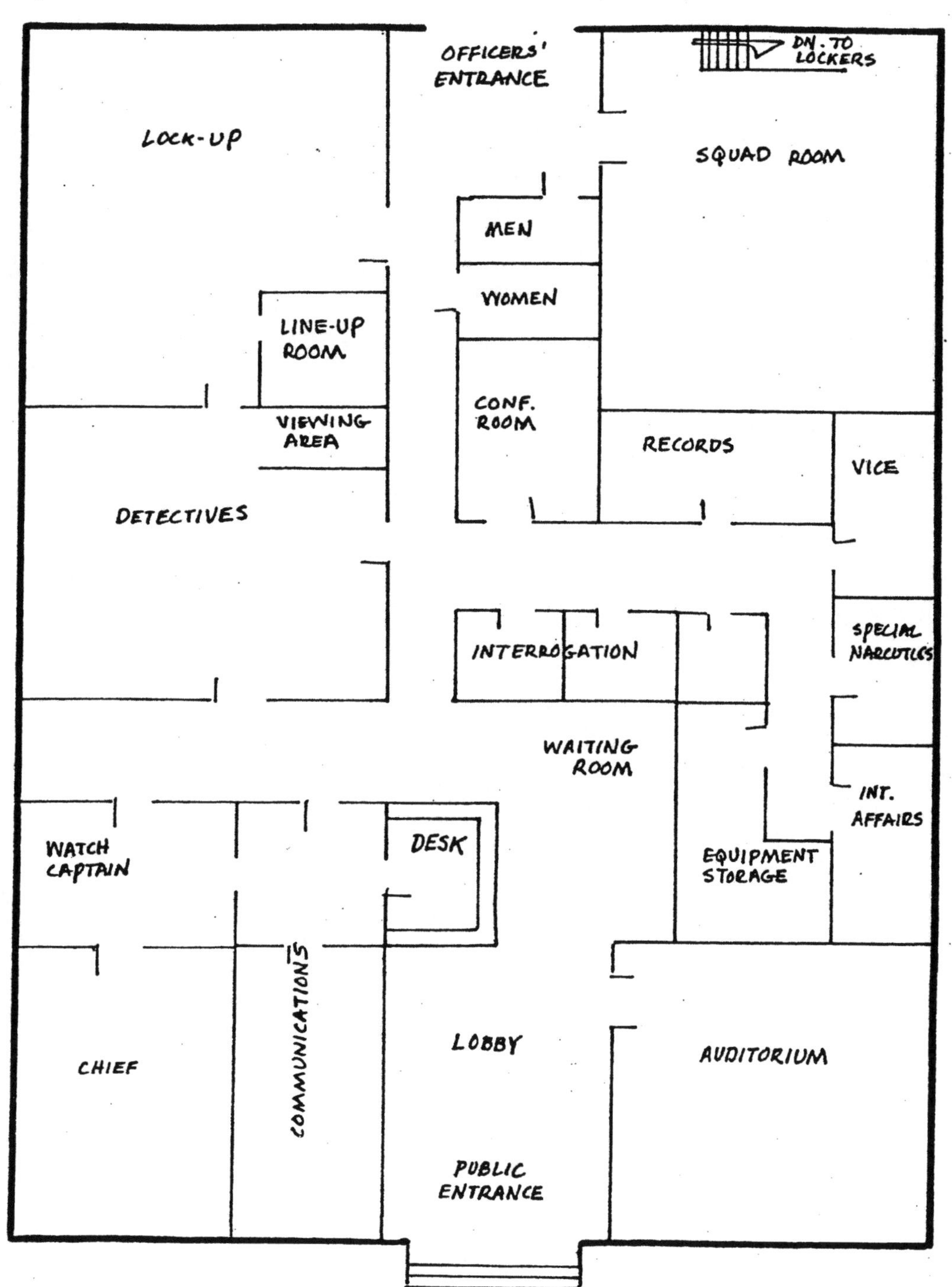

BAYSHORE POLICE DEPARTMENT BUILDING PLAN

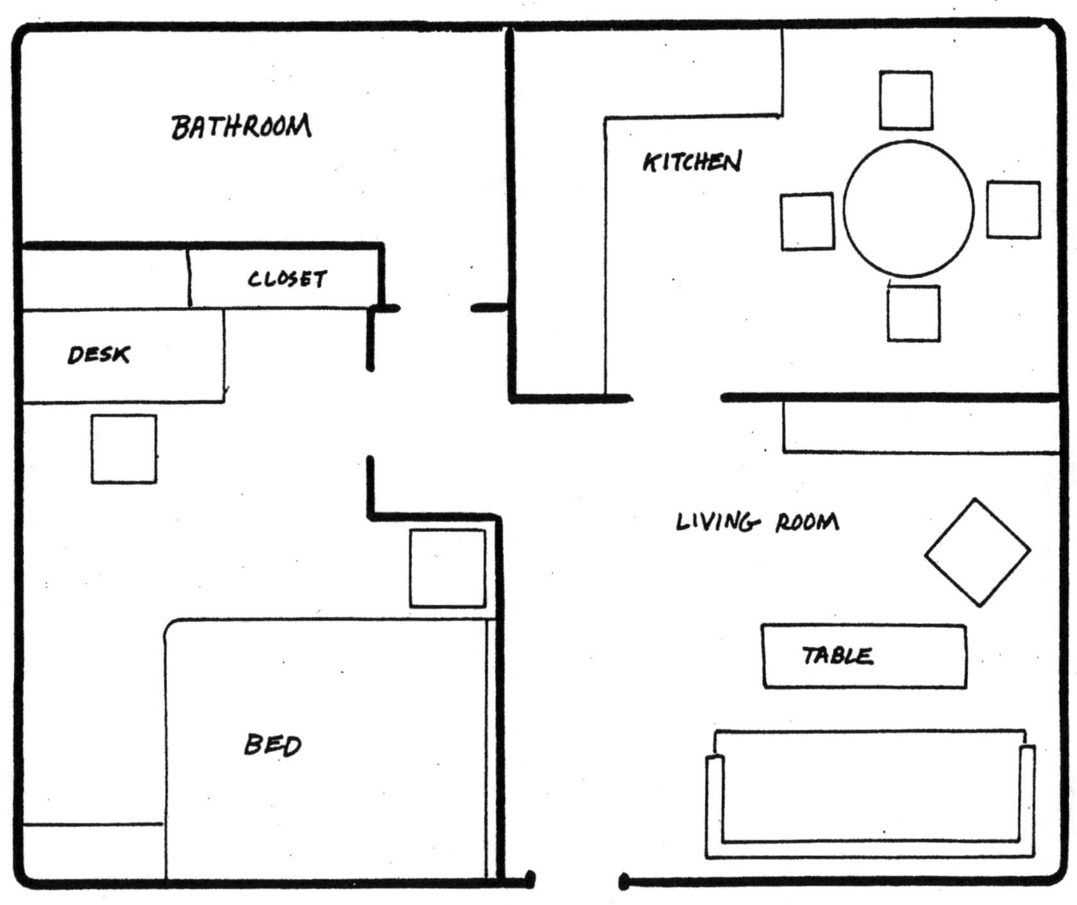

ROBERT MEADOWS' APARTMENT PLAN

CITY OF BAYSHORE

✪ POLICE DEPARTMENT "TO SERVE AND PROTECT"

LEGAL RIGHTS ADVICE FORM

Before we ask you any questions, you must understand your rights.

1. You have the right to remain silent.

2. Anything you say can and will be used against you in court.

3. You have the right to consult with a lawyer before we ask you any questions, and to have the lawyer present with you during questioning.

4. If you cannot afford a lawyer, one will be appointed for you before any questioning if you wish.

5. If you decide to answer questions now without a lawyer present, you will still have the right to stop answering at any time.

WAIVER

I have read this statement of my rights and I understand what my rights are. I understand that I may ask for clarification and explanation of my rights if I do not understand them. I am willing to make a statement and answer questions. I do not want a lawyer at this time. I understand and know what I am doing. No promises or threats have been made to me, and no pressure or coercion of any kind has been used against me.

Date: Jan. 27, YR-0 Signature: Robert H. Meadows

Witness: Andrew Sutton Witness: Wm Friedman

Time: 2:15 pm Place: Bayshore PD Bldg

STATEMENT OF OFFICER ROBERT MEADOWS

DATE : January 27, YR-0

PLACE : Bayshore Police Department

PRESENT: Officer Robert Meadows, Sgt. Andrew Sutton,
Capt. William Friedman, Lt. Carolyn Smith,
Assistant District Attorney James Byers,
Lawrence Boardman (attorney for Robert Meadows),
Stenographer Walter Steering

BY MR. BYERS: For the record, this is an informal interview with Robert Meadows, special narcotics officer, shield number 921, under suspicion of bribery and possession of cocaine. Present in the room are: Officer Meadows, represented by Lawrence Boardman, an attorney for the Police Benevolent Association; Sgt. Andrew Sutton and Captain William Friedman of internal affairs; Lt. Carolyn Smith of special narcotics; Walter Steering is the stenographer, and I am James Byers from the District Attorney's office. The date is January 27, YR-0, and the time now is 2:30 p.m.

Officer Meadows, you understand that you are under suspicion of these charges and that the case may be sent to the grand jury, that you have the right to remain silent, that if you give up this right anything and everything you say here will be recorded and may be used against you in court?

MR. MEADOWS: Yes.
Q: Have you discussed giving this statement with your attorney?
A: Yes.
Q: Are you satisfied with Mr. Boardman's advice?
A: Yes.
Q: Are you willing to make a statement voluntarily, of your own free will?
A: Yes.
Q: Have any promises been made to you, or threats, or coercion of any kind?
A: No.
Q: All right. For the record, you are Officer Robert Meadows of special narcotics employed by the Bayshore Police Department?
A: Yes.
Q: You've been on the force for nine years?

A: Yes, five on patrol and the last four in special narcotics.
Q: You were born April 14, YR-32?
A: Yes.
Q: You live in an apartment at 1012 North Park Street?
A: Yes.
Q: You were disciplined in March YR-8, were you not?
A: Yes. I was suspended for thirty days.
Q: According to your file, you were found grossly negligent by an Internal Affairs hearing board for losing $6,000 taken from a suspect during an arrest. Is that correct?
A: Yes. My partner and I arrested a suspect for sale of narcotics. He had $6,000 on his person. I put the money in an envelope and stuck it above the visor of the squad car. My partner went with the backup unit to book the suspect, and I was supposed to transport the evidence. On the way, I responded to a call for assistance at a fire. I foolishly left the car unlocked, and the money was gone when I got back to it.
Q: The narcotics suspect, one Jimmy Marlin, accused you of stealing the money.
A: That's right, but I did not steal it. The inquiry board acquitted me of that charge. I've never taken a dime from anyone.
Q: You are currently divorced?
A: Yes, since July, YR-4. My wife couldn't stand the long hours and didn't like my friends on the force. She said I was too moody. Lisa got custody of our son, and I pay $900 a month child support.
Q: How much is your salary?
A: $48,000 a year, gross. My take-home pay is about $3000 a month.
Q: Would you say you're hard-pressed financially because of the child support?
A: Yes. After the $900 for child support and the $1000 I pay for the apartment and $500 for my car, I have to live on $600 a month.
Q: Turning to the events at issue, do you recall arresting Nancy K. Hatton on January 3, YR-0?
A: Yes I do.
Q: Tell us about it.
A: I was on routine patrol in the area near Bryan Park, a major drug-trafficking area. It was a cold evening, so there didn't seem to be much drug business. About 9:00 p.m., I stopped Hatton for making an illegal right turn. She turned right through a red light without stopping. I was in an unmarked vehicle. I put on the flashers and pulled over Hatton's car. As I approached her vehicle, I recognized her as a known narcotics dealer. I'd been involved in a couple of investigations that involved her. When I got to her car, I asked for her license. As she opened her purse, I saw a

plastic bag on the seat in plain view that contained a white powder. I suspected it might be cocaine. I asked her to get out of the car. She hesitated and leaned forward. I knew she sometimes carries a gun, so I pulled open the door, grabbed her and pulled her out of the car. I put the cuffs on her, and placed her under arrest. I retrieved the white powder.

Q: Did you tell Hatton you were glad to see she was out of prison?
A: I don't remember.
Q: Did you pull her out of the car by her hair?
A: No, I grabbed her left arm.
Q: Did you search her car?
A: Yes, for weapons, but I didn't find any.
Q: In the course of that search, did you look under the front seat?
A: Yes.
Q: Did you find anything under the seat?
A: No.
Q: Where was the white powder?
A: Like I said, on the front seat in plain view.
Q: Did you say anything to Hatton about this being her third felony?
A: Yes. When I picked up the bag of powder, I said, "This means another felony--your third, right?" She said, "Don't you wish. That's just sugar. Why don't you send it to the lab and find out?"
Q: Anything else?
A: Yes. I said that if it was a felony, she could do thirty years, but that was later at the station. I took her to an interrogation room at the station. I gave her her rights, and told her that she could get thirty years as an habitual offender. She again repeated that the stuff was not cocaine.
Q: Did you think it was cocaine?
A: No. When I arrested her, I had dipped my finger in the powder and rubbed a little of the stuff on my gums. If it was coke, you should feel numbness. I didn't feel anything at all.
Q: By the way, do you normally make traffic arrests?
A: No, but there wasn't any action in that area on January third, so I was looking for something to do.
Q: All right. Did you say anything else?
A: At the station?
Q: Yes.
A: Yeah. I said that if it turned out to be cocaine, maybe we could work something out so she wouldn't have to do the thirty years. She asked what she would have to do.

I said that we'd have to wait and see what the lab report said. Hatton said, "The lab report won't show anything." I said, "Lots can happen to this bag on the way to the lab."
Q: What did you mean?
A: Well, I wanted her to think that I might doctor the stuff by adding some real cocaine to it so the lab report would show a controlled substance. Hatton knows a lot about the drug business and I was hoping she would panic and offer to become an informer.
Q: Did she?
A: No. She stayed cool and asked whether I was going to hold her on this charge when we both knew the powder was not cocaine. I said she would have to stay in jail until morning when the judge would decide.
Q: What did you do with the powder?
A: I put it in an evidence bag and dropped it off at the night depository at the lab.
Q: You're sure about that?
A: Pretty sure.
Q: Did you alter that substance, add anything to it, or substitute anything for it?
A: No.
Q: So, what you delivered to the lab was exactly what you took from Ms. Hatton?
A: Yes.
Q: What happened to it?
A: The lab report came back negative. I called the lab and they told me it was sugar, like I thought. I informed the district attorney's office on January 7, I believe, and they dismissed the charge against Hatton.
Q: Were you in court on January 4th?
A: Yes, that was Hatton's arraignment.
Q: Did you recommend to the judge that Ms. Hatton be released without bail?
A: Yes. I was pretty sure she was telling the truth about the powder being sugar rather than coke. I felt I had an obligation not to keep her locked up.
Q: Directing your attention to January 5th, YR-0, do you recall that day?
A: Vaguely.
Q: What do you mean by "vaguely"?
A: Nothing unusual happened that day that I recall. I have no reason to remember it.
Q: Do you know what you were doing?
A: Not explicitly. I was patrolling the Bryan Park area in the evenings all that week, but Hatton was the only person I arrested. So I assume I was patrolling on that night as well, but don't know for sure.
Q: What time did you leave the station?

A: I have no idea. You'd have to check the log.
Q: The log indicated you signed out at 10:20 p.m. Is that correct?
A: Sure. I always put down the right time when I sign out.
Q: Where is the log kept?
A: By the door in the special narcotics muster room.
Q: Is anyone there to see what time you're signing out in the evenings?
A: Not usually.
Q: On January 5th?
A: I don't remember. I doubt it.
Q: Did you go straight home?
A: Yes, as far as I can recall. Like I said, there was nothing special about that night, so I don't remember. I usually go straight home. I'd remember if there was any special occasion.
Q: You live alone?
A: Right.
Q: Can anyone verify that you were home at 11:00 on January 5th?
A: Not that I know of. Like I said, nothing about that night was special. I might have talked to someone on the phone, but I don't remember.
Q: Do you recall if John Summers called?
A: He calls sometimes with information so he knows my cell phone number, but I do not remember about that night.
Q: How long does it take you to get home form the police station?
A: About fifteen minutes.
Q: What door do you use to enter and leave the police station?
A: The rear door, the one that leads to the officers' parking lot.
Q: Do you ever leave by the front door?
A: Once in a while if I'm going to walk to a restaurant or go get a beer or something.
Q: Do you remember which door you left by on January 5th?
A: No. Probably the rear door.
Q: Did you see Nancy Hatton at any time on January 5th?
A: No.
Q: Did you see her or talk to her anytime between January 4th and 7th?
A: No.
Q: Has Ms. Hatton ever worked for you or your unit as an informant?
A: No.
Q: Did you at any time ask Ms. Hatton for cocaine?
A: No.
Q: Has she ever offered, given or sold you cocaine?

A: No.
Q: Were you in the courtroom on January 7 when charges were dismissed against Ms. Hatton?
A: No.
Q: All right. Turning to January 18, YR-0. Is it true that Sgt. Sutton searched your home at approximately 8:45 p.m. pursuant to a warrant?
A: Yes. He searched for about one hour.
Q: He found a bag of cocaine -- I believe one ounce or a little more -- and $2500 in cash, is that correct?
A: Yes.
Q: The cocaine was in a plastic bag in plain view on a table in your living room?
A: Yes.
Q: The money was found in a desk drawer?
A: Yes.
Q: Did he also find plastic bags and a scale?
A: Yes. I wrap sandwiches in the plastic bags and the scale is used to weigh drugs. When I pose as a buyer, I always bring the scale with me to impress the dealer that I am experienced.
Q: Where did the cocaine come from?
A: An informant named Johnnie Summers. I often pay him for valuable information. I had seen him on the street the morning of the 18th. He said that he had made connections with a new dealer known as Tony, selling cocaine. I asked if he could make a buy for me. He said sure, but he'd need some cash. I said I would meet him later, to set up a buy. I talked to Lt. Smith, who authorized me to withdraw $5000 to set up the buy. I met Summers at the park at about 7:00 p.m. I gave Summers half of it, and told him to buy some and bring it to me, and to tell this dealer that if the stuff was good, he'd have some friends interested in buying it too. I dropped Summers off on Hunter Street, one block from the bus station where he was supposed to meet this guy Tony. That was just before 7:30. Ten minutes later, Summers returned and gave me a bag of coke. I dropped him off back at the park and went back to my apartment, where I put the other $2500 in a desk drawer. I arrived home about 8:00. I was about to drive over to the lab to get the stuff tested, when Sutton arrived with a search warrant. I had set the suspected cocaine on the coffee table. I had heard the day before from a friend in internal affairs that I was under some sort of investigation, but I was not told why, and I had no idea because I have not done anything.
    Sutton went over and picked it up, and he searched my apartment and found the money, too. I tried to tell him it was part of an investigation, but he wouldn't

listen. He wouldn't even tell me what was going on.
Q: Isn't it standard police procedure to place controlled substances immediately into evidence bags and seal them at the scene?
A: Yes, but I had forgotten to bring any with me. I checked at home, but didn't have any there either. I was on my way downtown when Sutton took the coke from me.
Q: Do you know the street value of cocaine in this area?
A: Sure. In January, it was selling for about $2500 to $3000 an ounce.
Q: Yet this Summers person purchased one and three-eighths ounces for $2500?
A: I don't know the weight because I never got it to the lab. I sent him in with $2500 and he brought back what looked to be a little over one ounce. It's not unreasonable for a new dealer trying to attract customers to offer a good deal. I'd never heard of a dealer named Tony before and Summers verified that he was new.
Q: Do you have an address for Summers?
A: You'd have to look in my file, on my desk.
BY LT. SMITH: I have already done so. His address is 351 South Lincoln, Apartment 3A.
Q: Do you have anything else you wish to add?
A: No.
BY MR. BOARDMAN: Bob, you served as an M.P. in the service, didn't you, between YR-12 and YR-9?
A: Yes.
Q: And you received a distinguished service medal for saving the life of Ambassador Rothwell, our Ambassador to Great Britain?
A: Yes. I was in the embassy Marine detachment in London. I disarmed a terrorist trying to fire at the Ambassador's car, and was wounded in the process.
Q: And you received a meritorious duty citation in YR-7, didn't you?
A: Yes.
Q: That was for rescuing two people from a burning building?
A: Yes.
Q: You have consistently received annual evaluations as outstanding in the performance of your duty over the last five years, is that correct?
A: Yes. I'm very proud of my record.
Q: Did you have a fight with Sgt. Sutton a year ago?
A: Yes. I punched him at a party, though I don't remember why. He threatened that he was going to nail me one day to get even. I guess this is what he was talking about.
Q: On the 20th, after Summers made the buy, you went home. Why?
A: To use the bathroom. I know it sounds silly, but I don't like to use public restrooms.

I was having some digestive problems, and I needed the quiet of my own apartment for a bowel movement.

BY MR. BYERS: Oh, a few more things. You never filed a police report concerning this alleged drug investigation of Tony, did you?

A: No. I never made an arrest because my evidence was gone. Reports are usually prepared only when there is an arrest. But I do have my notes from both the third and eighteenth of January that I fill out as I'm working. They're pretty sketchy, though.

BY MR. BOARDMAN: Let's attach those two pages of notes to this statement as exhibits one and two.

Q: Sutton didn't arrest you on January 18th, did he?

A: No. I was arrested a few days later, on the twenty-second.

BY MR. BYERS: Thank you, that is all. We will have this typed up and ask you to read it to make sure it's accurate. I will ask that you sign it to verify its accuracy. Okay?

MR. MEADOWS: Okay.

Signature: *Robert H. Meadows*

1/3

Busted Nancy Hatton
cocaine
stopped for traffic light violation
cocaine plain view
front seat
Hatton uncooperative but might
be able to work out
<u>facing 30 years</u>

tested - probably <u>NOT</u> coke
send to lab

MEADOWS EX. 1

1/18

Summers — New dealer
"Tony"
set up buy
$5000 ok'd C. Smith
bus ~~stop~~ station

Summers made buy ~1930 hrs

Sutton Int. Affairs had warrant
searched my apt. 2045-2200 hrs.
took $ and cocaine
What the hell's going on?

Call Smith

MEADOWS EX. 2

LAW OFFICES
HOUSTON, MINNICK & DOS SANTOS
A PROFESSIONAL CORPORATION

DONALD L. HOUSTON
MEGAN STONE MINNICK
ROBERTO X. DOS SANTOS*
LYNDA A. MITCHELL
BARRY J. GREENBERG
*Also admitted in Florida

100 NORTH WALNUT
BAYSHORE

(811) 520-2020
FAX (811) 520-3477

NORTHSIDE OFFICE
4755 NORTH COLLEGE
(811) 639-3333

STATEMENT OF JOHN SUMMERS

Taken by Lawrence Boardman, attorney,
on January 29, YR-0, at the offices of
Houston, Minnick & DosSantos, 100 N. Walnut,

My name is John Summers, although I am known on the street as Candyman or Candy Summers. I am twenty-four old. I live alone in a rented room at 351 South Lincoln Street. I don't have a job and I haven't worked steadily since I was nineteen and worked on the loading dock at Ross Trucking Company. I got fired from that job for filling in too many hours on my time card. I get by from doing a little hustling, picking up odd jobs, and I sometimes do a favor for the cops. Sometimes I sell a little marijuana to college kids. I have a long record, but it's all small stuff. Lately, since I started working for the cops, I've been doing better and staying out of trouble.

I know Robert Meadows, a cop who works special narcotics. I've worked for him for two years. He's the one I give information to and he sometimes gives me money. I probably make a couple hundred a month. It's not much, but it pays the rent. If I hear anything or find out who's dealing, I let Meadows know. Sometimes he'll send me in to make a buy or get me to introduce him to a dealer. But I work on my own. You can't do this more than once or twice a month or it could be bad for your health if they start to suspect you.

I realize that by coming forward and agreeing to testify I am putting my life in danger. But I've got a couple thousand dollars saved up and I just bought myself a Buick that runs good, and I'm going to leave town when this is over. I like Meadows, and that drug dealer Hatton who is framing him is no good. It's my duty as a public citizen to come forward like this. Meadows did not threaten me or pay me to testify.

On January 16, I met a guy named Tony at a party. I don't know his last name. He said he could get me cocaine at a good price if I wanted any. I asked how much and he said he'd have to check, but he could do a couple hundred better than the going street price. I asked how I could tell if the stuff was any good, and he pulled some out and offered me a line. I snorted it and it was pretty good stuff. I have some experience with cocaine and I can tell the difference between good stuff and bad. Tony's a big guy, maybe six foot two and two-hundred twenty pounds, slightly bald. I'd guess he's an ex-college football player, about 35 years old. I'd never seen him around before. I said I might be interested and he said he only dealt with an ounce or more. He gave me a phone number to call and I wrote it on a matchbook cover that I have saved.

On January 18, I saw Meadows on the street near Bryan Park in the early afternoon. I told him about Tony and said that the word on the street was that he had good connections in New York. I asked Meadows if he wanted me to do anything. He asked me to set up a buy and meet him back at the park at 7:00. I told him I'd need at least $2500 because Tony said it had to be an ounce or more at $2500 an ounce.

I called the number and asked for Tony. I recognized the voice on the phone from the party as Tony's. He asked what I wanted. I told him I had met him at the party and was interested in his offer and that I'd have some money after 7:00. He gave me an address on First Street that I wrote down in the matchbook, and said I should come by at 7:30.

Meadows picked me up at the park a little after seven and I gave him the address. Meadows gave me $2500 and said he'd drop me off near the address. He told me to tell Tony that if the stuff was good, I knew some friends who would be interested. I suggested he drop me at the bus station and I would go from there so it wouldn't look suspicious.

Meadows dropped me off around 7:30 in front of the bus station. I went in the station, and left through another door. I went to the address and knocked on the door. A woman answered and I asked for Tony. She looked at me real close and then told me to wait. A couple of minutes later, Tony opened the door and told me to come in. He asked what he could do for me. I said I wanted to know what $2500 would get me. He said he'd take a look. He went in the back room and came back with a plastic bag with white powder. By my guess, it had over an ounce of coke in it. The guy must have been a real amateur because he told me it was one ounce, and a pro would have weighed it more accurately. I gave him the money and he gave me the coke. I told him I had some friends who might be interested and he said I could call that number any time, but that he used lots of different houses. I left and walked back to Meadows and gave him the stuff. He said he'd get it tested and if it was good stuff, he'd get me to set up a meeting. He gave me $50, and said I'd get more if it panned out. He dropped me back by the park about 8:00.

I have heard that this charge against Meadows is a frame by Nancy Hatton and the supplier she works for, Alvin Johnson. Apparently Meadows busted Johnson's other main dealer and Johnson lost a lot of business. He and Hatton are just evening the score. I heard this from a couple of guys who sell for Johnson.

I was busted for possession on January 5, YR-0, by a patrol officer. He picked me up about 8:30 near Bryan Park. I was locked up at police headquarters and I told them to contact Meadows. About 10:30 p.m., Meadows came into the lock-up and told me he'd get me released, and asked me to call him at home when I got out. It took about 30 minutes to get checked out and get my possessions back. As I was leaving the front door, I saw Nancy Hatton about 100 feet away walking toward the police station. She was carrying a large purse but I did not see any packages. I walked the other way so she wouldn't see me and wonder what I was doing at the police station. Meadows was nowhere around at that time. He had told me when he came into the lock-up that he was going home. I called him from a pay phone about 11:10 to thank him for getting me released. I remember the time because there was a bank time and temperature sign nearby. I know his cell phone number, 584-2199, because I sometimes call him for information. He was home when I called.

This is a true and accurate statement to
the best of my recollection.

Signed: *John Summers*
John Summers

UNITED STATES DEPARTMENT OF JUSTICE
FEDERAL BUREAU OF INVESTIGATION
IDENTIFICATION DIVISION
WASHINGTON, D.C. 20537

The following FBI record, NUMBER 3 093 211 R3 , is furnished for OFFICIAL USE ONLY. Information shown on this Identification Record represents data furnished FBI by fingerprint contributors. WHERE DISPOSITION DATA IS NOT SHOWN OR FURTHER EXPLANATION OF CHARGE OR DISPOSITION IS DESIRED, COMMUNICATE WITH AGENCY CONTRIBUTING THOSE FINGERPRINTS.

CONTRIBUTOR: IDENTIFIER (ORI) NAME CASE NUMBER (OCA)	SUBJECT: NAME STATE NUMBER	ARRESTED OR RECEIVED	C - CHARGE D - DISPOSITION
CO203010 PD, BAYSHORE COL 630140	SUMMERS, JOHN C #221311F	04/15/-5	C - CCC 484.8 MISD POSS DRUGS D - 04/17/-5 GUILTY 10 DAYS
CO203010 PD, BAYSHORE COL 632902	SUMMERS, JOHN C #221311F	08/04/-5	C - CCC 484.8 MISD POSS DRUGS D - 08/19/-5 GUILTY PROB 1 YR
CO203010 PD, BAYSHORE COL 636199	SUMMERS, JOHN C #221311F	01/29/-4	C - CCC 250.5 PUBLIC INTOX D - 01/3-/-4 DISMISSED
CO203010 PD, BAYSHORE COL 638421	SUMMERS, JOHN C #221311F	02/19-4	C - CCC 484.4 FEL SALE DRUGS D - 04/06/-4 GUILTY 30 DAYS
CO203010 PD, BAYSHORE COL 642166	SUMMERS, JOHN C #221311F	11/02/-4	C - CCC 250.6 LOITERING D - 11/04/-4 GUILTY TIME SERVED
CO203010 PD, BAYSHORE COL 650017	SUMMERS, JOHN C #221311F	06/23/-3	C - CCC 484.4 FEL SALE DRUGS D - 07/21/-3 GUILTY 60 DAYS
CO203010 PD, BAYSHORE COL 662562	SUMMERS, JOHN C #221311F	02/09/-2	C - CCC 484.4 FEL SALE DRUGS D - 04/11/-2 DISMISSED

UNITED STATES DEPARTMENT OF JUSTICE
FEDERAL BUREAU OF INVESTIGATION
IDENTIFICATION DIVISION
WASHINGTON, D.C. 20537

The following FBI record, NUMBER 3 093 211 R3 , is furnished for OFFICIAL USE ONLY. Information shown on this Identification Record represents data furnished FBI by fingerprint contributors. WHERE DISPOSITION DATA IS NOT SHOWN OR FURTHER EXPLANATION OF CHARGE OR DISPOSITION IS DESIRED, COMMUNICATE WITH AGENCY CONTRIBUTING THOSE FINGERPRINTS.

CONTRIBUTOR: IDENTIFIER (ORI) NAME CASE NUMBER (OCA)	SUBJECT: NAME STATE NUMBER	ARRESTED OR RECEIVED	C - CHARGE D - DISPOSITION
CO203010 PD, BAYSHORE COL 671752	SUMMERS, JOHN C #221311F	08/30/-2	C - CCC 250.2 DISORDERLY COND D - 09/16/-2 DISMISSED
CO203010 PD, BAYSHORE COL 681173	SUMMERS, JOHN C #221311F	03/03/-1	C - CCC 484.4 FEL SALE DRUGS D - 03/11/-1 DISMISSED
CO203010 PD, BAYSHORE COL 700080	SUMMERS, JOHN C #221311F	01/05/-0	C - CCC 484.4 MISD POSS DRUGS D - 01/06/-1 DISMISSED

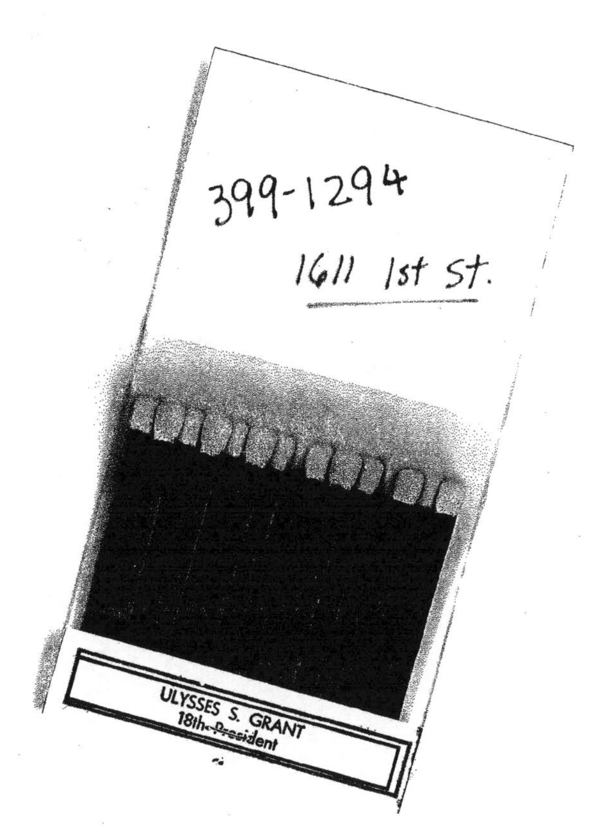
399-1294
1611 1st St.
ULYSSES S. GRANT
18th President

AFFIDAVIT

My name is Carolyn Jordan Smith. I am a lieutenant with the Bayshore Police Department. I am a shift supervisor for the Special Narcotics Unit and have been for three years. Before that, I was in public relations for eight years, concentrating on drug abuse community education. I am the superior officer to Robert H. Meadows, shield number 921. He takes his assignments from me and reports to me. The special narcotics unit is small, and we know each other well and support each other. In my opinion, Meadows is an honest cop and is not guilty of bribery or possession of narcotics. That's not his style. He is an outstanding officer, and I have given him that rating on his annual performance evaluation each of the last three years.

In special narcotics, we all work more or less independently. Since we use informants who can be untrustworthy, we rarely discuss the details of our investigation with each other, to assure against inadvertent leaks that could ruin our investigation.

On January 3, Meadows was patrolling Bryan Park. That's a major "drug supermarket" with lots of street sales, so someone has to pull that assignment each week. I know nothing of the details of the Hatton arrest except for having seen Meadows' report. All officers fill out such a report every time they make an arrest, and file a copy with their supervisor. It is not unusual for a report to be filed the next day after an arrest, particularly a night arrest. I do recall Meadows telling me on the fourth that he thought the bust would not stick, but I don't remember if he said why.

On January 18, Meadows came to me mid-afternoon and asked for money to make a buy. He said a reliable informant was on to a new dealer, but needed to make a big score so he needed $5000.00. I remember it because we don't usually give our officers that much. I trust Meadows, so I gave it to him and he signed a receipt. I have attached a true and accurate copy of that receipt to this affidavit as Exhibit A. The money was in random hundred dollar bills. We do not use marked money nor keep a list of serial numbers. It's too easy for the drug dealers to find out how to spot marked bills, and once the code is broken, we're out of business.

Meadows talked to me on January 19 about the internal affairs investigation. He seemed upset. I told him I knew nothing about it but would try to find out. Captain Friedman refused to tell me anything, but that's not surprising. He is a sexist who doesn't believe in women supervisors. I do not recall ever speaking to Sgt. Sutton about this case or any other matter. As far as I know, he never asked me for lactose. As far as I know, neither officer Meadows nor any others in my command had any lactose. Having any such substance would pose issues of the potential contamination of seized drugs which could jeopardize prosecution.

From what Meadows told me, he did not follow standard procedures in handling the cocaine buy on January 18. No officer is ever supposed to take money or narcotics to his home. They are supposed to bring them directly to the station. However, I am sure that they all bend the rules a little for the sake of convenience. Since Meadows lives alone, it's really no big deal that he went home before coming downtown.

Sgt. Grubb recalls that Meadows left work about 10:15 p.m. on January 5, saying he was going home.

Carolyn J. Smith

Carolyn J. Smith

Sworn to before me, this the 1st day of February YR-0

Marci Underwood

Notary Public of Monroe County

CASH RECEIPT

Number 5080

Date 1/18/YR-0

From Special narcotics Fund

$ 5,000.00

Amount Five thousand and no/100 Dollars

Purpose Controlled buy

[x] Cash [ ] Check / Money Order Signed *Robert H Meadows*

SELECTED COLUMBIA PATTERN JURY INSTRUCTIONS

Preliminary Instructions

Members of the Jury: This is a criminal case that has been brought by the state of Columbia. The state has charged the defendant with bribery and possession of cocaine. The state alleges that the defendant, Robert Meadows, was a police officer who solicited and accepted some cocaine from Nancy Hatton, in exchange for not prosecuting criminal charges on which she had been arrested.

The defendant is Robert Meadows, a Bayshore police officer. He has pleaded not guilty to the charges and denies committing the offenses. He is presumed to be innocent and may not be found guilty by you unless all of you unanimously find that the state has proved his guilt beyond a reasonable doubt.

The trial will begin with opening statements by the attorneys, in which they will preview the evidence they intend to offer. Then the State will present its evidence through witnesses and exhibits. The State must present enough evidence to convince you beyond a reasonable doubt of the defendant's guilt. The defendant will have the opportunity to present evidence on his own behalf, but is not required to do so. He does not have to prove his innocence. He is presumed innocent. Finally, the lawyers will present closing arguments in which they summarize their views of the case. What the lawyers say is not evidence.

At times during the trial, a lawyer may make an objection to a question asked by another lawyer, or to an answer by a witness. This simply means that the lawyer is requesting that I make a decision on a particular rule of law. Do not draw any conclusions from such objections or from my rulings on the objections. If I sustain an objection to a question you should not speculate on what the answer might have been. If I instruct you to disregard something, you may not consider it in your deliberations.

There will be occasional recesses during the trial. During these recesses you must not discuss the case with anyone, not even your friends. Nor may you look things up on the Internet. Please keep your cell phones turned off.

All people in this trial are fictional, and the events take place in an imaginary city called Bayshore, in the state of Columbia.

Concluding Instructions

Members of the Jury: You have now heard all the evidence in the case and will soon leave the courtroom to begin discussing this case in the jury room.

As I told you earlier, the state has accused the defendant, Robert Meadows, of committing the crimes of bribery and possession of cocaine. But this is only a charge. In order for you to find him guilty, you must be convinced beyond a reasonable doubt that he committed the crime as charged. If you are not convinced beyond a reasonable doubt that he committed the crime, you must find him not guilty.

Proof beyond a reasonable doubt is proof that leaves you firmly convinced of the defendant's guilt. There are very few things in this world that we know with absolute certainty, and in criminal cases the law does not require proof that overcomes every possible doubt. If, based on your consideration of all the evidence, you are firmly convinced that the defendant is guilty of the crime charged, you must find him guilty. If, on the other hand, you think there is a real possibility that he is not guilty, you must give him the benefit of the doubt and find him not guilty.

It is your duty to determine the facts and decide what happened. The only evidence you may consider is the evidence that was properly admitted at trial. You may not consider any matter that was rejected or stricken by the Court. You may not consider anything you read in the paper or hear from your friends about this case, nor may you do your own investigation or look anything up on the Internet.

Do not let sympathy, bias or prejudice affect your decision. In this case, the defendant is a law enforcement officer. He is to be treated like anyone else, neither more leniently nor more harshly because of his profession.

It is my job to instruct you on the rules of law that apply to the case. You must follow all of the rules as I explain them to you. You may not follow some and ignore others. Even if you disagree or do not understand the reasons for some of the rules, and even if you thought the rule of law was different than what I say, you are required to follow the instructions on the law as I give them to you.

As I have just reminded you, it is your job to decide if the state has proved the guilt of the defendant beyond a reasonable doubt. An important part of that job will be making judgments about the testimony of the witnesses, including the defendant, who testified in this case. You should decide whether you believe what each person had to say and how important that testimony was. In making that decision, I suggest that you ask yourself a few questions: Did the person impress you as honest? Did he or she have any particular reason not to tell the truth? Did he or she have a personal interest in the outcome of the case? Did the witness seem to have a good memory? Did the witness have the opportunity and ability to observe accurately the things he or she testified about? Did the witness's testimony differ from the testimony of other witnesses? These are a few of the considerations that will help you determine the accuracy of what each witness said.

The state has charged the defendant with two crimes, bribery and possession of cocaine..

First, the state has charged the defendant with the crime of bribery. To sustain this charge, the state must prove all of the following propositions beyond a reasonable doubt:

1. That the defendant was a public servant, judicial officer, or public administrator;
2. That the defendant solicited, accepted, or agreed to accept any benefit, service, or item of value from another person;
3. That the defendant agreed to perform some service related to his official duties in return; and
4. That the defendant thereby violated a known legal duty.

If you decide that the state has proved beyond a reasonable doubt that Robert Meadows is guilty of each and every element of the crime of bribery, it is your duty to find him guilty. However, if you have a reasonable doubt as to any one of these four elements, it is your duty to find him not guilty.

Second, the state has charged the defendant Robert Meadows with the crime of possession of a controlled substance, in this case, cocaine. To sustain this charge, the state must prove all of the following propositions beyond a reasonable doubt:

1. That the defendant possessed cocaine;
2. That the defendant did not have a valid prescription for it;
3. That the defendant possessed the cocaine knowingly or intentionally; and
4. That the defendant was not authorized to possess cocaine.

In this regard I instruct you that a state statute provides that a law enforcement officer acting in the course of legitimate law enforcement duties may lawfully possess controlled substances in order to seize, test, preserve as evidence, or destroy them.

If you decide that the state has proved beyond a reasonable doubt that Robert Meadows is guilty of each and every element of the crime as charged, it is your duty to convict him. However, if you have a reasonable doubt as to any one of these elements, it is your duty to find him not guilty.

The decision you reach in the jury room, whether guilty or not guilty, must be unanimous.

IN THE CIRCUIT COURT OF MONROE COUNTY
STATE OF COLUMBIA

THE STATE OF COLUMBIA)
)
vs.) Criminal Action No. 88396
)
ROBERT H. MEADOWS,) **VERDICT**
Defendant)

We the jurors of Monroe County in the above entitled action find the defendant:

1. ___Guilty

 of bribery in the first degree.

 ___Not Guilty

2. _____Guilty

 of possession of a controlled substance.

 ___Not Guilty

Signed:_______________________________________
Jury Foreperson